Studies of the Max Planck Institute Luxembourg for International, European and Regulatory Procedural Law

edited by
Prof. Dr. Dres. h.c. Burkhard Hess
Prof. Dr. Hélène Ruiz Fabri

Volume 16

Michel Erpelding | Burkhard Hess
Hélène Ruiz Fabri (eds.)

Peace Through Law

The Versailles Peace Treaty and Dispute Settlement After World War I

Nomos

Max Planck Institute
LUXEMBOURG
for Procedural Law

Coverpicture: © Australian War Memorial, [Order 14704090]

The Deutsche Nationalbibliothek lists this publication in the Deutsche Nationalbibliografie; detailed bibliographic data are available on the Internet at http://dnb.d-nb.de

ISBN 978-3-8487-5754-1 (Print)
978-3-8452-9916-7 (ePDF)

British Library Cataloguing-in-Publication Data
A catalogue record for this book is available from the British Library.

ISBN 978-3-8487-5754-1 (Print)
978-3-8452-9916-7 (ePDF)

Library of Congress Cataloging-in-Publication Data
Erpelding, Michel / Hess, Burkhard / Ruiz Fabri, Hélène
Peace Through Law
The Versailles Peace Treaty and Dispute Settlement
After World War I
Michel Erpelding / Burkhard Hess / Hélène Ruiz Fabri (eds.)
354 p.
Includes bibliographic references and index.

ISBN 978-3-8487-5754-1 (Print)
978-3-8452-9916-7 (ePDF)

Published by Nomos Verlagsgesellschaft, Baden-Baden, Germany 2019.
Printed and bound in Germany.

1st Edition 2019

Foreword

This edited collection of papers contains the presentations of the Versailles Peace Treaty conference, organized by the two departments of the Max Planck Institute Luxembourg for Procedural Law, from 6 to 8 December 2017 in Luxembourg. The leitmotif of the conference was 'peace through law', expressing a valuable aspiration of the 1920s and early 1930s.

The objective of the Conference was to bring together leading experts in dispute resolution in private and public international law on the eve of the centennial of the signing of the Treaty. The conference explored the enduring impacts of the Versailles Treaty with a specific focus on dispute resolution, thus combining the research fields of the two departments of the Institute. The conference started with two successive addresses by the ambassadors of France and Germany in Luxembourg, Their Excellencies Mr Bruno Perdu and Dr Heinrich Kreft, who shared their views on the Peace Treaties. This symbolic gesture, for which we express our gratitude, was followed by a deeply inspiring inaugural lecture by Nathaniel Berman outlining the historical context of the event's main theme. The next day of the conference addressed the establishment of the League of Nations and other aspects of the new world order (aiming at international cooperation) established by the Versailles Peace Treaty. The political and economic consequences of the war primarily concerned the transfer of territories and the protection of minorities. An additional issue related to the legal foundations and the rescheduling of payments of reparations between 1919 and 1930. The third day of the conference focussed on the various dispute resolution mechanisms under the Peace Treaties, the establishment of the Permanent Court of International Justice at The Hague and the various mixed arbitral tribunals, which gave individuals standing in proceedings under international law.

This publication is primarily the work of its authors, and we hereby express gratitude to them for the effort they have put into writing the papers. Special thanks are due to Derek Stemple for language editing and formatting of the manuscripts, and to Michel Erpelding, our co-editor, who—as a spiritus rector—conceived the conference and followed the progress of the publication of the papers. Finally, we would like to thank Nomos Verlag for its support and guidance in the publishing process of this book.

Luxembourg, 9 January 2019 Burkhard Hess and Hélène Ruiz Fabri

Table of Contents

Part 3: The Emergence of International Economic Law

Part 4: The Institutionalization of International Adjudication

Introduction: Versailles and the Broadening of 'Peace Through Law'

Michel Erpelding[*]

On 9 May 1919, a little more than forty-eight hours after the Allies had handed over the text of the Versailles Treaty to the representatives of Germany, a small ceremonial dinner was held at the Hôtel Bedford, in the fashionable 8th arrondissement of Paris. As one American attendee later wrote to his wife, it was a high-brow affair. The guest list included a grand-nephew of Napoleon I, Prince Roland-Napoléon Bonaparte, and Albert I, Prince of Monaco. However, like their host, the British barrister and academic Sir Thomas Barclay, most of the twenty or so diners were highly regarded authorities on international law. They were also members of the *Institut de Droit International* (IDI), which, a few hours earlier, had concluded an extraordinary two-day session at the Ceremonial Hall of the Paris Law Faculty. All were gathered to honour the man whose ideas were profoundly changing the way people thought about international relations and international law: the President of the United States of America, Woodrow Wilson.[1]

The IDI had not convened since its Oxford session in August 1913—its subsequent session, meant to take place in Munich in September of the following year, had been cancelled after the summer of 1914 had ended in mobilization and war.[2] Founded in 1873 as a reaction to the Franco–Prussian war of 1870–1871, the IDI had vowed to 'promote the progress of international law'. By declaring that they would '[strive] to formulate the general principles of the subject, in such a way as to correspond to the legal conscience of the civilized world', its members had openly challenged the monopoly of governments over international law.[3] The idea that international disputes might be better resolved by legal experts rather than governements or diplomats had also been gaining ground among a somewhat

* Senior Research Fellow, Max Planck Institute Luxembourg for Procedural Law.
1 'Avant-propos' (1919) 27 Annuaire IDI V–XII.
2 ibid.
3 Martti Koskenniemi, *The Gentle Civilizer of Nations: The Rise and Fall of International Law, 1870–1960* (CUP 2001) 47.

broader public. 'Realist' pacifist associations, such as the British International Arbitration League, founded in 1870, or the French *Association de la Paix par le Droit* ('Peace through Law Association'), established in 1887, were advocating compulsory international arbitration as an alternative to classic diplomacy. As an exclusive academic society, the IDI had always steered clear of pacifism. However, it had actively supported and contributed to the development of international arbitration as a means to avoid war.[4]

Its efforts, and those of other groups of international lawyers, such as the *American Society of International Law* (ASIL), created in 1906, had had a particular resonance with decision-makers in the Americas, particularly in the United States. That very same year, Theodore Roosevelt had become the first statesman to be awarded the Nobel Peace Prize, both for his having negotiated peace between Russia and Japan in 1905 and for having resorted to arbitration in a dispute with Mexico. In 1912, Roosevelt's former Secretary of State Elihu Root—who, like almost all Secretaries of State of that period, was a member of the ASIL and, also, an associate member of the IDI—had also been awarded the Nobel Peace Prize for his pro-arbitration policies. Roosevelt's successor, the lawyer—and ASIL member—William Howard Taft, was an even stronger proponent of international arbitration. On the eve of the First World War, it was therefore a widely-shared belief among international lawyers that their impartial technical expertise would eventually replace diplomacy as the main instrument of international dispute settlement. The Peace Palace, inaugurated at The Hague in August 1913 as the seat of the Permanent Court of Arbitration, seemed to embody the hope for a world in which a small community of international lawyers would prevent sovereign nations from going to war against each other.[5]

By 28 July 1914, when Austria-Hungary declared war on Serbia, that hope had vanished. International law, however, had not. Over the following years, the Allies had consistently claimed the international-legal high ground, while the Germany had tried—although not very successfully—to reciprocate in kind. On the Allied side, the 'war to end all wars' had quickly become a 'war in defence of international law'. The Allied claim to estab-

4 Charles De Visscher, 'La contribution de l'Institut de droit international au développement du droit international' in Institut de droit international (ed), *Livre du Centenaire 1873–1973: Évolution et perspectives du droit international* (S Karger 1973) 128, 144–145.

5 Mark Mazower, *Governing the World: The History of an Idea* (Penguin 2013) 81–93, 120.

lish a stable postwar order based on international law had raised high hopes among the peoples of Europe and beyond.[6] This claim had become somewhat more tangible when the United States had eventually joined the fight against the Central Powers in April 1917. Before entering the war, Woodrow Wilson had outlined, based on earlier proposals, a 'peace without victory' backed by a universal 'League for Peace'.[7] In January 1918, he had re-affirmed this commitment as part of his 'Fourteen Points'.[8] After arbitration alone had proved insufficient to prevent war, the idea of creating an international body that would effectively guarantee world peace had become a central element for proponents of 'peace through law'. In the United States, William Howard Taft and Elihu Root had been among the founders of the *League to Enforce Peace* in 1915. In France, the *Association de la Paix par le Droit* had campaigned for it in 1916–1917. After the Allied victory against Germany in November 1918, Wilson had made sure to put it at the top of the agenda of the Paris Peace Conference. After some initial misgivings, the other Allied Powers eventually obliged, with the British taking an especially proactive role in the drafting of what would become known as the Covenant of the League of Nations.[9]

The Covenant and its 26 Articles stood out as the most important common feature of the post-war settlement reached at the Paris Peace Conference. Its pre-eminence was materialized by its inclusion, as Part I, in all the peace treaties negotiated between the Allied and Associated Powers and the Central Powers, ie the Treaties of Versailles (Germany),[10] Saint-Germain (Austria),[11] Neuilly (Bulgaria),[12] Trianon (Hungary),[13] and Sèvres (Ottoman Empire).[14] The creation of the first permanent international or-

6 Isabel V Hull, *A Scrap of Paper: Breaking and Making International Law during the Great War* (Cornell University Press 2014) 2–8.

7 Wilson to Senate (22 January 1917) 40 The Papers of Woodrow Wilson 533–537.

8 Wilson to Congress (8 January 1918) 45 The Papers of Woodrow Wilson 534–539.

9 Florian Couveinhes-Matsumoto, 'Les travaux préparatoires' in Robert Kolb (ed) *Commentaire sur le Pacte de la Société des Nations* (Bruylant 2015) 7, 11–52.

10 Treaty of Peace between the Allied and Associated Powers and Germany (signed 28 June 1919, entered into force 10 January 1920) 225 CTS 188.

11 Treaty of Peace between the Allied and Associated Powers and Austria (signed 10 September 1919, entered into force 8 November 1921) 225 CTS 482.

12 Treaty of Peace between the Allied and Associated Powers and Bulgaria, and Protocol (signed 27 November 1919, entered in force 9 August 1920) 226 CTS 332.

13 Treaty of Peace between the Allied and Associated Powers and Hungary (signed 4 June 1920, registered 24 August 1921) 6 LNTS 187.

14 Treaty of Peace between the Allied and Associated Powers and Turkey (signed 10 August 1920) 28 LNTS 225.

ganization entrusted with '[promoting] international co-operation and [achieving] international peace and security ... by the firm establishment of the understandings of international law as the actual rule of conduct among Governments' had also raised important expectations among international lawyers. These expectations had been palpable during the IDI's extraordinary two-day session in Paris on 8–9 May 1919. In his opening statement, Sir Thomas Barclay had expressed the hope that the Versailles Peace Treaty would make international law—and its professionals—even more relevant than before the war:

> To deride international law, the Hague Conventions, and the peaceful means [of dispute settlement] because the most terrible war the world has ever known has taken place despite them is just as reasonable as deriding engineers, architects, and all construction work because an earthquake has destroyed some of humanity's finest creations.
> Wars are explosions of national wrath, and as long as the tumult is ongoing, nations are not more reasonable than individuals in midst of a violent argument.
> Today, the tumult subsides and men are returning to their normal state of mind. Moreover, the reaction to that tumult has been the creation of the League of Nations, providing international law with the binding force that it lacked.[15]

It seems fair to assume that Barclay's reception at the Hôtel Bedford in honour of Woodrow Wilson was not merely intended as a way of paying private homage to an old acquaintance of his. Inviting the main instigator of the League Covenant to a reception mostly attended by scholars and practitioners of international law was likely to be interpreted as a collective celebration of international law and its professionals. Whatever Barclay's intentions had been, Wilson made clear that he was there to celebrate the

15 'Séance d'ouverture du 8 mai 1919' (1919) 27 Annuaire IDI 295–296. Original French: '*Railler le droit international, les conventions de La Haye, les méthodes pacifiques, parce que la plus terrible guerre que le monde ait jamais vue a éclaté malgré eux, est aussi raisonnable que de railler les ingénieurs, les architectes et la science de la construction en général, parce qu'un tremblement de terre a détruit une partie de la plus belle œuvre de l'homme. Les guerres sont des explosions de colère nationale et, tant que dure le tumulte, les nations ne sont pas plus raisonnables que ne le sont les individus au milieu d'une violent dispute. Le tumulte s'épuise et les hommes reviennent à un état d'esprit normal, et déjà le jeu de la réaction produit dans la création d'une Société des Nations ce qui manquait pour donner au droit international la force obligatoire qui lui manquait.*'.

former rather than the latter. He agreed with Barclay that the war had only strengthened international law:

> I thought it a privilege to come here tonight, because your studies were devoted to one of the things which will be of most consequence to men in the future, the intelligent development of international law. In one sense this great unprecedented war was fought to give validity to international law, to prove that it had a reality which no nation could afford to disregard; that, while it did not have the ordinary sanctions, while there was no international authority as yet to enforce it, it nevertheless had something behind it which was greater than that—the moral rectitude of mankind. If we can now give to international law the kind of vitality which it can have only if it is a real expression of our moral judgments, we shall have completed in some sense the work which this war was intended to emphasize.[16]

However, Wilson clearly dissented from Barclay's contention that the ineffectiveness of pre-war international law had mainly been the result of 'unreasonable' nations. For the originator of the League Covenant, the 'engineers' and 'architects' of that international law also deserved part of the blame. Wilson's conclusion was that the new international order would still need international lawyers, but that they would not any longer be its driving force:

> International law has perhaps sometimes been a little too much thought out in the closet. International law has—may I say it without offense?—been handled too exclusively by lawyers. Lawyers like definite lines. They like systematic arrangements. They are uneasy if they depart from what was done yesterday. They dread experiments. They like charted seas, and if they have no chart, hardly venture to undertake the voyage. Now we must venture upon uncharted seas to some extent in the future. In the new League of Nations, we are starting out upon uncharted seas, and therefore, we must have, I will not say the audacity, but the steadiness of purpose which is necessary in such novel circumstances.[17]

Wilson's critique of the international legal profession was not limited to the stereotypical overcautiousness of lawyers. It had also a markedly social

16 'After-Dinner Remarks' (Paris, 9 May 1919) 58 Papers of Woodrow Wilson (1988) 598, 599.
17 ibid.

component. In fact, by invoking the 'moral rectitude of mankind' as the ultimate foundation of international law, Wilson was openly challenging the IDI's ability to reflect the 'legal conscience of the civilized world'. This must have become suddenly very clear to his exclusive audience when, later in his speech, he specified that 'when I think of mankind, I must say that I do not always think of well-dressed persons'.[18]

Although his words were hardly gracious toward his audience, Wilson would turn out to be right. In the post-Versailles world, the implementation of 'peace through law' would no longer be the exclusive province of a small community of diplomats and highly-trained legal experts. It would be a markedly more inclusive matter. Of course, diplomats and political decision-makers would still play a central role. But they would now do so partly in public, defusing urgent crises within the Council of the League of Nations or discussing more general issues within its Assembly. As for the professional international lawyers, the multiplication of international conventions, organizations, and dispute settlement bodies provided them with numerous new research topics and career opportunities. However, the stage would also increasingly open up to other actors. Journalists would cover each session of the Assembly of the League of Nations and comment on various provisions of the Peace Treaties. Humanitarian activists would try to lobby Assembly delegates for more effective international rules on the repression of the slave trade or trafficking in women or children. Members of the League Secretariat would comment on the answers to legal questionnaires provided by member states. Minorities would send petitions to the League Council. Non-European populations subject to League mandates would try to protest the violation of their rights before the Permanent Mandates Commission. At the International Labour Organization, worker delegates would participate in the negotiation of international conventions. Populations of disputed territories would determine their future in legally binding plebiscites. Allied creditors of pre-war debts would sue the Entente Powers before one of 36 Mixed Arbitral Tribunals. Small-town lawyers would learn to help working class communities sue their own state before localized international bodies.

Of course, with the benefit of hindsight, the lofty ideals invoked by Woodrow Wilson and others before, during, and after the Paris peace negotiations stand in stark contrast to the eventual fate of the world they were supposed to protect. Far from producing 'peace through law', they re-

18 ibid. On Wilson's conception of international law, see: Leonard V Smith, 'The Wilsonian challenge to international law' 13 JHIL (2011) 179–208.

sulted in contradictions that would lead to its very opposite. By basing their peace on legal principles that they presented as universally binding, the Allies raised expectations of justice that they were unwilling to meet while simultaneously limiting their own ability to decisively overpower those they had vanquished.[19] And yet, from the perspective of international dispute settlement, the extreme variety and innovativeness of procedural and substantial 'experiments' attempted as a result of the Treaty of Versailles and the other Paris peace treaties of 1919–1920 remain striking even today. Moreover, although they have largely disappeared from the collective memories of the profession, many of these 'experiments' have had a lasting impact on international law and international dispute settlement after the Second World War. How did the Paris peace treaties try to resolve war-related and future international disputes? What institutions and dispute settlement mechanisms did they create? How did these institutions and mechanism operate in practice? What is their relevance for contemporary international law? These are some of the questions that this book, based on a conference held at the Max Planck Institute Luxembourg for Procedural on 6–8 December 2017, will address.

1. *Peace Through Law?*

In Chapter 1, which is intended to serve both as a general opening and a caveat, Nathaniel Berman invites us to take a step back from the main theme of this book. In his view, describing the Versailles Treaty as an illustration of 'peace through law' constitutes 'a dramatic gesture', 'a surprise, a provocation, a defiance of conventional wisdom'. If anything, the international legal system created by the Treaty of Versailles and the other post-WWI peace treaties showed that the dialectic between peace and violence lies not exclusively between the national and the international, but is often internal to the international itself. Setting aside the effectiveness of the Versailles regime in achieving or developing international dispute settlement, Berman analyses the way in which this regime has constructed the very frame in which the drama of international law—with its characters, its disputes and the means devised to settle them—still unfolds today. In particular, despite a few subsequent additions, the *dramatis personae* of the international stage created at Versailles remains globally familiar to a contempo-

19 Marcus M Payk, *Frieden durch Recht? Der Aufstieg des modernen Völkerrechts und der Friedensschluss nach dem Ersten Weltkrieg* (De Gruyter Oldenbourg 2018) 658–659.

rary public. While holding on to national states as the protagonists of the international stage, Versailles formally introduced many new characters to it, such as international organizations, peoples in search of self-determination, 'not-yet-able' peoples, 'advanced nations', inhabitants of internationalized territories, or members of national minorities.

Insofar as it limited the state's monopoly on the international scene, the Versailles *dramatis personae* could be seen as an attempt to end the 'anarchy of sovereignties' that had led to the outbreak of the First World War. However, to such an extent as its characters—although originally presented as complementary—were often limiting each other, competing with each other, or undermining each other, it also had a definitively agonistic dimension. This agonistic dimension was further exacerbated when actors assumed parodic versions of Versailles *personae* to better undermine the system. Such was the case when Fascist Italy tried to use its prestige as an 'advanced nation' to recast Ethiopia as a conglomerate of 'not-yet-able' peoples in order to invade it. More generally, apart from proving unable to resolve the antagonisms between its characters, Versailles failed to produce a *dramatis personae* that the majority of the world could identify with. As a matter of fact, by barring certain actors—such as peoples living under colonial rule but not under a League mandate—from the list of authorized *personae*, the Versailles Treaty tacitly condoned their oppression and provoked their resistance. In doing so, it contributed to undermine the new international order it had created. Far from resolving its internal dialectic between peace and violence, the present-day international order—which, despite several major changes, is in many ways the continuation of the one established at Versailles—has perpetuated it. In this sense, the fact that 'peace through law' remains a promise, an aspiration, and a belief shared by many 'internationalists' should not prevent them from questioning its inherent limitations.

2. *The Establishment of a New International Order of Peace*

By incorporating the Covenant of the League of Nations, the Paris peace treaties instituted a greatly enhanced and systematized version of the scattered 'peace through law' mechanisms that had existed prior to the First World War. Whereas these mechanisms had been generally limited to 'peace through arbitration', the Covenant adopted a broader approach. The main element of this approach may be summed up as 'peace through dispute settlement'. Pursuant to Articles 12–15 of the Covenant, member states were no longer left alone with disputes that might lead them to wage war against each other, but had the obligation to submit these disputes either to arbitration or judicial settlement or to the multilateral forum of the League Council. As demonstrated by Thomas D Grant in Chapter 2, both forms of dispute settlement benefitted from the League's (theoretically) universal and (mostly) egalitarian character. True, as the product of a still largely Eurocentric international environment in which sovereign equality remained a matter of contestation, the League was far from perfect in both respects. While the League's openness was unprecedented for an international body, for non-Western states such as Afghanistan and Ethiopia joining the organization would turn out to be an uphill battle. Similarly, although the League placed its members on an equal footing where voting rights were concerned, it nevertheless granted certain privileges to the Allies and the powers that they decided to co-opt into the Council. However, despite these limited departures from the principle of sovereign equality, the League still institutionalized this principle and provided its less powerful members with multiple procedural avenues. Moreover, inequalities within the political dispute settlement organs of the League were not essential to the functioning of the legal procedures that were independent of the League itself. It might even be said that the existence of a certain degree of formal equality between League members contributed to a climate of congeniality that facilitated the recourse to international adjudication.

The procedural requirement imposed upon League members to prevent armed conflicts between them fell short of an outright prohibition of war as a means to settle disputes—the substantive obligation which, pursuant to Article 2(4) of the United Nations Charter, constitutes the foundation of the present-day international order.[20] Partly because of that limitation, the League's dispute settlement system would prove unable to prevent or end wars of aggression such as Japan's attack on China in 1931 and Italy's invasion of Ethiopia in 1935. However, it did resolve other serious crises where pre-1914 international dispute settlement mechanisms had clearly failed. One such case is presented in Chapter 3 by Michael D Callahan. On 9 October 1934, King Alexander I of Yugoslavia and the French Foreign Minister Louis Barthou were assassinated in Marseille by a member of an anti-Yugoslav group based in Italy and trained in Hungary. The attack was clearly reminiscent of the one carried out on Archduke Franz Ferdinand of Austria and his wife Sophie a little more than twenty years earlier in Sarajevo,

20 Robert Kolb, 'De la S.D.N. à l'O.N.U. en matière de maintien de la paix' in Robert Kolb (ed) *Commentaire sur le Pacte de la Société des Nations* (Bruylant 2015) 1331, 1334–1342.

which had led to the outbreak of the First World War. But this time, the League and its dispute settlement organs helped prevent the crisis from escalating into armed conflict. Eventually, discussions at the League would result into two conventions that, had they ever entered into force, would have constituted the first legal regime defining international terrorism and the organization of its repression.

Despite the League's primary focus on the settlement of disputes between member states that had already reached some degree of escalation, the Covenant's contribution to world peace was not limited to that aspect. By addressing the rights of minorities, as well as social, economic, and colonial issues, it also targeted the underlying causes of war. Granted, the Covenant did not acknowledge the relationship between these issues and the maintenance of international peace quite as clearly as Article 1 of the United Nations Charter, with its 'contextualized' definition of peace, would after the Second World War.[21] However, far from assuming that the League minimalistically considered peace as the absence of war, contemporary literature and practice suggest that even the Covenant's provisions on 'technical' issues were understood as a vital contribution to its 'political' role of preserving international peace.[22]

The contribution to world peace of the League of Nations' mandates system, established by Article 22 of the Covenant, might not seem apparent at first. For the peoples subject to A, B, or C mandates, whom that provision defined as 'not yet able to stand by themselves under the strenuous conditions of the modern world', the concept of the 'sacred trust of civilization' was hardly evocative of a clean break with aggressive 19th century imperialism and colonialism. And as Mamadou Hébié and Paula Baldini Miranda da Cruz remind us in Chapter 4, the whole mandates regime, in its formalization of Great Power interests and its great reliance on classical racial stereotypes, was essentially a slightly modernized and more institutionalized form of pre-war colonialism. And yet, by denying the great colonial powers the right to simply annex former German colonies and Ottoman provinces, the Paris peace treaties partly reflected President Wilson's commitment to the principle of non-annexation. By doing so, they effectively contributed to removing one of the main incentives for future wars of conquest and, eventually, to outlawing war itself. Similarly, the obliga-

21 ibid.

22 See, eg: Olof Hoijer, *Le Pacte de la Société des Nations: Commentaire théorique et pratique* (Spes 1926) 387–388; Jean Ray, *Commentaire du Pacte de la Société des Nations selon la politique et la jurisprudence des organes de la Société* (Sirey 1930) 661.

tion to maintain an 'open door policy' in mandated territories towards other members of the League was also a way of reducing the economic benefits commonly associated with territorial ambitions (while giving industrial nations with no or few colonies, such as the United States, access to colonial markets). As for the peoples governed under this regime, their limited right to petition the Permanent Mandates Commission not only reflected their embryonic right to self-determination. It also institutionalized a form of international oversight that contributed to establishing the way populations were treated as a matter of international concern and, therefore, as one of the foundations of international peace.

León Castellanos-Jankiewicz's contribution on minority rights in Chapter 5 offers a similarly contradictory image. During the 19th century, the Great Powers, as part of the Concert of Europe, had regularly used minority rights to further their individual interests. The institution of a supervisory mechanism before the League Council as part of the different minorities treaties concluded during the Paris peace conference was clearly intended as a way to prevent such unilateral interference. Moreover, by conferring individual rights upon minorities, the minorities treaties were meant to strike a balance between assimilation and group protection. However, by prohibiting minorities from having direct recourse to the League Council, the minorities treaties pushed them toward seeking the intercession of their 'kin-states' and acting—or appearing to act—disloyally toward their territorial state. Another major flaw of the minorities treaties was their selectiveness: just as the peacemakers had alienated Japan by rejecting its racial equality clause, they alienated many Central European states by failing to impose minority protection obligations on Germany, let alone on themselves.

3. *The Emergence of International Economic Law*

The League of Nations was not the only international organization established in 1919–1920 with the intent to guarantee international peace. Expressly noting that '[universal] peace can be established only if it is based upon social justice', the Paris peace treaties also created an International Labour Organization (ILO). Not unlike the League Covenant, the ILO's Constitution was directly incorporated into each individual peace treaty. It eventually formed Part XIII of the Treaties of Versailles, Saint-Germain, and Trianon, and Part XII of the Treaties of Neuilly and Sèvres. In Chapter 6, Guy Fiti Sinclair examines the role of the ILO within the post-war settlement and the interwar period, and assesses its impact on post-WWII international organization. Against the backdrop of wide-spread social unrest in many parts of the world and a successful revolution in Russia, the ILO's avowed objective was to turn away the workers from revolution, which the Preamble of its Constitution obliquely described as 'unrest so great that the peace and harmony of the world are imperilled'. Instead, the creators and officials of the ILO advocated liberal reformism within the capitalist system. In this context, they heavily relied on law as a technology of liberal government *par excellence*. However, rather than putting the emphasis on hard norms of labour law, they were mostly concerned with institutional structures and procedures. One of their most remarkable achievements in this regard was the ILO's tripartite structure, which brought together groups with conflicting interests—governments, employers, and workers representatives—to resolve differences and adopt standard-setting conventions and recommendations by a majority vote. Moreover, with the ILO's growing expert and legal authority, it would also be increasingly concerned with economic issues, especially in the aftermath of the Great Depression.

While the drafters of the Versailles Treaty devoted considerable attention to universal labour issues, they refrained from adopting similarly far-reaching and detailed provisions with respect to international trade and finance. Article 23(e) Versailles Treaty merely comprised the broad commitment 'to secure and maintain freedom of communications and of transit and equitable treatment for the commerce of all Members of the League'. However, in combination with Article 24, which stated that 'international bureaux and all commissions for the regulation of matters of international interest hereafter constituted shall be placed under the direction of the League', this provision would allow the League to become a major actor in the economic reconstruction of Europe.[23] These provisions would also have a major impact on private international law and on commercial arbitration.

As explained by Herbert Kronke in Chapter 7, Article 24 Treaty of Versailles served as the legal basis for the creation of the International Institute for the Unification of Private Law (*Institut International pour l'Unification du Droit Privé*, UNIDROIT). Established in 1926 as an auxiliary organ of the League of Nations, UNIDROIT had the mission to harmonize and coordinate domestic legislations in the field of private law, with the aim of fostering mutually beneficial commercial exchange. Like other auxiliary

23 Throughout the 1920s and 1930s, the League would progressively develop its agency in economic and financial affairs, eventually laying the groundwork for post-WWII international economic organization: Patricia Clavin, *Securing the World Economy: The Reinvention of the League of Nations, 1920–1946* (OUP 2013) 10–12.

organs or the League, UNIDROIT made an extensive use of independent experts, such as Antonio Scialoja, Ernst Rabel, and René David. Many of the legal creations of these experts are still of relevance today. For instance, although Rabel had to abandon his work on the harmonization of the law of the international sale of goods after his forced exile to the United States in 1939, it would have a major influence on the two Hague Conventions of 1964. However, UNIDROIT was not the only organization during the interwar period that claimed to promote peace through trade: in particular, the International Chamber of Commerce produced the 1923 and 1927 Geneva instruments on commercial arbitration that would in part inspire the 1958 New York Convention.

The sparseness of universal economic provisions in the Treaty of Versailles lies in stark contrast to its detailed regulations on German war reparations, of which two separate aspects are addressed here. In Chapter 8, Jean-Louis Halpérin describes the creation and functioning of the Reparations Commission, a dispute settlement mechanism established pursuant to Article 233. Its mission was to define the amount of the damage for which Germany had to pay reparations pursuant to Articles 231–232, to draw up a schedule of payments, then to modify it according to the evolution of German resources. It also provided the German government the opportunity to have its interests heard. Between 1920 and 1923, in order to assert its authority, the Reparations Commission tried to present itself as an independent quasi-judicial body. However, due to its composition—its members were Allied politicians and diplomats—and its procedural practice—its proceedings were held in private and were not subject to any particular predetermined rules—it could hardly qualify as such. Already bypassed by government conferences and bilateral agreements, the Reparations Commission was soon plagued by deadlock as a result of disagreements among the Allies, before being disbanded in 1930 as a result of the Young Plan. A full account of how German reparations evolved into sovereign debt between the entry into force of the Versailles Treaty in 1920 and the final German payment—made in 2010—is given by Pierre d'Argent in Chapter 9. It shows how moral principles turned into overly rigid legal rules—with its 'war guilt clause' in Article 231, the Versailles Treaty can be described as a reversion to the idea of a 'just peace', which European nations had abandoned since the 16th century[24]—were gradually replaced

24 Randall Lesaffer, 'Peace Treaties and the Formation of International Law' in Bardo Fassbender and Anne Peters (eds), *The Oxford Handbook of the History of International Law* (OUP 2012) 71, 88–91.

by pragmatic financial arrangements. While underlining the potentially catastrophic consequences of naïve legal expectations, this evolution also provides an additional illustration of the increasing influence that economists would acquire over political decision-makers during the interwar period and beyond.

4. The Institutionalization of International Adjudication

The growing impact of economic expertise on political decision-making during the interwar period did not coincide with a marginalization of international lawyers. Actually, by institutionalising international adjudication, the Treaty of Versailles and other international treaties created in its wake opened many new avenues for practitioners of international law.

Prior to the First World War, several attempts had already been made to create permanent international dispute settlement bodies that would be composed of sitting judges or arbitrators, rather than of adjudicators appointed by the parties for each individual case. Supporters of international judicial institutionalization hoped that permanent courts and tribunals would be able to develop a more consistent case law, thus contributing to the further development of international law. However, institutionalization during this period remained hesitant at best. Although the 1899 Hague Peace Conference resulted in the creation of the Permanent Court of Arbitration, this institution merely provided a more stable framework for individual disputes decided on an ad-hoc basis by party-appointed arbitrators. For the proponents of international judicial institutionalization, the outcome of the 1907 Hague Peace Conference was even more disappointing: rejecting the United States' proposal to create a Court of Arbitral Justice, the participating states approved the Convention Relative to the Creation of an International Prize Court only to see this project founder after the British Parliament failed to ratify it.[25] The only fully institutionalized international court of the period, the Central American Court of Justice, had many limitations. For example, although individuals could file complaints before it, it only had jurisdiction over the five Central American republics

---

25 Cornelis G Roelofsen, 'International Arbitration and Courts' in Bardo Fassbender and Anne Peters (eds), *The Oxford Handbook of the History of International Law* (OUP 2012) 145, 165–166.

(Costa Rica, Guatemala, Honduras, Nicaragua, and Salvador) and was not able to rule on more than 10 cases during its short existence (1907–1918).[26]

With these precedents in mind, the establishment of the Permanent Court of International Justice (PCIJ) pursuant to Article 14 Versailles Treaty in 1922 must be considered one of the most substantial and lasting contributions of that treaty to the materialization of 'peace through law'. However, as Christian J Tams explains in Chapter 10, with its optional rather than compulsory jurisdiction, the PCIJ was a markedly less ambitious project than its abortive predecessors from the pre-war period. Moreover, its integration into the larger framework of the League of Nations also implied a more modest conception of 'peace through law'. While states were ready to submit certain disputes to international adjudication, they were definitely not ready to renounce traditional 'political' means of dispute settlement, such as bi- and multilateral negotiations. In practice, this resulted in a level of judicial activity in the PCIJ that may be described as limited, but regular. While the Court was rarely handed over the most serious disputes, it made itself a solid reputation by solving smaller and midlevel conflicts, as well as by giving legal advice to international organizations. Moreover, the PCIJ effectively realized at least one of the hopes that many international lawyers had placed in the idea of institutionalized international adjudication: by systematically publishing its decisions and advisory opinions, the PCIJ produced a consistent body of case law that effectively contributed to the development of international law.

Today, the PCIJ remains the most prominent example of international judicial institutionalization after the First World War. However, the interwar period provides us with other compelling illustrations of this phenomenon. The Mixed Arbitral Tribunals (MATs), analysed in Chapter 11 by Marta Requejo Isidro and Burkhard Hess, are a case in point. Pursuant to Article 304 Versailles Treaty and similar provisions in the other post-WWI peace treaties, their mission was to adjudicate various disputes regarding the treatment of private rights. This included settling monetary claims arising out of pre-war contracts and awarding compensation to Allied nationals for wartime measures taken against their property by the Central Powers' domestic courts. Numerically speaking, the 36 MATs—especially those between Germany and the Allied and Associated Powers—were undoubtedly the busiest international courts of the interwar period. Taken together, they decided on more than 70,000 cases. This caseload is

26 Rosa Riquelme Cortado, 'Central American Court of Justice' in Rüdiger Wolfrum (ed), *Max Planck Encyclopedia of Public International Law* (OUP 2013).

even more impressive if one considers that their existence generally did not exceed 10 years, as most of the MATs were discontinued pursuant to the 1930 Young Plan. The MATs are similarly remarkable from a procedural point of view. First and foremost, their respective rules of procedure—several models were used due to the differences in legal traditions among the Allies—were so detailed that contemporaries described them as 'miniature civil procedure codes.' Another major innovation was the position of individuals before the MATs. Despite having to deal with mass claims, and although technically the right to submit and waive claims had been left to the states parties, the MATs nevertheless allowed the individuals whose rights were at stake to become directly involved in the proceedings. Due to their sheer number and the diversity of both the procedural and substantial rules that they applied, the MATs eventually failed to produce a universally consistent body of case-law. Nevertheless, their collection of published decisions was a major source for legal doctrine in the 1920s and 1930s and remains of interest for international lawyers today. In addition, although many accounts of the post-WWII era fail to mention the MATs, it should be noted that they served as a source of inspiration for the creators of the ECJ and might similarly inspire potential future negotiations over institutionalized investment tribunals.

Based on the model of the MATs but endowed with broader jurisdiction and an even wider range of procedural tools, the Arbitral Tribunal for Upper Silesia, which I describe in Chapter 12, is another example of international judicial institutionalization. Despite having been all but forgotten by international legal scholars and practitioners, it stands out as perhaps the most innovative international judicial body of its time. Its creation was the indirect result of Article 88 Versailles Treaty which provided for the division of Upper Silesia, one of Europe's major industrial regions, between Germany and the newly reborn Polish State. The partition of the ethnically mixed Upper Silesia was eventually implemented via the German–Polish Convention of 15 May 1922—an intricate legal system that was at least partly the brainchild of the League of Nation's first Deputy Secretary-General, Jean Monnet. Although its duration had been limited to 15 years, the Convention established several major innovations. Most notably, it created two local, yet international, organs to ensure its effective implementation: the Mixed Commission for Upper Silesia and the Arbitral Tribunal for Upper Silesia. While the Mixed Commission has left an important mark in the field of minority rights, even bringing the Nazi authorities to temporarily suspend anti-Jewish legislation in German Upper Silesia between 1934 and 1937, the Arbitral Tribunal, which could publish generally binding decisions on complaints filed by individuals against their own state and receive preliminary referrals from national judges, might have served as an inspiration for both the ECtHR and the ECJ.

5. Beyond 'Peace Through Law': The Use of Law and Its Records as Vehicles of Resistance and Change

The League of Nations and the international adjudicatory bodies created as a result of the 1919–1920 Paris peace treaties introduced new mechanisms for the resolution of international disputes and provided effective international guarantees for certain individual rights. Yet, they ultimately failed to fulfill their assigned mission, namely 'to achieve international peace and security.' After the Second World War, political decision-makers and scholars were often keen to point out the insufficiencies of the 'peace through law' approach. For them, the drafters of the Versailles Treaty and the other Paris peace treaties had placed too much faith in legal principles and procedures instead of harnessing the military might of the world's great powers to organize their effective implementation. Therefore, the replacement of the League of Nations by the United Nations and its beefed-up collective security system has been described as 'peace through law' making way for 'peace through power.'[27]

To be sure, the post-WWII triumph of realism over legalism was far from absolute. In Europe, especially after the failure of the European Defence Community in 1954, regional integration has relied heavily on law and legal experts, and has further refined legal techniques that had already been experimented with by the League of Nations. On a global level, the considerable development of international adjudication after the end of the Cold War might be seen as a partial rehabilitation of post-WWI legalism and the ideal of 'peace through law.' However, as the current context makes clear once again, the multiplication of international legal rules and tribunals provides no ultimate guarantee against nationalism, unilateralism, and war. Nonetheless, as shown in the last part of this book, law itself also provides various means to overcome its inherent limitations as a peacemaker.

First, although law is predominantly associated with reconciliation and peace, it is also a formidable tool to organize public mobilization and resistance—including in times of war. As Dider Boden demonstrates in Chapter 13, even under occupation, judges are by no means bound to adopt a reconciliatory approach between the occupier and the occupied—although

27 Robert Kolb, *Theory of International Law* (Bloomsbury 2016) 387–388.

historical precedents have shown that many are likely to do so under the circumstances. In 1915, rather than adding a veneer of legitimacy to certain German wartime impositions, two Belgian judges, Raymond de Ryckère and Maurice Benoidt, decided to use principles of international law—both public and private—to declare these measures illegal, thus openly questioning the occupier's authority. After initially rejecting this act of defiance, de Ryckère's and Benoidt's colleagues and superiors would eventually follow their lead, prompting a nation-wide strike of the judiciary that would leave the German occupier in awe and contribute to its eventual defeat.

Second, even when legal norms or proceedings fail to establish peace in the short term, the records they leave behind may be used as a later stage to foster mutual understanding and reconciliation between former enemies and, more generally, to contribute to societal change. The history of the Versailles Peace Treaty and the other post-WWI peace treaties is riddled with failures, unfulfilled hopes, and silences. Prominent examples include their incapacity to achieve a lasting peace between Germany and its neighbours, to bring to justice those responsible for the Armenian genocide, or to establish a principle of racial non-discrimination. In Chapter 14, Jennifer Balint, Neal Haslem and Kirsten Haydon argue that law, despite its silences and failures, can nevertheless effect societal change in the long run. For this to happen, the records that legal instruments and proceedings leave behind need to be 'translated' to the individuals and society to which they are directed. In their view, art is a potent vehicle to achieve this because it creates personal spaces within public spaces. These personal spaces facilitate engagement with, and recognition of, the meaning of law and its failures, as demonstrated by two art projects realized in Australia. The first of these projects, *Minutes of Evidence*, combines archival records and theatrical performance to address the unequal relations between Aboriginal residents and European settlers. The second project, *Flowers of War*, combines historical objects and visual arts to convey the enormity of war to a public that has never been confronted with it. Similar initiatives, based on international court proceedings, petitions filed before the League of Nations, or archival records of the interwar period, might perhaps one day address the various instances in which the Paris peace treaties eventually failed to establish peace through law.

Part 1:
Peace Through Law?

Chapter 1 Drama Through Law: The Versailles Treaty and the Casting of the Modern International Stage

*Nathaniel Berman**

1. Prologue: Noël, 1913

One hundred four years before our conference, almost to the day: the journal of the French *Association de la Paix par le Droit* features on its cover a mythological image of the group's ideals, an engraving in the style of the Symbolist painter Gustave Moreau. The engraving, by a now-obscure artist, André Galland, depicts three archetypal figures. In the center stands an exhausted young warrior with bandaged head, clutching sword and shield with downcast arms. On the warrior's right, a cherub-like child is prying the sword from his hand; on the warrior's left, a winged ephebe hovers over him, gazing intently at his face. The ephebe, who could pass for the warrior's younger self, gestures forward with his hand, perhaps guiding the warrior to a path better than violence. Two objects lie on the ground, evidently posing the choice before the warrior. To the right lies a skull, near where the sword will land when it ultimately falls from the warrior's hand. To the left lies a ploughshare, presumably to be taken up when the warrior foreswears the sword. Below the three figures, tomblike stones announce the morals of the engraving, in solemn Latin: '*Pax*' and '*Labor*.' Above the figures, bold letters proclaim the title of the journal: '*La Paix par le Droit*.' Slightly off to the side, a banner announces the date, '*Noël, 1913*.'

* Rahel Varnhagen Professor of International Affairs, Law, and Modern Culture, Brown University.

Maurice Galland, Cover of La Paix par le Droit, *December 10, 1913. © Adagp, Paris, 2019. Source: Princeton University Library.*

And thus, less than eight months before the 'guns of August,' an evocative mythological depiction of Peace-through-Law stands before the journal's readers. From the distance of more than a century, we cannot but contemplate this image with terror, as we helplessly watch the pacifists of December, 1913, daydreaming at the edge of a volcano. One cannot fully know the intent of the artist and editors in foregrounding this image, the only time in the journal's history an art-work thus appeared. Was the image to be an inspirational beacon for a program to be implemented in the here-and-now? Or did it originate in an intuition that the ideal of Peace-through-Law was becoming a fantasy separated from reality? Melding these two possibilities, I would pose yet a third: perhaps the artist, as the sensuous unconscious of this thoroughly rational, endlessly discursive Association, sought to act as a kind of conjurer, to bring these archetypal figures into being, to place on the world stage the mythical *dramatis personae* who might have made possible a different 20th century narrative than the one we know all too well.

We gather here, in December, 2017, under the slogan, 'Peace through Law,' in part as an after-effect of long-ago conjurations like those of the group who commissioned this artwork of December, 1913. The French *Association de la Paix par le Droit* was, as far as I can determine, the first group to gather under that slogan. It was founded in Nîmes, in 1887, by six *lycéens*, all offspring of staunch Protestant families.[1] The Association's foundational meeting itself presents something of an archetypal scene. It transpires in the kitchen of one of the *lycéens*' widowed mother and ailing grandmother, the latter a 'fervent Huguenot.' In the manner of idealistic youth, the founders draft a simple, but radical, two-article program: the 'suppression of all permanent armies' and the 'constitution of an international arbitrage tribunal.' This primal scene prefigures the engraving by Galland, commissioned on the eve of the catastrophe that would decisively inflect the ideals of the Association. At this founding moment, however, the two-article program stands as a discursive equivalent of Galland's image of the cherub and ephebe. Both depict a campaign of Peace-through-Law as something that comes *after* war: first to disarm the warriors, then to inaugurate a peaceful era governed by law.

From these simple beginnings, the Association steadily grew into an influential force in mainstream French political debate, attracting thousands of members, and publishing major French public intellectuals in its jour-

---

1 Ernest Roussel, 'Les Origines de la Paix par le Droit' (January 1928) 38 La Paix par le Droit 10–11.

nal—including international lawyers like Georges Scelle and Charles Rousseau. Its position as the dominant forum for French pacifism in the interwar period may have only been made possible, though, by a change in the meaning of that pacifism wrought by the Association's response to World War I. Like most other center-left groups in Europe, the Association supported the war, particularly the oft-repeated assertion by the Entente Powers that they were fighting a 'war of law.' Already in November, 1914, Théodor Ruyssen, the president of the Association, proclaimed, '[T]his war is ... a war against war ... The cause of France and its allies is truly the cause of law and liberty.' In April, 1918, the philosopher Gustave Belot wrote in the Association's journal, '[T]he true idea of Pacifism is that of a *Regime of International Law*, which the state of war can in no way annul, but, on the contrary, specifies and stimulates...'[2]

These pronouncements present a very different idea of the role of law than do the founding myths of the Association: rather than a force external to war, coming after violence to disarm and govern, it is inextricably bound up with war. Indeed, war may even be required to construct law, serving to 'specify and stimulate' it, by transforming the *dramatis personae* on the world stage: in Galland's archetypal imagery, converting the Warrior into a Tiller of the Soil. The *dramatis personae* necessary for an unfolding of a historical drama structured by law do not come by an act of grace from a mythological elsewhere; rather, their forceful construction is an indispensable prerequisite for that drama, its *hors-scène* prehistory.

The tenacious idea that law comes *after* war, as measured reason follows unbridled passion, is a powerful myth, expressed even by those who have reason to know better. In his magisterial 1939 opus, *The International Experiment of Upper Silesia*, Georges Kaeckenbeeck described the 1922 Geneva Convention for that region thus: 'The elimination of chaos and violence through legal order and legal process was its purpose.'[3] The 'chaos and vio-

---

2 Gustave Belot, 'Encore le Mot Pacifisme' (April 1918) 28 La Paix par le Droit 109.

3 Georges Kaeckenbeeck, *The International Experiment of Upper Silesia* (OUP 1942) 25. I note that I have gradually developed many of the arguments that have culminated in this paper in a long series of studies. Many of these have been collected in Nathaniel Berman, *Passion and Ambivalence: Colonialism, Nationalism, and International Law* (Brill 2011). Other studies of mine particularly relevant to this paper are Nathaniel Berman, '"The Appeals of the Orient": Colonized Desire and the War of the Riff' in Karen Knop (ed), *Gender and Human Rights* (OUP 2004) and Nathaniel Berman, 'The International Law of Nationalism: Group Identity and Legal History' in David Wippman (ed), *International Law and Ethnic Conflict* (Cornell University Press1997). In the last-named of these studies, I developed the notion of 'protagonist-positions,' a forerunner of the notion of '*dramatis personae*' that I use here.

lence' evoked by Kaeckenbeeck were those of World War I and the ethno-nationalist civil strife in Upper Silesia that followed in its wake. The complex 'international experiment' constructed by the Geneva Convention sought to impose the 'solid basis of legal principle' upon the 'elemental forces' of 'nationalist passion.'[4]

However, the seeming homologies between the three oppositions—internationalism/nationalism, law/passion, and peace/violence—do not suit the complex story of Upper Silesia after the War, as Kaeckenbeeck's own narrative demonstrates. The immediate post-war story of Upper Silesia comprised a complex dialectic of discourse and violence, of both internationalist and nationalist origin. The Versailles Treaty provided for a plebiscite for the region, an attempt to provide a rational way to resolve its tangle of ethnic, linguistic, national, and religious identities. However, Kaeckenbeeck declares:

> Though the decision to hold a plebiscite had an appearance of principle, it was in reality a *pis aller* … [It] became the signal for a veritable orgy of propaganda and polemics; the right of self-determination was met by the organization of all manner of pressure … [I]nsurrection and self-help soon became rampant …[5]

Moreover, after the plebiscite, the international community, a *dramatis persona* played in this context variously by a Committee of Experts, the Council of the League of Nations, and the Supreme Allied Council, ordered the partition of the region between Germany and Poland, to be followed by the conclusion of a treaty between the two states. Kaeckenbeeck described the internationally-mandated partition as a 'dangerous political operation' for which the similarly mandated Geneva Convention 'prescribed a regime of convalescence.'[6]

The dialectic between peace and violence, which one might have thought was homologous to that between the international community and nationalist forces, thus proves to be internal to the international itself. The 'regime of convalescence' of the international legal regime sought to heal the 'dangerous operation' of the international political decision, itself taken in the wake of the plebiscite mandated by the Treaty—a plebsicite whose imminence, Kaeckenbeeck argues, had itself inflamed the internecine violence. Ironically, the very plebiscite that sought to determine

---

4 Kaeckenbeeck (n 3) 361.
5 ibid, 112.
6 ibid, 23.

the identity of the Upper Silesian 'self' played a major role in dividing the hybrid Upper Silesian population between German and Polish ethno-national 'selves,' which the subsequent international legal regime would attempt once again to bring into harmony. This complex story of conflict and pacification was thus repeatedly reshaped by the *personae* whose contours and even existence were shaped by international legal and political texts and practice.

2. *A Dramatic Gesture*

To choose 'Peace through Law' as the title of a conference about the Versailles Treaty is a dramatic gesture. The most common view of the Versailles Treaty is that it did anything *but* bring about peace, let alone 'through law.' The title, 'Peace through Law,' therefore, is dramatic in both the metaphorical and literal senses of the word. It is a surprise, a provocation, a defiance of conventional wisdom—the metaphorical sense of 'dramatic.' But it also sets up a more literally dramatic, even theatrical, tension for our meeting: how will the organizers, the speakers, the participants vindicate the hypothesis announced in the title, how will they respond to the inevitable retorts about the brevity of the peace that followed the treaty's signing? One cannot help but surmise that the organizers consciously intended that this dramatic tension set the tone of our proceedings, that a certain frisson pervade our discussions, as we cast our gaze on a legal and political drama that, in retrospect, seems to have been a tragic tale culminating in unspeakable horror.

Whenever scholars—of law, history, or politics—cast their gaze on the Versailles regime, as they have done repeatedly over the past century, they endeavor to provide novel insight into its guiding conceptions and institutional details and to draw enduringly edifying lessons from their fate. That all know the circumstances attending the demise of the regime does not diminish these aspirations. The classical Greek tragedians, after all, demonstrated their art primarily by their creative presentation of mythical tales known to all, not by varying the outcomes. A portrayal of an Oedipus who had courteously made way for his father at the crossroad might have offered a cheery account of the avoidance of disaster, but would not have served for millennia as an inexhaustible resource of aesthetic, moral, and psychoanalytic reflection, a goad for countless re-tellings.

Rather than essaying a retelling of the entire story of the Versailles regime, I will focus, as hinted above, on its narrative precondition, the frame of any drama: the construction of the *dramatis personae*, the characters to be set in motion by the tale. When a drama appears in written form, the list of *dramatis personae* appears on the page that precedes the action. It does not form a part of the drama itself, but without it the drama cannot go forward. Indeed, at least according to some theorists, particularly those under Hegelian influence, the construction of the *dramatis personae* largely predetermines the course of a drama. The characters of Oedipus and Hamlet govern the unfolding of their respective tragedies, even if their respective classical and modern configurations lead them to do so in divergent ways. And it is Oedipus and Hamlet who continue to structure the Western imagination, rather than the details of their stories.

Hence, I propose reformulating our optic on the Versailles treaties (a phrase in which I include the whole gamut of post-World War I treaties, wherever signed). I urge setting aside, at least as a first step, the effort to test the historical importance and enduring relevance of the treaties by their effectiveness in achieving 'dispute settlement.' Instead, I propose that we see the treaties as constructing the *dramatis personae* which have decisively shaped the world, and its disputes, ever since—the world in which we continue to live, the disputes in which we continue to engage. The treaties constructed the ensuing narrative of world history in which we ourselves figure on the list of *dramatis personae*—that is, to the extent that we had not already been constructed by the *lycéens* of Nîmes.

This perspective shifts the emphasis away from the efficacity or normative value of this or that particular technique of dispute settlement. Instead, it refocuses attention on the Versailles regime's construction of the enduring actors who have continued, with manifold variations, to play the roles designed by the dramaturges of Versailles. We may embrace or reject particular features of the Versailles regime, but we ineluctably act on its stage, the modern international stage. We are the players created by those who wrote, implemented, and interpreted the Versailles treaties. Versailles may not have settled our disputes, but it continues to decisively shape our participation in them.[7]

---

7 I note that the field of 'law and performance' has been gradually growing over the past couple of decades, though generally along lines quite different than those I pursue here. For a sense of the range of this scholarship, see, eg, Julie Stone Peters, 'Law as Performance: Historical Interpretation, Objects, Lexicons, and Other Methodological Problems' in Elizabeth S Anker and Bernadette Meyler (eds), *New Directions in Law and Literature* (OUP 2017); Lucy Finchett-Maddock, *Protest, Property and the Commons: Performances of Law and Resistance* (Routledge 2016); Alan Read, *Theatre and Law* (Palgrave 2015); Julie Stone Peters, 'Theatrocracy Unwired: Legal Performance in the Modern Mediasphere' (2014) 26 Law & Literature 31;

Before proceeding, I present a selected list of the most prominent of these *dramatis personae*, along with their key legal claims:

- National states, purporting to embody pre-existing nations, with claims to full sovereignty
- Peoples or nations seeking self-determination
- Minority groups with internationally proclaimed civil and cultural rights for 'persons belonging to' those groups
- Internationalized territories with internationally defined 'inhabitants'
- 'Not-yet-able' peoples under League mandate, whose welfare forms a 'sacred trust of civilization'
- 'Advanced Nations' responsible for the welfare of 'not-yet-able' peoples
- The International Community, embodied in a variety of internationalist institutions and individuals

These *personae* are familiar to all, whether or not one has the training to recognize them as legal categories. These *personae*, and other, newer ones, such as internationally recognized indigenous peoples, structure our world to such an extent that they can even come to seem like natural persons rather than legal constructs.

3. *The* Dramatis Personae *and the Actors: Dynamics and Indeterminacy*

If my project is both possible and urgent today, it is because we live in a world undergoing destabilization. The internationally constructed identities through which we have come to recognize ourselves and others can no longer be taken for granted. The widespread sense of destabilization in this latter part of the second decade of the 21st century, moreover, comes only a generation after the last major destabilization, wrought by the fall of the Berlin Wall. I need not belabour here the reasons for the current sense of

---

Joshua Takano Chambers-Letson, *A Race So Different: Performance and Law in Asian America* (New York University Press 2013); Martha M Umphrey 'Law in Drag: Trials and Legal Performativity' (2012) 21 Columbia Journal of Gender and the Law 114; Catherine M Cole, *Performing South Africa's Truth Commission: Stages of Transition* (Indiana University Press 2010); Julie Stone Peters, 'Legal Performance Good and Bad' (2008) Law, Culture and the Humanities 179; Robin Chapman Stacey, *Dark Speech: The Performance of Law in Early Ireland* (University of Pennsylvania Press 2007).

destabilization, the myriad upheavals in the US, Europe, the Middle East, Africa, and elsewhere. But I maintain that it is at such times of destabilization, when the basic structures of our world appear to be bursting apart, when our taken-for-granted identities are put into question, that we can reflect on their origins and meanings. It is at such moments when we can observe ourselves, become something like the anthropologists of our own societies.

In 1974, the anthropologist Clifford Geertz published an important, if unfortunately entitled, article, 'From the Native's Point of View : On the Nature of Anthropological Understanding.'[8] Geertz presents an alternative to the impasse between empathy and analytical distance as the primary stance of the ethnographer. Rather, he declares, the latter should seek to determine how human beings 'define themselves as persons, what enters into the idea they have (but ... only half-realize they have) of what a self ... is.'[9] The achievement of this task requires 'searching out and analyzing the symbolic forms—words, images, institutions, behaviors—in terms of which, in each place, people actually represent themselves to themselves and to one another.'[10]

Turning to the Balinese, a people among whom Geertz spent considerable time, or rather, to what he saw as the 'never-changing pageant that is Balinese life,' Geertz writes:

> The Balinese have at least a half dozen major sorts of labels, ascriptive, fixed, and absolute, which one person can apply to another (or, of course, to himself) to place him among his fellows. ... To apply one of these designations or titles (or, as is more common, several at once) to a person is to define him as a determinate point in a fixed pattern, as the *temporary occupant of a particular, quite untemporary, cultural locus*.[11]

The term Geertz favors for these 'cultural loci,' provisionally occupied by individuals, is, indeed, *dramatis personae*.

> It is *dramatis personae*, not actors, that endure; indeed, it is *dramatis personae*, not actors, that in the proper sense really exist. Physically men come and go ... But the masks they wear, the stage they occupy, the

8 Clifford Geertz, 'From the Native's Point of View': On the Nature of Anthropological Understanding' (October 1974) 28 Bulletin of the American Academy of Arts and Sciences 26.

9 ibid 30.

10 ibid.

11 ibid 35.

> parts they play, and, most important, the spectacle they mount remain and comprise not the façade but the substance of things, not least the self.[12]

Geertz's depiction of the enduring power of the *dramatis personae* of Balinese society illuminates the enduring power I attribute to the *dramatis personae* of the Versailles regime—as well as to the shifting multiplicity of roles particular actors can play. One can readily, for example, think of a number of groups who have spent all or part of the past century cycling through a wide range of such *personae*. In the first half of the twentieth century, for example, the 'Sudeten Germans,' or portions of that population, successively played the roles of the following *dramatis personae*: a part of an empire's *Staatsvolk* prior to 1914, one of the legion of self-determination aspirants at the Paris Peace Conference in 1919, an internationally protected minority in the 1920s, again a self-determination aspirant in the early 1930s, agents of an irredentist foreign power in the mid-1930s, part of the majority of a racial-nationalist state from 1938–1945, and a group of expelled refugees with international claims after 1945. One can list a similarly wide range of *dramatis personae* played by other groups, such as the Jews, the Kurds, the Palestinians, and so on.

I immediately note that the way I have just portrayed this phenomenon is itself misleading, for terms like the 'Sudeten Germans,' 'Jews,' and so on, do not name stable, let alone natural, human collectivities that proceed to take on a variety of artificial roles. Rather, such terms simply bring us to another layer of *dramatis personae,* each with its genealogical layers of construction and reconstruction. From this perspective, in which *dramatis personae* 'comprise not the façade but the substance of things, not least the self,' there is no collective self, no natural 'actor,' which stands outside the shifting occupation of various 'cultural loci.'

To be sure, groups, as well as individuals, may at times deliberately, even cynically, mask themselves in available *personae* for instrumental purposes. As a result, when confronted by any particular affirmation of group identity, one may wonder whether one faces an instrumentally assumed, rather than a constitutive, *persona*. Indeed, partisans in ethno-national conflicts commonly accuse their opponents of not authentically incarnating the *dramatis persona* to which they claim title, particularly that of a 'nation' or 'people.'

12 ibid.

Judith Butler expresses this alternative thus:

> Does this mean that one puts on a mask or *persona*, that there is a 'one' who precedes that 'putting on,' …? Or does this miming, this impersonating, precede and form the 'one,' operating as its formative precondition rather than its dispensable artifice?[13]

Butler's emphasis is on the latter, the constitutive effect of 'impersonation.' She is, nonetheless, also attuned to its former, voluntaristic, sense, that of instrumental masking, especially for political purposes. In the legal arena, one might call the instrumental use a 'litigation strategy'; in the political arena, an act of 'propaganda.' In any particular case, discerning the difference between constitutive and instrumental acts of self-presentation may be difficult to determine, indeed may remain indeterminate even for the group itself. The intractability of this indeterminacy is underscored if one maintains, as would Butler, that any such instrumental masking is itself undertaken by a *dramatis persona*.

4. *The Agon of the Personae*

Key texts from the interwar period give an acute sense of the constitutive, yet constructed, quality of the Versailles *personae*, as well as their complex imbrication with each other. It is not only the case that, as in the 'Balinese pageant' of Geertz's telling, actors on the international stage may assume a variety of *dramatis personae*. Rather, the *dramatis personae* themselves engage in a variety of relationships with each other, including both complementarity and competition. They may reciprocally legitimate each other, or, on the contrary, usurp each other's authority, often through rhetorical maneuvers such as irony and parody.

Consider, for example, the Preamble to a treaty signed the same day as the Versailles Treaty, variously, and symptomatically, known as the 'Treaty of Peace with Poland,' the 'Polish Minority Protection Treaty,' and the 'Little Treaty of Versailles':

> Whereas the Allied and Associated Powers have by the success of their arms restored to the Polish nation the independence of which it had been unjustly deprived …

13 Judith Butler, 'Critically Queer' in Julian Wolfreys (ed), *Literary Theories: A Reader and Guide* (New York University Press 1999) 575.

> The [Allied and Associated Powers], ... confirming their recognition of the Polish State, ... as a sovereign and independent member of the family of nations, and being anxious to ensure the execution of...[Versailles Treaty] Article 93 ...[14]

On the one hand, we might read this Preamble as casting the 'Polish nation' as a natural, pre-existing entity, one which had been 'unjustly deprived' of its independence. This reading justifies the notion that the text is a 'Treaty of Peace *with Poland*,' with a Poland that pre-exists the treaty. On the other hand, we might focus on the Preamble's emphasis that Poland owes its newfound independence to the Allies, literally to 'the success of their arms'—implying that this independence is a product of the newly founded international community, even the first-born progeny of the emergent 'family of nations.' Read together with the text's express citation of Versailles Article 93, these phrases justify the appellation, the 'Little Treaty of Versailles'—whose namesake was concerned, above all, with the construction of a new international community. Finally, we might foreground the primary substantive content of the Treaty, which, in fulfillment of Versailles Article 93, protects members of 'racial, religious or linguistic minorities'—justifying its third, and most common, name, the 'Polish Minority Protection Treaty.' The treaty, in short, proclaims the existence of four of Versailles' main *dramatis personae*: national states, nations, minorities, and the international community. It does so, however, in such a way that highlights their constructedness—even their conjuring up by the text itself—and their irreducible dependence on each other.

The Preamble and the treaty's primary content underscore the constitutive, rather than merely instrumental, function of the international *dramatis personae*. This constitutive function makes it impossible to name the group that 'puts on' the dramatic *persona* without referring *ad infinitum* to previously donned *personae*—a feature particularly evident in relation to the 'minorities' who formed the main substantive concern of the treaty. For example, the group known in 1919 as the 'German minority' of Poland was formerly part of the *Staatsvolk* of the Prussian and Austrian empires. Only as a result of the War do its members become primarily an ethnic group defined by their German language, and become legally constructed as an internationally protected 'minority.' This shift exemplifies the notion I have advanced that both the existence of many of the Versailles *personae*

14 Treaty Between the Principal Allied and Associated Powers and Poland (signed 28 June 1919, entered into force 10 January 1920) 112 BSP 232.

and the 'occupation' of these 'cultural loci' by particular groups issue from the War that 'stimulated and specified them.'

The reciprocal dependence of distinct principles, which I have highlighted in discussing the Polish treaty's Preamble, does not suffice to portray the complexity of the inter-relationships of the *dramatis personae*. Rather, the *dramatis personae* often shadow each other, limit each other, compete with each other, even undermine each other. These struggles often occur on the concrete terrain of political, cultural, and military conflicts, but they always have a discursive dimension, an acceptance or contestation of the list of *dramatis personae* and of which groups should occupy particular 'cultural loci.' Since my primary archive in this essay is composed of texts, I focus on this discursive dimension, as expressed by scholars, jurists, official documents, and political leaders.

The following proclamation from CA Macartney, one of the foremost interwar experts on international minority rights, renders explicit the agonistic potential lurking in the seemingly static list of *dramatis personae*:

> The [Minority Protection] Treaties [seek] to put an end to the whole movement towards so-called national self-determination ... in favor of a true 'self-determination' based on feelings of political loyalty.[15]

Macartney here expresses a variant of a widely held view concerning the primary purpose of the minority protection treaties—viz, that they primarily sought to secure the loyalty of the minority groups to the states of their new citizenship. Macartney's distinctive formulation foregrounds the rivalry between two *personae*, that of 'nations' and 'minorities.' He approvingly anticipates the dominance of the latter, to be achieved by its salutary usurpation of the phrase denoting the deepest aspiration of the former: the usurpation of 'national self-determination,' in which the primary *persona* is the 'nation' with normative primacy over the state, by 'a true "self-determination,"' in which the primary *persona* is the state with normative primacy over the nation. The scare-quotes around 'self-determination' show that this linguistic, as well as legal and political, usurpation is a kind of deliberate 'impersonation' of one category by the other. Such 'impersonation' demotes the usurped category into something one no longer takes fully seriously—in short, a subversive parody. I will return to a very different use of such subversive parody later in this paper.

A resolution adopted by the Council of the League in 1923 enables us to witness, *en direct*, the legal construction of McCartney's favored *persona*,

---

15 CA Macartney, *National States and National Minorities* (OUP 1934) 278.

the internationally protected minority group. The resolution laid down the conditions for admissibility to the League of petitions for redress submitted by such groups.[16] Among other conditions, the resolution declared:

> ...(b) in particular, they must not be submitted in the form of a request for the severance of political relations between the minority in question and the state of which it forms part;
> (c) they must not emanate from an anonymous or unauthenticated source;
> (d) they must abstain from violent language ...

This historically contingent construction is so familiar that it may seem to many a description of a natural entity. The 'minority' *persona* cannot, by definition, ask for political independence. It must also be willing to name itself, to present openly its identity papers for scrutiny by the agents of power. It must, finally, engage only in civil, one might say, 'civilized,' discourse. These conditions take on particular poignancy when one considers the newness of the 'minority' *persona*, both generally (despite its foreshadowings in the late 19th century) and in relation to the particular actors who assumed this role. The Versailles-constructed minority *persona* required the reconstruction of the identities of millions of people in central and eastern Europe, their 'impersonation' of a new *persona*. Appearance on the Versailles stage required these groups to name themselves as subjects structured by these international demands.

The Council resolution provides a quintessential example of the pervasive mechanism of identity-formation called 'interpellation' by Althusser: the 'hailing' of individuals by an agent of power and their subsequent recognition of themselves in the identities thus imposed upon them.[17] In laying down conditions for the authorial voice of the *persona*, 'minority,' the Council constructs the conditions for *existing* as a 'minority' on the international stage.

I turn to two other novel Versailles constructions, an examination of whose similarities and differences both with each other and with precursor legal regimes sheds crucial light on the agonistic relationships of the treaties' *personae*. I refer to the territories within Europe placed under a va-

16 Resolution of the Council of the League of Nations, September 5, 1923. See Report by M de Rio Branco, and Resolutions adopted by the Council on September 5th, 1923, Council Document C 552 (1). 1923. I, 1, 6.

17 See Louis Althusser, 'Ideology and Ideological State Apparatuses (Notes towards an Investigation)' in Althusser, *Lenin and Philosophy and Other Essays* (Verso 1970) 11.

riety of forms of international governance, whose purest form was the League government for the Saar, and the non-European territories placed under League mandate, whose governance was entrusted to 'advanced nations' as a 'sacred trust of civilization.' Both constructions effected various forms of an internationalization of territory, legal regimes wholly or partially outside the state system.

Both kinds of regimes sought novel solutions to conflicts between incompatible territorial claims and principles. In the internationalized European territories, these conflicts arose from: clashes between the ethnic identity of the population and economically-motivated claims by neighboring states (the Saar and Danzig); the hybrid and contested ethnic identity of the population (Upper Silesia); and competing historical claims (all three of the territories). In the non-European territories, all regions wrested from the defeated and collapsed pre-War empires (Ottoman and German), the colonial ambitions of the French and British Empires conflicted with the internationalizing and self-determinationist élan of Wilsonian and European reformists. Both kinds of regimes imposed various forms of government by non-local rulers; both were, consequently, shadowed by accusations of imperial or colonial rule in internationalist mask; and both sought to differentiate themselves from such critiques, indeed to achieve legitimacy precisely through such differentiation.

Legal partisans of both kinds of regimes portrayed them as coexisting with the 'normal' allocation of territory to sovereigns. One way of describing this co-existence was that state sovereignty over such territories was 'in abeyance.' This term appears in relation to the Saar in a major early 1920s work on the Versailles Treaty, as well as in a key 1950 portrayal of the Mandate System by ICJ Judge Arnold McNair.[18]

The notion that the allocation of territory to sovereigns was merely 'in abeyance' reinforces the sense of the constructed and provisional quality of the internationalized territories and their associated *personae*. It is all the more striking, therefore, that the partisans of these regimes celebrated them as the crowning achievements of the Versailles system—a status to which they were entitled precisely by virtue of their departure from the traditional legal notions of statehood which many held responsible for the catastrophe of the War.

---

18 On the Saar, see HWV Temperley, *A History of the Peace Conference of Paris*, vol. 2 (Henry Frowde 1920) 180. On the Mandate System, see *International status of South-West Africa* (Advisory Opinion) 1950 ICJ Rep 128, 150 (sep op McNair).

In the introduction to his remarkable 1925 monograph on the Saar regime, Henri Coursier expresses this common held view:

> To the 'anarchy of Sovereignties,' an anarchy allowed, indeed, by public law since the formation of modern states and whose most disastrous consequence was the 'unlimited right of war,' the Covenant of the League of Nations substitutes an international organization which, without abolishing individual sovereignties, limits the exercise of their freedom by justice.[19]

While this passage refers to the creation of the League itself, many saw the internationalized territories as the ultimate expression of this 'substitution.' In the words of a 1920 League report on the Saar:

> The appointment of a Governing Commission of a State created under the auspices of the League of Nations will be the first characteristic act of the League after leaving its theoretical existence to enter upon its practical life. It constitutes, so to speak, the incarnation of the lofty principles that inspired its creation and which are to guide its work of pacification and later of organisation and adjustment.[20]

This ultimate 'incarnation' of the League nonetheless left the normal sovereign structure intact, perhaps proving its superiority precisely by contrast with that structure:

> In relation to the Saar, the drafters of the Treaty … did not claim to modify *de jure* the juridical concepts of Sovereignty, Statehood, Nationality, [and] State Property … [T]hey simply instituted the … *international personality* … of the Governing Commission. The latter has completed its oeuvre by promulgating … the status of an 'inhabitant of the Saar.' And thus the Territory of the Saar was organized as a *de facto* State [*État de fait*].[21]

Over vociferous and repeated German objections, the Governing Commission proceeded with 'determination' toward the goal of the 'constitution of a Sarroise political personality [*l'individualité politique sarroise*].'[22] Coursier thus proclaims the construction of a key *dramatis persona* of the Versailles system to be a self-conscious act by internationalist authorities.

---

19 Henri Coursier, *Le Statut International du Territoire de la Sarre* (Pedone 1925) 5.

20 'Report on the Saar Basin Presented by Monsieur Caclamanos' (1920) 2 LNOJ 45, 49.

21 Coursier (n 19) 35–36 (emphasis added).

22 ibid 104.

I emphasize the two key *personae* to emerge from this 'constitution': the Saar as a new kind of polity and its people as a new kind of collectivity. First, the Governing Commission, through a series of acts and decrees, established the Saar as a new kind of 'state,' even if a '*de facto* state.' The Governing Commission, for example, secured the Saar's adherence to international conventions, despite its non-conformity with traditional notions of statehood—a key symbol of the establishment of the Saar as an international *persona*.[23]

Second, the Governing Commission established a new international legal status for those residing within the Saar, under the seemingly anodyne phrase, 'inhabitant of the Saar.' Just as the status of sovereignty over the Saar had not formally been altered, neither had the citizenship status of its residents. Nonetheless, in a 1921 ordinance, the Commission declared that 'all inhabitants of the Territory of the Saar, whatever their nationality, are equal before the law in the Territory.'[24] This ordinance effected a change in the prevailing (German) law, which limited to citizens the various rights traditionally predicated upon political allegiance, such as participation in certain organs of local government. In defiance of the German position that the Versailles Treaty phrase 'inhabitant of the Saar' was merely an empirical description of those living in the region, the Commission declared that the 'status of "inhabitant of the Saar" constitutes a *new kind of legal subject*.'[25]

The Saar regime thus introduced two new *dramatis personae* on the international stage: the internationalized '*de facto* State of the Saar' and the internationalized human beings, the 'new legal subjects,' called the 'inhabitants of the Saar.' The partisans of the Saar regime fully acknowledged that the 'Saar Territory, as determined by the Treaty, has no roots in the past and is, politically, a purely artificial creation.'[26] Yet it was precisely this 'artificial' regime that was said to 'constitute at once the most complete and the most solidly constructed of all the experiments in international government.'[27] My one gloss here would be to affirm that to characterize as 'artificial' the *personae* of the '*de facto* State of the Saar' and 'inhabitants of the Saar' is misleading if one intends thereby to contrast them with the purported 'naturalness' of *personae* like 'Poland,' the 'Polish nation' and the

---

23 See ibid 79–82.

24 ibid 98 (quoting Ordonnance portant définition de la qualité d'habitant de la Sarre [15 June 1921] Journal officiel de la Commission de Gouvernment, art 1).

25 ibid 99 (emphasis added).

26 Michael T Florinsky, *The Saar Struggle* (Macmillan 1934) 11.

27 Coursier (n 19) 37.

'German minority.' Rather, all the *personae* ushered onto the stage of the Versailles drama were, and remain, contingent, though enduring, constructions.

I turn to the Mandate System, another bold innovation in international governance, at least in its founding documents and legitimating texts. To be sure, the mandates' genealogy in colonialism, particularly reformist colonialist projects of the late 19th century, made them seem less of a break with the past than the Saar regime. Nonetheless, it was precisely in their supposed contrast with their proximate colonialist precursor that many saw their superior legitimacy. Indeed, what could be more attractive to the internationalist imagination than a government by idealistic agents of the international community, conscious of their task to fulfill the 'sacred trust of civilization'? These features are highlighted in Judge McNair's crucial portrayal in his separate opinion in the 1950 *Southwest Africa Case*.

In addition to the Mandate System itself, McNair focuses on two *personae* homologous to those I have highlighted in relation to the Saar: the Mandatory government and the people under mandate. In McNair's formulation, the mandate was a 'new international institution,'[28] which established

> a new relationship between territory and its inhabitants on the one hand and the government which represents them internationally on the other—a new species of international government, which does not fit into the old conception of sovereignty and which is alien to it ... Sovereignty over a Mandated Territory is in abeyance ...[29]

The creation of the Mandate System thus created three *personae* on the international stage. First, it created the 'new institution' itself. Its very name was an international innovation, borrowed, but only through an imperfect analogy, from private law.[30] Second, it created the *persona* of the Mandatory Power, a state charged with administering territory on behalf of 'civilization.' Versailles Article 22 defined such states as 'advanced nations'—*personae* familiar from the colonial stage, but newly defined and internationally codified. The system's partisans described the Mandatory Powers as something like functionaries of the international community. The Mandatory Power's rights are 'tools given to him in order to achieve the work assigned

28 *Southwest Africa Case*, sep op McNair (n 18).
29 ibid 150.
30 ibid 148–149.

to him'; he has 'all the tools necessary for such end, but only those.'[31] The subjection of the conduct of the mandate to international scrutiny was often taken as the sign of the difference of this 'new institution' from colonial sovereignty. The Court in the *Southwest Africa Case* emphasized this feature by deciding that this subjection survived the demise of the League —in fulfillment of Geertz's notion of the endurance of the *dramatis personae*, in contrast with their always-provisional actors.

Article 22 also created the new *persona* of the peoples under Mandatory rule: 'peoples not yet able to stand by themselves under the strenuous conditions of the modern world.' Like every other term associated with the Mandate System, this phrase, while an obvious progeny of colonial discourse, sought its legitimacy precisely in its difference from its analogues in that discourse. In contrast with the essentialist racism of the conceptualization of the colonized in most colonial discourse, Article 22 constructs what we could call a 'provisional racism.' The 'not yet' suggests an eventual emergence of this new category of peoples into full membership in the international community. [32] The provisionality of its racism could even allow the Mandate System's advocates to deny the racist dimension, arguing that the 'not yet' was subject to some form of objective empirical evaluation.[33]

From this perspective, we can discern an implicit legitimating function in the contrast between the peoples under 'A,' 'B,' and 'C' mandates, three sub-*personae* created by the Mandate System. Article 22 called for 'provisional' recognition of the peoples under 'A' mandates as 'independent nations,' albeit 'subject to the rendering of administrative advice and assistance by a Mandatory until such time as they are able to stand alone.' The prospect of imminent independence for the 'A' peoples highlights the contrast with the 'B' and 'C' peoples, for whom the Article mentions no path

---

31 JL Brierley, 'Mandates and Trusts' (1929) 10 BYIL 217, 219 (quoting Pierre Lapaulle, 'An Outsider's View-point of the Nature of Trusts' [1928-1929] 14 Cornell Law Quarterly 52, 61).

32 Antony Anghie's seminal analysis of Vittoria persuasively argues that a form of the provisional racism of the 'not yet' constitutes a central strand of colonial ideology as early as the 16th century. See 'Franscisco de Vittoria and the Colonial Origins of International Law' (1996) 5 Social and Legal Studies 321. However, this early notion concerned the possible acquisition of 'civilization' by the colonized as individuals, rather than as nations, excluding any re-acquisition of national sovereignty. The latter notion only begins to appear in the late 19th and early 20th century in the reformist strands of colonial ideology, as in certain French interpretations of the protectorates over Tunisia and Morocco.

33 See, eg, Walter H Ritsher, 'What Constitutes Readiness for Independence?' (February 1932) 26 American Political Science Review 112–122.

to independence. This contrast serves to give a certain 'reality effect' to the 'not-yet-ness' of the 'A' mandates. The contrast between the essentialist racism directed at the colonized under colonialism and the provisional racism of the 'not yet' *personae* under the Mandate System is thus replicated within the latter itself.

Regimes like the Saar and the mandates shared a dynamic conception of the new *personae* created for their respective populations. The construction of the 'not yet' *persona* for peoples under mandate explicitly incorporated this dynamism from the start, although it seemed only seriously intended for the 'A' peoples. The dynamism of the *persona*, 'inhabitant of the Saar,' was an artifact of the imaginative activity of the Governing Commissioners, for whom the identity of the people in the Saar was malleable. The Commissioners codified their refusal to treat the category as a merely empirical description in a series of legal provisions concretizing the notion that 'inhabitant of the Saar' constituted a new 'legal status.' Moreover, they sought to create a culture in the Saar that would make it plausible that these legally constructed 'inhabitants' would vote for the continuation of the League regime in the 1935 plebiscite. The Governing Commission thus took its subjectivity-constructive activity very seriously—even if unsuccessfully, as the 1935 plebiscite, which decided in favor of unification with Nazi Germany, demonstrated.

5. Dramatic Anomalies

The two regimes' respective defects and failures aside, their proponents envisioned them as potentially creating unprecedented legal and political forms, inhabited by utterly novel *dramatis personae*. They viewed them as foreshadowing a world in which rulers governed as trustees of civilization, rather than as power-hungry sovereigns, and people would see their primary allegiance as due to the international community, rather than narrowly national states. This vision would culminate in a completely different world stage, one which would leave the old *personae* in permanent 'abeyance.' However, the defects and failures of both kinds of regimes also reveal the extent to which any authoritative construction of *dramatis personae*, even if ideal in the eyes of its architects, inevitably leaves out many important roles, mis-casts many groups, and provokes resistance.

Indeed, we can find a striking verification of the decisive importance of the Versailles construction of *dramatis personae* precisely by turning to a key form of resistance to it: colonized peoples claiming a place on the international stage in defiance of the authorized list of *personae*. The War of the

Rif of the 1920s, a revolt by the Berber people of the Rif mountains against Spanish and French colonial rule, provides the clearest example of this phenomenon. By 1912, Spain and France had formalized their increasing control over Morocco, dividing the country between them in colonial 'protectorates.' The Rif region, on the border between the French and Spanish zones, had historically resisted outside domination, whether by the Moroccan central government or by Europeans. In the early 1920s, rebels led by Mohamed ben Abd el-Krim el-Khattabi (known popularly as Abd el-Krim) fought a highly successful battle against Spanish control. By mid-1925, French attempts to reinforce the colonial division of Morocco brought them into full-scale war with the Riffans. The war provoked vigorous cultural and political contestation in France. The rebels also garnered widespread international solidarity, from Latin America to Indonesia. The French conducted their war against the Riffans in a particularly inhumane fashion.

The brutality of the French campaign brought some on the French center-left to place their hope in international intervention. The French Human Rights League sought an opinion from Georges Scelle about the legal possibility of League of Nations action to stop the carnage. Scelle responded, however, that the League of Nations had 'no competence at all in the Moroccan affair.'[34] As a conflict within a French protectorate, the War of the Rif, as well as all of its non-state participants, simply had no existence on the international stage.

> The Rif, the Riffans, Abd el-Krim, have no international personality of any degree. Morocco is a country under protectorate with two protecting States and the League of Nations has no capacity to intervene in the domain of a protectorate ... [L]egally, one cannot even say that there is a war... [35]

This 'non-existence' of the Riffans and their charismatic and increasingly world-famous leader strikingly confirms Geertz's dictum that 'it is *dramatis personae*, not actors, that in the proper sense really exist.' Even the war itself could not appear on the international stage, regardless of how much deadly firepower was directed against the Riffans.

In 1925, there simply was no international legal *dramatis persona* for a non-European people fighting for self-determination. More than three

34 'Rapport de M. Georges Scelle' (1925) 25 Les Cahiers des droits de l'homme 496 (emphasis added).

35 ibid (emphasis added).

decades would pass before that *dramatis persona* would be authoritatively included in the international legal drama—or, to use technical international legal language, for anti-colonial self-determination to ripen into a right of customary international law.

The War of the Rif underscores the continency, constructedness, and contestability of the *personae* of the international drama. As all jurists know, international law develops in ways both centralized and decentralized, with the relative weight of these two poles varying over time. The construction of *dramatis personae* sometimes proceeds from above, as in the pronouncements of treaties and international organs. However, those *personae*, as well as the aptness of particular groups to play them, are subject to the re-appropriations, resistances, and diversions of people around the world. The Riffans were trying to introduce a new *persona* into the Versailles drama. Abd el-Krim tried to enclothe the Riffan cause with a number of *personae* in his many epistles to the world, his soliloquies on the international stage: from a secular Republic of the Rif to an Islamic Caliphate and much else in between. Abd el-Krim portrayed his failure as due to his having 'come too early.'[36] But eventually the 'anti-colonial combatant' would become a powerful *persona* on the international stage, one that would change the map of the world, a coveted role even at times claimed by those with dubious title to it.

For established legal opinion in 1925, however, the only way to bring the war's participants into 'existence' was to bring them under one of the authorized *dramatis personae*. Accordingly, Scelle, searching for a legal way to apply his humane ideals, declared:

> It is obviously regrettable that the [Versailles] Treaty does not cover all situations of this type … I have already wondered if, in the future, it would not be beneficial to transform the Rif into a territory under Mandate …[37]

Scelle here explicitly states the condition for these actors to appear on the international stage: their impersonation of one of the already authorized *dramatis personae*.

Scelle's opinion about the fatal anomalousness of the Riffans and its possible remedy was embedded in his overall vision of the Versailles drama. Ten years later, this vision continued to inform his response to crucial

36 See M Tahtah, *Entre Pragmatisme, Réformisme et Modernisme: Le rôle politico-religieux des Khattabi dans le Rif (Maroc) jusqu'à 1926* (Peeters 2000) 165.
37 ibid.

international events, specifically the Italian invasion of Ethiopia. The Italian invasion was, of course, a decisive event in the Versailles drama, the opening scene of its final act. While we can attribute the League's failure to take effective action to many factors, a central issue was Ethiopia's anomalousness within the Versailles construction of *dramatis personae*. The Versailles construction of 'Africa' placed the continent's peoples among those 'not advanced' enough for full membership in the international community, perhaps never destined to be 'ready' for the 'strenuous conditions of the modern world.' This racist construction of the *dramatis persona*, 'Africa,' stood in tension with the existence of an African state as a member of the League. Defenders of the Italian invasion foregrounded this inconsistency, stressing the illegitimate anomalousness of Ethiopian sovereignty.

Scelle vigorously condemned the Italian invasion. Nonetheless, he made it clear that his defense of Ethiopian sovereignty rested only on formal legal grounds, rather than on his distinctive sociological theory of law. On the level of principle, he agreed that Ethiopia's casting as a full member of the League was an anomaly on the international stage. Echoing his search for a remedy to the Riffan anomaly a decade earlier, he declared that a more proper casting for Ethiopia would have been as a mandated territory.

> Personally, we believe that it is one of the weaknesses of the conception of the Covenant of the League of Nations to have established in principle the identity of the legal and functional situation of all the member States ... Taken in itself, the plan [proposed by a League committee to resolve the conflict] ... comes close to the regime that it would have been reasonable to adopt from the start ... It is a regime analogous to that of the mandates, apt to guide towards progressive emancipation those 'peoples not yet able to govern themselves' (art. XXII of the Covenant); ... This system ... would constitute an excellent formula ... if it were not associated with the transformation [of Ethiopia] into an *Italian* Mandate.[38]

Scelle's position was thus very far from opposition to changing Ethiopia's international status. On the contrary, he declared the mis-casting of Ethiopia as a full League member to be a crucial blunder committed at the inception of the Versailles drama. He only objected to the proposed plan for resolving the conflict because it compounded that mis-casting with an additional one: the placing of a fascist state in the role of an 'advanced na-

38 Georges Scelle, 'La politique extérieure française et la S.D.N.' (1935) 10 Année politique française et étrangère 257, 282 (emphasis added).

tion.' The entrustment of the governance of Ethiopia to a truly 'advanced nation' would have been the ideal rectification of this anomaly in the Versailles drama. By 1935, however, it was too late for such fine-tuning.

6. *Destructive Parody*

I have shown that understanding international legal group identities as *dramatis personae* illuminates their contingent and constructed quality, the ways that they possess enduring power to shape the international drama and yet are subject to continual re-confirmation by the players on the stage or to being re-shaped and even resisted by them. Macartney's approving portrayal of the usurpation of 'self-determination' by proponents of minority rights provides a clear example of discursive *agon*, pitting one *dramatis persona* against another. Abd el-Krim's manifold efforts to enclothe the Riffan cause with a variety of conventional and unconventional *personae*, in an attempt to somehow place it on the world stage, provide examples of an attempted re-configuration of the Versailles list. Scelle's comments on the Rif and Ethiopia provide examples of an attempt to re-cast the actors to make them conform to an overall vision of the drama.

I turn now to the most effective, indeed deadly effective, re-appropriation of the *dramatis personae* of the Versailles drama: the Munich Accords of 1938.[39] Those seeking legal edification from the Versailles system rarely discuss the Munich Accords—except as a 'political' attack by Germany on law and the failure of political will by the West. If, however, all the Versailles *personae* are both contingent and constructed, subject to continual re-confirmation, re-appropriation, and resistance, we must fully acknowledge the Munich Accords as an integral part of the Versailles legal drama.

When read closely (and out of context), the Munich Accords have the power to startle us precisely due to their similarity to the Versailles treaties, rather than by any direct rejection of the Versailles principles. The Munich Accords do, of course, stage the penultimate scene of the closing act of the Versailles drama. They do not, however, attack it from without, but unfold one of its intrinsic possibilities. Far from renouncing the Versailles principles, they endorse them, even cite them for authority, all the while re-appropriating them in such a way as to empty them of their prior meaning.

39 Agreement for the Cession by Czechoslovakia to Germany of Sudeten German Territory, with Annex, and Declarations (done 29 September 1938) (1938) 142 BSP 438.

The Munich Accords are, in short, a close parody of Versailles, a parody undertaken with destructive intent.

A brief comparison of key Versailles principles with the Munich Accords should suffice to give a sense of this technique. The following is only a partial list of the overlap between the two:

a) Versailles Principle: division of territory predominantly according to the 'objective' principle of nationalities, anticipated in Wilson's call for the reconstitution of Poland on territory with 'indisputably Polish populations':[40]
b) Munich: paragraph 4 called for the cession by Czechovakia of 'predominantly German territory':
c) Versailles Principle: plebiscites to be held for territories whose national character was in dispute, implementing 'subjective self-determination,' as in the Saar and Upper Silesia;[41]
d) Munich: paragraph 5 provided for a plebiscite in territories not included in paragraph 4, 'taking as a basis the conditions of the Saar plebiscite'; these 'conditions' even included the occupation of the disputed territories by 'international bodies,' as in the Saar and Upper Silesia
e) Versailles Principle: treaties on minority rights as supplements to the main territorial divisions, as in Poland and all the new and 'greatly enlarged' states of central and eastern Europe;
f) Munich: two months after Munich, the Czechs and Germans concluded an agreement to protect their respective 'national minorities';[42]
g) Versailles Principle: international guarantee of territorial integrity to all recognized states, embodied in Article 10 of the Covenant;
h) Munich: an Annex to the Agreement bound the French and British to an immediate guarantee of the new Czech border.

In imitating, even citing, the Versailles Treaty, the Munich Accords effected a plot twist within the Versailles drama rather than a break from it. In Aris-

40 Woodrow Wilson, 'The Fourteen Points Address' (1918) in Arthur S Link (ed) *The Papers of Woodrow Wilson*, vol 45 (Princeton 1984) 536, 539.

41 For the provisions for the Saar Plebiscite, see Treaty of Versailles, art 49; for the Upper Silesia plebiscite and International Commission, see Treaty of Versailles, art 88.

42 The agreement is reprinted in 12 Documents Diplomatiques Français 798 (2d ser 1938). See also Hubert Ripka, *Munich: Before and After* (Ida Sindelkova and Edgar Young tr; H. Fertig 1969, first pubished 1939) 269.

totelian terms, the Accords were more of a *peripeteia*, a reversal within the logic of the drama,[43] rather than a *deus ex machina*, some new *persona* introduced from the outside. The new weight given to the 'predominant Germans' of Munich indeed reversed the fortunes of the established characters of the Versailles drama. This character, however, did not introduce a new kind of *persona* from the outside, for similar *personae*, like Wilson's 'indisputable Poles,' were long well-established in the tale.

As so often in Greek drama, this *peripeteia* was achieved through the use of language. To be sure, the reversal did not occur through language which reveals a previously unknown truth, as in plays like *Oedipus Rex*. On the contrary, the Munich Accords used familiar language, but in a way which emptied out the previous truth of its meaning. This linguistic subversion is characteristic of parody, here undertaken with the most heinous aims. The parody was so effective that the French and British who acclaimed the Accords did not even sense its destructive power until it was too late.

7. *No Exit?*

Despite the Versailles drama's elaborate and powerful constructions, there were those who proclaimed their refusal to participate in it, despite, or even because of, its promise of Peace-through-Law. Some of these refusals can be found in the responses to the War of the Rif published in the journal *Clarté*, a far-left literary journal, in 1925. The journal had invited such responses in an 'Open Letter' condemning France's attack on the Rif's 'independence and national sovereignty,' to which it was entitled by virtue of the 'inalienable right of the self-determination of peoples.'[44] The radical French writer Henry Poulaille[45] responded as follows:

> The war in Morocco?
> Obviously against.
> Against all wars.

---

43 Aristotle, *Poetics* 1452a.

44 Editors of Clarté, 'Lettre Ouverte aux Intellectuels pacifistes, anciens combattants, révoltés' (1925) 75 Clarté 1.

45 Poulaille was a somewhat unclassifiable left-wing political and cultural radical. He founded the 'proletarian school' of French literature and participated in anti-war and anarchist activism, while opposing the Communist Party and supporting Victor Serge, a Trotskyist imprisoned by Stalin.

> On the subject of this new 'last' war, what happens to the question of *Law?*
> Is the war in Morocco also a war of law?
> Then against law.[46]

And thus, in a few pithy phrases, Poulaille systematically rejected the kind of pacifism represented by the *Association de la Paix par le Droit*. Poulaille's contempt for the 1914–1918 'war of law' led him not only to reject all wars, but even all law. To declare a 'regime of law' to have been 'specified and stimulated' by war would be the ultimate condemnation of both.

A more well-known cultural and political radical, Louis Aragon, responded to the War of the Rif by directing his scorn at some of the key Versailles *dramatis personae*. Because the war was being waged 'in the name of France,' he declared that the very 'idea' of France, 'like all national ideas,' should 'disappear from the Earth.' [47] But he also addressed himself to the *Clarté* editors, condemning the principles upon which they based their own opposition to the war.

> [L]et me reproach you ... for having used expressions drawn from nationalist language: *independence, national sovereignty, inalienable right of peoples to self-determination*. For me, *there are no 'peoples.'* I can barely understand this word in the singular.[48]

Aragon here rejects not only key *personae* of the Versailles drama but also of the anticipated leftist revision of that drama to include anti-colonial *personae*: nationalism, national sovereignty, self-determination, even 'peoples.' Indeed, Aragon refuses even the ultimate *persona* of the Marxist imagination, 'the people' in the singular. I note that the Aragon of this declaration is the Dadaist and Surrealist rebel, not the later Aragon who joined the Communist Party—a party with a fixed sense of who comprised the legitimate *dramatis personae* on the international stage, even if drawn from a radically different list than that of Versailles.

8. *The 'Art of Justice' and the 'Smoking Crater'*

In 1930, Robert Redslob, professor of international law at Strasbourg, published *Le Principe des Nationalités,* a monograph on nationalism in histori-

46 'Réponse de M. Henry Poulaille' (1925) 76 Clarté 21.
47 'Réponse de M. Louis Aragon' (1925) 76 *Clarté* 23–24.
48 ibid 24 (emphasis added).

cal, philosophical, and legal perspective.[49] Redslob's career straddled the divide between German and French sovereignty over his native Alsace. This 1930 work was thus a mid-career reckoning with a force that powerfully shaped his life. *Le Principe des nationalités* is a stylistic and substantive *tour de force*, whose paradoxes, reversals, enthusiasms, and erudition I have explored at length elsewhere.[50]

By 1930, the Versailles drama was past its zenith. In September, the Nazis became the second largest party in the German parliament, increasing the number of their seats nearly ten-fold. A 1930 monograph optimistically appraising international law's engagement with nationalism, even if fully acknowledging the many difficulties, can only appear to us, like the journal cover with which I began this paper, as resembling a daydream at the edge of a volcano.

It is, therefore, somewhat startling when we recognize Redslob's acute awareness of his situation, as in the following description of law's relationship to nationalism:

> One must not delude oneself with the hope that one can fully illuminate this crater filled with flames and smoke ... [In relation to nationalist conflicts], justice is no longer a science but an art ... It is here that its imperfection appears, but it is here that, at the same time, its sovereign grandeur reveals itself.[51]

The 'sovereign grandeur' of an 'art' attempting to 'illuminate' a 'crater filled with flames and smoke': Redslob's stance is that of a tragic nobility, determination in the face of an indomitable, ungraspable force.

Indeed, the context of the passage from which I have taken the above quote suggests that a full consciousness of the indeterminacies, dangers, and yet unavoidability of the legal construction of *personae* lies behind Redslob's evocative imagery:

> In the dogma of nationalities, true and false conceptions, all irreducible, are intermixed. ... The world of the living is made of light and shadow. ... [H]umanity will always be pursued by Pilate's tragic apostrophe: 'What is truth?' [John 18:38].

49 Robert Redslob, *Le Principe des Nationalités* (Sirey1930).

50 Nathaniel Berman, '"But the Alternative is Despair": European Nationalism and the Modernist Renewal of International Law' (1993) 106 Harvard Law Review 1792, 1808–1821.

51 Redslob (n 49) 38.

The passage from the Gospel of John to which Redlsob refers concerns precisely the quest by Pilate to determine the *persona* of Jesus, indeed the legal question of whether he is a sovereign ['Are thou the King of the Jews?,' John 18:33]. Jesus then engages him in a riddling colloquy about the different possible meanings of sovereignty, playing with the polysemousness of the word 'kingdom.' The context of Redslob's citation of Pilate startlingly implies his identification, and that of international law generally, with this figure charged with adjudicating the most famous trial of identity in the Western imagination. His reading of Pilate's enigmatic question ('What is truth?') as 'tragic' implicitly proclaims the necessity, the intrinsic uncertainty, and the perils of the legal determination placed before the Roman Prefect. For Redslob, the 'sovereign grandeur' of law lies in its perseverance in the tragedy it which must act. And, of course, given the horrors that would shortly unfold in Europe, the anti-Jewish propaganda in the service of which the Gospel of John has historically been recruited compounds the fraught implications of Redslob's quote.

I have, in earlier studies, taken up Reslob's invitation to treat international law's engagement with nationalism as an 'art' in a number of ways. Given the themes of this paper, I will here read it in terms of the art of drama, especially the construction of the *dramatis personae*. I will examine Redslob's imputation of 'tragedy' and 'sovereign grandeur' to this art in relation to its most developed and subtle instantiation: the construction of the *personae* of the 'international experiment of Upper Silesia,' truly the *Gesamtkunstwerk* of Versailles dramaturgy. This art-work included an attempt to subtly balance the following *personae*:

- *National states*: the region was partitioned between German and Poland;
- *Supranational economic entity:* the Geneva Convention contained many provisions seeking to ensure the economic unity of the partitioned region for fifteen years;
- *Minorities*: the Convention granted Polish and German minorities on the two sides of the partition line extensive substantive and procedural rights, unparalleled elsewhere;
- *Transnational ethnic identity*: in contrast to the rest of the minority protection system, which denied 'kin-states' any role in protecting their ethnic 'kin' in other states, Germany and Poland played a variety of roles in such protection in Upper Silesia;
- *Supranational adjudicatory system:* the Mixed Commission' and 'Arbitral Tribunal,' comprised of international, German, and Polish of-

ficials, were entrusted with hearing disputes brought by individuals under the Geneva Convention;

- *Domestic legal systems partially integrated in a supranational system*: many cases could be brought directly in the Arbitral Tribunal; cases that began in domestic courts could also be referred to the Arbitral Tribunal at the request of the parties if they implicated questions under the Convention;
- *Internationalized individuals*: Upper Silesians attained an unprecedented international legal status by virtue of their ability to bring cases before the supranational Arbitral Tribunal; Upper Silesians who had opted for citizenship in the state in which they did not reside could remain in the state of their residency—creating a 'special category' of Upper Silesians who would have been considered mere 'aliens' under previous international law, 'an entirely new departure in international law'[52] that constructed a new legal *persona*.

It is by virtue of this complex list of *personae*, drawn from a variety of frameworks of political, economic, and judicial governance, that I dub the Upper Silesia regime the *Gestamtkunstwerk* of Versailles dramaturgy. The explicitly temporary nature of this 'experiment,' destined to lapse after fifteen years, emphasizes the constructed and contingent quality of its *personae*.

Nonetheless, many of these *personae* were to endure on the international stage long after the demise of their original instantiation in the Upper Silesian theater. The 1947 Palestine Partition Plan, for example, echoed the Upper Silesia regime in many of its key features and *personae*. The Dayton Accords for Bosnia also echoed, in revised form, many of the key features and *personae* of the Upper Silesia regime. Indeed, the European Union itself, a supranational regime providing economic unity, the partial integration of domestic legal systems in a supranational system, and a new legal status for individuals, even while maintaining the sovereignty of its member states, may justly be considered the chief progeny of the Upper Silesia regime.

If Upper Silesia was the site of the Versailles drama's *Gestamtkunstwerk*, it was also the site of its final scene. When the Nazis decided to finally destroy the Versailles treaty, they did so with an action that thoroughly confounded this site of the most delicate balancing of the Versailles *personae*. On August 31, 1939, German troops wearing civilian clothes attacked a ra-

52 Kaeckenbeeck (n 3) 187–188.

dio station on the German side of the Upper Silesian partition border, broadcast an announcement that the station was in Polish hands, and left behind a dead concentration camp prisoner dressed in Polish army uniform. This murdered prisoner was a German Upper Silesian who had fought on the Polish side during civil unrest in the region in 1921.[53] This elaborately conceived dramatic gesture, which served as the pretext for the invasion of Poland, was something other than the subversive parody of the Munich Accords. It was a direct assault on the *dramatis personae* of Versailles, their literal, as well as gestural, murder.

9. *Conclusion … or Not?*

Some might think it would be fitting to close this portrayal of the Versailles drama with August 31, 1939, the final scene of the tragedy, and the opening scene of the unimaginable horror that followed. I have asserted, however, that the Versailles drama did not end with the demise of its founding treaties. On the contrary, I maintain that its dramatis personae endure a century later, even if continually revised, expanded by some new *personae*, contracted through the demise of some old ones. If it has indeed lived on to our day, is it appropriate to call it a tragedy?

In the Preface to *The International Experiment of Upper Silesia*, dated October 5, 1939, Kaeckenbeeck declares:

> This is no war literature. The present work was written before the war broke out, and was conceived as a contribution to peace and international law. The horror into which Europe has now been plunged has not been permitted to influence its spirit … Should it succeed in giving useful inspiration for future settlements, one of my fondest hopes would be fulfilled.[54]

While Kackenbeeck no doubt intended the term 'war literature' as a synonym for 'propaganda,' I propose reading it as the designation of a literary genre, that of a tragedy that ends in war. Kaeckenbeeck is trying to prevent us from reading his *chef-d'œuvre* as such a tragedy. He insists that he completed the work when the outcome of the drama was still open, when the

53 See Leonard Mosley, *On Borrowed Time: How World War II Began* (Random House 1969) 430–34; Donald C Watt, *How War Came: The Immediate Origins of the Second World War, 1938–1939* (Pantheon 1989) 532.

54 Kaeckenbeeck (n 3) vii.

happy end of a comedy was still possible. He sought to make a 'contribution to peace and international law,' even, in light of his other statements, 'peace-*through*-international-law.'

He urges us to read his 'literature' in that optic, not to view the horror of the new World War as that in which the Versailles drama inevitably culminated. On the contrary, he envisions a future in which the apocalypse of the war might seem like just an episode in a continuing drama. He addresses himself to those who might someday still identify with the *personae* of the Versailles-era internationalists, to those who might seek in the 'international experiment of Upper Silesia' the 'inspiration' for the 'settlement' of conflicts yet to come. He is thus addressing himself to the future authors of the Palestine Partition Plan, of the Dayton Accords, of 'international experiments' we can only imagine—and to the scholars who will study, interpret, and draw lessons from them. In short, he addresses himself to us, beseeching us to see the Versailles drama as perpetually open, its outcome always in the future. And that outcome depends, in part, on how we take up the *personae* of the 'internationalists' to whom Kaeckenbeeck implicitly addresses himself.

The 'internationalist' *persona* (whether or not designated by that term), was not invented by the Versailles treaties, but the institutionalized international community and the 'new international law' they inaugurated gave it a far more central role. 'Internationalist' can designate at least two distinct *personae*. The first includes those whose specialty, either as practitioners or scholars, is international law. The second includes those who advocate the ideology of internationalism, the advancement of greater cooperation and understanding among nations, often accompanied by advocacy of the attenuation of the political and legal prerogatives of sovereignty. These *personae* often overlap: international legal scholars and practitioners often commit themselves to creating a world of peace and understanding, one in which sovereigns can no longer initiate and conduct war in an unfettered manner. Most of the best-remembered international jurists of the interwar period fit this description. This overlap, however, has no logical necessity: one may be an ideological internationalist but possess no legal training; one may be an international jurist and dedicate oneself to a fierce defense of sovereign prerogatives.

Moreover, the deepest differences divide even those who fit both senses of the 'internationalist' *persona*. They include both pro-colonialists and anti-colonialists, Communists and anti-Communists, feminists and those indifferent to the issue of international patriarchy. Despite these and other radical differences, most of those I have just named have understood themselves as believers in Peace-through-Law—including both principled pacifists and those who have believed that the establishment of a just world requires armed force to restructure the world stage, in order to 'specify and stimulate' a legal regime worthy of respect.

Thus, while the 'internationalist' persona is a legacy of the long drama in which we act, we can, and indeed must, take up that role in a way that chooses among its prior, widely divergent, performances, or that invents new ones. To borrow and adapt the words of Judith Butler:

> In a sense, all signification takes place within the orbit of the compulsion to repeat; 'agency,' then, is to be located within the possibility of a variation on that repetition ... The injunction *to be* a given [*persona*] ... takes place through discursive routes ... in response to a variety of different demands all at once. The coexistence or convergence of such discursive injunctions produces the possibility of a complex reconfiguration and redeployment; it is not a transcendental subject who enables action in the midst of such a convergence. There is no self that is prior to the convergence or who maintains 'integrity' prior to its entrance into this conflicted cultural field. There is only a taking up of the tools where they lie ...[55]

The injunction, or aspiration, '*to be*' a persona, can be 'taken up' in many different ways, and must always be taken up anew. This dictum applies to the 'internationalist' *persona*, just as it applies to *personae* such as 'state,' 'people,' and 'minority'—or to personae such as 'Germans,' 'French,' 'Jews,' and so on. Even the *persona* of 'rebel against all the official *personae*,' is one that has been bequeathed to us by precursors as different as the Riffan Abd el-Krim and the Parisian Louis Aragon.

In the conclusion to my 1993 study of the interwar period's 'modernist renewal of international law,' I quoted Adorno's famous 1949 dictum 'To write poetry after Auschwitz is barbaric.'[56] At a time of post-Cold War international legal exuberance, I asked whether this condemnation of European high culture for its failure to prevent, or even for its complicity in, Auschwitz might apply to international law, an artifact of that same culture. In our very different time of disintegration and disillusionment, I would like again to contemplate Adorno's revision of that statement published in 1966:

---

55 Judith Butler, *Gender Trouble: Feminism and the Subversion of Identity* (Routledge 1999) 185.

56 Theodor W Adorno, 'Cultural Criticism and Society' (1944) in *Prisms* (Samuel & Sherry Weber tr, MIT Press 1981) 17, 34. See discussion in Berman, '"But the Alternative is Despair..."' (n 50) 1900–1901.

> Perennial suffering has as much right to expression as a tortured man has to scream; hence it may have been wrong to say that after Auschwitz you could no longer write poems. But it is not wrong to raise the less cultural question whether after Auschwitz you can go on living—especially whether one who escaped by accident, one who by rights should have been killed, may go on living. ... By way of atonement he will be plagued by dreams such as that he is no longer living at all, that he was sent to the ovens in 1944 and his whole existence since has been imaginary, an emanation of the insane wish of a man killed twenty years earlier.[57]

There is, similarly, something 'insane' about continuing to inhabit the 'internationalist' persona after World War II, the war which the 'new international law' of the Versailles drama did not prevent—as well as after Vietnam, after the Bosnian genocide, the Rwandan genocide, and the numerous other horrors perpetrated in full public view, long after the re-imagination of the international stage by the dramaturges of Versailles.

But, we may ask: was it not also 'insane' to invent the 'new international law' after the 'Great War,' the war that the idealists of the *Association de la Paix par le Droit* did not prevent, despite their conjuration of the disarming cherub and the edifying ephebe who sought to transform the Warrior into a Tiller of the Soil?

It is, in short, a dramatic, maybe even 'insane,' gesture to entitle a conference on the Versailles Treaty, 'Peace through Law.' But we, who have chosen to live on as 'internationalists'—even after the repeated murder of that *persona* over the past century—must take up that gesture, 'reconfiguring and redeploying' it in ever-new ways.

What is the fate of the Versailles drama within which we all live? It is too early to tell.

57 Theodor W Adorno, *Negative Dialectics* (EB Ashton tr, Seabury 1973) 362–363.

Part 2: The Establishment of a New International Order of Peace

Chapter 2 The League of Nations as a Universal Organization

Thomas D Grant[*]

1. Introduction

The attainment by the United Nations of nearly universal participation of states, joined with the 'turn to history' in the study of international law, imparts interest to the topic of participation in the League of Nations. A relatively well-known, if still incompletely understood, dimension of the international environment of the time was the emergence of new dispute settlement mechanisms and the vivification of existing ones. Dispute settlement mechanisms are the central focus of the works contained in this book. It is not at first obvious, perhaps, what effect universality of membership in the League, or the striving toward it, might have had on dispute settlement mechanisms. Universality and the principle of sovereign equality that underlay it were themselves, however, a dimension of the same environment in which those mechanisms functioned. This chapter considers how universality and sovereign equality may have affected dispute settlement in other forums in the interwar era.

The League, though a political body, was congenial to sovereign equality, which, in turn, lent support to legal procedures for dispute settlement, because sovereign equality is indispensable to any legal procedure that purports to be binding as between states. States in the decades before the League by no means had rejected legal procedures as a means to settle inter-state disputes; nor did states suddenly arrive at a complete acceptance of such procedures in the League era. Far from it.[1] However, as other chapters in this volume attest, the interwar era witnessed an efflorescence of inter-state dispute settlement.

As the dispute settlement machinery of the interwar era was not entirely new, so too was society at large characterized by a mixture of innovation and continuity. After a century, we still think of World War One as the end

---

* Fellow, Lauterpacht Centre for International Law, University of Cambridge. The views expressed in this chapter are those of the author and do not reflect those of any other individual or institution.

1 See Erpelding (Introduction).

of a social order, and 1919 as the start of something very different. Professor Nathanial Berman has noted that, after the war, it seemed as though 'everything [had] changed.'[2] One is reminded of the Foreword to Thomas Mann's *The Magic Mountain,* that favourite of international lawyers, in which the third person narrator attributes the 'extraordinary pastness' of his story to 'its having taken place *before* a certain turning point, on the far side of a rift that has cut deeply through our lives and consciousness... back then, long ago, in the old days of the world before the Great War, with whose beginning so many things began whose beginnings, it seems, have not yet ceased.'[3] The changes no doubt were momentous, and the people who experienced them were shaken by the transition. Even so, in and after 1919, vestiges of an earlier epoch remained. Much of the old social order was gone, but, in truth, not everything had changed. This was no less the case in regard to international law in particular than in society at large. Because formal equality of parties is an indispensable principle in judicial and arbitral procedure, it is salient for present purposes to recall that certain vestiges of sovereign inequality remained very much visible in 1919.

2. *Sovereign Equality Emerging—But not Entrenched*

It was still accepted in 1919 that not all states were equal, even in the formal, legal sense. Inequality was reflected in the Treaty of Versailles itself.

Part V of the Treaty—the Military, Naval and Air Clauses[4]—famously placed Germany under special constraints. There were also the financial clauses[5] and the articles relating to the internationalization of certain rivers passing through Germany.[6] In defence of the drafters, it might be said that those constraints were the substantive rules of the treaty. They implement-

---

2 See Berman (ch 1).

3 Thomas Mann, *The Magic Mountain* (John E Woods tr, Alfred A Knopf 1995) xi–xii. The passage in full in the German language original, *Der Zauberberg* (S Fischer Verlag 1924), is as follows:'*Um aber einen klaren Sachverhalt nicht künstlich zu verdunkeln: die hochgradige Verflossenheit unserer Geschichte rührte daher, daß sie vor einer gewissen, Leben und Bewußtsein tief zerklüftenden Wende und Grenze spielt... Sie spielt, oder, um jedes Präsens geflissentlich zu vermeiden, sie spielte und hat gespielt vormals, ehedem, in den alten Tagen, der Welt vor dem großen Kriege, mit dessen Beginn so vieles begann, was zu beginnen wohl kaum schon aufgehört hat*.'

4 Arts 159–213.

5 Part IX—arts 248–263.

6 See Part XII, Section II, Chapters III and IV (arts 331–362) (relating to the Elbe, the Oder, the Niemen, and the Danube; and the Rhine and the Moselle). Cf *Territorial*

ed political decisions taken in the aftermath of a war in which the victors insisted on maximum terms against the Central Powers. In themselves, the punitive provisions of the Treaty did not entail a loss of sovereign equality. They were burdensome, but they did not indicate that the state to which they applied was anything less than a legal person having the same formal rights and obligations under general international law as other states. At least the formal indicia of state consent were present; these were terms to which a state had acceded in the normal way, even if the circumstances were anomalous.

Less often noted are the provisions of the Treaty of Versailles that really did reflect a formal, juridical imbalance in the relations among states. The most striking examples related to third states—that is, to states not parties to the treaty. For example, Germany in Article 142 re-affirmed that it recognized the French Protectorate in Morocco. In Article 147, it did the same in respect of the British Protectorate in Egypt. Morocco and Egypt, under Protectorate, did not possess the full scope of rights that we expect a state today to hold.[7] These protectorate provisions reflected a generally accepted reality of the day, as was seen in the response to the Rif rebellion in the French and Spanish Protectorates of Morocco.[8]

Also sometimes overlooked are the guarantee provisions of Article 433 regarding Eastern Europe. German troops were to remain in the Baltic States until the Principal Allied and Associated Powers said otherwise. One

Jurisdiction of the International Commission of the River Oder, PCIJ Rep ser A no 23 (Judgment, 10 September 1929).

7 It is true that protectorates, too, were understood to result from treaty engagements between the protecting and the protected states, and, to that extent, might be considered as simply another example of substantive treaty rules imposing an agreed burden on a state: see *Nationality Decrees Issued in Tunis and Morocco*, PCIJ Rep ser B no 4 (Advisory Opinion, 7 February 1923) 27–28. However, in balance, at least some of the protectorates were not 'sovereign' in the fullest sense. Relevant in this regard were the extreme extent to which their competences were curtailed and doubts as to whether they were free to renounce the protectorate treaty. The Advisory Opinion on the Austro-German customs régime furnishes a comparison, where the Permanent Court addressed Article 88 of the Treaty of Saint-Germain, under which Austria's independence was affirmed to be 'inalienable otherwise than with the consent of the Council of the League of nations...' PCIJ Rep ser AB no 41 (Advisory Opinion, 5 September 1931). Also salient in this connection is the example of Egypt. That state formally ended the capitulatory rights of various states in its territory, and this was an important development in opening the way to its admission as a member of the League. See Manley O Hudson, Editorial Comment (1937) 31(4) AJIL 681–83.

8 See Berman (ch 1).

might ask whether this is consistent with sovereign equality. Lithuania, Latvia, and Estonia were not parties to the Treaty of Versailles. Yet under Article 433 very large numbers of foreign troops remained in those territories, in effect with the imprimatur of the victorious powers.

Even though provisions such as these were still included in treaties—or perhaps because they were—sovereign equality was a topic of high interest at the time. The third edition of Oppenheim's *International Law*, the first edition of that work published after the war, had the following to say about equality of states:

> The equality before International Law of all member States of the Family of Nations is an invariable equality derived from their International Personality. Whatever inequality may exist between States as regards their size, population, power, degree of civilization, wealth, and other qualities, they are nevertheless equals as International Persons.[9]

Oppenheim's editor went on to say that sovereign equality had three consequences, which he expressed as follows:

> (1) that, whenever a question arises which has to be settled by the Family of Nations, every State has a right to a vote but to one vote only
> (2) that—legally though not politically—the vote of the weakest and smallest State has quite as much weight as the vote of the largest and most powerful
> (3) that—according to the rule *par in parem non habet imperium*—no State can claim jurisdiction over another full Sovereign State.

The Oppenheim treatise here expressed the first two points in terms of voting procedure; the third as a matter of jurisdiction. To express sovereign equality as a matter of jurisdiction—as it was expressed in the third point —is unremarkable. But to express sovereign equality as a matter of voting procedure merits note. The third edition of Oppenheim was published in 1920. The League's First Assembly was on 15 November 1920; the first session of the Council had been in January. So Oppenheim was speaking of sovereign equality as a matter of voting procedure; then linked the point to the principle that a sovereign does not exercise jurisdiction over another sovereign (*par in parem non habet imperium*); and this was practically at the same time as the inauguration of the League. It is to be suggested that the

---

9 Ronald Roxburgh (ed), *Oppenheim's International law: A Treatise* (3rd edn, Longmans, Green and Co 1920) Section 115.

arrival on the scene of a body of states in which decisions were to be reached by it as a body, and in which those decisions were to be reached by votes, and in which the votes were to be cast on the basis of sovereign equality, had captured the imagination of international lawyers.

To be sure, there were situations before the League came into existence where states might cast votes. Diplomatic conferences well before 1914 had sometimes been conducted under voting procedures. However, it was not self-evident that the way to speak about sovereign equality was to speak about voting procedures. Indeed, diplomatic conferences of the earlier era were characterized by variable rights and precedence, depending on the status or power of particular states participating. Compared to the particular rules adopted for diplomatic conferences, under which different states had different rights, the Covenant of the League indeed inspired a new way of seeing things. With the Covenant, the idea started to take hold that international relations might now be coming under the rule of law. Moreover, the League appeared to promise that international relations would be institutionalized, as well as legalized, to a degree heretofore unknown. And so it was becoming natural to speak about sovereign equality as a matter of *procedural* equality. The equality of states was no longer a matter of abstract principle. It instead was beginning to have practical consequences in decision-making mechanisms.

Thus the United States Secretary of State, Charles Evans Hughes, speaking in 1923 about the Monroe Doctrine, which asserted the supremacy of United States power in the New World, placed unmistakeable emphasis, instead, on the sovereign equality of states in that region and upon the value of cooperation among them.[10] Writers at the time took keen interest in sovereign equality. More particularly, it was noted how the League of Nations was giving effect to sovereign equality through its rules and procedures. Schücking and Wehberg addressed this development in *Die Satzung des Völkerbundes* (2nd edn);[11] Georges Scelle in various works concerning the League,[12] and Edwin Dickinson in his dissertation on *The Equality of*

10 See James Brown Scott, Editorial Comment (with the Secretary of State's statement) (1924) 18 AJIL 117–19.

11 Walter Schücking and Hans Wehberg, *Die Satzung des Völkerbundes* (Franz Vahlen 1924).

12 See, eg, Georges Scelle, 'La troisième Assemblée de la Société des Nations', *L'Europe Nouvelle* (Paris, 7 October 1922) 1257; 'Ce que nous attendons de l'Assemblée de Genève', *La Paix par le droit* (August–September 1921) 274, for discussion of which see Jean-Michel Guieu, *Les juristes français, la Sociéte des Nations et l'Europe* (colloquium paper, 2005) 6–8.

States in International Law published around the same time in the United States.[13] And the connection between the League, sovereign equality, and dispute settlement was observable not only in the writings of publicists or inferrable from the pronouncements of foreign ministers. The constitutive texts of the contemporary international order reflected it.

To consider the conceptual connection between the League, sovereign equality, and dispute settlement, it helps to recall how the Treaty of Versailles, the Covenant of the League, and the dispute settlement machinery of the interwar era were connected as texts. It has been recalled that the Treaty of Versailles was not a stand-alone document; it was one in a series of treaties.[14] Part I of the Treaty of Versailles was a common part repeated and incorporated into each of them. The Covenant was, figuratively speaking, a long preamble to the peace itself—or at least to the written instruments whose purpose was to secure the peace.

As to the dispute settlement machinery, this was two-fold: there would be the League Council in which disputes might be addressed at diplomatic level; and there would be the legal procedures of arbitration, now supplemented by a standing judicial organ, the Permanent Court of International Justice.[15] The Council, in this arrangement, was available under Article 12 of the Covenant as a forum for resolving any dispute between members of the League. The Covenant also conferred on the Council the function of a backstop: where members had a dispute and did not submit it to arbitration or to the Permanent Court, they were to submit it to the Council. In accordance with Article 15, the Council then would conduct a dispute settlement procedure itself (or refer the matter to the Assembly if so requested by either party to the dispute). The benefits of universal membership in the League for this dispute settlement apparatus were obvious: the apparatus was open to members, and so the closer the League approached universal membership, the fewer the bilateral disputes not potentially subject to the Council's dispute settlement function. Universality would close the gaps.

Then there was the standing judicial organ, the Permanent Court. Its Statute provided that '[o]nly States or Members of the League of Nations

13 Edwin DW Dickinson, *The Equality of States in International Law* (HUP 1920). Dickinson saw as particularly important the rules and apparatuses established under the Covenant to remove self-help from international relations; with recourse to force no longer a normal part of international relations, juridical relations among states had a chance, in Dickinson's view, to come to the fore. ibid 347–48.

14 See Erpelding (Introduction).

15 See further Tams (ch 10).

can be parties in cases before the Court.'[16] The Statute indicated that the 'conditions under which the Court shall be open to other States' were to be 'laid down by the Council, but in no case shall such provisions place the parties in a position of inequality before the Court.' In light of these provisions, it might appear that universality of membership in the League was not centrally important to the functioning of the Court. After all, the Statute expressly identified non-member states as potential parties in the Court's cases. The subsistence of a number, or even a large number, of non-members for that reason would not seem necessarily to have impeded the Court's dispute settlement function. A degree of separation seemed to exist between the Court and the League.

The manner in which the Court came into being also suggested that these institutions might not be absolutely integral to one another. The Covenant itself did not bring the Permanent Court into being. Instead, Article 14 required the League Council to 'formulate and submit to the Members of the League for adoption plans for the establishment of a Permanent Court...' This provision stands in contrast to the ICJ, which Chapter XIV of the UN Charter with reference to the annexed Statute of the Court constitutes as a principal organ of the UN. The link between the PCIJ and the League of Nations was not quite so tight.

One should take care, however, not to overstate the degree of separation. The Statute of the Permanent Court envisaged a role for the Council. It was, for example, for the Council to say what conditions a state not a member of the League would have to meet in order to participate as a party in proceedings of the Court. Article 13 of the Covenant provided for referral of legal disputes to the Court. Article 14 provided for the competence of the Court in contentious matters between states, to the extent that states submitted such matters to it. And the Covenant provided for advisory jurisdiction. Advisory jurisdiction was to be based on referral by the League Council or by the League Assembly. Advisory jurisdiction in this way was a further illustration of the nexus between the League and the Court.

3. *Admission, Voting, and Sovereign Equality in the League*

There was a less direct, but perhaps just as important, connection between the League and the dispute settlement system then taking shape. This was

16 Statute of the Permanent Court of International Justice (adopted 16 December 1920, entered into force 20 August 1921) 6 LNTS 389, art 34.

in the character of the League as a permanent international body predicated on the equality of its members. When it came to the Council itself, insofar as it might perform dispute settlement functions, the equality of the members was of direct importance, because a body in which certain members had formal, legal privileges of general scope placing them above others in matters of decision-making could not have performed dispute settlement functions in a manner compatible with modern principles of law or justice. There was also the supporting role that the political organs might perform in respect of decisions reached by the judicial organ. When it came to the judicial machinery as such, that is to say, the Permanent Court, and all the more so the various arbitral procedures, these, it is true, functioned on their own terms, separately from the political organs of the League; one could have had political organs in which sovereign equality was curbed or ignored altogether, and still have had dispute settlement organs in which it was respected in full. It may be submitted, however, that sovereign equality in the Council and Assembly were nevertheless important to judicial and arbitral procedures in the interwar era. Before considering how sovereign equality in the League's political organs supported the judicial and arbitral procedures, some observations are in order in respect of the rules and procedures of the League—in particular, the rules and procedures regulating participation in the League.

The states parties to the Peace Conference needed to answer a threshold question about participation, if they were to build a permanent international body of states. Namely, they needed to say what states would be members of that body. The states parties answered the question in two parts.

First, in an Annex to the Covenant, they set out a list of states which Article 1, paragraph 1, of the Covenant designated '[t]he original Members' of the League. The category 'original Members' itself had two subsidiary parts. The first subsidiary part consisted of 'Signatories [of the Treaty] which are named' in the Annex; the second consisted of 'such of those other states named in the Annex as shall accede without reservation' to the Covenant. The list of signatories included 32 states. (Not all states on the list in fact ratified the Treaty, most famously the United States). The second group in the Annex consisted of 13 states 'invited to accede to the Covenant.'

Then there was the possibility of the League admitting states in addition to the original members. That is to say, it was open to the League to admit states in addition to those included by name in the Annex. Admission of such states required agreement of two-thirds of the Assembly. Admission also required that a state seeking admission 'shall give effective guarantees of its sincere intention to observe its international obligations, and shall accept such regulations as may be prescribed by the League in regard to its military, naval and air forces and armaments.' These requirements were contained in Article 1 of the Covenant. In principle, any state was able to meet such requirements. This held for the defeated states as well as others. There was no special reference to defeated or enemy states, and so nothing prevented the states on the losing side of the Great War from requesting and gaining admission to the League. Even the mandates provision, Article 22, which addressed certain territories and colonies of Germany and the Ottoman Empire, referred to the change of status of those territories and colonies as 'a consequence of the late war,' saying simply that the territories to come under mandate 'have ceased to be under the sovereignty of the states which formerly governed them...' The language here was neutral. It did not place any special disability on the defeated states, and it did not address them as a special class for purposes of participation in the League.

As to the procedures of the League under which its members operated, these guaranteed the formal equality of members. Under Article 3, paragraph 4, of the Covenant, 'At meetings of the Assembly each member of the League shall have one vote.' The Council was somewhat different. The Principal Allied and Associated Powers were guaranteed membership in the Council. Further members were selected by the Assembly. So a degree of unequal treatment was entailed by the manner in which the League constituted the Council. It is natural to compare this provision for preferential treatment in the League Council to the UN Security Council, with its permanent five members. Nevertheless, each state in the League Council had one vote; and, at least as a formal matter, each vote was equal. The Covenant in this way placed the member states on an equal procedural footing even where, in the Council, a certain precedence was given to the main powers. The one-state, one-vote formula in the Assembly was striking for its institutionalization, and proceduralization, of sovereign equality. While the Council embodied a preference for its guaranteed members, this was not a general purpose denial of equal rights.

Another provision of the Covenant that holds interest for present purposes is Article 1, paragraph 2. That provision described what entities were eligible for admission to the League. The UN Charter, in its article 4, paragraph 1, concerning admission of new members, does not distinguish between different types of 'peace-loving states.' The Covenant of the League, by contrast, indicated that the entities that 'may become a Member of the League' included '[a]ny fully self-governing State, Dominion or Colony.' So there were three possible subjects under Article 1, paragraph 2 of the Covenant. Article 1, paragraph 2, presents a question of interpretation. It might be that the modifying phrase 'fully self-governing' is the center of gravity in Article 1, paragraph 2. The requirement that the entity be 'fully self-governing,' perhaps, was what really controlled the matter. On that view, the drafters of the Covenant intended to adopt a requirement of independence, tantamount to statehood. On that view, whether the entity was designated 'state,' 'dominion,' or 'colony' was less important than the substance of what it was.

The practice of the League, however, suggested that independence was not an absolute requirement. As at 1919, the dominions that belonged to the British Empire were in the process of attaining full independence, but even as to the dominions furthest along the road to independence—Canada, Australia, New Zealand, South Africa—it could be asked at the time whether the journey was complete. As to India, it clearly was not. India was not an independent state in 1919. It was however, by virtue of its inscription in the Annex, a member of the League. The League practiced openness as regarded membership.

At least to a degree. The only Dominion to be admitted under paragraph 2 of Article 1 was the Irish Free State. Its representatives having taken their places in Geneva, the Irish Free State was mindful to distinguish its position from that of a dependency of the British Empire. Any suggestion of dependency roused sharp protest from the Irish delegates. Indicative of the priority that the Irish attached to their equal representation in the League, there was this observation from the Permanent Representative of the Free State to his superiors in Dublin:

> it would perhaps also be well to consider the prejudice that may be caused to the Saorstát [the Free State] by the meetings of the delegates of the 'Empire' whilst at Geneva. It is because of these meetings that the British delegate has frequently pretended to speak to his Colleagues in the name of the Dominions as well.[17]

The point was that Ireland did not intend to tolerate another state speaking in its name. This new Assembly was to be a forum of equal rights, regardless of size or history. A member that enjoys sovereign equality with other members might voluntarily assign its rights to another, but for another member to purport to exercise its rights, even procedural rights such

17 Memorandum, para V, with letter of Michael MacWhite [Irish Permanent Representative to the League] to Joseph P Walshe (Dublin), (M L 04/0130), dated 14 April 1928: no 136 NAI DFA LN 1/7.

as the right to speak in the Assembly of the League, would be incompatible with that equality.

Apart from the Free State, no other party was admitted as a member of the League under the dominions or colonies provision. The potential openness of the membership provision of the Covenant thus remained a possibility, but not a generally realized fact. Two states that were plainly states—Afghanistan and Ethiopia—discovered that gaining admission was an uphill battle.[18] The League admitted them, but it seems only begrudgingly. The subsequent maltreatment of Ethiopia in the League at the time of the Italian invasion was one of the low points in the League's declining years.[19]

Other national communities at the margins of international relations asked for admission but were refused. There were the independent states at the edges of the former Russian empire for example. Ukraine's pleas to the League were emotionally moving,[20] but ultimately did not move the Assembly to admit Ukraine.[21] Georgia and Armenia were not admitted either.[22]

---

18 Request for Admission to the League of Nations from the Empire of Ethiopia: C.562.1923.IX (31 August 1923). See further Antoinette Iadarola, 'Ethiopia's Admission into the League of Nations: An Assessment of Motives' (1975) 8(4) International Journal of African Historical Studies 601–622. As to Afghanistan, see Manley O Hudson, Editorial Comment (1935) 29 AJIL 110–11. Upon Afghanistan's eventual admission to the League, the French delegate, M Aubert, said that its admission 'was a further stage towards the universality which all desired.' Assembly, Sixteenth Meeting (26 September 1934) 94. Other delegates invoked universality as well in the same connection (eg, Tevfik Rüstü Bey for Turkey: ibid 93).

19 See, for example, the doubts expressed as to Ethiopia's credentials following the invasion:'The question seemed to the Committee an extremely delicate one. No member suggested that it should be settled in the negative, and that the credentials in question should accordingly be declared to be manifestly not in order. None the less, all the members of the Committee felt some doubt whether they really were in order.' (Politis [Greece], as Rapporteur of the Committee on Credentials). LoN, Assembly, 17th ordinary session, 4th plenary meeting, 23 Sept 1936: *LONS*, VR (Ass) 1–2, cols 2, 1. No legal basis existed for denying credentials to the representatives of Ethiopia after Italy had purported to extinguish that member state's independence by force.

20 See Letter of A Margolin, Ukrainian Diplomatic Mission in the United Kingdom, to Sir Eric Drummond, Secretary-General of the League of Nations (14 April 1920) 20/48/5 VII.

Another episode was similarly instructive about the attitude in the League toward states and political communities at the peripheries of international relations. The King of Yemen, in 1936, wrote to his counterpart, Edward VIII, asking about admission to the League. He asked,

> [W]e hasten to request Your Majesty, thus placing us under a debt to Your Majesty and to Your Beloved Government, kindly to intercede personally on our behalf by placing our request to join the membership of the League of Nations from this time onwards in company with those who are already sincere members of it. By this means, Your Majesty will have both rectified the omission made by the Foreign Minister [sic] … and also accomplished a praiseworthy act by being the means of commencing a golden age for the Yemen, as a result of Your Majesty's gracious intervention.[23]

The matter in the end was referred to the British governor at Aden, a rather minor colonial official.[24] There is no record that Yemen's request received consideration at Geneva.

4. *Other Aspects of Participation*

This is not to depreciate the developments toward greater equality which took place under the Covenant. As already noted in this chapter, there was the formal equality of states in the Assembly and Council as reflected in voting procedure.

There were other examples as well. Article 18 of the Covenant provided for the registration of treaties. This was the precursor to Article 102 of the UN Charter. At first glance, treaty registration might not appear to have anything to do with sovereign equality. However, it was not only League

---

21 See Admission of new members: Ukraine; Report Presented by 5th Committee to the Assembly, 20/48/180 VII (6 December 1920). The 5th Committee's objection was that Ukraine lacked a stable government exercising authority over the whole of Ukraine's territory.

22 See Admission of New Members: Georgia; Reported Presented by the 5th Committee to the Assembly, 20/48/208 VII (10 December 1920); Armenia, 20/48/209 VII (10 December 1920).

23 His Majesty the King of Yemen, Imam Yahya bin Muhammad Hamid Ud Din, to His Majesty King Edward VIII, King of Great Britain and the British Dominions beyond the Seas, Emperor of India (25 March 1936) FO 141/455/9, 6.

24 Foreign Office text of letter, from the King to the King of the Yemen (dated 27 July 1936) FO 141/455/9, 8–9.

member states that availed themselves of the treaty registration apparatus. States not parties to the Covenant of the League from time to time communicated treaties to the Secretariat. Moreover, Wilson's call for 'open covenants of peace, openly arrived at' was one of the foundation stones of the post-war peace as envisaged.[25] The principle of openness (to be implemented through publication) is a famous one; less remarked is the other branch of this Wilsonian precept: the peaceful character of the treaty. Proposals were made in the Fifth Session of the League Council by Council President Léon Bourgeois and at the Second Assembly by the representative of Greece that a treaty which the Council determined to be 'contrary to international public order' was to be declared null and void and not to be registered; Arnold McNair was among the jurists in sympathy with such proposals.[26] If they had been implemented, then Article 18 would have evolved into a system of treaty certification as against fundamental international law rules—a sort of permanent advisory procedure to test the lawfulness of the treaty engagements of states.[27] The idea of a substantive certification for treaties was ahead of its time (and it remains so today!). It nevertheless highlighted another way in which participation in the functions of the League tended to support international dispute settlement. Even though Article 18 never entailed a system of formal, centralized scrutiny of treaties, it prescribed an open and transparent procedure under which treaties henceforward would be published and thus available to any interested party. Under that procedure, a state, regardless of its size or political power, could comment upon and, as it wished, object to, treaties that concerned it, including treaties to which it was not a party. This was, in effect, a decentralized procedure of review. In its decentralization, Article 18's effects fell short of the ambitions of those who wished the League to perform custodial functions in a centralized way. The new transparency nevertheless was valuable to certain states, especially those having less political influence and adversely affected by treaty-making carried out by others in

---

25 This being the first of Wilson's Fourteen Points. See (1919) 13 AJIL 161.

26 Arnold D McNair, 'Equality in International Law,' (1927) 26(2) Mich LR 131, 150 with citations at footnotes 55 and 56 to the Council and Assembly proceedings.

27 Such a procedure would have accorded with McNair's view that a reservation to a multilateral treaty should not be effective unless all parties assent to it, a view that he expressed in 1938 in *The Law of Treaties* (Clarendon Press 1938) 106 and which was reflected in the joint dissent in the *Reservations* advisory opinion in 1951: 'We believe that the integrity of the terms of the Convention is of greater importance than mere universality in its acceptance.' *Reservations to the Convention on the Prevention and Punishment of the Crime of Genocide*, Dissenting Opinion of Judges Guerrero, McNair, Read, and Hsu Mo (28 May 1951): ICJ Rep 1951 at 47.

their absence.[28] The earlier practice of secret treaty-making had often been used to derogate the rights of third states; in this way secret treaty-making had undermined the practical value of sovereign equality. Article 18 tended to level the playing field.

And there were still other steps toward equality, in a wider social sense, going beyond the treatment that international organization accorded to states. Article 7 of the Covenant provided that '[a]ll positions under or in connection with the League, including the Secretariat, shall be open equally to men and women.' Seen through present-day eyes, this provision does not suggest any great progressive ambition. It was not however written by 21st century drafters. It was a product of its time, and as such may it be read. The social milieu in which the Covenant came into force was not the same as that before the Great War, but by no means had Europe been catapulted to a completely new social order in 1918. To paraphrase Mann, so many things had begun whose beginnings, it seems, even today have not yet ceased ... To give a taste of the milieu in the immediate post-war period, one might consult the first volume of the *Cambridge Law Journal*. This was published in February 1920. The *Journal* that month reported on two debates at the Pembroke College Law Society.[29] The Michaelmas Term debate was on the motion 'That in the opinion of this House the power of women has increased and ought to be diminished.' The motion prevailed. Then in Lent Term the motion in the Law Society was 'That this House welcomes the advent of women on the jury.' That motion 'was finally defeated by a substantial majority.'[30] So this was a time in which basic propositions of the equality of individuals in civic life had not been settled.[31] The provision in Article 7 of the Covenant opening League positions equally to men and women is a more significant step than it might at first appear. It was of a piece with a general theme of openness and participation that, modest as its particular mechanisms were, marked a step toward a different attitude than had prevailed before.

28 Noteworthy in this connection were Ethiopia's protests against an Italian–British treaty allocating rights in Ethiopia between those two parties. See 'Italy and Abyssinia,' 12 (2) Bulletin of International News (Chatham House, 27 July 1935) 35–38.

29 Pembroke College is one of the constituent Colleges of the University of Cambridge.

30 (1921) 1 (1) Cambridge L J 106.

31 Addressing restrictions on industrial employment, see *Interpretation of the Convention of 1919 concerning Employment of Women during the Night*, PCIJ Rep ser AB no 50 (Advisory Opinion, 15 November 1932).

5. Conclusion

This movement toward equality was significant to the dispute settlement machinery emerging after 1919. Dispute settlement was assisted, albeit in subtle ways, by the movement toward equality, in particular, by the sovereign equality of participants in the League and the relative, if still incomplete, openness of the League to new participants.

A political organ may be governed by rules that give some states more power, and more rights, than others. This is visible for example in the system of quotas for member states in the International Monetary Fund.[32] Such an arrangement is perfectly able to co-exist with a mechanism for the settlement of legal disputes that operates on the principle of equality. The procedures of ICSID are in no way frustrated by the weighted voting procedures of a related institution. Equality of the parties is a principle embedded in those procedures.[33] Political organs and judicial or arbitral organs are different things. Each operates on its own terms.

And so the existence of a League of Nations under rules that treated the states comprising it as equals, and which also recognized individual equality in certain respects, does not seem to 21st century observers as relevant in any particular way to the creation of a machinery for interstate adjudication and arbitration. The League might have had a highly restrictive approach to participation, and it might even have had rules giving some members more rights than others in its Assembly. In fact, the Covenant did give some states more rights than others, namely by giving some of them permanent seats in the Council. Such an arrangement did not impede the functioning of an international court or arbitral procedure. From the standpoint of formal legal rules, the voting procedures in a political organ have nothing to do with the decision-making procedures of a court or arbitral tribunal. Because that observation is valid generally, it must have

---

32 For the allocation as at November 2018, see <https://www.imf.org/external/np/sec/memdir/members.aspx> accessed 28 November 2018.

33 The principle has been acknowledged repeatedly in ICSID jurisprudence. See, eg, *Enron Creditors et al* v *Argentine Republic,* ICSID Case no ARB/01/3, Decision on Application for Annulment (30 July 2010) (Griffith, President; Robinson & Tresselt, *ad hoc* Committee Members), para 197; *Amco Asia Corp et al* v *Republic of Indonesia,* ICSID Case no ARB/81/1, Decision on Application for Annulment (16 May 1986) (Seidl-Hohenveldern, President; Feliciano & Giardina, *ad hoc* Committee Members), para 88. See also in the 1984 version of the ICSID Rules of Procedure for Arbitration Proceedings (Arbitration Rules) Rule 2, Note D; Rule 3, Note B; Rule 33, Note A (reprinted in (1986) 4 International Tax & Business Law 362.

been valid as well for the League of Nations and for the dispute settlement machinery that was emerging at that time. The League and the emergent dispute settlement machinery merit consideration as formal legal institutions functioning under particular constitutive instruments interpretable by the ordinary methods of legal interpretation. There is no formal imperative to consider the social and political milieu in which that machinery operated.

But the machinery did not operate in a vacuum. These institutions came into being in a particular setting. To implement sovereign equality of states in an inter-state organ was not a self-evident solution to the questions faced by states at the time. The 19th century, when most of the statesmen present at Versailles had come of age, was not an era in which sovereign equality was a presumption in all interactions among states. In this historical setting, the creation of a body open in principle to all states and the establishment of sovereign equality among the states in that body was to set an example. In the circumstances that existed immediately after the First World War, sovereign equality was still a matter of contestation. It was a momentous step to affirm sovereign equality in a general political organ of the international community.

The League was not a perfect organization of state equality. Its record was particularly lacking in respect of states at the periphery. States that were not part of the Peace Conference were certainly present. The further that one went, however, from the core of European states, and states closely modeled on European states, the less equal was their treatment in the League. The League's behaviour toward Ethiopia was a debacle. China, too, struggled at the time against a 19th century legacy.[34] The League had difficulty accommodating certain states even in Europe, especially the smallest ones.[35]

Nevertheless, an international political body that opened itself as widely as did the League was unprecedented. The openness reflected a commitment to sovereign equality which, though incomplete, it may be submitted lent support to the judicial and arbitral procedures that were emerging at the time. It is possible to have procedurally unequal states in a political

34 The damage to the prestige of the League following Japan's invasion of Manchuria is a centrepiece in the historical narrative. Less frequently noted is the skirmish between China and Belgium at the Permanent Court. The Court's Order of 8 January 1927 protected Belgian capitulatory rights under the Treaty of 2 November 1865 between China and Belgium: PCIJ Rep ser A no 8.

35 Consider the rejection of Liechtenstein's application: 20/48/178 VII (6 December 1920).

body; it is not in a court. The procedures of a court, if the court is to be worthy of the name, must treat the parties who come before it as equals. The League was a political body, and its creators had all the discretion and all the choices that inhere in political decisions. They decided that their organization should strive to be universal in scope, and its states should participate, mostly, on a footing of juridical equality. Their decisions in this regard were not essential to the functioning of dispute settlement under legal procedures independent from the League itself. They did however help make the environment for judicial and arbitral procedures more congenial than it would otherwise have been. The rules and procedures of the League in respect of participation in it in this way helped set the stage for the dispute settlement machinery that followed.

Chapter 3 Preventing a Repetition of the Great War: Responding to International Terrorism in the 1930s

Michael D Callahan[*]

On 9 October 1934, King Alexander I of Yugoslavia was assassinated as he arrived in Marseilles to begin a state visit to France.[1] Louis Barthou, the French foreign minister, was wounded during the chaos and died later. Evidence quickly established that anti-Yugoslav terrorist groups based in Italy and trained in Hungary had carried out the attack. The terrorists' ultimate goal was to destabilize the multi-ethnic Yugoslavia and create new nation states. Much like the shooting of the Archduke Franz Ferdinand at Sarajevo twenty years before, Alexander's murder sparked an international crisis that threatened the peace of Europe. France supported Yugoslavia; Italy the Hungarians. In the background were alliances and individual states interested in either defending or changing the European status quo. All the ingredients of the July Crisis of 1914 seemed suddenly there again.

While these two terrorist attacks had important similarities, their repercussions were very different. According to its Covenant, the main purposes of the League of Nations were 'to promote international co-operation and to achieve international peace and security.'[2] These central aims were in fact accomplished in 1934, an achievement that represents the League at its most effective. With strong leadership from Britain and France, the League made it possible for states to adopt a unanimous resolution that preserved the peace that all sides wanted.

During its successful mediation the League Council decided to confront the serious problem of international terrorism. Jurists and officials from several countries would spend nearly three years exploring ways to classify specific terrorist acts, and conspiracies to commit them, as international

---

* Professor of History and Frances Willson Thompson Professor of Leadership Studies, Kettering University.

1 This essay draws on a larger recent study. For more, including a list of all references and archival sources, see Michael D Callahan, *The League of Nations, International Terrorism, and British Foreign Policy, 1934–1938* (Palgrave Macmillan 2018).

2 Covenant of the League of Nations (adopted 28 June 1919) 225 CTS 195.

crimes. These efforts were significant milestones in the history of modern international law and legal procedure. Yet the League's legal response to terrorism was designed to deter or punish emulators of Alexander's assassination, not contend with the sorts of challenges that Adolf Hitler posed. In the end, few governments supported the organization's anti-terrorism project in itself. In contrast to the League's success in helping states use the security provisions of the Covenant and find common ground through diplomacy to preserve peace in 1934, the collective attempt from 1935 to 1938 to combat state-supported terrorism through the development of experimental legal methods and institutions illustrates the increasing limits on the organization's effectiveness.

*

'The King and M. Barthou are dead and the future is darkly uncertain,' *The New York Times* declared the day after the terrorist attack at Marseilles. All of Europe feared 'grave complications.' In London, *The Times* called it 'a horrible crime' that 'shocked the conscience of civilised Europe.' According to *Le Temps* in Paris, the shootings were a 'criminal act' that could have 'profound political repercussions.' Since Alexander's assassination was captured on film, it was not long before cinemas across Europe and North America were adding to the sense of deepening international crisis.[3] Given the sensationalist nature of the newsreels, the British government warned the film industry against showing unedited versions in the United Kingdom.[4] In France, Yugoslavia, and elsewhere the newsreels were eventually banned or heavily censored. Few needed the press pointing out that 'no one forgets tonight that it was the assassination in Sarajevo that started the World War.'[5]

Memories of 1914 underpinned the overall sense of dread in the first few volatile days after the terrorist attack at Marseilles in 1934. Govern-

3 *The New York Times* (New York, 10 and 11 October 1934) 1 and 2; *The Times* (London, 10 October 1934) 15; *Le Temps* (Paris, 11 October 1934) 1; and 'Alexander Murdered' (9 October 1934) Universal International News, Newsreels 1932–35, DVD50, compiled by Steven Schoenherr, available at <http://history.sandiego.edu/gen/newsreels> accessed 20 June 2018.

4 Meeting of the Cabinet (17 and 24 October 1934) National Archives (United Kingdom) CAB 23/80 and 'Assassination of King Alexander and M. Barthou: Cinematographic Film. Memorandum by the Home Secretary' (22 October 1934) CAB 24/251.

5 *The New York Times* (New York, 10 October 1934) 15.

ments quickly reexamined their policies. Italy and Hungary scrambled to deny responsibility and divert attention, even as evidence increasingly implicated both. If Yugoslavia made formal accusations or issued any sort of ultimatum, a violent reaction would be almost inevitable.

The Marseilles attack also made the larger question of terrorism a matter of serious public and private debate. While most states routinely condemned political violence and expected the French police to conduct a criminal investigation, some now began to advocate international action against terrorist organizations. Others feared alienating Italy or provoking Hungary, thereby risking an end to plans for greater political cooperation in Europe, especially in containing Nazi Germany and maintaining peace. By 1934 most European statesmen understood that the League could itself never require such international action, particularly not of a great power determined to oppose it.

The news from France shocked Britain. After receiving intelligence substantiating Yugoslavia's charges against Italy and Hungary, British Foreign Secretary Sir John Simon exerted British influence to urge calm. In a speech timed to coincide with Alexander's funeral, Simon called political assassination 'not only the most wicked, but the most stupid of political crimes' because it seldom accomplished its intended result.[6] He also was certain that no state could want to repeat the catastrophe of 1914–1918.

> Now we have had the bitter experience of four years of war, and when we survey this stricken and shattered world, we can realise not only the horror, but the uselessness of slaughter. The antiquated method of blood-letting as a cure for national fever is rejected, not only by conscience, but by the experience of mankind.[7]

But Britain likewise wanted no new commitments in Europe and had no intention of addressing the complicated question of state-supported terrorism. The British government's policy in October 1934 was therefore to do what they thought should have happened in July 1914: joining other great powers to urge restraint and keep the peace despite a provocative act of terrorism.

French officials were in a quandary. France and Yugoslavia were allies under terms of a Treaty of Friendship signed in 1927. The new French foreign minister, Pierre Laval, worried about undermining the League, worsening Yugoslavia's relations with Italy, or having to take sides publicly be-

6 For the text of the speech, see *The Times* (London, 20 October 1934) 14.
7 ibid.

tween Belgrade and Rome. Like Britain, France was willing to placate both the Italians and Hungarians in order to preserve peace, but was finding this difficult in the face of growing pressure from the Yugoslavs and their other allies in Eastern Europe.

The Yugoslav government demanded accountability for Alexander's murder as well as an international effort to prevent future terrorist attacks. In November 1934 the Yugoslav government filed a formal request with the League to address the 'odious crime of Marseilles.'[8] This appeal put renewed focus on international law and the security provisions of the League Covenant. The kingdom did not call on League members to fulfill their obligations under Article 10 to respect and preserve its 'territorial integrity and existing political independence' against an act of 'external aggression.' Instead the Yugoslavs cited Article 11(2), exercising their 'friendly right' to bring to attention 'any circumstance' threatening 'to disturb international peace or the good understanding between nations upon which peace depends.' Without mentioning Italy or even implicating the Hungarian government, the Yugoslavs accused 'certain Hungarian authorities' of assisting the terrorists who murdered Alexander. As a consequence, Yugoslavia declared that peace with Hungary was now endangered. While the complaint insisted that the circumstances of the crime 'must be completely brought to light,' it identified only 'the responsibility of the Hungarian authorities' as requiring 'just punishment.' Only the Council could 'restore confidence in international morality and justice' in this situation. But the attack at Marseilles exposed the larger problem of state-supported terrorism which was a threat to 'any civilised nation.'[9]

> This is not the case of a political murder which is the work of an isolated individual, nor of shelter given to political emigrants; the question involved is that of drilling and training on the territory of a foreign State of professional criminals intending to commit a series of outrages and assassinations for a specific political purpose.[10]

The Yugoslavs warned that if the League, 'the guardian of peace and of the international morality on which peace depends,' did not confront this dangerous problem and attempt to put an end to such crimes, '[a]n era of anarchy and international barbarism would overwhelm the civilised world.'[11]

---

8 LoN, Council, 83rd (extraordinary) session, Annex 1523: The Government of Yugoslavia to the League of Nations (22 November 1934) 15 LNOJ 1765–1766.

9 ibid 1766.

10 ibid.

11 ibid.

Reactions varied. Both Romania and Czechoslovakia supported Yugoslavia. Each insisted that its own relations with Hungary were also endangered, as were 'the general conditions on which peace in Central Europe depends.' Hungary protested that it was the victim of 'the most far-fetched accusations,' which were 'not only full of serious dangers for the ordinary relations between certain States of Europe' but were also 'capable of affecting even the peace of the world.' It insisted on an opportunity to 'defend its honour' at Geneva and reminded the Council of its right under Article 4 of the Covenant to address 'any question' concerning global peace. Italy backed Hungary's demand that the Council consider the matter as soon as possible.[12]

The League Council helped to end this dangerous international crisis. Despite initial reluctance, London agreed that Anthony Eden, the British member of the League Council, would serve as *rapporteur* for the dispute. The Council met from 5 to 11 December. For two days the representatives of Yugoslavia and Hungary, along with other members of the League, took turns speaking in an open forum. All appealed to public opinion, tried to score political points at home and abroad, staked out negotiating positions, and attempted to bend the League's moral authority to serve their national interests.[13] The Soviet representative insisted 'post-war terrorism' was 'an immense danger to the maintenance of international relations and general peace' and the League needed 'to work out measures for combating this international evil.'[14] None of the organization's member states wanted war, but 1914 had taught them that war could come through miscalculation rather than intent. Publicly addressing disputes at Geneva was meant to diminish that possibility. Council speeches did not resolve the crisis, but they exposed areas of common ground and created conditions necessary to make subsequent private negotiations successful.

The Council's resolution adopted during a special midnight session made specific and far-reaching proposals for settling the Yugoslav-Hungarian dispute. Eden's brief report to the Council that night illustrates why the League's peacekeeping functions were successful in 1934.[15] As with all of the Council's previous major decisions, the settlement he recommended was the result of a process of conciliation and compromise. He reminded

12 ibid Annex 1523a, 1523b, and 1523c.

13 LoN, Council, 83rd (extraordinary) session, 3rd and 4th meeting (7 and 8 December 1934) 15 LNOJ 1691–1842.

14 4th meeting (8 December 1934) ibid, 1734.

15 6th meeting (10 December 1934) ibid, 1759–1760; 14 League of Nations Monthly Summary 283.

the public that the League had a circumscribed role in resolving international disputes. The Council was not a parliamentary but a diplomatic body. The League relied on the information that sovereign states, acting in good faith, provided the organization and on the willingness of member states to carry out international obligations they freely accepted.

> It must be observed that the Council is not a court of justice. It has no means at its disposal for undertaking judicial enquiries. Its function is to assist the parties to re-establish the political relations which are desirable between Members of the League.[16]

Eden offered the carefully worded conclusion that even 'if the whole question of responsibility has not been completely elucidated,' there was enough evidence to convince him that 'certain Hungarian authorities may have incurred, at any rate through negligence, certain responsibilities relative to acts connected with the preparation of the Marseilles crime.' For this reason, the Hungarian government should punish anyone 'whose culpability may be established' and report 'the measures it takes to this effect' to the Council.[17] This tightly limited and highly equivocal finding of guilt met Yugoslavia's demand for achieving a measure of accountability for Alexander's murder.

Another reason for the League's success was that Britain and France had satisfied Yugoslavia's other demands as well. To prevent the sort of terrorist acts witnessed at Marseilles in the future, Eden noted that the French delegation had presented a series of propositions on the subject, including specific suggestions for 'the effective suppression of political crimes of an international character' and the creation of an international criminal court to try accused terrorists. Admitting that the rules of international law concerning the repression of terrorist activity were not yet 'sufficiently precise to guarantee efficiently international co-operation in this matter,' he suggested that a 'committee of experts' study the problem and produce a preliminary draft convention 'to assure the repression of conspiracies or crimes committed with a political or terrorist purpose.'[18] While the British government previously opposed discussion of an anti-terrorism convention, London was now willing to go along if it resolved the current crisis peacefully and did not oblige Britain to do anything. This committee would have members from Britain, France, Italy, and the Soviet Union, the

---

16 ibid 1759.
17 ibid.
18 ibid.

four most powerful states in the League. Several other governments interested in the question were invited to participate, including Belgium, Chile, Hungary, Poland, Romania, Spain, and Switzerland. The French proposals would serve as the starting point of the committee's work.

The Council's settlement of the Hungaro–Yugolsav dispute was greeted with genuine relief and widespread praise. Behind the scenes, the League Secretariat began the work necessary to carry out technical aspects of the Council's resolution. The secretary-general, Joseph Avenol of France, also used his personal influence to put pressure on the Hungarians and ensure the final outcome. Eden later concluded that the Yugoslav appeal to Geneva 'was a dispute of the type which the League of Nations was well qualified to handle.'[19] In announcing the results to parliament, Simon called it a victory for the forces of 'reconciliation and appeasement,' moderation, and international cooperation. 'But there can be no doubt,' he declared, 'that the favourable position which has been reached from a situation which so recently appeared to threaten grave consequences, is due first and foremost to the existence and the effective use of the League of Nations.'[20]

The League's achievement, however, had been neither inevitable nor easy. Keeping the peace in 1934 depended on the leading members of the Council. France worked to pacify its Eastern European allies and Laval was responsible for hammering out many details of the final resolution. Italy ultimately gave only half-hearted support to Hungary in favor of other priorities, particularly the promise of an accord with France. Britain portrayed itself as impartial and Eden was willing to disappoint both sides of the dispute, particularly the Yugoslavs, in order to keep everyone calm and to promote international cooperation. Other states also urged cooperation while some took the opportunity to defend their opposing interpretations of the Treaty of Versailles. All sides were willing to ignore the course of justice in order to serve the cause of peace by overlooking Italy's complicity in Alexander's murder. Avoiding another needless war in Europe remained the overriding moral imperative.

*

The Committee for the International Repression of Terrorism first met in Geneva in early 1935. Using the French proposal as a starting point, the

19 Earl of Avon (Anthony Eden), *The Eden Memoirs: Facing the Dictators* (Houghton Mifflin 1962) 132.

20 296 *House of Commons Debates* (11 December 1934) cols 213–214.

Committee approved several articles of an anti-terrorism convention. Some of the Committee's ideas were bold and innovative, others only made a confusing and difficult undertaking more so. These deliberations demonstrated that the League could foster international cooperation, but they also exposed deep divisions between—and within—member states over the definition of 'terrorism,' the limits of extradition law, the rights of political refugees, and the practicality of an international criminal court.[21]

While initial reaction to the Committee's accomplishments was generally favorable, Nazi Germany's unilateral rearmament and remilitarization of the Rhineland, Italy's attack on Ethiopia, and the outbreak of civil war in Spain affected the way many governments approached the subject of international terrorism and altered attitudes toward the League of Nations in general. Most British officials never supported an international criminal court. Many also were dubious about adopting new domestic legislation to criminalize international terrorism. Yet it was primarily because Eden had proposed the Council's resolution in the first place that the British government agreed to help draft an international anti-terrorism convention, but were careful not to promise to ratify such a convention.[22]

The League's committee on terrorism held its second session in early 1936. All of the original members, including Italy and Hungary, participated. Their efforts, however, became increasingly technical and symbolic as governments considered other threats to global peace and security more important. Still, they drafted two conventions: one to criminalize international terrorism and the other to establish an international criminal court.[23] The first convention raised particularly difficult questions in Britain. The Home Office was convinced that parliament would never accept an anti-terrorism convention requiring any significant changes to British law. Eden, however, now foreign secretary, saw diplomatic benefit in cooperating in drafting the conventions and convening a diplomatic conference to consider them, even if ultimately the British government refused to sign or ratify either one. When in late 1936 several other states at the League Assembly attempted to impede the organization's anti-terrorism project, France and Britain joined to give the experts one last chance to revise the conventions. Preserving the prestige of the League and carrying

21 *Report to the Council on the First Session of the Committee* CRT (8 May 1935) C.184.M102.1935.V.

22 See Callahan (n 1) ch 7.

23 *Committee for the International Repression of Terrorism: Report to the Council Adopted by the Committee on January 15th, 1936* CRT (10 February 1936) A.7.1936.V [C.36(I).1936.V].

out the Council's resolutions still mattered to both great powers, even if the anti-terrorism project itself did not.[24]

The Committee's third and final session was in April 1937.[25] After more than two years of work, the Council accepted the revised drafts and agreed to summon a diplomatic conference on terrorism in November, a decision that fulfilled all conditions of the Hungaro-Yugoslav settlement.[26] Eden could claim success, but he, and the rest of Europe, was already dealing with larger concerns. When Britain's attorney-general, solicitor-general, and home secretary continued to see legal and political difficulties in the latest draft anti-terrorism convention, Eden quietly abandoned it.[27]

The International Conference on the Repression of Terrorism opened in Geneva on November 1, 1937.[28] Thirty-five member states, along with an observer from Brazil, attended. Instead of further delaying or diluting the organization's efforts, the delegates produced two conventions that largely preserved—and in certain respects even strengthened—the expert committee's drafts. Determined delegates from France and a few other countries took control of the conference to accomplish their own diplomatic objectives. A number of jurists who served as delegates remained committed to innovative ideas for combating terrorism, particularly those concerning conspiracy and incitement to commit terrorist acts. They also continued to advocate incremental reforms, including those regulating firearms and ammunition, enhancing international police cooperation, and tightening passport controls. The chairman of the conference, Henri Carton de Wiart, formerly the prime minister and minister of justice of Belgium, used his opening speech to advocate the emerging modern concept of a shared global community that needed to undertake active and collective legal responses to new and different threats to security. He observed that

> we cannot but realise with shame and disquiet how advancing knowledge and improved communications have served in their turn to menace the security of persons and property and helped to promote acts designated by that new term 'terrorism' – acts which, by reason of their gravity and contagious nature, are prejudiced not only to the interests

---

24 See Callahan (n 1) ch 8.

25 *Report Adopted by the Committee on April 26th, 1937* CRT (26 April 1937) C.222.M.162.1937.V.

26 League Council, 97th session, 4th meeting (27 May 1937) 18 *Official Journal* 308–310.

27 See Callahan (n 1) ch 9.

28 LoN, *Proceedings of the International Conference on the Repression of Terrorism: Geneva, November 1st to 16th, 1937* (Geneva 1938) C.94.M.47.1938.V.

> of individuals as such or of one or more specific States, but may affect mankind as a whole.

Others, including the Czech delegate, strongly agreed and used the conference as a means to bolster the League's ability to work collectively to defend the interests of smaller states through 'the organisation of international action against terrorism.' France, Romania, Yugoslavia, and Spain worked together to strengthen both conventions or ensure that they were not to change much from the preliminary texts that had emerged the previous April. In general, the states most threatened by internal and external enemies in late 1937 did the most to shore up both drafts.

Twenty-five governments representing peoples from across Europe, Latin America and the Caribbean, the Middle East, and Asia signed 'The Convention for the Prevention and Punishment of Terrorism.' According to Article 1, 'acts of terrorism' were defined as 'criminal acts directed against a State and intended or calculated to create a state of terror in the minds of particular persons, or a group of persons or the general public.' The list of criminal offenses included not only attempts to kill political leaders, but also 'any wilful act calculated to endanger the lives of members of the public.'[29]

Most states, however, opposed the proposed international criminal court. 'The Convention for the Creation of an International Criminal Court' was eventually signed by only thirteen states, including Belgium, Czechoslovakia, France, Greece, the Netherlands, Romania, Spain, Turkey, the USSR, and Yugoslavia.[30] Since Britain and a number of other states strongly opposed linking the court to the League, the conference decided that the Permanent Court of International Justice should select the judges and the new court's seat should be at The Hague, not Geneva. After signing it, the Czech delegate attempted to put the best face on it he could by observing that the fact that states representing 'upwards of a hundred million persons' had accepted the idea of an international criminal court was 'a landmark in the development of international criminal law.'[31] France made sure to remind everyone that both conventions were based on a

29 Convention for the Prevention and Punishment of Terrorism (adopted 16 November 1937) (1938) Série de publications de la Société des Nations / 5 SdN Doc C.546.M.383.1937.V.

30 Convention for the Creation of an International Criminal Court (adopted 16 November 1937) (1938) Série de publications de la Société des Nations / 5 SdN Doc C.547(1).M.384(1).1937.V.

31 *Proceedings of the International Conference on the Repression of Terrorism* (n 28) 178.

French proposal and maintained an ongoing interest in the states that signed them.[32]

In the end, India was the only signatory to ratify the anti-terrorism convention. None ratified the court convention. Britain did not sign either one. Denmark considered adhering to both conventions early in 1939, but after consulting the British government did not.[33] Neither convention ever went into force. Nonetheless, delegates from smaller powers, defended both conventions. For them, the League's anti-terrorism project was a success, if only in a technical and symbolic sense. Romania called the conclusion of the two conventions 'a red-letter day' for the development of international criminal jurisdiction and international cooperation.[34] The Yugoslav delegate reminded everyone that the League had not only settled the international crisis resulting from the terrorist attack at Marseilles in 1934, but had fulfilled its duty to address the underlying cause of that crisis. Yet, for the Yugoslavs, the value of the conventions was 'primarily as a moral achievement' and 'a demonstration of international solidarity,' not as effective instruments to suppress and punish state-supported terrorism. In a reference to the darkening international climate, he expressed a hope that the 'moral force and preventative influence' of the two conventions might serve 'the future happiness of generations more fortunate than our own.'[35]

*

From its beginnings the League of Nations defined 'peace' and 'security' in terms of the experience of the First World War. In order to achieve this peace and security, as well as promote international cooperation, League member states promised not to resort to war, to foster good relations between governments, to observe international law, and to respect all treaty obligations. The vast majority of the world's sovereign states were League members by 1934. But both within and outside of the organization some observed that preventing war required an understanding of the root causes of political instability. Peace depended on changing the way that states viewed themselves in relation to each other. The League of Nations handled dozens of international disputes, many of which centered on the

32 French Foreign Ministry to League (16 June 1938) United Nations Archives at Geneva, 3A/33882/31742.

33 Callahan (n 1) 220.

34 *Proceedings of the International Conference on the Repression of Terrorism* (n 28) 179–180.

35 ibid 175–76.

Balkans. Indeed, managing the myriad sources and symptoms of political violence in Southeastern Europe was vital to the organization from its origins. Yet the League's peacekeeping authority was always circumscribed by international power constraints beyond its control.

Many statesmen in the interwar period were convinced that if the League of Nations had a role to play in international relations, it was to help maintain the peace that all governments genuinely desired, even if this required pressing smaller states to accept unpleasant concessions, sweeping inconvenient truths under the rug, and leaving intractable issues to be sorted out in the indefinite future. The settlement of the dispute between Yugoslavia and Hungary exemplified this conception of the League's utility. The League proved it could carry out its essential peacekeeping duty, and could do so in constructive and often creative ways. Yet as with earlier settlements under the auspices of the League, successful resolution of the international crisis of late 1934 was imperfect and limited. It was the sort of diplomatic compromise that states aligned on all sides of an international dispute could choose to accept when genuinely determined to prevent war for fear of where it might lead. Such determination was absent in 1914 and would be again in 1939.

Blaming the League for failing to accomplish what was always impossible, or condemning its most powerful members for not reading Hitler's mind, has obscured what the organization actually could and did attain in light of the bitter experience of the Great War. Even with its many defects, the League could mediate between states that wanted a peaceful resolution to their difficulties in cooperation with great powers that feared repeating the avoidable catastrophe of 1914. It also could make it possible for states to collaborate in creating new legal methods and institutions designed to diminish the underlying causes of international conflict. The organization had the power to defuse a crisis centering on the Balkans and to keep governments from blundering into another collective tragedy that they wished to avoid and could not control. With the active support of its most influential members, it was able to carry out its main purposes 'to promote international co-operation and to achieve international peace and security.'

The League's capacity to settle international disputes of any sort, however, rapidly dissipated after 1935 as great powers abandoned it and smaller ones lost faith. This erosion of political support also severely undercut Geneva's ability to confront other threats to peace, including state-supported terrorism. Still, Geneva's two anti-terrorism conventions were significant for a number of reasons. Together, they, if ratified, might have given states a way to reduce acts of terrorism by putting greater pressure on governments that harbored terrorists, increasing international police collaboration and intelligence sharing, and making it more difficult for terrorists to acquire weapons and false passports. The League's proposals also could have given governments a means for criminalizing conspiracies to commit terrorist acts while providing an external and more neutral process for prosecuting accused terrorists.

None of this happened. The conventions never prevented or punished state-supported terrorism. Their value was mostly technical and symbolic, largely divorced from the political realities of the late 1930s. The League's legal response to terrorism was a success only in the narrowest sense and went largely unnoticed. But despite devoting decades to the subject, the United Nations too has yet to resolve many of the dilemmas that the League identified in the 1930s.[36]

Condemning the League as a 'failure' has obscured what the organization actually attained and why that matters. Geneva could not stop 'Hitler's War' of 1939, but it did help in 1934 to avert a repetition of the 'Great War' of 1914. Resolving the dispute between Yugoslavia and Hungary demonstrated the value of Article 11, perhaps the most effective security provision of the Covenant. The League also enabled its members to co-operate in exploring ways to combat state-supported terrorism, a problem that remains among the most important and difficult in international relations. In order to assess the Treaty of Versailles as well as Geneva's contributions to peace through law after the First World War, it is necessary to know how the League of Nations responded to international terrorism in the 1930s.

36 See United Nations Security Council Res 2178, 'Threats to international peace and security caused by terrorist acts' (24 September 2014) UNDoc S/RES/2178 (2014).

Chapter 4 The Legacy of the Mandates System of the League of Nations

Mamadou Hébié[*] / *Paula Baldini Miranda da Cruz*[**]

1. *Introduction*

The mandates system of the League of Nations was based on two principles which were considered to be of paramount importance: the principle of non-annexation of the territories of the defeated powers, and the principle that the well-being and development of the populations inhabiting those territories formed 'a sacred trust of civilization.'[1] Both principles went against long-standing practices of European powers relating to the conquest and the treatment of the populations of colonial territories. This chapter examines the legacy of the mandates system based on the motives underlying the consecration of these two principles during the peace conferences, as well as its implementation in an international society that had never seen a world without colonies and conquests. It will show how the mandates system infused new ideas in international relations (2), while still remaining embedded in the traditional framework justifying European colonialism (3).

2. *The Innovative Character of the Mandates System of the League of Nations*

International law recognized the right to acquire territorial sovereignty upon a lawful use of force, even in the relations between member states of the European Family of Nations. Except for the case of *debellatio*,[2] where '[a] peace treaty [was] not needed nor customary nor even very easy to con-

* Special Assistant to the President of the International Court of Justice.
** PhD candidate at Leiden University, Netherlands.

1 *International Status of South-West Africa* (Advisory Opinion) [1950] ICJ Rep, at 131.

2 It was with reference to *debellatio* that the Permanent Court of International Justice held that: 'Conquest only operates as a cause of loss of sovereignty when there is war between two States and by reason of the defeat of one of them sovereignty over territory passes from the loser to the victorious State.' *Legal Status of Eastern Greenland (Denmark/Norway)* (1933) PCIJ Rep Series AB no 22, 47.

ceive juristically',[3] the acquisition of territorial sovereignty in the course of a lawful war between member states of the European Family of Nations required the conclusion of a peace treaty.[4] Established as a requirement since the 1713 Utrecht Peace Treaty,[5] the conclusion of a peace treaty extinguished the right of *postliminium*, that is to say, the right of the defeated state to attempt to recover the territory lost, forcibly if necessary.[6] Before the peace conferences, only Latin-American states had attempted to establish a general rule prohibiting the recognition of the acquisition of territorial sovereignty through force.[7]

The mandates system marks a departure from the practice of victorious states acquiring territorial gains from defeated powers through peace treaties (2.1.). Mandatory powers were granted only administering powers in the territories subject to this regime. The scope of those rights was based on the content of the treaties conferring the mandate and compliance with the obligations imposed in favour of the populations of territories under mandate (2.2.). The system was completed by oversight mechanisms (2.3.).

2.1. *The Principle of Non-Annexation of Territories Upon Military Victory*

Since the beginning of the war, the Allied powers[8] presumed that their victory would entitle them to acquire territorial gains.[9] For this purpose, they

---

3 Jan HW Verzijl, *International Law in Historical Perspective* (vol 3, Sijthoff 1970) 361.

4 See Marcelo G Kohen and Mamadou Hébié, 'Territorial Conflicts and Their International Legal Framework' in Marcelo G Kohen and Mamadou Hébié (eds), *Research Handbook on Territorial Disputes in international Law* (Elgar 2018) 22–24.

5 See art X of the Treaty of Peace and Friendship Between Great Britain and Spain (signed 13 July 1713) 28 CTS 295.

6 Emer de Vattel, *The Law of Nations or Principles of the Law of Nature Applied to the Conduct and Affairs of Nations and Sovereigns with Three Early Essays of the Origin and Nature of Natural Law and on Luxury* (Book III, Chapter XVI, Liberty Fund 2008) 607 [212].

7 See International American Conference, 'Recommendation on the Right of Conquest' (1890) 11 Reports of Committees and Discussions Thereon 1121.

8 For the purposes of this contribution, the term 'Allied powers' will refer to the Principal Allied and Associated powers as defined in the Treaty of Versailles—that is, the United States, the British Empire, France, Italy, and Japan (preamble to the Treaty of Peace between the Allied and Associated Powers and Germany (signed 28 June 1919) 225 CTS 188).

9 See 'The Ambassador in Austria-Hungary (Penfield) to the Secretary of State, 12 January 1917', in Office of the Historian, *Papers Relating to the Foreign Relations of the United States, 1917: Supp 1 (The World War)*, File no 763.72119/368 <https://histo

signed, during the war, several secret treaties establishing the terms of their mutual support, including how they would divide the spoils of war.[10] Promises of territorial concessions and threats of territorial dismemberment were used as bait to recruit states to join their side in the war or to try to prevent them from joining their enemies. Whereas Italy and Romania joined the Allied powers upon promises of territorial compensation,[11] Turkey was warned that it would keep its territorial integrity only if it stayed neutral during the war.[12] Even the United States attempted to negotiate an early peace with Austria-Hungary by promising the preservation of its territorial integrity upon the end of the war.[13] The proposal was unsuccessful, as Austria-Hungary refused to negotiate peace without its allies.[14] In line with the old spirit of conquest, France and Great Britain occupied militarily the territories they intended to acquire at the end of the war.[15]

It is therefore somewhat surprising that the peace settlement negotiations consecrated the principle of non-annexation. This achievement is due to the position adopted by the United States during the negotiations. On 8 January 1918, president Wilson made a speech identifying the principles to govern the peace negotiations to end World War I. In one breath, Wilson rejected the plans of the other Allied powers to acquire sovereignty at the

---

ry.state.gov/historicaldocuments/frus1917Supp01v 01/d10> accessed 21 November 2018.

10 'Telegram from the Russian Minister of Foreign Affairs (M Sazonoff) to the Russian Ambassador at Paris 5 March 1915', in Frederick Seymour Cocks, *The Secret Treaties and Understandings: Text of the Available Documents with Introductory Comments and Explanatory Notes* (Union of Democratic Control 1918) 17–18; 'Telegrams exchanged between French and Russian representatives between 24 February 1916 and 20 February 1917', in ibid 65–74.

11 See arts 4–8, 9–13 of the Treaty with Italy (Britain, France, Russia, and Italy) (signed 26 April 1925), in ibid 30–41; See also the communications exchanged between Romanian and Russian officials between 12 and 18 August 1916, in ibid 49–59.

12 'Speech of Sir Edward Grey in the House of Commons (13 October 1915), and internal communications of Russia from 6 March 2017', in ibid 41–47.

13 'The Secretary of State to the Ambassador in Austria-Hungary (Penfield)' (22 February 1917) in Office of the Historian (n 9) File no 763.72119/10094a <https://history.state.gov/historicaldocuments/frus1917Supp01v 01/d50> accessed 21 November 2018.

14 The Ambassador in Austria-Hungary (Penfield) to the Secretary of State (27 February 1917) ibid, File no 763.72119/8389 <https://history.state.gov/historicaldocuments/frus1917Supp01v 01/d53> accessed 21 November 2018.

15 See Quincy Wright, *Mandates Under the League of Nations* (University of Chicago Press 1930) 26–27.

end of the war, as well as the secret treaties which supported them. For Wilson:

> The day of conquest and aggrandizement is gone by; so is also the day of secret covenants entered into in the interest of particular governments and likely at some unlooked-for moment to upset the peace of the world.[16]

Instead, Wilson explained in the fifth point of the Fourteen Points that the United States aimed for

> [a] free, open-minded, and absolutely impartial adjustment of all colonial claims, based on a strict observance of the principle that in determining all such questions of sovereignty the interests of the populations concerned must have equal weight with the equitable claims of the government whose title is to be determined.[17]

One month after the Fourteen Points speech, Wilson was again before the United States Congress to explain his goals in the peace negotiations. He listed four of them, which would replace the equilibrium of power among European states in the mission of maintaining international peace. In the new world order that Wilson intended to establish,

> peoples and provinces [would not] be bartered about from sovereignty to sovereignty as if they were mere chattels and pawns in a game, even the great game, now forever discredited, of the balance of power.[18]

At the end of the war, the Allied powers secured the renunciation by Germany and the Ottoman Empire to their titles of sovereignty over the territories they intended to place under the mandates system. Germany renounced to its titles over its colonies by virtue of Article 119 of the Treaty of Versailles. Although the Ottoman Empire had agreed to the loss of its territory through the 1920 Treaty of Sèvres, it failed to ratify this agreement. Therefore, it was only in the 1923 Treaty of Lausanne that Turkey renounced its titles of sovereignty over territories that were subsequently placed under the mandates system.[19]

---

16 Wilson to Congress (8 January 1918) 45 The Papers of Woodrow Wilson 534–539.

17 ibid.

18 Wilson to Congress (11 February 1918) 46 The Papers of Woodrow Wilson 318–324.

19 *Territorial Sovereignty and Scope of the Dispute (Eritrea/Yemen) (Award in the First Stage of Proceedings)* [1998] 22 RIAA 209 [151]–[152].

The renunciation by Germany and the Ottoman Empire to their titles of territorial sovereignty did not, however, lead to the annexation of these territories by the Allied powers. Despite difficult negotiations with Great Britain and France which threatened not to support the creation of a League of Nations,[20] Wilson remained firm in his stance against the annexation of the territories of the defeated powers. Only when annexation ceased to be an option due to domestic and international pressure, Great Britain and France expressed support for the mandates system, which they perceived as a lesser evil.[21] As a consequence, the only territory of Germany that was attributed to an Allied power following the First World War was Alsace-Lorraine. However, the Allied powers did not see the transfer of Alsace-Lorraine to France as an acquisition of territorial sovereignty through conquest. Instead, they considered the conquest of this territory by Germany in 1871 as null and void *ab initio*, characterizing it as the result of an unlawful war. The return of Alsace-Lorraine to France was therefore described as a 'moral obligation to redress the wrong done by Germany in 1871'.[22]

Mandatory powers rarely attempted to proclaim formally their sovereignty on territories under the mandates system. When they did so, the League systematically rejected these claims. In 1926, South Africa claimed openly that it possessed 'sovereignty over the Territory of South-West Africa' in a boundary treaty with Portugal.[23] This claim caused some commotion among the members of the Permanent Mandates Commission and prompted a firm rebuttal by the Council.[24] In 1927, a representative of New Zealand made a public speech referring to Western Samoa as 'part of the British Empire' and its inhabitants as 'British subjects'. The choice of words was unfortunate. Again, the Permanent Mandates Commission was vigilant and requested explanations from New Zealand on this statement

20 Robert Lansing, *The Big Four and Others of the Peace Conference* (Houghton Mifflin Company 1921) 50–52.

21 See Michael D Callahan, *Mandates and Empire: The League of Nations and Africa, 1914-1931* (Sussex Academic Press 2008) 42–43.

22 Introduction to Section V of the 1919 Treaty of Peace with Germany (n 8).

23 'Agreement Between the Government of the Union of South Africa and the Government of the Republic of Portugal in Relation to the Boundary Between the Mandated Territory of South-West Africa and Angola (22 June 1926)' 7 LNOJ 1530, 1533.

24 League of Nations, General Council, 58th session, 2nd meeting (13 January 1930) 11 LNOJ 69, 69.

before clarifying that this country did not hold sovereignty over Western Samoa.[25]

Hence, despite some resistance, the mandates system was able to establish the principle of non-annexation upon military victory. The choice for the principle of non-annexation was rather voluntary and cannot be construed as imposed by or reflecting a general international law rule at that time. Nonetheless, its adoption was a strong policy choice that would evolve later into the principle of non-recognition of the acquisition of territories by force.[26] The ensuing internationalization of the status of territories under mandate was coupled with the recognition of certain rights to the populations living therein.

2.2. *The Internationalization of the Treatment of Certain Colonial Populations*

Traditionally, international law contained primarily rules applicable to the relations between states. Thus, in the *Lotus (France v Turkey)* case, the Permanent Court of International Justice held peremptorily that '[i]nternational law governs relations between independent States.'[27] The rare exceptions were a few rules regarding minorities,[28] the capitulation regimes,[29] and those relating to slavery.[30] Issues relating to the domestic treatment of

25 League of Nations, Permanent Mandates Commission, 'Report on the Work of the Twelfth Session of the Commission,' (1927) Doc C.564.1927.VI, 7.

26 See *Legal Consequences of the Construction of a Wall in the Occupied Palestinian Territory* (Advisory Opinion) [2004] ICJ Rep 171 [87] (holding that 'the principles as to the use of force incorporated in the Charter reflect customary international law … ; the same is true of its corollary entailing the illegality of territorial acquisition resulting from the threat or use of force.')

27 *The case of the SS 'Lotus'* (Judgement) PCIJ Rep Ser A no 10, 18.

28 See, eg, art 5(31) and (32) of the Treaty of Osnabruck (signed 24 October 1648) 1 CTS 231.

29 See, eg, Treaty of Amity and Commerce Between Japan and the United States (signed 29 July 1858) 119 CTS 253.

30 See, eg, the Treaty Between Great Britain, Austria, France, Prussia, and Russia, for the Suppression of the African Slave Trade (signed 20 December 1841) 92 CTS 437; Treaty Between Great Britain and Venezuela, for the Abolition of the Slave Trade (signed 15 March 1839) 88 CTS 359. See, especially, the 1815 declaration by Austria, France, Portugal, Prussia, Russia, Spain, Sweden-Norway, and the United Kingdom, during the Congress of Vienna (Declaration of the Eight Courts Relative to the Universal Abolition of the Slave Trade) (signed 8 February 1815) 63 CTS 473.

individuals which were not governed by international agreements were considered as falling under the *domaine réservé* of states.[31]

The end of the First World War witnessed a substantial increase in the number of treaties concluded for the protection of minorities. This increase was a consequence of the need to protect at the international level the minority groups in the states created in the territories formerly under the sovereignty of the Austro-Hungarian Empire.[32] Revealing the legal perceptions that existed at that time, the Permanent Court of International Justice explained in the advisory opinion relating to the *Jurisdiction of the Danzig Tribunals* that

> … an international agreement, cannot, as such, create direct rights and obligations for private individuals. But it cannot be disputed that the very object of an international agreement, according to the intention of the contracting Parties, may be the adoption by the Parties of some definite rules creating individual rights and obligations and enforceable by the national courts.[33]

In cases not covered by existing treaties, states enjoyed almost full discretion when it came to dealing with their nationals. The international legal system had not yet matured to reach the stage where it could be held that '[i]t would be a travesty of law and a betrayal of the universal need for jus-

---

31 *Nationality Decrees in Tunisia and Morocco* (Advisory Opinion) PCIJ Rep ser B no 4, 26.

32 See, among others, arts 62–69 of Treaty of Peace Between the Principal Allied and Associated Powers and Austria (signed 10 September 1919) 226 CTS 8; arts 49–57 of the Treaty of Peace Between the Allied and Associated Powers and Bulgaria (signed 27 November 1919) 226 CTS 332; arts 54–60 of the Treaty of Peace Between the Allied and Associated Powers and Hungary (signed 4 June 1920) (1923) 113 BSP 486; arts 37–45 of the Treaty of Peace with Turkey (signed 24 July 1923) 28 LNTS 11; art 2, 7–12 of the Minorities Treaty Between the Principal Allied and Associated Powers and Poland (signed 18 June 1919) 225 CTS 412; arts 2, 7–11 of the Treaty Between the Principal Allied and Associated Powers and the Serb-Croat-Slovene state (signed 10 September 1919) 226 CTS 182; arts 2, 7–14 of the Treaty Between the Principal Allied and Associated Powers and Czechoslovakia (signed 10 September 1919) 226 CTS 170; arts 2, 8–12 of the Minorities Treaty Between the Principal Allied and Associated Powers and Romania (signed 9 December 1919) 226 CTS 447; arts 2, 7–16 of the Treaty Between the Principal Allied and Associated Powers and Greece (signed 10 August 1920) 13 UNTS 196.

33 *Jurisdiction of the Court of Danzig* (Advisory Opinion) PCIJ Rep ser B no 15, 17–18.

tice, should the concept of State sovereignty be allowed to be raised successfully against human rights'.[34]

In the *Bernheim* case which arose from the enactment of discriminatory measures against 'non-Aryans', especially Jews, Germany claimed before the Council of the League of Nations that it had a right to treat its citizens as it saw fit.[35] When examining the complaint submitted by Mr Bernheim, the League of Nations Council concluded that the laws of Germany had violated the German–Polish Convention of 15 May 1922 because the measures adopted discriminated against the Jewish minority living in Upper Silesia.[36] However, the Council was careful to emphasize that the German–Polish agreement applied only to the region of Upper Silesia. As such, it did not apply to minority groups residing in the rest of the territory of Germany. For the Council, Germany could fix the breach of its international obligations if it excluded the Upper Silesian region from the scope of application of the discriminatory laws.[37]

The mandates system expanded the 'very loosely-set bars' of the 'iron cage'[38] through which individuals could reach for international legal protection by granting rights to the populations of territories under mandate and imposing obligations bearing upon mandatory powers.[39] Some of the rights arose directly from Article 22 of the League of Nations Covenant. This provision guaranteed that the populations of territories under B and C mandates would have 'freedom of conscience and religion', while prohibiting 'abuses such as the slave trade, the arms traffic and the liquor traf-

34 International Criminal Tribunal for the Former Yugoslavia, *The Prosecutor v Dusko Tadic a/k/a 'Dule'*, Decision on the Defence Motion for Interlocutory Appeal on Jurisdiction, IT-94-1-AR72, Appeals Chamber, Decision of 2 October 1995, para 58.

35 Franz Bernheim, 'The Bernheim Petition to the League of Nations' (1934/1935) 35 Am Jewish YB 74.

36 For the text of the Convention on Upper Silesia, see 'Deutsch-polnisches Abkommen über Oberschlesien' [1922](2) Reichsgesetzblatt 238, in particular arts 66–67, 75, 80, and 83. See also Erpelding (ch 12).

37 League of Nations, 'Application of the German-Polish Convention of May 15th, 1933, Relating to Upper Silesia, Opinion of the Committee of Jurists' (1934/1935) 35 Am Jewish YB 99.

38 See Nicolas Politis, *The New Aspects of International Law* (Washington 1928) 31–32.

39 We use the term 'right' in a manner similar to that of the International Court of Justice in the *Lagrand* case concerning the right to consular notification. *LaGrand (Germany v United States of America)* (Judgment) [2001] ICJ Rep 497 [89].

fic.' Other rights arose from specific provisions of mandate treaties and included the right to education,[40] as well as the prohibition of forced labor.[41]

By providing rights based on international treaties to the populations of territories under mandate, the mandates system removed the question of their treatment on these matters from the *domaine réservé* of the mandatory powers. In theory, all states parties to the mandates system were therefore entitled to request compliance with the legal obligations arising under these agreements. Furthermore, all mandate treaties had a compromissory clause granting jurisdiction to the Permanent Court of International Justice over disputes arising from their interpretation and application.[42] During the League era, these provisions were not used to secure compliance with the rights of the populations under mandate. In the 1960s, Ethiopia and Liberia relied on the compromissory clause in South Africa's mandate agreement to hold this country accountable for the implementation of racist policies in South West Africa. Reversing its 1962 preliminary objections decision,[43] the International Court of Justice held that these jurisdictional clauses were not sufficient for the Court to decide on the case at the merits stage. Ethiopia and Liberia were required to demonstrate their right to request compliance by South Africa with the obligations stipulated in favour of the populations of territories under the mandate. The Court held

40 See, eg, art 8 of the 'French Mandate for Syria and the Lebanon, 24 July 1922' Doc C.528.M.313.

41 See, eg, art 6 of the 'British Mandate for East Africa, 1 October 1922,' Doc C.449(1)a.M.345(a).1922.VI; art 4 of 'British Mandate for Cameroons, 1 October 1922,' Doc C449.1.C.M.345(C)1922.VI.

42 All mandates had a dispute resolution clause granting jurisdiction over all disputes on the interpretation of mandate obligations. See, eg, art 17 of the Treaty of Alliance (Great Britain–Iraq) (signed 10 October 1922) 17 LNTS 629; art 12 of the 'French Mandate for Togoland, 12 October 1922,' C.449(1)b.M.345(b).1922.VI.

43 In the preliminary objections decision, the Court had held – rightly it is submitted that 'The language used [in the compromissory clause of the mandate agreement] is broad, clear and precise: it gives rise to no ambiguity and it permits of no exception. It refers to any dispute whatever relating not to any one particular provision or provisions, but to 'the provisions" of the Mandate, obviously meaning al1 or any provisions, whether they relate to substantive obligations of the Mandatory toward the inhabitants of the Territory or toward the other Members of the League or to its obligation to submit to supervision by the League under Article 6 or to protection under Article 7 itself. For the manifest scope and purport of the provisions of this Article indicate that the Members of the League were understood to have a legal right or interest in the observance by the Mandatory of its obligations both toward the inhabitants of the Mandated Territory, and toward the League of Nations and its Members.' *South West Africa Cases (Ethiopia v South Africa; Liberia v South Africa)* (Preliminary Objections) [1962] ICJ Rep 343.

that member states of the League, unlike the League itself, did not have *locus standi* to require such compliance.[44]

Besides the possible recourse to the Permanent Court of International Justice, which was never used in practice,[45] the mandates system also provided for an institutional framework to monitor compliance with the obligations under the mandates system.

2.3. *The Institutionalization of a Droit de Regard with Respect to the Treatment of Certain Colonial Populations*

The web of treaties that composed the mandates system was anchored in Article 22 of the Covenant of the League of Nations.[46] Article 22 specified that the powers of the mandatories over the territories under mandate would be 'previously agreed upon by the members of the League' or 'explicitly defined on each case by the Council [of the League of Nations].' Moreover, Article 22 of the Covenant indicated that mandatories were acting 'on behalf of the League.' The legal interest of the League of Nations in the implementation of the mandate treaties was therefore not contentious.[47]

Foreshadowing some contemporary human rights monitoring bodies, the League institutionalized its right to monitor compliance with the obligations arising under the mandates through a subsidiary body. Established in 1920 under Article 22 of the Covenant, the Permanent Mandates Com-

44 *South West Africa Cases (Ethiopia v South Africa; Liberia v. South Africa)* (Judgment) [1966] ICJ Rep 28–30, [33]–[36].

45 The International Court of Justice subsequently changed its approach to the question of *locus standi* in Belgium v Senegal (*Questions relating to the Obligation to Prosecute or Extradite (Belgium v Senegal)* (Judgment) [2012] ICJ Rep [68]–[69]) following the recognition by the Court of *erga omnes* obligations in the *Barcelona traction case (Barcelona Traction, Light and Power Company, Limited (Belgium v Spain)* (Judgment of 5 February 1970) [1970] ICJ Rep [33]. Interestingly, in the *Whaling case*, the Court seems to have considered as irrelevant, at least for this case, the question of the *locus standi* of a party to a multilateral treaty to request compliance with the obligations therein (*Whaling in the Antarctic (Australia v Japan: New Zealand intervening)* (Judgment) [2014] ICJ Rep, 226).

46 Thus, it has been contended that the mandates system had a 'conventional and constitutional character.' See, Giovanni Distefano, 'Article 22' in Robert Kolb, Djacoba Liva Tehindrazanarivelo & Markus G Schmidt (eds), *Commentaire sur le Pacte de la Société des Nations* (Bruylant 2015) 896–907.

47 See *South West Africa* (1966) (n 44) [26].

mission was an advisory organ. Initially composed of nine experts in colonial administration, the Commission's membership expanded subsequently to ten members, in addition to a representative of the International Labour Organization who participated in discussions relating to labor issues. The members of the Commission were mostly nationals from non-mandatory powers.[48] To avoid conflicts of interest, they could not hold any political appointment during the duration of their term in the Commission. Six out of the ten members of the Commission had to be nationals from non-mandatory states.[49] Although the Commission was not a political organ and its members were prohibited from holding governmental position, it was unusual for commissioners to criticize the actions of the state of their nationality.[50]

The Commission exercised its control mostly based on periodical reports submitted by mandatory powers and the individual petitioning mechanism. Reports were presented annually by mandatories to the Commission and provided general information on steps and measures taken in the previous year to fulfill their obligations under their mandate agreements. The Secretariat of the League could also provide additional information. In addition to the annual reports, the Commission could request special reports relating to emergencies, as it did during the Bondelswarts rebellion in South West Africa.[51]

Populations of territories under mandate could petition the League and report situations of misconduct and lack of performance by mandatory powers of their obligations. Before 1923, individual complaints regarding mandates were informally submitted to the Secretariat, but there was no assurance that they would be, indeed, examined by the League or by the Commission. After 1923, the Council formalized a procedure whereby individuals of territories under the mandates system could petition to the Permanent Mandates Commission.[52] However, this procedure had limitations. There was no protection for petitioners against retaliation, as anony-

---

48 Art A of the 'Constitution of the Permanent Mandates Commission' (1920) 1 (8) LNOJ 87.

49 ibid.

50 On the role of the Permanent Mandates Commission and its members, see Susan Pedersen, *The Guardians: The League of Nations and the Crisis of Empire* (OUP 2015) 58–69.

51 LoN, Permanent Mandates Commission, 'Minutes of the Third Session, 20 July–10 August 1923' Doc A.46.1923.VI[A], 290–296.

52 LoN, Council, 'Twenty-Third Session' (1923) YB of the League of Nations 57–58.

mous petitions were not accepted.[53] Furthermore, petitioners were required to submit their petitions through mandatory powers. The disclosure allowed the latter to have access to the information in the petition, and to append their comments before forwarding it to the League.[54]

Although evidence of retaliation against petitioners is hard to find, it was not uncommon for mandatory powers to discourage individuals from petitioning the League.[55] The system anticipated this possibility by authorizing petitioners to forward a copy of their petitions directly to the Secretariat of the League. Nevertheless, informing mandatory powers of the content of the petitions gave them the opportunity to hamper procedures by, for instance, withholding evidence of their misconduct.[56] The complexity and restrictions of the petitioning system led members of the League Council to question its effectiveness.[57]

The Commission could not issue binding decisions. Its primary role was, on the one hand, to interpret the mandates treaties and relating documents, and, on the other hand, to formulate standards of best practices.[58] Nonetheless, the mere exercise of oversight and scrutiny by the Commission influenced mandatory powers and their colonial agents to take their

53 LoN, Permanent Mandates Commission, 'Minutes of the Seventh Session' (19–30 October 1925) Doc C.648.M.237.1925.VI[A], 133–134.

54 LoN, Council, 'Petitions from Mandated Territories', art A, available in 'Twenty-Third Session' (1923) (n 52) 57–58; LoN, 'Procedure in respect of Petitions Regarding Inhabitants of Mandated Territories, 1 February 1923', C.37.M.91.1923.XI.

55 See eg, when New Zealand was called in to provide explanations for why it withheld information from the Permanent Mandates Commission regarding disturbances and complaints by the Western Samoa population. LoN, Permanent Mandates Commission, 'Minutes of the Twelfth Session, 24 October–11 November 1927' (1928) 9 LNOJ 1220, 1222, and LoN, Permanent Mandates Commission, Report on the Twelfth Session (1927) (n 25) 7. For a more detailed account of the incident, see Pedersen (2015) (n 50) 170.

56 See LoN, Permanent Mandates Commission, 'Minutes of Twelfth Session (1927)' (n 55) 1222.

57 Thus, the Norwegian representative observed during the Council's fifth session that '[h]e had occasionally seen it stated that there is no such right [to petition to the Mandates Commission], and, more frequently, that the Rules of Procedure were so rigid that they almost invariably nullified, in practice, the theoretical right which did exist.' in League of Nations, General Council, 'Fifth Meeting, 16 September 1927' 8 LNOJ 19.

58 See the President's speech in League of Nations, Permanent Mandates Commission, 'Minutes of the First Session 4–8 October 1921' Doc C.416.M.296.1921.IV, 2.

obligations seriously.[59] The Commission's oversight, including the review of periodical reports, the petitioning system, and its focus on the well-being of the populations under the mandates system, may have been successful in inducing mandatory powers to comply with their obligations and improve the living conditions of these populations. For ease of administration, colonial powers often applied in their neighbouring colonies the obligations applicable to their mandates by creating administrative unions.[60]

Wilson's idealism is at the roots of the mandates system of the League of Nations. However, the departure from old practices was not complete. The non-application of the mandates system to the Allied powers' colonies is the most obvious evidence of this fact.

3. *The Mandates System of the League of Nations as a Continuation of Colonialism*

During the first session of the Permanent Mandates Commission, M William Rappard, director of the mandates section of the Secretariat of the League, commented that

> [t]he mandatory system formed a kind of compromise between the proposition advanced by the advocates of annexation and the proposition put forward by those who wished to entrust the Colonial territories to an international administration.[61]

Since its origins, the idealistic and innovative spirit of the mandates system had to accommodate the more traditional interests of the Allied powers. It is therefore not surprising that the mandates system still served their economic and political interests (3.1.). Moreover, the mandates system still relied on the criterion of civilization which justified colonialism (3.2.). This reliance, along with the lack of clear criteria for accession to independence made it difficult, if not impossible, for the mandates system to bring colonialism to an end (3.3.).

---

59 In 1924, Hugh Clifford, responsible for the administration of Nigeria, could not fail to observe that the obligations applicable to the 'Mandated Territory and the League of Nations stupidities ... despite their folly have to be treated seriously.' 'Clifford to Gowers, 30 November 1924,' in Gowers Papers, RH, Mss Afr S 1149. See also Callahan (n 21) 103.

60 Distefano (n 46) 872–873.

61 LoN, Permanent Mandates Commission, First Session (1921) (n 58) 4.

3.1. The Mandates System as a Formalization of the Interests of Colonial Powers

Agreements conferring mandates were not concluded with the League but between mandatory powers and the Allied powers themselves. The refusal of the United States to accede to the Covenant of the League of Nations, as well as the desire of the Allied powers to keep full control of decisions relating to the fate of the territories under mandate, justified this choice. During the first session of the Permanent Mandates Commission, its members confessed that the Allied powers, not the League, were the ones in control of the mandates and that the League had been only entrusted with oversight and control powers over the system.[62] The origins of the system leave no doubt on its consistency with the interests of the colonial powers themselves.

The allocation of territories placed under the mandates system closely followed the territorial interests of the mandatory powers. As those territories could not be annexed due to the principle of non-annexation, they were transformed into mandates of the state that had militarily occupied them during the war.[63] Colonial powers did not see the institution as temporary nor as entailing any less control over territories under the mandates system than colonies. In 1926, the British Secretary of State for the Colonies, explained about Tanganyika, a B mandate, that:

> Our mandate in Tanganyika is by no means temporary tenure or lease from the League of Nations. We hold it under obligation to the League, but in our own right under the Treaty of Versailles, and the foundations of East Africa for the future are as sure and as permanent in Tanganyika as any other of the East African territories.[64]

In a correspondence addressed to the Permanent Mandates Commission on the issue of nationality of the inhabitants of territories under mandate, the South African General Smuts said that '[w]e must only recognize the fact that C mandates are in effect not far removed from annexation.'[65] To use the words of Lord Balfour, colonial powers seem to have considered

---

62 ibid.

63 For information on the territories occupied by the Allied powers and the exchanges between them, see Wright (1930) (n 15) 26–27.

64 As quoted in EFW Gey van Pittius, 'Whither South-West Africa?' (1947) 23 Intl Affairs 202.

65 Smuts to Rappard (sent 4 July 1922), available in LoN, Permanent Mandates Commission, 'Minutes of the Second Session, 1–11 August 1922' Doc A.36.1922.VI[A], 91.

the mandates system as a 'self-imposed limitation by the conquerors on the sovereignty which they obtained over conquered territory'.[66]

In reality, the mandates did not imply an effective transfer of territory. It placed the territories concerned under an international legal regime.[67] However, at the moment of the negotiations, the legal significance of the new regime was somewhat unclear.[68] This constructive ambiguity facilitated its acceptance by Great Britain and France as a second-best alternative to dividing the territorial spoils of the war. In addition, there was no fixed deadline for the termination of the mandates, while the degree of international supervision over mandates remained unclear during the negotiations. Besides, no one could predict how the institution would develop in the future.[69] Finally, the mandates system gave to mandatory powers a title to administer the territory at the exclusion of any other colonial power. Although it did not grant to mandatory powers the fulness of the territorial competencies inherent to sovereignty, mandatory powers still enjoyed a high level of control over the economic and political life of the territories under mandate. The C mandates were the ones with the least control over their internal affairs because they were fully subject to the laws of their mandatory powers, save only for some special protections. The B mandates were not subject to the laws of their mandatories, but the latter had never-

---

66 LoN, Council, 18th session, 11th meeting (17 May 1922) 3 LNOJ 547.

67 *International Status of South-West Africa* (n 1) 141. See also Marcelo G Kohen, *Possession contestée et souveraineté territoriale* (PUF 1997) 88–86.

68 Scholars from the time provided very different interpretations on the wording of Art 22 of the League Covenant and the nature of the mandates system. Among others, some scholars believed that sovereignty over territories under mandate belonged to the League (eg James C Hales, 'Some Legal Aspects of the Mandate System: Sovereignty—Nationality—Termination and Transfer' (1937) 23 Transactions of the Grotius Society 85; Hersch Lauterpacht, 'The Mandate in the Covenant' in *International Law Being the Collected Papers of Hersch Lauterpacht* vol. 3 (CUP 1977) 68–69; Ramendra Nath Chowdhuri, *International Mandates and Trusteeship Systems* (Martinus Nijhoff 1955) 8–10). For others, sovereignty rested with the populations of the territories under mandate (Duncan Campbell Lee, *The Mandate for Mesopotamia and the Principle of Trusteeship in English Law* (The League of Nations Union 1921) 19). A last group of scholars thought that sovereignty belonged to the mandatory powers (Quincy Wright, 'Sovereignty of the Mandates' 17 AJIL 691 (1923); Frederik Lugard, *The Dual Mandate in British Tropical Africa* (William Blackwood and Sons 1922) 50–59).

69 Andrew J Crozier, 'The Establishment of the Mandates System 1919–1925: Some Problems Created by the Paris Peace Conference' (1979) 3 J of Contemporary History 483, 485 and 491.

theless full control over the administration of their territories.[70] Even the A mandates, which were considered as quasi-independent territories, granted mandatory powers at least control over their military,[71] over judicial system,[72] and diplomatic affairs,[73] as well as the right to draft some of their domestic laws.[74]

The mandates system also satisfied the economic interests of the states concerned. The internationalization of the status of the territories under mandate placed them beyond the sovereignty of the mandatory powers. Consequently, the latter could not discretionarily proclaim a monopoly of trade and commerce in these territories, as they could do with their colonies. One of the governing principles of the mandates system was openness to international commerce.[75] All mandates contained a clause guaranteeing to all members of the League of Nations freedom of trade and commerce in territories.[76] As a consequence, even non-mandatory members of the League of Nations enjoyed the open-market policy applicable to these territories. Significantly, freedom of commerce and trade was established in territories under mandate, especially access to the Iraqi oil market, which was one of the main objectives of the United States in the negotiations.[77]

In sum, the international legal regime created by the mandates system allowed the accommodation of the different interests of the Allied powers. The idealism underlying the mandates system made way for pragmatism. It also succumbed to the prevailing prejudice and racial stereotypes prevailing during that period.

---

70 See, eg, art 9 of the 1922 French Mandate for Togoland (n 42).

71 Art 2 of the 1922 French Mandate for Syria and the Lebanon (n 40); art 17 of the 'Mandate for Palestine (24 July 1922) Doc C.252.1922.VI; art 7 of the 1922 Treaty of Alliance (Great Britain–Iraq) (n 42).

72 Art 6 of the 1922 French Mandate for Syria and the Lebanon (n 40); arts 1 and 14 of the 1922 Mandate for Palestine, ibid; art 9 of the 1922 Treaty of Alliance (Great Britain–Iraq) (n 42).

73 Arts 3, 4, 5, and 7 of the 1922 French Mandate for Syria and the Lebanon (n 40); art 12 of the 1922 Mandate for Palestine, ibid; arts 4 and 5 of the 1922 Treaty of Alliance (Great Britain–Iraq) (n 42).

74 Arts 1, 14 and 15 of the 1922 French Mandate for Syria and the Lebanon (n 40); arts 1 and 21 of the 1922 Mandate for Palestine, ibid; arts 3 and 14 of the 1922 Treaty of Alliance (Great Britain–Iraq) (n 42).

75 See LoN, Permanent Mandates Commission, First Session (1921) (n 58) 4.

76 See, eg, art 6 of the 1922 French Mandate for Togoland (n 42).

77 See John A DeNovo, 'The Movement for an Aggressive American Oil Policy Abroad, 1918–1920' (1956) 61 Am Historical Review 854, 861.

3.2. The Reliance of the Mandates System on the Right of Civilization

Despite their divergence on the principle of annexation, the Allied powers agreed all on the existence and the practical consequences of the right of civilization. Since 1492, colonial powers had justified colonialism through a theory of social evolution that put European civilization at the apex of a purported universal standard of human civilization. Thus, during the Spanish epoch of international law, populations considered as slaves by nature, in light of their sociopolitical organization, were deemed incapable of governing themselves.[78] The papal bull *Inter Caetera* of 1493 implemented this worldview when Alexander VI granted to the Spanish Sovereigns sovereignty over the territories of the populations encountered by Christopher Columbus during his first trip to the Americas. The mission assigned to King Ferdinand and Queen Isabella was to instruct them 'in the Catholic faith and train them in good morals.'[79] Since then, the right of civilization has remained a constant feature of European colonial ideology.[80]

The mandates system endorsed the criterion of civilization in at least two ways. First, the mandates system categorized the populations of the territories under mandate in accordance to their degree of civilization. The initial draft of Article 22 of the Covenant, which was proposed by General Smuts, was based on the idea that certain races were incapable of ever becoming fully civilized. Smuts proposed, therefore, the annexation of German colonies and the transitional application of the mandates system only to former empires, such as Austria-Hungary and Turkey.[81] The last version of Article 22, granting independence to nations under the Austrian-Hungarian Empire, and applying the mandates system to former colonies, was a result of the pressure imposed by the United States. [82]

---

78 On this issue, see Mamadou Hébié, *Souveraineté territoriale par traité: une étude des accords entre puissances coloniales et entités politiques locales* (PUF 2015) 130–136.

79 'Bull Inter Caetera of Pope Alexander VI, 4 May 1493', in Wilhelm Grewe (ed), *Fontes Historiae Iuris Gentium: Sources relating to the History of the Law of Nations* (Vol 2, Walter de Gruyter 1988) 108 (Doc 10).

80 Jo-Anne Claire Pemberton, 'The So-Called Right of Civilisation in European Colonial Ideology, 16th to 20th Centuries' (2013) 15(1) JHIL 25–52.

81 Jan C Smuts, *The League of Nations: A Practical Suggestion* (London & Stoughton 1918) 15.

82 According to Wright, although the final version of Article 22 was introduced by Lloyd George, its drafting was actually mostly done by Smuts, thus making Smuts the one to prepare both the original and the final drafts of Article 22. See Wright (1930) (n 15) 32.

Article 22 of the League Covenant distinguished between A, B, and C mandates. Class A mandates were composed of '[c]ertain communities formerly belonging to the Turkish Empire [which had] reached a stage of development where their existence as independent nations [could] be provisionally recognized.' Although the communities that formed part of this class still needed the administrative advice and assistance of a mandatory power, their wishes had to be a 'principal consideration in the selection of the mandatory.' Class B mandates were composed not of 'communities,' but of 'peoples' which were considered to be '*at such a stage* that the Mandatory must be responsible for the administration of the territory' under certain international safeguards stipulated for their inhabitants. As for Class C mandates, they were merely referred to as

> territories, such as South-West Africa and certain of the South Pacific Islands, which, owing to the sparseness of their population, or their small size, or their remoteness from the centres of civilisation, or their geographical contiguity to the territory of the Mandatory, and other circumstances, can be best administered under the laws of the Mandatory as integral portions of its territory, subject to the safeguards above mentioned in the interests of the indigenous population.

Secondly, the identification of the states fit to act as mandatory powers was equally based on the criterion of civilization. Only states ruled by Europeans or their descendants were entitled to act as mandatories. Japan is the only exception to this rule. Japan had adopted the European standard of civilization and was considered to have made progress in this regard.[83] Despite the rejection of the Japanese proposal for the inclusion of a clause on the equality of races in the Covenant,[84] Japan was still considered as an 'advanced nation' under Article 22 of the Covenant, and therefore capable of undertaking the tutelage of populations 'not yet able to stand by themselves under the strenuous conditions of the modern world'.

---

83 On Japan's process of westernization, see Susumu Yamauchi, 'Civilization and International Law in Japan During the Meiji Era (1868–1912)' (1996) 24 Hitotsubayashi Journal of Law and Politics 1–25.

84 'Preliminary Peace Conference, Protocol No 5, Plenary Session of April 28, 1919', in Office of the Historian, *Papers Relating to the Foreign Relations of the United States, The Paris Peace Conference, 1919* (Vol 3), File no Paris Peace Conf.180.0201/5, at 289–291 <https://history.state.gov/historicaldocuments/frus1919Parisv 03/d7> accessed 21 November 2018. See also Castellanos-Jankiewicz (ch 5).

Japan was therefore assigned some of the C mandates over the Pacific Islands.[85] States that were part of the British Empire became responsible for the other C mandates: South West Africa was assigned to South Africa,[86] New Guinea to Australia,[87] Western Samoa to New Zealand,[88] and Nauru to Great Britain.[89] Among the B mandates, 'East Africa' was awarded to Belgium[90] and Great Britain.[91] Cameroon[92] and Togoland[93] were divided among Great Britain and France. Finally, the A mandates of Iraq[94] and Palestine[95] were also granted to Britain, while France kept the Syrian-Lebanese mandate.[96]

Article 22 of the Covenant gave a conventional foundation to the right of civilization and categorized the populations of the territories under mandate based on their level of sociopolitical development. As the mandates system relied heavily on the very ideology which had justified colonial expansion, it could not bring it to an end.

3.3. *The Mandates System as an Entrenchment of Colonial Domination*

While during colonial expansion a 'backward nation' could be placed summarily under the sovereignty of a colonial power, advocates of the mandates system believed that societies evolved in a Darwinist manner. Just like children are only able to fully exercise their personality rights when they reach a certain age, a given society would only be able to fully become independent upon reaching a certain level of civilization, as defined

85 Mandate for the German Possessions in the Pacific Ocean Lying North of the Equator (17 December 1920) 2 LNOJ 84, 87.
86 'Mandate Agreement Regarding German South West Africa' (17 December 1920) 2 LNOJ 84, 89.
87 'Mandate for the German Possessions in the Pacific Ocean Situated South of the Equator, Other than German Samoa and Nauru' (17 December 1920) 2 LNOJ 84, 85.
88 'Mandate for German Samoa' (17 December 1920) 2 LNOJ 84, 91.
89 'Mandate for Nauru' (17 December 1920) 2 LNOJ 84, 93.
90 'Belgian Mandate for East Africa' (1 October 1922) C.449.(1)f.M.345(f).1922.VI..
91 1922 British Mandate for East Africa (n 41).
92 1922 British Mandate for the Cameroons (n 41); 'French Mandate for the Cameroons' (1 October 1922) C.449.(1)e.M.345(e).1922.VI.
93 1922 French Mandate for Togoland (n 42); 'British Mandate for Togoland' (1 October 1922) C.449.(1)b.M.345(b).1922.VI.
94 1922 Treaty of Alliance (Great Britain–Iraq) (n 42).
95 1922 Mandate for Palestine (n 71).
96 1922 French Mandate for Syria and the Lebanon (n 40).

through European lenses. Although theoretically possible, independence remained largely an illusion.

The division of mandates in Article 22 of the League Covenant presumed that territories under mandate should, and eventually would, follow a linear development towards the European standard of civilization – or, in the words of Article 22, until they were 'able to stand by themselves under the strenuous conditions of the modern world.' Under this logic, C mandates would eventually evolve to B, and then to A mandates, and would be terminated once they had achieved the required level of civilization. However, neither the League Covenant nor the mandate agreements clarified under what conditions a class A mandate would be considered fulfilled and terminated. The A mandate agreements, the only ones to have any mention of the possibility of independence, merely provided that, upon the end of the mandate, the Council would continue to monitor and pressure mandatory powers to fulfill their international obligations.[97]

The lack of any provision on how to terminate mandates or to upgrade a territory from one category to the other suggests that a subsequent agreement or an amendment to article 22 of the League Covenant would be necessary. Such a negotiation would, therefore, be political, rather than legal, and would rely largely on the impressions and political will of the members of the League.

During the entire existence of the mandates system, the only territory under mandate which became independent was Iraq, an A mandate that was under Great Britain's administration. The termination of Iraq's mandate and approval of its membership to the League was described by member states as an evolution from 'adolescence to the full status of manhood.' It was also presented as evidence that the mandates system was not a cloak perpetuating colonial domination.[98]

Great Britain advocated for Iraq's independence before the Permanent Mandates Commission and the League Council.[99] Its decision to withdraw from Iraq, however, was less motivated by actual confidence in Iraq's capacity to 'stand on its own' than by Great Britain's financial difficulties in keeping a governmental structure in Iraq, coupled with the Iraqi resistance

97 Art 19 of the 1922 French Mandate for Syria and the Lebanon (n 40); art 28 of the 1922 Mandate for Palestine (n 71).

98 League of Nations, Permanent Mandates Commission, 'Minutes of the Twenty-Second Session, (3–6 November 1932)' C.772.M.364.1923.vi, at 37.

99 For details on the negotiations on Iraq's independence at the League of Nations, see Susan Pedersen, 'Getting Out of Iraq—in 1932: The League of Nations and the Road to Normative Statehood' (2010) 115 The Am Historical Review 975.

to British presence. The resistance to foreign intervention had already granted Iraq considerable advantages when compared to other mandates. Along with Syria, Iraq was the only territory under mandate that had its sovereignty officially recognized[100] and that had the right to conduct its diplomatic relations, albeit under limited British supervision.[101] Still, when negotiating the termination of the mandate, Iraq had to grant to Great Britain a series of military and economic concessions that survived the mandate.[102] Iraq's independence was, therefore, attributable to particular circumstances, and not to an alleged right to independence under the mandates system.

The absence of a concrete right to independence under the mandates system has an important theoretical consequence. Despite several references to 'self-determination' or to the word 'people' during the period of the League of Nations, there is no filiation between those references and the principle of equal rights and self-determination of peoples consecrated as an objective of the Organization under Article 1, paragraph 2 of the United Nations Charter. Thus, the Court explained in the *Namibia* advisory opinion that it is '[t]he subsequent development of international law in regard to non-self-governing territories, *as enshrined in the Charter of the United Nations*', which made 'the principle of self-determination applicable to all of them'.[103] However, the Charter itself did not impose decolonization.[104] Similarly to the mandates system, it continued to regulate colonialism. Under Article 73 of the Charter, states administering non self-governing territories 'recognize[d] that the interests of the inhabitants of these territories are paramount' and 'accept[ed] as a sacred trust the obligation to promote to the utmost ... the well-being of the inhabitants of these territories'. Consequently, under Article 73 (b) administering powers accepted to 'develop self-development ... and to assist [the peoples of non-self-govern-

100 League of Nations, Permanent Mandates Commission, 'Minutes of the Twenty-Second Session' (3–6 November 1932) C.772.M.364.1923.vi, at 37.

101 Art 5 of the 1922 Treaty of Alliance (Great Britain–Iraq) (n 42). PMC, Seventh Session (1925) (n 53).

102 Treaty of Alliance (Great Britain and Iraq) (signed 30 June 1930) [1932] CMD.3797.

103 *Legal Consequences or States of the Continued Presence of South Africa in Namibia (South West Africa) notwithstanding Security Council Resolution 276 (1970)* (Advisory Opinion) [1971] ICJ Rep 31 [52].

104 Huntington Gilchrist, 'Colonial Questions at the San Francisco Conference' (1945) 39 American Political Science Review 982, at 987; Michel Virally, 'Droit international et décolonisation devant les Nations Unies' (1963) 9 AFDI 508, 509.

ing territories] in the progressive development of their free political institutions'. Under Article 73 (e), administering powers accepted 'to transmit regularly to the Secretary-General for information purposes, subject to such limitation as security and constitutional considerations may require, statistical and other information of a technical nature relating to economic, social, and educational conditions in the territories'. None of these obligations can be equated with an obligation to decolonize. It is only with the adoption of Resolution 1514 (XV) by the General Assembly that

> the international law of self-determination developed in such a way as to create a right to independence for the peoples of non-self-governing territories and peoples subject to alien subjugation, domination and exploitation.[105]

Resolution 1514 (XV) rejected the idea of a universal concept of civilization. Giving full meaning to the principle of equal rights of peoples and self-determination, it declared that '[i]nadequacy of political, economic, social or educational preparedness should never serve as a pretext for delaying independence'.[106]

The entire social Darwinism underlying the mandates system had finally been set aside. With Resolution 1514 (XV), the United Nations established the right to self-determination as a right of peoples to freely determine their political status and freely pursue their economic, social and cultural development.

4. *Conclusion*

You cannot put new wine into an old wineskin. Old wineskins have suffered from fermentation; they have been stretched to their limits and are brittle. Putting new wine into them would most probably tear them apart, thus losing both, the wine and the wineskin. The only way of effectively preserving new wine is by putting it into a new skin that is ready to accommodate it. The link between wines and wineskins reflects a common issue involving new ideas and old institutions. New ideas and paradigms usually arise and are first implemented in traditional contexts and institutions that

105 *Accordance with International Law of the Unilateral Declaration of Independence in Respect of Kosovo* (Advisory Opinion) [2010] ICJ Rep 436 [79] (emphasis added).

106 United Nations, General Assembly, 'Resolution 1514, Declaration on the Granting of Independence to Colonial Countries and Peoples' (14 December 1960) UN Doc A/RES/1514(XV).

were not designed nor prepared for them. They have been developed to sustain old paradigms and their structures lack the plasticity to adapt to new ones. As a result, these old structures may end up contaminating these new paradigms and their implementation up to the point of distortion.

The mandates system was, in this sense, some drops of new wine in the old wineskin containing colonialism, not enough to tear it or to fundamentally change its content and nature. The principle of non-annexation that the mandates system embraced was a right step towards the universalization of the prohibition of the acquisition of territorial sovereignty through the use of force. The Permanent Mandates Commission provided the first laboratory of an institutional mechanism for the protection of human rights at the international level. A century later, the periodic reports system and the right to petition at the international level, despite their imperfections, remain established features of quasi-judicial human rights monitoring bodies.

Chapter 5 Negotiating Equality: Minority Protection in the Versailles Settlement

León Castellanos-Jankiewicz[*]

1. *Introduction*

Although they are not considered the legacy precedents of human rights today, the interwar minorities treaties contributed to developing the legal standard of equality before the law, which would become the keystone of the international human rights regime after the Second World War. The minority protection standards were also the first international rights that were embedded in an international organization. This regime is therefore useful in providing us with an understanding of the origins of later human rights treaties, since the notion of equality they contained is not dissimilar to that outlined in the Universal Declaration and subsequent international instruments of a binding nature.[1]

This chapter reviews the *travaux préparatoires* of the interwar minorities treaties, which reflect a broad concern for equality and non-discrimination. Its central proposition is that the international protection of minorities was primarily designed to develop a liberal-democratic agenda premised on equality before the law in order to allay the concerns of national minorities in Eastern Europe. This cause was supported by United States President Woodrow Wilson, whose democratic outlook set the tone of the 1919 Paris peace conference.

The first section of the chapter begins by presenting the plight of minorities during the Great War and surveys the war aims of the Great Powers in relation to this problem. It emerges that minority protection was regarded as instrumental in achieving the Allied objectives of spreading democracy and fulfilling nationalist aspirations. The role of self-determination in reconciling the contradictions of these competing notions is also explained through a discussion of Woodrow Wilson's Fourteen Points and their connection to the protection of national minorities.

---

* Researcher, TMC Asser Institute for International and European Law, The Hague.

1 Max Sørensen, 'The Quest for Equality' (1956) 31 International Conciliation 291–346.

The chapter's second section focuses on the drafting process of the minority protection regime, which, it is argued, came close to becoming a universal human rights regime premised on the internationalization of equal treatment with regard to certain rights. This claim is supported through an examination of several high-profile proposals to incorporate racial and religious equality into the Covenant of the League of Nations as generally binding norms. Religious freedom clauses were put forward by Woodrow Wilson and supplemented by Britain's Lord Cecil, whereas a much more contentious racial equal equality clause was championed by Baron Makino from Japan. All these proposals floundered, but the setbacks prompted Wilson to press on with the minorities issue in Central Europe. The chapter concludes by presenting the drafting of the equality clauses in the influential Polish Treaty, which would be included in subsequent human rights instruments.

2. *National Minorities and the Great War*

This section discusses the liberal ideas that defined nationalist causes during World War I and their relationship to the debates about the equal treatment of minorities. It begins by presenting the most notable wartime incidents of minority abuse with an emphasis on government-sanctioned mistreatment of citizens, such as the massacres of Armenians in Turkey. This is followed by a discussion of the Allies' war aims, where the welfare of national minorities was treated as a distinct priority. An additional section presents the Wilsonian idea of democracy to understand the rationales behind the President's insistence on protecting minorities. Finally, Woodrow Wilson's major wartime speeches are presented, and it emerges that minorities featured prominently therein, especially in the Fourteen Points and the Four Principles. The discussion of these pronouncements concludes the section and is followed by the drafting process of the minorities provisions for the League of Nations Covenant.

2.1. *Wartime Mistreatment of Minorities*

Soon after the Versailles Peace Conference opened on 18 January 1919, the peacemakers created the Commission on the Responsibility of the Authors of the War and on Enforcement of Penalties. This body was charged with reporting on the violations of international law committed by the Central

Powers (Germany and Austria-Hungary) and their allies (Turkey and Bulgaria). The Commission's mandate included the controversial question of responsibility for the outbreak of the war, the facts surrounding breaches of the laws and customs of war and the possible constitution of an international criminal tribunal that would adjudicate on offenses committed.[2]

In its summary, the report presented instances of mistreatment of minorities. It documented a massacre in Turkey of 200,000 Armenians 'systematically organized with German complicity' and committed by Turks. Also listed against Turkey was the abduction of Greek girls and women for the purpose of enforced prostitution, as well as the pillage of some 600 Greek villages. A section entitled 'Attempts to denationalise the inhabitants of occupied territory' mentioned the imposition of national characteristics on the population, the destruction of schools and churches, and beatings for saying 'good morning' in Serbian.[3]

The massacres of Armenian minorities in the Ottoman Empire received considerable attention and the Allies actively sought to bring those responsible to justice. Turkey's campaign against its Armenian citizens claimed between eight hundred thousand and 1.3 million lives in 1915.[4] A joint diplomatic note issued by France, Great Britain and Russia denounced these purges as 'crimes against humanity and civilization' noting the connivance or assistance of Turkish authorities and vowing to bring those responsible to account.[5]

---

2 'Report of the Commission on Responsibility of the Authors of the War and Enforcement of Penalties' in *Violation of the Laws and Customs of War, Reports of Majority and Dissenting Reports of American and Japanese Members of the Commission of Responsibilities, Conference of Paris, 1919* (Clarendon 1919) 1, 2. The Commission's Minority Report is reproduced in 4 AJIL (1920) at 95–154. The 1919 edition is cited here as 'Minority Report of the Commission on Responsibility'. Members of the Commission included James Brown Scott, Nicolas Politis, and Édouard Rolin-Jaequemyns. It was chaired by U.S. Secretary of State Robert Lansing, and Albert de Lapradelle acted as Secretary. Scott and Lapradelle would later have a prominent role in the drafting of the *Déclaration des droits internationaux de l'homme* issued on 1929 by the *Institut de Droit International.*

3 Report of the Commission on Responsibility… (n 2) 30, 34, 39, 40.

4 Toynbee circumscribes the Armenian massacres within the first 'war of extermination' carried out in the name of the principle of nationalities during the Greco-Turkish War of 1919–1922A. Arnold Toynbee, *The Western Question in Greece and Turkey* (Constable 1922) 259–319.

5 'Diplomatic note dated 28 May 1915', quoted in the Armenian Memorandum presented by the Greek delegation to the Commission of Fifteen of the Paris Peace Conference on 14 March 1919, cited in Arthur Beylerian, *Les Grandes Puissances,*

The American Ambassador to the Ottoman Empire also reported persecutions of 'unprecedented proportions' and warned the United States Secretary of State that a 'campaign of race extermination' was underway.[6] Five years later, in the Treaty of Sèvres, the Allies duly amputated the Armenian territories from the Ottoman Empire and sought to punish those responsible for the atrocities.[7] But the attempts at redressing the plight of minorities in Turkey were short-lived. The collapse of the Sultanate took the demobilized Allies by surprise and was quickly followed by Mustafa Kemal's seizure of power. When Kemal refused to ratify Sèvres, the resulting Lausanne Treaty made no mention of accountability for the genocide of Armenian minorities. Instead, it granted a blanket amnesty to all the inhabitants of Turkey and Greece for offenses that occurred during that conflict and the Greco-Turkish war of 1919–1922.[8]

This episode underscored the need to develop general international rules to protect minority populations from their abusive governments during armed conflict. Given the minorities' sacrifices, the Paris Peace Conference was sympathetic to their rehabilitation, not least because of the pressing need to establish stable borders in Central and Eastern Europe. In his opening speech to the Conference, for instance, Raymond Poincaré, the French President, honored the 'captive nationalities' that had rallied to the Allied colours:

> The Yugo-Slavs, the Armenians, the Syrians and Lebanese, the Arabs, all the oppressed peoples, all the victims long helpless or resigned, of great historic deeds of injustice, all the martyrs of the past, all the out-

---

l'Empire ottoman et les Arméniens dans les archives françaises (1914-1918) (Publications de la Sorbonne 1983) 29.

6 Morgenthau to Secretary of State, telegram of 16 July 1915: 'Deportation of and excesses against peaceful Armenians is increasing and from harrowing reports of eye witnesses it appears that a harrowing campaign of race extermination is in progress under pretext of a reprisal against rebellion.' Reprinted in: Alan Whitehorn, *The Armenian Genocide: The Essential Reference Guide* (ABC-CLIO 2015) 295.

7 Art 88 provided that 'Turkey...hereby recognises Armenia as a free and independent State.' Treaty of Peace between the Allied and Associated Powers and Turkey (signed 10 August 1920) 28 LNTS 225 (Treaty of Sèvres).

8 That is, for acts committed between 1 August 1914 and 20 November 1922. 'Declaration of Amnesty' in 18 AJIL Supplement: Official Documents (1924) 92–95, art 3 at 93. Moreover, all judicial decisions pronounced in this regard were to be annulled, and any ongoing proceedings were to be stayed: art 5 at 93. The Treaty of Lausanne was signed on 24 July 1923 and is reprinted in 18 AJIL Supplement: Official Documents (1924) 4–53.

> raged consciences, all the strangled liberties, revived at the clash of our arms and turned towards us as their natural defenders.[9]

Poincaré's sympathies reflected the espousal of the principle of national self-determination that had been incorporated to the Allies' war aims by the end of the conflict. These aims are briefly presented in the next section and are followed by a detailed treatment of Woodrow Wilson's novel ideas on 'democratic diplomacy' and self-determination, which foreshadowed the inclusion of the equality clauses.

2.2. *The Allies' War Aims and National Minorities*

We need to understand the attitudes of the Allied Powers towards nationalism as captured in their war aims in order to grasp the *ethos* of interwar minority protection, since these objectives greatly defined the development of equality and non-discrimination during the interwar period.[10] In Eastern Europe, the Allies focused on stabilizing the region through the creation of new liberal states in the wake of the dissolution of the Austro-Hungarian, German and Ottoman Empires.

More than any other Allied leader, Woodrow Wilson sought to outline preconditions for peace prior to the Paris peace conference. His note to the belligerents contains the first reference to a permanent international organization that would replace the old structure, as each power should be 'ready to consider the formation of a league of nations to ensure peace and justice throughout the world.'[11] The Allied governments engaged actively with Wilson's outlook, as demonstrated in their response to a German note linking sovereign equality with the principle of nationalities that underpinned minority protection:

---

9 'Plenary Session of 18 January 1919' in David Hunter Miller, *My Diary of the Conference at Paris, with documents* (20 vols, Appeal Printing Company 1925), vol 3, 399 (hereinafter *Diary*).

10 The Principal Allied Powers were the British Empire, France, Italy and Japan. When the United States declared war on Germany in April 1917, it entered the war as an 'Associated Power.' Thenceforth, the coalition was referred to as the Allied and Associated Powers.

11 'Note of President Wilson of 18 December 1918' in James Brown Scott (ed), *Official Statements of War Aims and Peace Proposals December 1916 to November 1918* (Carnegie Endowment 1921) 12–15.

> no peace is possible as long as ... the acknowledgement of the principle of nationalities and of the free existence of small States shall not be assured; as long as there is no assurance of a settlement to suppress definitely the causes which for so long a time have menaced nations and to give the only efficacious guarantees for the security of the world.[12]

The Allies further outlined the implications of these ideas for minorities in a reply to Wilson's note. There, they called for the reorganization of Europe based on 'respect for nationalities and on the right to full security and liberty of economic development possessed by all peoples, small and great.'[13] They also sought the liberation of Rumanians and Czecho-Slovaks from foreign domination and the enfranchisement of European peoples in Turkey.[14] By the end of 1917, British Prime Minister Lloyd George was calling for the liberation of the peoples subject to the Ottoman Empire (notably the bereaved Armenians), and for the self-determination of the German Empire's holdings. The future of these colonies, he declared, should be settled upon the principle of respecting the desires of the peoples themselves.[15]

In addition to self-determination, the Entente's objectives aimed at securing stability in Central and Eastern Europe on the basis of national affinities. In a draft memorandum of 1916, the Foreign Office recognized that the fulfillment of nationalist aspirations through statehood would ensure peace.[16] However, the satisfaction of nationalist claims was impracticable when confronted with promises made in the form of territorial concessions to other allies.[17] Beyond these commitments, it was clear that certain minorities would remain enclosed in states whose predominant nationality

12 'Entente Reply to German Proposals of 29 December 1916' in Brown Scott (n 11) 28.

13 'Entente Reply to President Wilson of 10 January 1917' in Brown Scott (n 11) 35–38.

14 ibid 37. See also: Robert de Caix, 'War Aims of the Allies' (1917) 205 The North American Review 530, 532.

15 'Full text of Lloyd George's Speech on War Aims in House of Commons' *The New York Times* (New York, 24 December 1917) 3.

16 A tentative memorandum of the Foreign Office reveals this much. *See* the memorandum reproduced in David Lloyd George, *The Truth about the Peace Treaties* (Gollancz 1938) vol 1, 31, 32: 'no peace can be satisfactory to this country unless it promises to be durable, and an essential condition of such a peace is that it should give full scope to national aspirations as far as practicable.'

17 The Sykes-Picot secret agreement was one such instance where Great Britain and France established their spheres of influence in Southwestern Asia in anticipation of the collapse of the Ottoman Empire. See 'The Sykes-Picot Agreement: 1916' in

was unlike their own, further complicating matters. The minority protection regime was the answer to these problems, for it recognized the personal attachment of irredentist persons to their heritage and nation without impinging on the territorial integrity of states while ensuring a modicum of equal treatment.

Problematically, Wilson assumed that American democratic values could be imported to the European context. But, instead of kindling the liberal spirit of deliberative democracy, he provoked the ethnic and conservative nationalisms that had lain dormant in Eastern Europe since the abortive revolutions of 1848.[18] His pledge to fight for 'the rights of nations great and small and the privilege of men everywhere to choose their way of life and of obedience' resonated with European national minorities, but also across the colonial world where imperial footholds had shown their first signs of wear.[19] Of course, the European Allies would later refuse to release their colonial possessions, and confined themselves to dismantling the empires of the defeated Central Powers. Instead of annexing these territories, they took it upon themselves to administrate them through the League's mandate system, and to establish the minority protection regime.[20] Despite these setbacks, the projection of Wilson's principles of self-government onto America's war aims marked a turning point. His insistence that they should also define the parameters of the peace negotiations would be reflected in the Conference's final outcome. For the first time, a major international peace conference took a principled stance on democratic governance, as evidenced in the creation of new states along national lines, the use of plebiscites, and the provisions on minority protection.

Reeva S Simon and Eleanor H Tejirian (eds), *The Creation of Iraq, 1914–1921* (Columbia University Press 2004) 165–68.

18 Mohammad Shahabuddin, 'The Ethnic Dichotomy of "Self" and "Other" within Europe: Inter-War Minority Protection in Perspective' in Duncan French (ed) *Statehood and Self-Determination: Reconciling Tradition and Modernity in International Law* (CUP 2013) 407–426.

19 Erez Manela, *The Wilsonian Moment: Self-Determination and the International Origins of Anticolonial Nationalism* (OUP 2007).

20 Susan Pedersen, *The Guardians: The League of Nations and the Crisis of Empire* (OUP 2015).

2.3. Woodrow Wilson's Fourteen Points and Self-Determination

When Wilson cast his war aims around the Fourteen Points, his ideas gave expression to the aspirations held by Europe's national minorities for political autonomy and equality of treatment. The foremost of these principles was national self-determination, which originates from the political statements made by Wilson during the Great War, and which was synonymous with democratic self-government, although it stopped short of advancing external independence. The term's meaning has varied since, and self-determination went on to become the banner of independence from colonial rule after 1945.

Wilson emphasized that self-rule and democratic representation were the keystones of peace. Although he did not coin the term himself, 'self-determination'—understood as the political independence of nations through the exercise of democracy—emerged as a corollary of his ideas on self-government:

> No peace can last, or ought to last, which does not recognize and accept the principle that governments derive all their just powers from the consent of the governed.[21]

Wilson's program was a democratic one and his ideas found resonance among Europeans at large, but especially among national minorities still under the imperial yoke. Self-determination thus became the vessel for nationalist aspirations. The tensions resulting from this unusual mixture of American democratic ideals and European nationalism significantly dominated the lifespan of the League of Nations and was embodied in various forms, including the creation of national states, the establishment of the mandates system, the reliance on democratic plebiscites to determine territorial frontiers, the multilateral system of minority protection, reciprocal emigration arrangements and population exchanges.[22]

The most iconic of Wilson's wartime statements was the Fourteen Points speech of 8 January 1918, where he outlined America's war aims while denouncing the European practices of annexation, conquest and secret

---

21 'President Wilson's Address of January 22, 1917' 11 ASIL Supplement: Official Documents (1917) 318–323 (hereinafter referred to as Wilson's 'Peace without Victory' speech).

22 Nathaniel Berman, '"But the alternative is despair": European nationalism and the modernist renewal of international law' (1993) 106 Harvard Law Review 1792–1903.

covenants.[23] The importance of the Fourteen Points is compounded by the fact that Germany surrendered to the Allies on the understanding that the peace treaties would be concluded around these principles. In his speech, Wilson also made his first public reference to what later became the League of Nations by speaking of 'a general association' that could guarantee the territorial and political integrity of all states after the war.[24]

Although they did not contain an explicit reference to self-determination, the Fourteen Points espoused the nationalities principle in full. Frontiers were to be readjusted along national lines in Italy, Austria-Hungary and the Balkans. The Italian state was to have 'clearly recognizable lines of nationality' and the subject peoples of Austria-Hungary were to be accorded 'the freest opportunity to autonomous development.' In the former Ottoman Empire, the (Christian) nationalities under Turkish rule 'should be assured an undoubted security of life and an absolutely unmolested opportunity for autonomous development.' The Polish state was to resurface and would comprise vast territories 'inhabited by indisputably Polish populations.' Finally, relations among the Balkan states should be determined 'along historically established lines of allegiance and nationality.'

In his 'Peace without Victory' address to the Senate, Wilson expounded his ideas on representative government and the equality of states. No nation, he prayed, 'should seek to extend its polity over any other nation or people.' Every people should be free to determine its own polity 'unhindered, unthreatened, unafraid.'[25] Wilson considered the equality of nationalities to be inextricably linked to the equality of nation-states. To him, these were two sides of the same coin. He took the equality of states to mean a formal 'equality of rights' that did not differentiate between powerful and weak states. Since geography and historical happenstance ruled out equality of territory and resources, equal rights among nations could only be achieved 'in the ordinary peaceful and legitimate development of the peoples themselves.'[26]

Wilson's worldview centered on the free development of peoples and groups. He used the words 'nations' and 'peoples' in a loose, equivocal way. The terms oscillate between the idea of states and that of ethnic na-

23 Woodrow Wilson, 'The Fourteen Points Address of 8 January 1918' in Arthur B. Keith (ed), *Speeches and Documents on International Affairs (1918-1937)* (OUP 1938) 1–8.

24 Joachim Schwietzke, 'Fourteen Points of Wilson (1918)' in Rüdiger Wolfrum (ed), *Max Planck Encyclopedia of Public International Law* (OUP 2007).

25 Wilson, 'Peace Without Victory' (n 21) 323.

26 ibid 321.

tionalities. Yet, he never suggests that individuals should be entitled to international rights and always used the language of collectives to advance his democratic agenda.[27]

It follows that, for Wilson, good governance is a precondition to individual freedom. The recognition of disenfranchised collectives through the elimination of state-based discrimination was his goal. In other words, he was agitating for the 'right to have rights' of persons regarded as second-class citizens or stateless persons because of their identification with a national or ethnic minority.[28] He sought to achieve this by ensuring their equal rights in the peace settlement. Almost overnight, the expansive individual entitlements of the minorities treaties that had been, until then, reserved only to some, became accessible to a broader range of subjects in those states. In the same stroke, as it were, the equality of all nationals 'before the law' became an international standard of treatment for the first time ever in the minorities treaties.[29]

The nineteenth-century treaties protecting certain minorities had never offered so broad an interpretation of equality and instead confined themselves to piecemeal equality, that is, they granted equality in selected aspects of public and private life: equal access to, concurrently or alternatively, public offices, dignities, the courts, civic rights and political rights.[30] Similarly, the pre-1919 practice alludes to the equal right to, concurrently or alternatively, peaceable existence, religious equality, or equality of economic opportunity. Equality 'before the law,' as it appeared in the minorities treaties, was altogether different. It would later be enshrined in Article

27 '[H]enceforth inviolable security of life, of worship, and of industrial and social development should be guaranteed to *all peoples* who have lived hitherto under the power of governments devoted to a faith and purpose hostile to their own.' ibid, emphasis added.

28 The 'right to have rights' was articulated by Hanna Arendt in *The Origins of Totalitarianism* (Meridian Books 1958). For a recent survey of the concept, see: Stephanie DeGooyer, Alastair Hunt, Lida Maxwell and Samuel Moyn, *The Right to Have Rights* (Verso 2018).

29 See art 7 Polish Minority Treaty: 'All Polish nationals shall be equal before the law *and* shall enjoy the same civil and political rights without distinction as to race, sex, language or religion.' Emphasis added. Note that the presence of the word 'and' makes the 'equality before the law' guarantee a self-standing one. Treaty Between the Principal Allied and Associated Powers and Poland (signed 28 June 1919, entered into force 10 January 1920) 112 BSP 232.

30 For the most recent surveys, see Patrick Thornberry, *International Law and the Rights of Minorities* (Clarendon Press 1991) ch 2; Alfred W Brian Simpson, *Human Rights and the End of Empire: Britain and the Genesis of the European Convention* (OUP 2004) ch 3.

7 of the Universal Declaration[31] and in Article 26 of the International Covenant on Civil and Political Rights.[32] The minorities regime elevated the principle of equality before the law to the international legal plane as a rule, but also as an interpretative tool for the formulation of other individual rights. Herein lies the unique contribution of the minorities treaties, which, in seeking to construct inclusive societies through group-levelling, broadened the scope of internationally-protected rights to include any class of invidious treatment or discrimination on the part of governments. To Wilson, this was not simply a matter of domestic stability, but also one of international peace. 'Nothing,' he ventured, 'is more likely to disturb the peace of the world than the treatment which might in certain circumstances be meted out to minorities.'[33]

Barely a month after outlining his Points, Wilson declared that 'every territorial settlement involved in this war must be made in the interest and for the benefit of the populations concerned, and not as a part of any mere adjustment or compromise of claims amongst rival states.'[34] In that address, known as the Four Principles, he explicitly refers to ethnic minorities as sub-state entities.[35] The foremost concern for minorities is much more explicit in this speech: 'peoples and provinces are not to be bartered about

31 Universal Declaration of Human Rights (adopted 10 December 1948 UNGA Res 217 A(III) (UDHR) art 7: 'All are equal before the law *and* are entitled without any discrimination to equal protection of the law. All are entitled to equal protection against any discrimination in violation of this Declaration and against any incitement to such discrimination.' Emphasis added. As in the Polish Treaty, the 'equality before the law' construction is also a self-standing guarantee.

32 International Covenant on Civil and Political Rights (adopted 19 December 1966, entered into force 23 March 1976) 999 UNTS 171 (ICCPR) art 26: 'All persons are equal before the law *and* are entitled without any discrimination to the equal protection of the law. In this respect, the law shall prohibit any discrimination and guarantee to all persons equal and effective protection against discrimination on any ground such as race, colour, sex, language, religion, political or other opinion, national or social origin, property, birth or other status.' Emphasis added.

33 'Speech by President Wilson of May 1st, 1919, Plenary Session of the Peace Conference' in Louis B Sohn and Thomas Buergenthal (eds), *International Protection of Human Rights* (Bobbs-Merrill 1973) 217.

34 Wilson to Congress (11 February 1918) 46 The Papers of Woodrow Wilson 318–324. The address is known as the Four Principles and was intended to supplement Wilson's Fourteen Points. Hereinafter referred to as Wilson's 'Four Principles' speech.

35 ibid. The plight of 'small nations and of nationalities' stemmed from their lack of unity, which in turn impeded their ability to 'determine their own allegiances and their own forms of political life.' Ultimately, the war 'had its roots in the disregard of those rights' and new Covenants would avoid this.

from sovereignty to sovereignty as if they were mere chattels and pawns in a game, even the great game, now forever discredited, of the balance of power.[36] The challenge for Wilson to reconcile the state sovereignty and imperial rivalries with minimal guarantees for minorities was considerable by any measure.[37] His vision involved an understanding among nations through the language of democracy, not statehood; he believed the state was merely instrumental, its existence and purpose subordinate to its constituent parts. These images of a pan-democratic world alliance informed Woodrow Wilson's advocacy for the new concept of self-determination.

America's position as the single most important power in 1919, combined with Wilson's messianic persona, stoked these sentiments and raised expectations that – for the most part – would never be fulfilled. But, at Paris, Wilson insisted on designing the peace treaties on the basis of national lines and ethnographic affinities as outlined in the Fourteen Points. Speaking at the plenary of the Paris Peace Conference, he stressed that a peaceful settlement would entail making 'an equitable distribution of territories according to the race, the ethnographical character of the people inhabiting those territories'.[38] He even hectored his British, French and Italian counterparts to accept these terms:

> Except where nearly impassable frontiers forced themselves upon us, such as the one drawn by the crests of the Alps, we have followed the boundaries traced by ethnographic affinities, according to the right of self-determination.[39]

The states subject to minorities obligations were latecomers to the nation-building process who had yet to fully develop representative political institutions; yet, their European heritage disallowed their subordination to mandates, and colonial claims were out of the question lest the European civilizing mission be tarnished and ridiculed. For postwar planners, the challenge was to channel their primitive nationalism into the orbit of west-

36 ibid.

37 Carole Fink, 'The Minorities Question at the Paris Peace Conference: The Polish Minority Treaty, June 28, 1919' in Manfred F Boemeke, Gerald D Feldman and Elisabeth Glaser (eds), *The Treaty of Versailles: A Reassessment After 75 Years* (German Historical Institute/CUP 1998) 249, 250.

38 Lloyd George (n 16) vol 2, 1377.

39 Paul Mantoux, *The Deliberations of the Council of Four: (March 24–June 28, 1919): Notes of the Official Interpreter*, (Arthur S Link tr, Princeton University Press 1992) vol 2, 226.

ern liberal values. The eastern and western conceptions of group identity being different, the minority protection system would fill that gap.[40]

3. *Equality and the Covenant: Failure or Qualified Success?*

This section presents the drafting history of the minority protection regime at the Paris Peace Conference of 1919. It shows the inherent contradictions that plagued the system from the outset, such as the hypocrisy of the Great Powers in refusing to accept the principle of equal treatment as a universal standard. The principle's introduction to the League of Nations Covenant by Japan was explicitly rejected, with Woodrow Wilson presiding over its dispatch while maintaining (rather unconvincingly) that the idea of equality permeated the entire League structure. Minority protection was also excluded from the Covenant, lest the subjects of Britain's dominions obtain full status equality as regards their imperial overlords.

The few minorities provisions that were ultimately adopted were fraught with ambiguities; two unresolved questions would carry into the regime over the years to come. The states containing minorities pushed to assimilate the hitherto diverse populations inhabiting their newly minted borders. The Great Powers were sympathetic to their arguments: the goal, as Lloyd George put it, was to turn minorities into 'satisfied and faithful citizens.' And yet, the Allies maintained that past instances of minority abuse would recur: 'I greatly fear,' said Balfour ominously, 'that the Jewish problem will become one of the most serious in the future.'[41] Torn between setting up strong client states, on the one hand, and the assertion of their humanitarian sentiments, on the other, the Allies took a Solomonic stance by granting international rights to minorities while making it extremely difficult for them to assert these claims. Ultimately, the assimilation-versus-autonomy debate forced minorities and majorities into uncompromising positions, which, compounded by the Great Powers' aloofness, condemned the minorities regime to a stillborn existence. The second matter of contention was the international character of minority protection. It was a pioneering idea–the first multilateral guarantee of individual rights under modern international law–but its procedural intricacies prevented

40 To Berman, the debate opposed 'two different cultural conceptions of group identity – those of Western and Eastern Europe.' Nathaniel Berman, 'The International Law of Nationalism: Group Identity and Legal History' in David Wipmann (ed), *International Law and Ethnic Conflict* (Cornell University Press 1998) 25, 40–42.

41 Council of Four, Meeting of 23 June 1919, in Mantoux (n 39), vol 2, 527.

the minorities from having direct access to its machinery. This changed in 1920, when an informal petition system was established. Over the years, this mechanism was formalized and streamlined, but its efforts came to naught when Hitler began disrupting European politics in the early 1930s.

Despite these setbacks, the main problem facing the incorporation of minorities into the general population was resolved by granting them citizenship, equal rights, and special measures of protection. Although not reflected in the Covenant, they subsisted in the exceptional regime of minority protection, thereby giving 'the right to have rights' to formerly disenfranchised peoples.

The League of Nations Covenant contains no clauses on minority protection and does not recognize equality and non-discrimination as standards of individual treatment, attesting to the exceptional nature of minority obligations and their limited application to a handful of states. The first American and British drafts of the League of Nations Covenant ignored the minorities question altogether.[42] Although Woodrow Wilson was enthusiastic about the inclusion of minority provisions, his British counterparts preferred to solve the matter with border readjustments. This is perhaps why, instead of a minority protection clause, Woodrow Wilson's first draft of the League Covenant provides that all territorial readjustments following the war should be made in accordance with principle of self-determination (art 3).[43] Attempts made to incorporate general clauses on racial equality and freedom of religion into the Covenant failed. An overview of

42 The earliest draft Covenant was circulated informally by the Phillemore Committee: 'The Phillemore Plan' dated 20 March 1918, in David Hunter Miller, *The Drafing of the Covenant* (GP Putnam's Sons 1928), vol 2, 3 (hereinafter *Covenant*). Upon receiving this document, Woodrow Wilson commissioned his advisors to venture a draft, and the task fell on Colonel House: 'Draft of Colonel House' dated 16 July 1918, ibid, vol 2, 7. Wilson wrote his first draft on the basis of House's text: 'Wilson's First Draft' ibid, vol 2, 12. Two other documents exercised considerable influence during the drafting process: the memorandum by General Jan Smuts, and Lord Robert Cecil's 'draft sketch' of the League. See Jan Smuts, 'The League of Nations: A Practical Suggestion' dated 16 December 1918 in Miller, *Diary* (n 9) vol 3, 31–64; and 'The Cecil Plan' dated 14 January 1919, in Miller, *Covenant*, vol 2, 61. Of the latter two, only Smuts refers to minorities.

43 The relevant passage reads: 'it is understood that between [the Powers] that such territorial readjustments, if any, as may in the future become necessary by reason of changes in present racial conditions and aspirations or present social and political relationships, pursuant to the principle of self-determination, and also such territorial readjustments as may in the judgment of three fourths of the Delegates be demanded by the welfare and manifest interest of the peoples concerned, may be effected, if agreeable to those peoples.' 'Wilson's First Draft of August 1918', in

their fate is instructive in highlighting the main issues that were at stake before examining the minorities provisions in detail.

3.1. *Wilson's Equal Treatment Clauses*

Despite their leaders' reluctance, American and other officials had reached the preliminary conclusion that some form of international protection would be necessary in certain localities. A memorandum on American foreign policy and international law admitted this much in respect to the Balkans.[44] Tellingly, the influential paper authored by General Smuts also singled out the plight of oppressed minorities in considerable detail, noting that the welter of multinational empires had constrained the freedom of their constituent nations. Any peace agreement made on the basis of inequality, bondage, and oppression of the smaller nationalities would fail, and a new approach was necessary.[45] Smuts' program of nationalist emancipation reads as a blueprint for the systems of minority protection and mandated territories that were to come:

> The vital principles are: the principle of nationality involving the ideas of political freedom and equality; the principle of autonomy, which is the principle of nationality extended to peoples not yet capable of complete independent statehood; the principle of political decentralization, which will prevent the powerful nationality from swallowing

Miller, *Covenant* (n 42) vol 2, 12–13. That article also contained a clause that was striking for its narrow construal of reserved domain: '... The Contracting Powers accept without reservation that the peace of the world is superior in importance to every question of political jurisdiction or boundary.'

44 'The American Program and International Law: Draft Memorandum by David Hunter Miller,' dated 31 July 1918 in Miller, *Diary* (n 9) vol 2, 323–475, 422-23: 'Experience has shown that treaty provisions on the protection of racial and religious minorities are in no sense self-executing. In the case of such states as the Balkans, beyond the mere agreement of religious freedom and personal liberty must be effective provisions for publicity and remedy when essential rights are threatened or violated.'

45 Smuts (n 42) 36. Smuts blended his idealism with considerable doses of realism: 'The nationalities of Europe are in many cases animated by historic hostility to one another; the tendency will be for them to fly at one another's throats on very slight provocation ... In this and many other respects, the league will have a very real rôle to play as the successor to the empires. ibid 48.

> the weak autonomy as has often happened in the now defunct European empires.[46]

The crowning jewel of these ideals was the League of Nations, coupled with an international guarantee to stabilize this decentralized system. In time, the small nations would become self-sufficient: 'Government by consent of the governed is our formula.'[47] It is no coincidence that Smuts' recipe for international stability chimed with Woodrow Wilson's ideas on self-determination.[48]

At Paris, the first discussions on minorities took place in the League of Nations Commission, which was charged with drafting the new organization's Covenant.[49] During its first meeting, Wilson, who insisted on chairing the proceedings, introduced a non-discrimination provision relating to religious freedom:

> Art. 19. The High Contracting Parties agree that they will make no law prohibiting or interfering with the free exercise of religion, and that they will in no way discriminate, either in law or in fact, against those who practice any particular creed, religion, or belief whose practices are not inconsistent with public order or public morals.[50]

This clause already contains the notion of equality 'in law or in fact,' which became ubiquitous in the minorities treaties. Deeming it too general in nature, Lord Robert Cecil proposed an amendment to Wilson's article. The result was an extremely progressive text aimed at staving off state-based religious intolerance and authorising the League Council to make direct representations towards ill-behaved governments on behalf of religious minorities:

> Art. 19. Recognising religious persecution and intolerance as fertile sources of war, the High Contracting Parties agree that political unrest arising therefrom is a matter of concern to the League and authorise

46 ibid 50.

47 ibid 53.

48 Smuts is credited for drafting the UN Charter's Preamble. For an account linking the Preamble episode with his views on the Commonwealth, see: Peter Marshall, 'Smuts and the Preamble to the UN Charter' (2001) 358 The Round Table, 55–65.

49 The (sometimes inconsistent) English and French minutes of these meetings are in Miller, *Covenant* (n 42) vol 2, 229–33; 395–500. The meetings were held at the Hôtel Crillon, where the American delegation had been put up.

50 'First Meeting [of the League of Nations Commission] of 3 February 1919,' ibid, vol 2, 237.

> the Executive Council, wherever it is of opinion that the peace of the world is threatened by the illiberal action of the Government of any State towards the adherents of any particular creed, religion or belief, to make such representations or take such other steps to put an end to the evil in question.[51]

If Wilson's proposal had been daring, Cecil's amendment was completely unacceptable. The clause was rejected outright, a clear sign that equality in religious matters were not considered as generally binding under international law. Indeed, David Hunter Miller, Wilson's chief legal advisor in Paris, informed the President that the text went 'very far, and, I think, farther than any other provision in the Covenant'.[52] Nor was the article well received by Wilson's colleagues in the Commission, who were clearly apprehensive about extending the pale of recognition to their own subnational groups.[53] In response, Wilson watered down the clause by incorporating a public order exception:

> The High Contracting Parties agree that they will make no law prohibiting or interfering with the free exercise of religion, and they resolve that they will not permit the practice of any particular creed, religion, or belief, whose practices are not inconsistent with public order or with public morals, to interfere with the life, liberty or pursuit of happiness of their people.[54]

This article was adopted in the Committee's Seventh Meeting, with Léon Bourgeois approvingly noting its resemblance to the religious freedom

51 'Sixth Meeting [of the League of Nations Commission] of 8 February 1919', ibid, vol 2, 276.

52 ibid vol 1, 196.

53 Hymans (Belgium) flatly rejected the proposition of enabling the League to pronounce itself on domestic matters; Batalha Reis (Portugal) deemed the clause unacceptable for governments that recognized an official religion; Italy's Orlando warned of potential conflicts with constitutional dispositions; and Bourgeois believed such instances were already covered in the Covenant's draft article 9 (final art 11(2)) which dealt with internal disturbances and the 'friendly right' of all League members to bring such matters to the Organization's attention. ibid vol 2, 273–27, 441.

54 'Seventh Meeting [of the League of Nations Commission] of 10 February 1919' ibid vol 2, 282, 286–87. The French text is better drafted: 'Les Hautes Parties Contractantes décident qu'elles ne permettront pas que leurs citoyens, adhérents d'une foi, religion ou croyance quelconque, qui ne porte pas atteinte a l'ordre ou aux moeurs publiques, soient pour cette raison inquiétés dans leur vie, leur liberté et leur poursuite du bonheur.' ibid vol 1, 196.

clause in the French Declaration of 1789.[55] But 'in view of the complications', the article was removed from the draft Covenant in the Ninth Meeting.[56]

Wilson's provision on equality of treatment for ethnic minorities followed the same fate. This clause provides a clear indication that one of Wilson's main goals in establishing the minority protection regime was the elimination of the legal disabilities that were attached to group membership. Following the Treaty of Berlin of 1878, the clause conditions recognition to the equal treatment of minorities and presupposes that protected individuals could also be aliens:

> VI. The League of Nations shall require all new States to bind themselves as a condition precedent to their recognition as independent or autonomous States, to accord to all racial or national minorities within their several jurisdictions exactly the same treatment and security, both in law and in fact, that is accorded the racial or national majority of their people.[57]

When reviewing its wording, Miller told the President that this article would be unacceptable to his peers.[58] Wilson promptly amended the provision in his Second Paris Draft by restricting the equal treatment standard between minorities and majorities only to those states seeking admission to the League.[59] This would have entailed ubiquitous minority protection obligations for all new member states, but it would not bind the Great Powers. When this formulation too was rejected, it became apparent that

55 ibid vol 1, 282.

56 For the decision to omit the article, see: 'Ninth Meeting [of the League of Nations Commission]' of 13 February 1919, ibid, vol 2, 307. The minutes indicate that if there was 'a strong feeling in the Commission that some such provision should be inserted', the following drafting was suggested: 'The High Contracting Parties agree that they will not prohibit or interfere with the free exercise of any creed, religion, or belief whose practices are not inconsistent with public order or public morals, and that no person within their respective jurisdictions shall be molested in life, liberty, or in the pursuit of happiness by reason of his adherence to any such creed, religion, or belief. ibid vol 2, 307.

57 'Wilson's Second Draft or the First Paris Draft' dated 10 January 1919. ibid vol 2, 91. In his commentary, Miller observes that the article foreshadowed the subsequent minorities treaties. ibid 40.

58 ibid vol 1, 91. Miller's remarks are taken from his clause-by-clause commentary and suggestions to Wilson's First Paris Draft.

59 'Wilson's Third Draft or Second Paris Draft' dated 20 January 1919. ibid vol 2, 105.

self-determination would only be materially relevant for a limited number of states.

Wilson's draft articles on religious and political equality are relevant because they became the backbone of the minorities provisions in the Polish Treaty.[60] Their rejection from the Covenant stems from the reluctance to give the League too much supervisory power, from uncertainties surrounding the international standards of treatment required by the equality clauses and from the reluctance to extend favorable conditions to all persons in social, economic, and political matters.[61]

3.2. *Japan's Racial Equality Clause*

The Great Powers' apprehensiveness in extending equal treatment beyond European borders is illustrated through the well-known episode concerning the rejection of Japan's racial discrimination clause from the Covenant.[62] By 1919, Japan had become rapidly modernized, commanded a first-class fleet, and enjoyed international prestige as a 'middle power' for its recent military victories. However, the Japanese were frequently sidelined in Paris for strategic reasons. The expansion of their interests towards the Pacific interfered with the United States' two-ocean navy policy and

---

60 Wilson's clauses were forwarded to the Committee on New States for incorporation to the Polish Treaty: 'I should mention that President Wilson's draft in regard to the protection of religious minorities was generally agreed to be satisfactory. It was hoped that it might be possible to draw up provisions in regard to Poland.' 'Hankey to Dutasta,' Miller, *Diary* (n 9) vol 13, 13–14. Maurice Hankey annexed Wilson's 'religious' and 'political' clauses to his note addressed to the conference's Secretary-General.

61 Italy proposed a clause for the Covenant guaranteeing equal access to working conditions regardless of citizenship: 'All laws and regulations intended to protect the rights and interests of workpeople shall be applied in every country without distinction of nationality.' States could still limit foreign workers from accessing certain kinds of work. The proposal was not adopted. See: 'Draft Scheme for the Constitution of the Society of Nations presented by the Italian Delegation' reproduced in Miller, *Covenant* (n 42) vol 2, 246–247.

62 Paul G Lauren, 'Human Rights in History: Diplomacy and Racial Equality at the Paris Peace Conference' (1978) 2 Diplomatic History; Noriko Kawamura, 'Wilsonian Idealism and Japanese Claims at the Peace Conference' (1997) 66 Pacific Historical Review 503–526; Kristofer Allerfeldt, 'Wilsonian Pragmatism? Woodrow Wilson, Japanese Immigration, and the Paris Peace Conference' (2004) 15 Diplomacy and Statecraft 545–572; Naoko Shimazu, *Japan, Race and Equality: The Racial Equality Proposal of 1919* (Routledge 2009).

each side drew up precautionary war plans. In the United States, Asian industrialists and businessmen were the target of various discriminatory policies, including limitations on land acquisition and legal disabilities in the western United States.[63] To the Japanese delegation, then, racial equality became an important sticking point towards the signature of the Versailles peace treaty and their demands went furthest in articulating a desideratum for states in their relations with their inhabitants:

> The equality of nations being a basic principle of the League of Nations, the High Contracting Parties agree to accord, as soon as possible, to all other nationals of States Members of the League equal and just treatment in every aspect, making no distinction, either in law or in fact, on account of their race or nationality.[64]

The legal effects of this article were potentially widespread. Its wording and structure, which could be described as a multilateral national treatment clause, compelled states to treat the citizens of all League member states as they did their own nationals. Moreover, the reference to 'races' meant that national minorities could potentially benefit from this treatment. But Baron Makino, the former Japanese foreign minister who introduced the provision, downplayed its immediate legal consequences by noting that the realization of absolute equality was not envisaged and that the clause merely 'enunciated' a principle while leaving a wide margin for implementation to states.

Lord Cecil, who was chairing the meeting when Makino introduced his text, immediately objected on the grounds that it raised 'extremely serious problems within the British Empire.'[65] China's Wellington Koo was the only delegate to voice support for the Japanese initiative, and tepidly at that: although his delegation was 'deeply interested' in the proposition, he had not received specific instructions from his government to take a definite position.[66] Greek Prime Minister Venizelos, whose country had made exorbitant territorial claims from Epirus to Thrace and down to Asia Minor, conveniently suggested entrusting the matter of racial equality to the fu-

---

63 United States Supreme Court, *Yick Wo v Hopkins* (1886); Margaret Macmillan, *Peacemakers: The Paris Conference of 1919 and Its Attempt to End War* (John Murry 2009) 323.

64 'Tenth Meeting [of the League of Nations Commission]' of 13 February 1919, in Miller, *Covenant* (n 42) vol 2, 324.

65 ibid 323, 324.

66 ibid 325.

ture League.[67] The Australian delegation was among the foremost objectors, since the clause ran counter to its White Australia policy.[68] The position of the dominions was among the main reasons why Britain opposed this clause so forcibly. Australia and New Zealand had made great sacrifices during the war, and although not embracing self-determination, they were quietly assessing their options for negotiating increased autonomy from the metropolis.

Other leading delegates also objected to the generalization of equality that Japan advocated. In a characteristically sulky remark, British Foreign Secretary Arthur Balfour privately told the Americans that the notion that all men are created equal was 'an eighteenth-century proposition', which he did not believe was true. All men 'of a particular nation' were equal, but the principle did not apply to a Central African man when compared to a European one.[69] The mid-level American delegates generally supported the Japanese proposal, but understood it was unrealistic. After laboring over its wording, Miller soon realized that its approval would 'of course, be impossible'.[70]

Baron Makino duly withdrew his clause from the Covenant's body and refocused his energies to include it in the Preamble. He redrafted the provision to read as a *voeu*, removing all coercive language. Once modified, his expansive racial equality article became a mere symbolic expression proposing 'the endorsement of the principle of equality of nations and just treatment of their nationals'.[71]

This text, put forward during the Commission's Fifteenth Meeting, was welcomed in speeches made by the Italian, French, Chinese, Greek, and Czech delegations, primarily because it omitted the previous reference to 'races', that is, national minorities. Venizelos, his fears allayed, was now in favor: it would be very difficult to reject a preambular expression of equality among nations and their citizens, especially considering that racial minorities and immigration were excluded from its scope. He was even prepared to accept the insertion of a religious liberty clause in the Preamble to

67 ibid 325.

68 Warwick A McKean, *Equality and Discrimination under International Law* (Clarendon 1983) 18; Paul G Lauren, 'First Principles of Racial Equality: History and the Politics and Diplomacy of Human Rights Provisions in the United Nations Charter' (1983) 5 Human Rights Quarterly 1–26.

69 Miller, *Covenant* (n 42) vol 1, 183.

70 ibid 184.

71 'Fifteenth Meeting [of the League of Nations Commission] of 11 April 1919. ibid vol 2, 389.

boot.[72] Italy's Orlando also believed that invoking the notion of equality was fitting for a League that was regrouping nations of a democratic character; its explicit rejection, he continued, would represent a jarring setback.[73] But both Wilson and Cecil dug in their heels. In an extremely careful speech, the President warned the Japanese delegation about the negative reception that his racial equality provision might receive outside the Commission. Cecil was markedly direct: either the formula was vague and therefore ineffective, or it had a practical significance. If the latter, it 'opened the door to serious controversy and to interference in the domestic affairs of States members of the League.'[74] But emboldened by the otherwise widespread support, Makino solemnly requested a vote. His preamble proposal marshalled eleven votes in favor out of seventeen (the nays were not called out). But Wilson – presiding over the meeting and therefore in control of procedural matters – insisted that unanimity was required for the motion to pass. At the French delegate's insistence that Japan had garnered the requisite votes, Wilson replied that given the 'strong opposition' that had manifested itself against the amendment, the resolution could not be considered as adopted.[75] The stoic Japanese did not question this dubious explanation and racial equality was excluded from the Covenant.[76]

The incident almost derailed the entire Conference and the Japanese later threatened to leave the proceedings without signing the treaties.[77] This would have proved catastrophic, for Italy's Orlando had already staged his exit (only to return eleven days later), and the Belgians were nearing that point. Ultimately, the controversial vote isolated Japan during the interwar

---

72 ibid 390–391.

73 ibid 390. As the speeches progressed, Colonel House slipped a note to Wilson: 'The trouble is that if this Commission should pass it, it would surely raise the race issue throughout the world.' Although somewhat obscure, this warning was likely referring to the issue of colored peoples in America and beyond. That Wilson tolerated—if not passively advocated—racial segregation is no secret. Macmillan (n 63) 329.

74 ibid 389, 390.

75 ibid 392. Cecil merely thought it better 'that the Covenant should be silent on these questions of right. Silence would avoid much discussion.' ibid.

76 According to the minutes, 'President Wilson said that no one would dream of interpreting the vote which had just been taken as a condemnation of the principle proposed by the Japanese Delegation.' ibid 392. A sympathetic statement of the American delegation regarding the Japanese proposal was prepared, but not officially distributed. ibid vol 1, 465–466.

77 Mantoux (n 39) vol 1, 314.

years. The Japanese steered away from the Western world, which they had enthusiastically orbited since the mid-nineteenth century, and fell back on aggressive nationalism.

In its final form, then, the Covenant remained silent about racial and religious equality, and contained no provisions on the equality of nations. As the drafting history shows, equality of all persons in domestic jurisdictions had not reached the level of internationally agreed rules. This is not to say that equality was not a matter of international concern under the League Guarantee, but the standard would only apply to certain rights, certain groups and to the territorial holdings of states composing the so-called Minorities Belt running from Estonia to Iraq. It follows that, during the interwar period, there was no consensus as to the existence of a general rule requiring states to hold all persons equal under their jurisdiction as between themselves or before the law. However, these elaborate discussions show a swelling concern for equality in many quarters, and the discarded provisions were later taken up by the drafters of the minorities treaties.

Further attesting to the exceptional character of the minorities regime, the Great Powers did not bear the treaty obligations that required the defeated, new and enlarged states to protect minorities. No clauses established general principles of democratic government applicable to all states, nor did they aim at a general codification of minimum standards of treatment to aliens. Any rules on equality and non-discrimination aspiring to universal recognition would have been included in the Covenant, and, as we have seen, they were deliberately rejected. When it became obvious that minority protection would only be feasible in the former belligerents' and in the new client states, Wilson's grandstanding principles were cut down to size.

3.3. Equality in the Polish Treaty: Defining Moments

If the Great Powers took great pains to avoid the presence of minorities clauses in the Covenant, they were just as resourceful in cajoling the smaller states into accepting these obligations. Alongside the problem of discrimination against the Jews and other minorities, the avoidance of statelessness emerged as a major concern during the drafting process of the peace treaties with the defeated and new states. Minorities living 'beyond the pale' of the law needed adequate recognition. This explains why citizenship provisions and minorities clauses were the mainstay of the so-called minorities treaties.

The main deliberative organ at Paris was the Council, which sat at the Quai d'Orsay and was modeled around the body that had coordinated the Allied wartime efforts.[78] Presided over by French Prime Minister Georges Clemenceau, the Council entrusted the minorities question to the 'Committee on New States and the Protection of Minorities', composed of expert mappers and mid-level advisors.[79] In the course of its sixty-four meetings, this Committee would redraw the map of Eastern and Central Europe along the lines of national self-determination and would also draft the main provisions on minority protection.[80]

The minorities provisions in the treaty with Poland were the first to be adopted and their well-documented drafting history provides important insights into the purposes of the regime. Poland was first notified that the peace arrangement would tie her to international guarantees for minorities in a memorandum signed by Clemenceau, which recalled a string of nineteenth-century minority protection precedents in Europe. The Polish delegation was not amused by the prospect of giving special rights to non-Poles, but the Germans had insisted upon this guarantee to protect their co-nationals who, under the new arrangements, would find themselves outside the *Mutterland*. In fact, following the dissolution of Austria-Hungary, and the appearance of Poland, Czechoslovakia and Yugoslavia, the largest minority in Europe was German-speaking.[81]

---

78 That is, the Supreme Inter-allied War Council. Clive Day, 'The Atmosphere and Organization of the Peace Conference', in Edward M House and Charles Seymour (eds), *What Really Happened at Paris: The Story of the Peace Conference, 1918–1919 by American Delegates* (Charles Scribner's Sons 1921) 15, 17.

79 The British members were Edward H Carr and James W Headlam-Morley, whereas Manley O Hudson represented the United States with David Hunter Miller, President Wilson's closest advisor. Philippe Berthelot represented France and Mineichirō Adatci was the Japanese representative. Manley O Hudson, 'The Protection of Minorities and Natives in Transferred Territories' in House and Seymour (n 78) 204, 211.

80 See David Hunter Miller's prefatory note in *Diary* (n 9) vol 13. Some experts complained that they had little guidance beyond the vague principle of self-determination. They were also unaware that most of their advice was adopted by the Great Powers without much discussion. See: Harold Nicolson, *Peacemaking 1919* (Grosset & Dunlap 1965) *passim*.

81 '*Le cas le plus caractéristique fut celui des minorités allemandes dispersées en nombre assez considérable dans presque tous les pays d'Europe centrale et orientale.*' Stevan Tchirkovitch, 'La règle de non-discrimination et la protection des minorités' (1951) 22 RGDIP 247, 253. See also Mark Mazower, *Governing the World: The History of an Idea* (Allen Lane 2012), 161–162.

The re-establishment of the Polish state remedied what had widely been regarded as a historical injustice. Its resurgence had been trumpeted in liberal circles since the Vienna Congress of 1815, and up until Wilson's Fourteen Points. Ignacy Paderewski, the pianist and composer who was also the foremost Polish spokesperson at Versailles, embodied this romantic ideal. But new borders meant new minorities, or, as Colonel House would have it, 'to create new boundaries is always to create new troubles', and the Allies rushed to appease the defeated German Empire lest they hand over a poisoned peace.[82] British Prime Minister David Lloyd George was well aware of the stakes, expressing in his Fontainebleau Memorandum that he was:

> strongly averse to transferring more Germans from German rule to the rule of some other nation than can possibly be helped. I cannot conceive any greater cause of future war than that the German people, who have certainly proved themselves one of the most powerful races in the world, should be surrounded by a number of small States, many of them constituting of people who have never previously set up a stable government for themselves, but each of them containing large masses of Germans clamouring for reunion with their native land.[83]

These reflections contain the stuff of prophecy, for Hitler would later instrumentalize and dismantle the League system by manipulating German minorities abroad. But in 1919, the prostrate Germans had sustained heavy territorial losses and were humiliated to see many of their co-nationals come under foreign rule. It was natural that their Government should speak honorably of the League Guarantee, given their insistence that Ger-

---

82 Colonel House, *Diary*, '29 June 1919', quoted in Carole Fink, *Defending the Rights of Others: The Great Powers, the Jews, and International Minority Protection, 1878–1938* (CUP 2004), 165.

83 Lloyd George's Fontainebleau Memorandum is dated 25 March 1919. Reproduced in Lloyd George (n 16), 405-406. Minorities in Central Europe had troubled the Great Powers in the years leading up to the Great War. There is some truth in the statement that this was a 'war of nationalities', not of states, and although the idea of minorities using states as proxies goes too far, they did come high on the political agenda of European governments after 1919. Leaders with a fascist and socialist bent benefited greatly from this *air du temps*. Stresemann later fashioned the new Weimar Republic as protector of German minorities abroad, a policy eagerly continued by National Socialism after 1933. Hitler's racist policies were the antithesis of minority equality, which might have something to do with equality's importance for post-war legal and constitutional developments in international organization. See Carole Fink, '"Defender of Minorities": Germany and the League of Nations, 1926–1933' (1972) 5 Central European History 330–337.

man kin-populations should be 'enabled to develop their German individuality, especially by being accorded the right to attend German schools and Churches.' Germany would do her part, for she was 'determined to treat the minorities on her territory in accordance with the same principles.'[84] With this in mind, the Allies persuaded Poland that the international guarantee was old wine in new bottles: just as the Balkan states had been enjoined to respect religious minorities after discarding the Ottoman yoke in 1878, so was Poland being committed at her coming of age.[85]

All of the minorities treaties were modelled around the Polish treaty, which was the first among them to be drafted.[86] The rationale behind the system of interwar group equality, as seen by the Great Powers, is captured neatly in Clemenceau's Fontainebleau memorandum to Paderewski. What is striking in this document is its reliance on old precedents, especially those emanating from the Congress of Berlin of 1878, where the Balkan states were recognized to the detriment of the Ottoman Empire:

> 1. In the first place, I would point out that this Treaty does not constitute any fresh departure. It has for long been established procedure of the public law of Europe that, when a State is created, or even when large accessions of territory are made to an established State, the joint and formal recognition by the Great Powers should be accompanied by the requirement that such State should, in the form of a binding international convention, undertake to comply with certain principles of government. This principle, for which there are numerous other precedents, received the most explicit sanction when, at the last general assembly of European Powers—the Congress of Berlin—the sovereignty and independence of Serbia, Montenegro, and Romania were recognised...[87]

its commitments were the Great Powers meeting in 1878. At Paris, the guarantor of the minority obligations was, for the first time, an interna-

---

84 The German reply to the Versailles treaty proposals, reproduced in LoN Publications, *Les Contrepropositions de l'Allemagne au projet du Traité de Paix de Versailles*, deuxième partie, II. i.b.

85 Fink, 'The Minorities Question...' (n 37), 249–274.

86 All the minorities treaties and other instruments negotiated after World War I containing minorities provisions are collected in *Protection of Linguistic, Racial and Religious Minorities by the League of Nations. Provisions Contained in the Various International Instruments at Present in Force* (Publications de la Société des Nations, I.B Minorités 1927).

87 'Letter of M Clemenceau to M Panderewski of 24 June 1919', reproduced in Sohn and Buergenthal (n 33), 214–15.

tional institution. An essential element of the peace, therefore, was 'the constitution of the League of Nations as the effective guardian of international right and international liberty throughout the world.'[88] The League was to mark the first instance of placing groups and their members under international protection. Clemenceau elaborated on the distinction between the old and new legal policies thus:

> 3. It is indeed that the new Treaty differs in form from earlier Conventions dealing with similar matters. The change of form is a necessary consequence and an essential part of the new system of international relations which is now being built up by the establishment of the League of Nations. Under the older system the guarantee for the execution of similar provisions was vested in the Great Powers ... Under the new system, the guarantee is entrusted to the League of Nations.[89]

In their first Report to the Council of Three, the members of the Committee on New States signalled their agreement that minorities clauses on religious and political equality would be 'essential' in the Polish treaty.[90] This was necessary, they argued, 'for the protection of the Jews and other minorities,' as the experience in Romania had painfully shown. They added that 'this has been very strongly pressed on us by the Jewish representatives whom we have seen; it will be equally important for other minorities.' Clauses defining citizenship would also be necessary in this context to avoid the problem of stateless minorities.[91] The Big Three agreed, with Wilson noting that:

> If we ask the new states to commit themselves purely and simply to grant equal treatment to their citizens, without providing a right of ap-

88 Lloyd George (n 16) 409.

89 'Letter of M Clemenceau to M Panderewski of 24 June 1919' (n 87).

90 On Wilson's initiative, a Council of Four comprising Wilson, Clemenceau, Lloyd George and Orlando had been established on 24 March 1919 to expedite the decision-making process. The Council of Ten continued to meet. Orlando suspended his participation when the Italian delegation walked away from the Conference over Fiume and other frustrated territorial claims on 24 April 1919. He returned with Baron Sonnino eleven days later, on 5 May, and resumed his participation in the Council. The Council's deliberations were transcribed and later published by Clemenceau's interpreter Paul Mantoux (n 39). Mantoux went on to establish the Graduate Institute of International Studies in Geneva with William Rappard in 1927.

91 'First Report to the Council of Three' dated 3 May 1919, in Miller, *Diary* (n 9) vol 13, 20, at 21–22: 'some clause binding Poland in respect of the citizenship and rights of these millions of her population which are not German is essential.'

> peal to the League of Nations, exactly what happened in Rumania in 1878 would happen in Poland.[92]

The Committee on New States finalized the draft minority protection clauses of the Polish treaty on 9 May 1919 and transmitted them to the Council of Four.[93] These were duly approved and forwarded to Paderewski. A cursory review may be made at this juncture to highlight their main features. First of all, the entire treaty was framed around the League's Guarantee, which Poland had to recognize as 'obligations of international concern.' The second part granted citizenship ipso facto to all persons habitually resident in Poland from 1 August 1914 onwards (in the final version, the critical date was changed to that of the treaty's entry into force.) In an accompanying report, the drafters deemed these clauses 'essential' to prevent statelessness and recalled the recurrent disenfranchisement of Jews of Romania.[94] In its third section, the draft treaty required Poland to protect the life and liberty of 'all inhabitants of Poland without distinction to birth, race, nationality, language, or religion.' Further clauses proclaimed equality before the law for citizens in the enjoyment of civil and political rights, freedom of religion to all inhabitants, and a special non-discrimination clause in respect of religion. All of these clauses became part of the final treaty. The article on special measures of protection for minorities followed. It would also remain largely unmodified in its final version, and ran thus:

> Polish citizens who belong to racial, religious, or linguistic minorities shall be granted the same treatment and security in law and in fact as the other citizens of Poland, and in particular shall have an equal right to establish, manage, and control at their own expense charitable, religious and social institutions, schools, and other educational establishments, with the free use in them of their own language and religion.[95]

---

92 'Conversation between President Wilson, Clemenceau and Lloyd George, and Barons Sonnino and Makino' dated 17 June 1919, Mantoux (n 39) 482. The Jews in Romania were still a concern, and Romanian assurances to guarantee 'the rights and liberties' of minorities and the 'free development in language, education and worship' to alien populations were considered as empty promises. See Annex (A) to the Thirteenth Meeting, 'Note of M. Bratiano to M. Berthelot dated 27 May 1919,' in Miller, *Diary* (n 9) vol 13, 89–90.

93 'Draft Treaty Between Poland and the Principal Allied and Associated Powers' (9 May 1919), in Miller, *Diary* (n 9) vol 13, 37.

94 'Second Report [of the Committee on New States]' dated 13 May 1919, ibid, 54.

95 ibid.

This clause was inserted verbatim in the other minorities treaties.[96] These special measures included the provision of adequate educational facilities in minority districts, and governmental funding for the establishment of social, religious, educational, and charitable institutions that were to be managed by the minorities. Language rights were also contemplated to accommodate for the German demands, but would also benefit Jews, Ruthenians and White Russians, especially as regards elementary education. In addition, the Polish draft treaty featured extensive provisions on the Jews, ensuring the communal authority of rabbis and the observation of the Sabbath. But the Jews' demand to be recognized as a separate nationality was not met.[97] All of these provisions were adopted by consensus, except for the clause on international guarantees.

Paderewski energetically protested the supervisory measures in a memorandum, while quickly adding that Poland fully subscribed to the provisions on equal rights for minorities.[98] He demanded that the international guarantee be removed on the grounds that it impinged on national sovereignty and prevented the development of a national conscience. If the minorities felt that they had external protection, they would be 'encouraged to lodge their complaints against the state to which they belong before a foreign court of appeal'. However, by his own admission, he regretted that the relations between Jews and Christians in Poland had become 'strained' and promised that Poland would grant 'full rights of citizenship' to all her subjects. He also opposed the far-reaching provisions on the Jews, which would result in the creation of an autonomous Jewish nation.[99] The Great Powers were sympathetic; Lloyd George, in particular, sheepishly admitted that they had gone 'perhaps a bit far' on certain points regarding the minorities clauses.[100] Protecting the Jews, he continued, did not require making them 'a state within a state' and the provisions on Jewish autonomy were duly relaxed.[101] As for the international guarantee, its re-

---

96 Albanian Treaty (art 6); Austrian Treaty (art 67); Bulgarian Treaty (art 54); Greek Treaty (art 8); Hungarian Treaty (art 58); Rumanian Treaty (art 9); Treaty with the Serb-Croat-Slovene State (art 8); Treaty with Czechoslovakia (art 8); Treaty with Turkey (art 40).

97 The Jews wanted separate electoral 'curias' allotted them in the Polish Diet and other elected bodies. 'Second Report', 'Second Report [of the Committee on New States]' dated 13 May 1919, in Miller, *Diary* (n 9) vol 13, 53 at 54, 56.

98 'Memorandum by M. Paderewski', ibid, 171.

99 ibid 175.

100 Council of Four, 'Meeting of 17 June 1919', in Mantoux (n 39), 482.

101 Council of Four, 'Meeting of 23 June 1919', ibid, 525.

moval was out of the question, but its forms of implementation remained an open issue.

The Great Powers also rejected the conditional application of the minorities clauses on the basis of reciprocity. Paderewski had requested that the rights offered to Germans in Poland should be extended to Poles in Germany in a separate convention, but the Allies insisted that the League should be the sole guarantor of the rights. The abandonment of the reciprocal system of individual rights was one of the major innovations of the League regime that became ubiquitous after World War II.

The matter of enforcement was among the most controversial issues that arose during the drafting process and a variety of options were put on the table. A first series of proposals focused on the Permanent Court of International Justice pursuant to the following alternative formulae: direct access for minorities to the PCIJ; seisin of the Court by a member of the League Council; seisin by any state-member of the League; or seisin by the Council itself. Others insisted that the Council alone was competent and proposed different modalities of referral thereto.[102] As these proposals circulated, Jewish lobbyists insisted that the minorities themselves should have access to the League to formulate complaints.[103]

Early proposals to give minorities a direct right of recourse repeatedly failed during the drafting of the peace treaties at the Paris Conference. Lord Robert Cecil had suggested that minorities and their members should be given direct access to the Permanent Court when local remedies proved futile:

> The Polish Government further agrees that, as soon as the Permanent Court of International Justice shall have been established and shall have settled the necessary procedure, *any Polish citizen or group of citizens* who shall have been aggrieved by the failure to carry out any of the provisions referred to in the last preceding Articles may appeal to that court, and the court may give such decision and make such order as it shall think right.[104]

---

102 The approaches are surveyed in Manley O Hudson's 'Memorandum to President Wilson' dated 6 June 1919, in Miller, *Diary* (n 9), vol 13, 141–142.

103 For a detailed account see Fink, *Defending the Rights of Others* (n 82), ch 8.

104 'Suggested Additions to the Polish Treaty (Rights of Minorities)' drafted by Lord Robert Cecil, 30 May 1919, in Miller, *Diary* (n 9) vol 13, 103. Emphasis added. The United States and Italian delegations supported this approach. The French, British, and Japanese experts preferred that the Court's jurisdiction be limited to state-based disputes. See Council of Four, 'Meeting of 6 June 1919', Mantoux (n 39) 331.

Cecil's idea was 'favourably received in principle,' but there was doubt 'as to whether the right of appeal could be conferred unconditionally on all individuals.'[105] A French counterproposal gave individuals and communities the right of refer violations to a member of the League Council.[106] An additional—rather odd—draft put forward by the United States and Italy would have enabled the PCIJ to attract disputes pertaining to minority groups or their members.[107]

Petitioning rights were also floated in the Council of Four, with Headlam-Morley reminding its members that the Covenant only enabled states to address disputes to the League. Could this right be granted to the representatives of minorities? Lloyd George was skeptical: giving 'propagandist associations' access to the League was dangerous, since the Jews were 'very litigious' and, in any event, anti-Semitism would not disappear overnight.[108] Wilson believed the responsibility should fall on all member states, mainly to allay the concerns of minor powers whose populations were being enclosed in new states. This would be in accordance with the principle of equality of all states, and consequently, removed any semblance of unwarranted intervention.[109] The final clauses are much more conservative and only members of the League Council were entitled to take conciliatory measures or bring legal action to the PCIJ.[110] This meant that states non-members of the Council that were immediately concerned by a breach could not obtain redress if a Council member did not espouse the claim on their behalf.

---

105 'Suggested Additions to the Polish Treaty' (n 104) 96.

106 ibid 104. The French proposal, drafted by Berthelot, provided that 'any violation of these obligations, of which a member of the Council of the League of Nations shall have been informed, may be referred by the latter to the Council...' The Cecil proposal is reproduced alongside the Berthelot proposal at Miller, *Diary* (n 9) vol 13, 105.

107 'Poland agrees that the Permanent Court of International Justice to be established by the League of Nations may take jurisdiction over claims of infraction of these obligations, and that she will submit to the exercise of this jurisdiction upon such conditions and under such procedure as, by general regulations, the Court from time to time prescribe.' See: 'Draft proposed by the American and Italian Delegations,' ibid, 141.

108 Council of Four, 'Meeting of 17 May 1919,' Mantoux (n 39) 90, 91.

109 Council of Four, 'Meeting of 6 June 1919,' ibid, 332, 333. Clemenceau limited himself to observing that the smaller states were 'very touchy' and should be dealt with carefully. ibid 332.

110 The final clause was drafted by the French, British, and Japanese delegations. See 'Draft Proposed by the French, British and Japanese Delegations,' Miller, *Diary* (n 9) vol 13, 141.

4. Concluding remarks

The establishment of international oversight for the minorities provisions was nothing short of revolutionary. By giving the League of Nations competence to ensure the implementation of the treaties, the peacemakers made redundant the methods employed by the Concert of Europe, which were an extension of the Great Powers' interests. They also established the first international supervisory mechanism concerning the rights of groups.

But in order to denounce violations of the regime, national minorities were not entitled to have direct recourse to the bodies of the League of Nations. This was a salient defect of the treaties. Instead, primary oversight of the obligations was given to states members of the League Council and to states having access to the PCIJ. Under that system, minorities sought the intercession of their kin-states and bypassed their territorial authorities in what was deemed to be an act of disloyalty.

When comparing the final outcome of the Paris Conference to Wilson's wartime desire to accord 'utmost satisfaction' to national aspirations, the achievements are considerably modest.[111] His attempt to generalize minority rights in the Covenant had failed and he resented the episode concerning Japan's racial equality clause. Moreover, the peacemakers also failed to impose minority protection obligations on Germany, and the attempt to develop minority protection obligations for Belgium, France, Denmark and Italy was a similar failure.[112] But the successful establishment of the League changed the international system forever, not least because the fate of populations and minorities had, for the first time in modern history, played an important role in the delimitation of borders, the creation of states and the establishment of a new Covenant for peaceful international relations.

The minorities clauses also stabilized the new international order by appeasing kin-states. But domestic peace was equally important, as the clauses also aimed at integrating their beneficiaries into their new polities. Although they were later criticized for their assimilationist bent, these two aspirations were believed to be mutually reinforcing at the time. The design of the treaties addressed this dual objective by adopting a group protection rationale to justify the conferral of individual rights. This ensured the delicate equilibrium between national and international forces and

111 Wilson, 'Four Principles' (n 34).

112 See Inis Claude, *National Minorities: An International Problem* (HUP 1955) 35.

fused national and international horizons.[113] That is to say, individual rights were given a new context of meaning after their elevation to the international plane. Unquestionably, liberal individual rights had enjoyed great currency in national laws before the Great War, especially in Western Europe and America. Their transnational development during the nineteenth century through reciprocity and nationality cemented their normative value. But these personal freedoms owe their international elevation to the principle of nationalities, which imbued them with its cosmopolitan international programme and its legal embodiment after the Great War through the internationalization of equality as a legal standard of protection.

113 To paraphrase Gadamer's dialectical concept. See Hans-Georg Gadamer, *Truth and Method* (Seabury Press 1975).

Part 3: The Emergence of International Economic Law

Chapter 6 Managing the 'Workers Threat': Preventing Revolution Through the International Labour Organization

Guy Fiti Sinclair[*]

1. *Introduction*

Writing in 1933, almost a decade and a half after the Versailles conference, the Columbia University professor James T Shotwell described the International Labour Organization (ILO) in vivid terms as 'an alternative to violent revolution'.[1] The ILO, he argued, had been created 'to meet the challenge of socialism and communism and prove to the workers of the world that the principles of social justice might be established under the capitalist system'. Its programs 'dealt with social justice the world over, rather than with the narrow issues of domestic economic warfare', envisaging 'national and international reform rather than revolution'.[2] Nor was Shotwell alone in viewing the ILO as a means of diverting energy away from revolution and towards class reconciliation. A major study of the organization by an American political scientist, published the next year, likewise described the ILO as 'patently a buttress against communism, as it stands for the collaboration of classes, though not always in fact their co-operation, within the present structure of society'.[3]

The same issue of the *Annals of the American Academy of Political and Social Science* in which Shotwell's paper appeared also carried contributions

---

* Senior Lecturer, Victoria University of Wellington Faculty of Law. Thanks to the organizers of the 'Peace Through Law: The Versailles Peace Treaty and Dispute Settlement After WWI' Conference held at the Max Planck Luxembourg in December 2017. A fuller account of the establishment and evolution of the ILO from 1919 to 1945 can be found in Guy Fiti Sinclair, *To Reform the World: International Organizations and the Making of Modern States* (OUP 2017) chs 1–2.

1 James T Shotwell, 'The International Labor Organization as an Alternative to Violent Revolution' (1933) 166 The ANNALS of the American Academy of Political and Social Science 18–25.

2 ibid 18.

3 Francis Graham Wilson, *Labor in the League System* (Stanford University Press 1934) 50–52.

by staff and supporters of the young organization. These included an introduction by Harold Butler, the recently-appointed Director of the International Labour Office;[4] a paper on 'How the International Labor Organization Operates' by Edward Phelan, an Assistant Director of the Office who had been instrumental in the design of the ILO;[5] and an essay on 'The Principles of International Labor Legislation' by Ernest Mahaim, a former chairman of the ILO's Governing body.[6] Other contributions addressed specific aspects of the ILO's functioning, from the standard-setting work of the Conference to the enforcement of those standards and the relatively routine research activities of the Office, while a whole section of papers addressed the relationship between the ILO and the United States. Comprising 25 separate papers in total, plus appendices including the ILO's constitution, the volume was squarely aimed at persuading members of the intelligentsia and policy-making elite in the United States of the benefits of ILO membership. The volume's editor, herself the ILO's Washington office manager, noted in the papers a 'tone of approval and the occasional exhor-

4 Butler (1883–1951) had worked in the Home Office of the British government before being transferred to the Ministry of Labour in 1917. He subsequently served as a substitute member of the Commission on International Labour Legislation at the Paris Peace Conference and as the Secretary-General of the first International Labour Conference, and was appointed the first Deputy Director of the International Labour Office, responsible for Central Services. See generally 'Harold Butler: Director-General of the International Labour Organization, 1932-1938', <www.ilo.org/global/about-the-ilo/how-the-ilo-works/ilo-director-general/former-directors-general/WCMS_192709/lang--en/index.htm>.

5 After joining the British Ministry of Labour in 1916, Phelan (1888–1967) was appointed Secretary of the Labour Section of the British delegation to the Paris Peace Conference, and had been one of the principal drafters of Part XIII and the originator of some of its most innovative features; he then served as assistant secretary of the organizing committee for the first Labour Conference held in Washington, DC, in 1919, and was appointed Principal Secretary of that Conference; and was among the first appointments to the International Labour Office, as the first Head of its Diplomatic Division. On Phelan's life and career, see generally 'Edward Phelan: Director-General of the International Labour Organization, 1941–1948', <http://www.ilo.org/global/about-the-ilo/who-we-are/ilo-director-general/former-directors-general/WCMS_192711/lang--en/index.htm>; and International Labour Office, *Edward Phelan and the ILO* (2009).

6 Mahaim (1865–1938) had been a founding member in 1900 of the International Association for Labor Legislation (IALL) and author of *Droit International Ouvrier* (1913), and was a Belgian government representative to the International Labour Conference for almost twenty years (1919–1938).

tations … that the United States join the Organization,' but modestly charged this 'to the personal responsibility of the contributors'.[7]

Appropriately for a professor of history, Shotwell's paper focused on the origins of the ILO in the work of the Commission on International Labour Legislation at the Peace conference. Outlining the difficulties facing the Commission, he addressed the particular ways the British proposal, which formed the basis of the Commission's discussions, had been adapted to meet the concerns of the American delegates—principally among them, the president of the American Federation of Labor, Samuel Gompers. This was history with a purpose, then, aimed at persuasion. Moreover, Shotwell wrote as an eye-witness to the events at Paris, indeed as an active participant in the negotiations over the ILO during which he had encouraged United States engagement in the nascent international institution. Shotwell's activism on behalf of internationalist causes reached perhaps its apotheosis in his work leading to the signing of the Kellogg–Briand Pact to outlaw war in 1928.[8] In 1934, Shotwell published a two-volume history of *The Origins of the International Labor Organization*;[9] his work as scholar and activist would continue for another three decades.[10]

This chapter approaches the establishment of ILO in 1919 not from the perspective of a historian, nor an activist, but that of an international lawyer, interested in international organizations and the rationales and technologies of power they embody. I have previously argued that the expanding powers exercised by international organizations have been imagined and understood to be necessary to the process of making modern states on a broadly Western model. I have further argued that twin processes of expansion of international organizations' powers and state formation are sustained by a logic of liberal reform that is at once external and internal to the law.[11]

---

7 Alice S Cheney, 'Foreword' (1933) 166 The ANNALS of the American Academy of Political and Social Science ix, ix.

8 See generally Oona Hathaway and Scott Shapiro, *The Internationalists and Their Plan to Outlaw War* (Simon & Schuster 2017).

9 James T Shotwell (ed), *The Origins of the International Labor Organization* (Columbia University Press 1934) 2 vols.

10 See generally Harold Josephson, *James T. Shotwell and the Rise of Internationalism in America* (Associated University Presses 1975).

11 See generally Guy Fiti Sinclair, 'State Formation, Liberal Reform and the Growth of International Organizations' (2015) 26 EJIL 445; Sinclair, *To Reform the World* (note preceding n 1).

Here, I take liberalism to be a critical ethos and practice that is constantly concerned with the problem of 'governing too much'.[12] Taking individual freedom as the principle and limit of governmental action, liberalism posits certain domains of liberty—including, importantly for our purposes, the market and economy—in which the state should interfere to the least extent possible. Yet, paradoxically, it also endorses and legitimizes numerous interventions in society and the individual: through mechanisms of 'social government' or the welfare state (social insurance schemes, old age pensions, programs of public health, and so on) which are seen as necessary to guarantee and support individual freedom in the face of the risks of modern society;[13] and by disciplinary practices that shape individual subjectivities and instil the self-mastery necessary for the responsible exercise of freedom. These contradictory pulls—don't intervene, but intervene in the right ways—are internal to liberal government and create a dynamic of liberal reform in both international organizations and states. In its various strategies of intervention and non-intervention, liberal government deploys a variety of techniques and associated sources of authority: legal, moral, and expert.[14]

What does all this have to do with the ILO and Versailles? The argument I wish to advance in this chapter is that the ILO was deeply shaped, in its origins and evolution, by the dynamic of liberal reform outlined above; and that, in turn, it contributed to the extension of that dynamic in its members. More broadly, I contend that the formation of the ILO articulated a new form of international governmentality that depoliticized, channelled, and managed the 'workers threat'. I begin by sketching the background to the formation of the ILO, before the Versailles moment and in the negotiations at the Peace Conference. Here, I am concerned with the ILO seen as an 'alternative to violent revolution', protecting workers and safeguarding the economy. The chapter then outlines three modes of liberal government that the ILO embodied, both in the terms of its constituent instrument and in the early actions of its leading officials. Broadly, these modes involve appeals to legal, moral, and expert authority—and frequently to a complex admixture of all three. The chapter concludes by noting

12 Michel Foucault, *Security, Territory, Population* (Graham Burchell tr, Palgrave Macmillan 2007) 385.

13 Here I follow the analysis of the welfare state set out in David Garland, 'The Welfare State: A Fundamental Dimension of Modern Government' (2014) 55 European Journal of Sociology 327.

14 Guy Fiti Sinclair, 'The International Civil Servant in Theory and Practice: Law, Morality, and Expertise' (2015) 26 EJIL747.

the significance of the ILO's early activities in each these technologies of government for more recent developments in global economic governance.

2. *From Revolution to Reform*

The ILO's formation must be seen as the culmination of a range of efforts, both public and private and on a national and international scale, over a period of at least a century, to address the 'social question.' The expansion of European commercial activity, spurred on by the industrial revolution, was accompanied by population growth, urbanization, the formation of an industrial proletariat, and growing concerns about social problems such as mass poverty, disease, crime, and immorality. These concerns were most sharply realized in the rise of revolutionary socialist movements, and ultimately in the Europe-wide revolutions of 1848, which had been heralded in the *Communist Manifesto*. As Charles Maier has argued, these revolutions —together with other traumatic upheavals around the mid-century, such as colonial wars and rebellions, civil wars, and wars of national independence —were followed by the reconstitution and consolidation of state power to an unprecedented degree.[15] In the latter half of the nineteenth century, European governments attempted to ameliorate social conditions, and thereby guard against social disorder, through the introduction of a variety of public measures.[16]

Internationally, efforts to address labour conditions in Western Europe proceeded on two separate tracks. On the one hand, trade unionists organized internationally through the 'International Working Men's Association' (the 'First International'), formed in 1864; through the 'Second International,' formed in 1889; and through a variety of international labour secretariats.[17] On the other hand, liberal reformists, with the Swiss government leading, promoted the idea of international labour legislation as a means of standardising conditions of labour in different countries. These efforts eventually led to the formation of the International Association for Labour Legislation (IALL), a semi-official body, partly funded by govern-

---

15 Charles Maier, 'Leviathan 2.0: Inventing Modern Statehood,' in E Rosenberg (ed), *A World Connecting* (HUP 2012) 29, at 69–170.

16 See generally Pat Thane, *Foundations of the Welfare State* (2nd ed, Longman 1996) 6–45.

17 See generally Lewis L Lorwin, *The International Labor Movement* (Greenwood Press 1953) 7–37.

ments, which in 1906 produced draft conventions on night work for women and the use of white phosphorous in matches.[18] Given their later connections with the ILO, it is noteworthy that participants at the 1900 Congress which founded the IALL included Arthur Fontaine, Ernest Mahaim, and Émile Vandervelde.[19]

The more immediate context of the ILO's creation was, of course, formed by the devastations of the First World War and their consequences. The outbreak of the Great War initially forced a nationalist wedge between workers in opposing European states, resulting in the dissolution of the Second International. As the War progressed, however, the international trade unions movement—in particular led by the International Federation of Trade Unions (IFTU, or 'Amsterdam International')—rallied to reassert the interests of workers.[20] In July 1916, an inter-Allied trade union conference held in Leeds passed resolutions, put forward by the French *Confédération générale du Travail*, demanding that the peace treaties to terminate the war incorporate provisions recognising workers' rights and setting minimum labour standards, including the right to work, the right of 'coalition' in trade unions, provisions on emigration and immigration, social insurance, hours of labour, hygiene and protection, and inspection and statistics. The resolutions further demanded the establishment of an international commission to supervise the application of these standards, and in international labour office to 'coordinate and consolidate the various inquiries, studies, statistics, and national reports on the application of the la-

18 On the IALL, see generally Sandrine Kott, 'From Transnational Reformist Network to International Organization: The International Association for Labour Legislation and the International Labour Organization, 1900–1930s', in Davide Rodogno, Bernhard Struck and Jakob Vogel (eds), *Shaping the Transnational Sphere: Experts, Networks and Issues from the 1840s to the 1930s* (Bergahn Books 2015) 239–257.

19 Fontaine (1860–1931) had served as Director of the French Ministry of Labor at the time, and was Chairman of the ILO's Governing Body from 1919 until his death. Vandervelde (1866–1938) was a member of the Belgian Workers' Party from 1886 and a Member of Parliament from 1894, serving at different times as Minister of Justice and Minister of Foreign Affairs and chair of the executive body of the Second International (1900–1918). See generally Jasmien Van Daele, 'Engineering Social Peace: Networks, Ideas, and the Founding of the International Labour Organization' (2005) 50 International Review of Social History 435.

20 Reiner Tosstorff, 'The International Trade-Union Movement and the Founding of the International Labour Organization' (2005) 50 International Review of Social History 399. On the IFTU, see generally Geert Van Goethem, *The Amsterdam International: The World of the International Federation of Trade Unions (IFTU), 1913-1945* (Ashgate 2006).

bor laws.'[21] A counter-conference held in Berne in October 1917, organized by the German leader of the IFTU and attended by Central Power representatives, proposed an even more far-reaching set of terms for inclusion in the peace treaties.[22] The next month saw the Bolsheviks' triumph in Russia.

The work of the International Labour Commission in Paris therefore took place against the backdrop of very real revolutionary possibilities. Waves of labour strikes, political strikes, and revolutions had swept across central Europe since 1917, and threatened to extend even to Western liberal democracies such as Britain and France. As Harold Butler put it, the months following the War ushered in a 'general metamorphosis of the social outlook' in England, including the rise of socialism among industrial workers, greater demand for public ownership and democratic control of industry, and widespread acceptance, across the political spectrum, of the need to extend social insurance, improve housing and education, and address extreme cases of poverty.[23] Describing the preoccupations of the British and French Prime Ministers at the time, David Lloyd George and Georges Clemenceau, Edward Phelan later wrote:[24]

> Both were fearful of an extension of Bolshevism … both realized how the trade-union movement had grown in power in their respective countries, how the unions had made sacrifices to secure war production and expected some return; and above all both were concerned with the problem of demobilization and its results, a proletariat trained to the use of arms and hardened to warfare.

A further trade union conference, held in Berne in February 1919, brought together representatives from Allied, Central Power, and neutral countries, and sought to build upon the demands made at the earlier Leeds and Berne conferences.[25] The members of the Commission who gathered in Paris in February–March 1919 were, by and large, moderate socialist and liberal reformers. Chaired by Samuel Gompers, the head of American Federation of Labour, which had a strict policy of avoiding politics, the Com-

---

21 'Standards of Labor Legislation Suggested in Resolutions of International Labor Conference at Leeds, July, 1916' (June 1917) 4/6 Monthly Review of the US Bureau of Labor Statistics 912–915.

22 Tosstorff (n 20) 409–413.

23 Harold Butler, *Confident Morning* (Faber & Faber 1950) 130–131.

24 Edward J Phelan, 'The Labor Proposals before the Peace Conference, in Shotwell, *The Origins…* (n 9), vol 1, 207.

25 Tosstorff (n 20) 418–421.

mission included Arthur Fontaine, Ernest Mahaim, Émile Vandervelde, and the French trade union leader Léon Jouhaux, who had played a leading role in the Leeds conference.[26] Behind the scenes, lawyers, economists, and other public servants and technical advisors – including Shotwell – played an essential role in attempting to balance the demands of workers with the competing interests of European governments, not to mention those of important extra-European countries such as the United States and Japan.[27]

Judged against these challenges, Part XIII of the Versailles Peace Treaty, which formed the constituent instrument of the ILO, was a remarkable achievement. Politically and diplomatically, the text managed to address and resolve the strongly-held concerns raised by the different parties; legally, in the drafting of its provisions, and in the structure of the institution it brought into being, it was highly innovative. In all respects, it renewed commitment to the liberal ideals of progressive social reform. As Emile Vandervelde put it:[28]

26 Other members of the Commission included, for the United States, in addition to Gompers, the President of the American Shipping Board (AN Hurley); for the British Empire, a Labour Member of the War Cabinet (George Barnes) and Assistant Under-Secretary of State (Sir Malcolm Delevingne); from France, in addition to Fontaine, the Ministers of Labour (Pierre Colliard) and Industrial Reconstruction (Louis Loucheur); from Italy, the Commissioner-General for Emigration (Baron Mayor des Planches) and Vice-President of the Supreme Labour Council (Angiolo Cabrini); from Japan, an Envoy Minister of the Japanese Emperor (K Otchiai) and a former Director of Commercial and Industrial Affairs in the Ministry of Agriculture and Commerce (Minoru Oka); from Belgium, in addition to Mahaim and Vandervelde, a Labour Party Senator (Henri Lafontaine); a professor from Havana University, Cuba (Antonio de Bustamente); a member of the Polish National Committee (Count Zoltowski) and Director-General of the Ministry of Labour (François Sokal); and the Minister of Foreign Affairs of the Czechoslovak Republic (Eduard Benes). See generally Edward J Phelan, 'The Commission on International Labor Legislation, in Shotwell, *The Origins…* (n 9), vol 1, 128–129; Van Daele, 'Engineering Social Peace' (n 19).

27 In his eyewitness account of the work of the Commission, Shotwell mentions significant interactions with (among others) James Brown Scott, Felix Frankfurter, Harold Butler, and Edward Phelan; as well as encounters with John Maynard Keynes, William Beveridge, Edward ('Colonel') House, and Jean Monnet. See generally James T Shotwell, *At the Paris Peace Conference* (Macmillan 1937). For other eyewitness accounts of the Commission, see generally Butler, *Confident Morning* (n 23), 155–176; Phelan, 'The Commission' (n 26).

28 Cited in Phelan, 'The Labor Proposals' (n 24) 209.

> If I dared to express my thoughts in a tangible way, I should say that there are two methods of making the revolution which we feel is happening throughout the world, the Russian and the British method. It is the British method which has triumphed in the Labor Commission ...

The following parts of this chapter explore how this 'British method'—that is to say, liberal reform, as opposed to revolution—was codified in Part XIII and manifested in the early actions of ILO officials.

3. *Legal Proceduralism versus Revolution*

Law is a technology of liberal government *par excellence*. The routinization of charismatic and traditional authority through a variety of legal-rational procedures and techniques has been the leading characteristic of modern, Western government since at least the nineteenth century, not to mention much earlier examples in other cultures and on other continents.[29] Law places limits upon state power, defining the boundaries between state power and the various domains of liberty carved out by liberalism, delineating institutional architectures, and assigning specific powers to different state organs. The institutions of liberal government—including 'disciplinary' institutions such as schools, prisons, and hospitals and mechanisms of 'social government' or 'security'—are interpenetrated and supported by a latticework of legal rules. Any perceived imbalance between freedom, discipline, and security thus requires a corresponding adjustment in law.

Looking at Part XIII today, with the benefit of a century's hindsight, it is perhaps surprising to observe that the founding instrument contained no 'hard' norms of labour law. Contrary to the hopes of the trade unionists who had recently gathered in Berne (twice) and Leeds, only Section II articulated a set of labour standards at all—and there only as an aspirational set of 'General principles', subject to important caveats and conditions. This 'charter of rights', as it came to be known, was a late addition to the text, intended to reflect the high ideals and goals towards which both the international labour movement and liberal social reformers had struggled

29 See generally Max Weber, *Economy and Society* (Guenther Roth and Claus Wittich eds, University of California Press 1978) 2 vols.

over decades. But they were carefully couched in non-binding language, as the following extracts illustrate:[30]

> … [T]here are methods and principles for regulating labour conditions which all industrial communities *should endeavour to apply, so far as their special circumstances will permit.*
>
> > Among these methods and principles, the following *seem* to the HIGH CONTRACTING PARTIES to be of special and urgent importance:
> > … [L]abour *should not* be regarded merely as a commodity or article of commerce …
> > The adoption of an eight hours day or a forty-eight hours week as *the standard to be aimed at* … The principle that men and women *should* receive equal remuneration for work of equal value …
> > Each State *should* make provision for a system of inspection in which women *should* take part, in order to ensure the enforcement of the laws and regulations for the protection of the employed.

In contrast, the binding provisions of Part XIII—where we find 'shall' instead of 'should'—were all concerned with creating an institutional structure and procedures. The 'permanent organisation' established by Articles 387–399 was to consist of a 'General Conference,' which would meet on a regularly recurring basis, at least once per year; a permanent 'International Labour Office, with a Director and staff; and a 'Governing Body,' comprising 24 members, including eight nominated by the members of 'chief industrial importance,' which would appoint the Director and exercise control over the Office. Articles 400–420 in turn related mostly to the operations of the Conference, though they also provided procedures for reporting, complaints, and enquiries. Though relatively brief, these various provisions introduced several remarkable innovations into international governance.

First and perhaps most inventive was the so-called principle of 'tripartism.' This principle entailed the separate representation of three distinct groups in both the Conference and the Governing Body, with half the delegates in each organ representing government members, a quarter representing workers, and another quarter representing employers. Already during the War, the British government's Ministry of Labour had introduced —with limited success—a scheme for 'self-government in industry' which

30 Treaty of Peace at Versailles (adopted 28 June 1919, entered into force 10 January 1920) 225 CTS 188, Part XIII ('Part XIII'), art 427 (emphasis added).

brought together employers and workers in joint councils, known (after its leading sponsor) as 'Whitley Councils'.[31] The structure suggested in the British proposal that formed the basis of Part XIII transformed this 'bilateral' principle into a 'trilateral' one, involving government. A quintessentially liberal mechanism, tripartism aimed to bring conflicting social classes together to resolve their differences through dialogue, debate, and voting.

The law-making functions assigned to the ILO comprised a second remarkable innovation introduced by Part XIII. Article 405 empowered the International Labour Conference to adopt, by a two-thirds majority of votes cast, one of two kinds of international instrument: a recommendation for consideration by governments, to be given effect by national legislation or otherwise; or a draft international convention for ratification by member governments. By virtue of the principle of tripartism discussed above, these procedures involved non-state actors in an international 'legislative'—that is, standard-setting—process with implications for state law, albeit without automatic or direct effect.[32] Article 405 allowed for the production of both draft conventions and recommendations, making it possible to work towards wider agreement; by not requiring the take-it-or-leave-it presentation of a draft convention, as Shotwell noted, these alternatives allowed the door to social progress to be left open.[33] Both options made international 'legislation' subject to national legislative action—conventions were only binding on member states that ratified them, and the implementation of recommendations likewise relied on state action—thus preserving the perquisites of state sovereignty. Moreover, the option of adopting recommendations rather than draft conventions allowed for the participation of federal states—in particular, the United States—where labour legislation lay within competence of state legislatures.

Third, Part XIII introduced novel institutional procedures with respect to implementation, notification, and accountability. Members were required to place the draft conventions and recommendations passed by the Conference before their relevant state authorities within 18 months, and inform the Secretary-General of the League of Nations of actions taken with respect to recommendations and the formal ratification of conventions.[34] Members further agreed to produce annual reports on the measures they had taken to give effect to the provisions of conventions to

---

31 Butler, *Confident Morning* (n 23) 136–139.

32 In this sense, the Conference was rightly described as a world 'Parliament of labour'. Albert Thomas, *International Social Policy* (ILO 1948) 39.

33 Shotwell, *At the Paris Peace Conference* (n 27) 62.

34 Part XIII, art 405.

which they were party, in a form to be determined by the Governing Body.[35] Complaints could be brought, through the Office, against any member which appeared to have 'failed to secure in any respect the effective observance within its jurisdiction of any convention to which it is a party.'[36] The Governing Body would communicate any such complaints (or 'representations') made by workers and employers associations to the relevant member government and, where no (or an unsatisfactory) response was forthcoming, could publish a complaint and any response received.[37] In the case of complaints made by one members against another in respect of a convention which both had ratified, the same procedure could apply; alternatively, the Governing Body could initiate a procedure for the appointment of a Commission of Enquiry, which ultimately allowed referral to, and final decision by, the Permanent Court of International Justice.[38]

In brief, then, the drafters of Part XIII created the ILO as a permanent mechanism, governed by law, capable of framing international standards, and able to resolve transnational disputes involving states and particular non-state actors. As such, the ILO offered an institutionalized mechanism of class reconciliation and cooperation that could, in theory, progressively implement higher labour standards and address new issues as they arose. The use of legal procedures to contain and channel political disagreement thus lay at the heart of the ILO's efficacy as 'an alternative to violent revolution.' Indeed, it is difficult to imagine even the suggestion of such an innovative mechanism without the backdrop and threat of actual revolution.

4. *Law and Morality: Towards Responsive Law*

In the 'social science strategy' proposed by Philippe Nonet and Philp Selznick, three modalities of law-in-society can be distinguished. In the first, law is an instrument of repressive power; in the second, it is 'a differentiated institution capable of taking repression and protecting its own integrity'; in the third, law is responsive to social need and exigencies.[39] Each of these types of law—repressive, autonomous, and responsive—identifies

35 Part XIII, art 408.

36 Part XIII, art 409.

37 Part XIII, art 410.

38 Part XIII, arts 411-417. It should be noted that this provision was not in fact used until 1961.

39 Philippe Nonet and Philp Selznick, *Law & Society in Transition: Toward Responsive Law* (Transaction Publishers 2001) 14.

a characteristic posture, and may be distinguished from the others along various dimensions. Thus, whereas repressive law is characterized by a communal morality or moralism, and autonomous law is identified with an 'institutional morality ... preoccupied with the integrity of legal process', responsive law expresses a 'civil morality', or 'morality of cooperation'. Likewise, repressive law employs an ad hoc, expedient mode of reasoning; autonomous law seeks to adhere strictly to legal authority, to the point of becoming formalistic; whereas responsive law is purposively oriented.[40] Moreover, each of these modalities is associated with one or more schools of jurisprudence.

In its creation and early operations, I will argue, the ILO was closely associated with the move from autonomous to responsive law, both nationally and internationally. Whereas 'classical legal thought' in nineteenth-century European and North American law was typically formalistic and in general expressive of an 'autonomous law' modality, by the early twentieth century attention to 'the social' had started to shift the over-all legal posture towards concern with social welfare, social justice, and social rights.[41] In the United States, this shift was most closely associated with the sociological jurisprudence of thinkers such as Roscoe Pound.[42] In Europe, figures such Léon Duguit similarly developed a jurisprudence that grounded the legitimacy of the state in its contribution towards social solidarity, through laws and other measures that guaranteed social security, public health, employment, and individual development.[43] In its advocacy for social interests, welfare, and rights, the ILO positioned itself at the forefront of an international movement to reconceptualize law in anti-formalistic, purposive, and responsive terms.

---

40 ibid 16.

41 Duncan Kennedy, 'Three Globalizations of Law and Legal Thought: 1850–2000' in David M Trubek and Alvaro Santos (eds), *The New Law and Economic Development* (CUP 2006), 37–42.

42 Pound (1870–1964) was the Dean of Harvard Law School from 1916 to 1936. His key articles on the topic include Roscoe Pound, 'The Scope and Purpose of Sociological Jurisprudence' (1910–1911) 24 Harvard Law Review 591, 25 Harvard Law Review 140; and 'The Theory of Sociological Judicial Decision' (1922–1923) 36 Harvard Law Review 641.

43 Duguit (1859–1928) taught in the Law Faculty at the University of Bordeaux from 1886 to 1928, where he was a friend and colleague of Émile Durkheim. His most important works include *L'État, le droit objectif et la loi positive* (Albert Fontemoing 1901), and *Le droit social, le droit individuel et les transformations de l'État* (Félix Alcan 1908). See generally JES Hayward, 'Solidarist Syndicalism: Durkheim and Duguit Part II' (1960) 8 The Sociological Review 185.

In this effort, ILO officials drew on the moral authority embedded in the new organization's purposes and principles. Part XIII thus began with a preamble asserting the ILO's high moral purpose:[44]

> Whereas the League of Nations has for its object the establishment of universal peace, and such a peace can be established only if it is based upon social justice;
>
> And whereas conditions of labour exist involving such injustice, hardship and privation to large numbers of people as to produce unrest so great that the peace and harmony of the world are imperilled …
>
> The HIGH CONTRACTING PARTIES, moved by sentiments of justice and humanity as well as by the desire to secure the permanent peace of the world agree to the following …

Likewise, the 'General principles' constituting the 'charter of rights' in Section II of Part XIII set out the social principles guiding the ILO's members, elevated to a moral code: 'The HIGH CONTRACTING PARTIES, recognising that the wellbeing, physical, moral and intellectual, of industrial wage-earners is of supreme international importance … ' Indeed, the same 'General Principles' suggested that the ILO's mission embodied a *universal* morality, extendable in principle to all countries and regions of the world, although 'differences of climate, habits and customs, of economic opportunity and industrial tradition, [made] strict uniformity in the conditions of labour difficult of *immediate* attainment.'[45] Accordingly, from a relatively early stage the ILO consciously extended its reforming mission to colonial territories and states in Asia and Africa; from 1922, India was recognized as a member 'of chief industrial importance' on the Governing Body; and the ILO occupied a seat on the League's Permanent Mandate Commission.[46]

ILO officials and supporters invoked these high moral purposes and principles in tandem with claims to formal legal or delegated authority. Described by the first Director of the Office, Albert Thomas, in a quasi-religious vocabulary—as 'a faith if not a doctrine,' constituting the sole means of 'salvation for the world'[47]—the 'charter of rights' comprised 'Nine Articles of faith,' upon which Thomas 'built up a great body of doctrine with

---

44 Part XIII, Section I.

45 Part XIII, art 427 (emphasis added).

46 Luis Rodríguez-Piñero, *Indigenous Peoples, Postcolonialism, and International Law: The ILO Regime (1919-1989)* (OUP 2005) 27–28.

47 Thomas (n 32) 40, 123.

all the dialectic of a medieval theologian.'[48] As such, they were available for deployment in a variety of ways, whether as a free-standing source of authority where no—or only weak—legal authority existed, or as a means to enhance and augment the latter. A 'hermeneutic of growth', quickly adopted in the ILO, thus framed Part XIII as a 'living constitution', at once a manifestation of 'autonomous' and 'responsive' law, in the terminology of Nonet and Selznick:

> [I]n these ten years that we have just been through, we have shown that the Constitution [Part XIII] as it was originally drawn up was a sound Constitution ... We are also in the process of demonstrating that it is a living institution, in the sense that it is capable of adaptation; that it is not just a static charter, ... but that it is a living organism which works and which is capable of expansion and modification in order to meet the needs of practical life. [49]

This view of the ILO's founding instrument encouraged and legitimized an expansive, 'responsive' approach to its activities. Convening workers' representatives together with those of governments and employers, the Conference already claimed to serve as a 'Parliament of labour', 'the social conscience of mankind', and 'the forum of the ordinary man in world affairs'.[50] A far-flung network of branch offices and correspondents, supplemented by ever-expanding 'missions' to member states, as well as personal contacts in the IFTU and through it to trade unions, extended the Office's influence even further and enabled it to respond to the energy of the international labour movement even better. As Thomas put it in an address to the IFTU Congress in 1922: 'The Office is nothing else but a great international thermometer. If there is ardour and activity in the labour movement, its action expands. If, on the contrary, the activity of the labour movement slows down and stagnates, our work too contracts'.[51]

The responsive approach taken by ILO officials, inspired by the broad moral purposes of Part XIII, rapidly took the organization into new areas of activity and activism. Some of these were 'natural', if contested, extensions of the organization's existing mandate, such as labour protections for migrants, refugees, maritime and agricultural workers, and worker hous-

48 Butler, *Confident Morning* (n 23) 173.
49 Harold Butler, 'Past, Present, and Future of the International Labour Organization', in Humphrey Milford (ed), *Problems of Peace* (OUP 1930) 43.
50 C Wilfred Jenks, 'Introduction', in International Labour Office, *Edward Phelan and the ILO* (n 5) 1, 6.
51 Thomas (n 32) 29.

ing. Others were more overtly 'political', including investigations into atrocities against workers by counter-revolutionary 'White Terror' in Hungary, the conditions of Russian prisoners in German internment camps, the compulsory labour service in Bulgaria, the effects of political disturbances on production and working conditions in Upper Silesia, and allegations of Fascist paramilitary violence against workers' organizations in Italy. These extensions of the ILO's ostensible legal authority attracted criticism and resistance, including challenges before the Permanent Court of International Justice, which in turn resulted in important advisory opinions rejecting a 'restrictive' interpretation of Part XIII and embracing of a theory of 'extended competence' instead.[52]

The first few years of its operations thus saw a rapid expansion of the Office to be much larger than the minimal secretariat support anticipated by all sides in the negotiations over Part XIII. A report on the organization of the Office dated 7 May 1921, prepared by a Commission of Experts appointed in accordance with a resolution of the League of Nations Assembly, gives a good sense of the functions that the Office was expected to perform at that time. Noting that the 'general policy' of the Office had already been criticized for being too innovative and promoting socialist ideas, the Commission expressed confidence that Office staff were 'controlled with a firm hand', were 'well aware of the grave dangers to the future of the Office which would attend any ventures outside the province which has been marked out for it', and were 'inspired with too great a confidence in its future possibilities, too lofty an idea of its mission, and too impassioned and rational a zeal for the accomplishment of its destiny, so to compromise the work which [had] been entrusted to them'. The Commission further considered that, 'generally speaking', the Office's work had remained 'clearly within the limits laid down by the Treaties', but warned that its authority

> might be compromised, especially when its enquiries lead it inevitably over the border line into adjoining, and often closely connected, fields of activity, such as, for instance, that of economics, unless the International Labour Office were to act with the greatest possible prudence and laid no claim to do more than supply the necessary element of co-

52 International Labour Office, *The International Labour Organisation: The First Decade* (1931) 99–101.

> ordination together with such data and statistics as it alone is in a position to provide.[53]

As the next part of this chapter shows, the danger to which the Commission averted—the possibility that the Office might trespass into the realm of economics—would soon be realized.

5. *Law and/as Expertise*

In championing a turn to responsive law, undergirded by a 'social' morality, early twentieth-century liberals regarded law as an instrument of 'social engineering' through which society could be reshaped. As a part of what Samuel Haber called 'an efficiency craze—a secular Great Awakening, an outpouring of ideas and emotions in which a gospel of efficiency was preached without embarrassment', the idea of social engineering was common to the Progressive movement in the United States, New Liberalism in Britain, and other, related movements, in Europe and elsewhere.[54] This 'gospel of efficiency' informed the emergence of scientific management and rationalization in the field of public administration,[55] while in the human sciences it influenced a range of social reform efforts, including, at the extreme, eugenics.[56] More broadly, the period saw a growing faith in the ability of experts to identify and implement solutions to social problems. Thus, for example, Roscoe Pound's sociological jurisprudence advocated the use of scientific expertise for social planning, and viewed the rise of the administrative state as a positive and natural outcome of recent social evolution.[57]

This intellectual milieu influenced the way the ILO was conceived and operated in its early years. Some seeds of the ILO's expert authority can be

---

53 Cited in 'Organisation of the Secretariat of the League of Nations and of the International Labour Office' (25 May 1921) 3:20 International Labour Office Official Bulletin 1, 6–7 and 9.

54 Samuel Haber, *Efficiency and Uplift* (University of Chicago Press 1964) ix.

55 See generally Dwight Waldo, *The Administrative State* (2nd ed, Holmes & Meier 1984) ch 3.

56 See generally Michael Freeden, 'Eugenics and Progressive Thought: A Study in Ideological Affinity' (1979) 22 The Historical Journal 645.

57 See generally G Edward White, 'From Sociological Jurisprudence to Realism: Jurisprudence and Social Change in Early Twentieth-Century America' (1972) 58 Virginia Law Review 999; Morton J Horwitz, *The Transformation of American Law* (HUP 1992).

discerned in the few provisions of Part XIII that indicated the Office's functions, such as:[58]

> ... the collection and distribution of information on all subjects relating to the international adjustment of conditions of industrial life and labour ... the conduct of such special investigations as may be ordered by the Conference ... duties ... in connection with international disputes ... edit[ing] and publish[ing] ... a periodical paper dealing with problems of industry and employment of international interest ... such other powers and duties as may be assigned to it by the Conference.

Each of these provisions became the basis for wide-ranging activities undertaken by the Office, mentioned above. Chief among other steps taken to enhance the Office's scientific or expert authority was the creation of a Scientific Division that initially was to serve as a 'clearing house of information', gathering and distributing reports from around the world and then producing its own reports, as well as syntheses of collected information, in a large range of publications including an *Encyclopaedia of Industrial Hygiene*; an annual *International Labor Directory*, *Legislative Series*, *International Survey of Legal Decisions on Labour Law*, and *Yearbook*; and a monthly *Summary* and *International Labour Review*.[59] The Office's—and more broadly, the ILO's—expert authority was further augmented through the establishment of other specialized sections within the Office, and the use of external experts in an array of conferences, advisory committees and correspondence committees addressing particular topics, such as anthrax, industrial hygiene, social insurance, and labour statistics.[60] Notable among many such endeavours was the ILO's landmark study of forced labour for the League's Temporary Slavery Commission, and subsequent appointment of an Expert Committee on Native Labor.[61]

Other actions taken by the ILO combined expert with legal authority. When it became overly cumbersome for the Governing Body to review the information provided by governments regarding their ratification of international labour conventions, the Conference resolved to establish a special committee of experts, who would be chosen 'on the ground of their tech-

58 Part XIII, Art 396.

59 'The Scientific Work of the International Labour Office' (December 1927) 12 Monthly Summary of the International Labour Organisation 7, 7.

60 See generally E Beddington Behrens, *The International Labour Office* (Leonard Parsons 1924) ch 8.

61 Rodríguez-Piñero (n 46) 31–36.

nical competence alone', to review the information provided by governments.[62] The same session of the Conference also created a separate conference committee to allow government representatives to submit additional information or explanations in relation to the expert committee's reports, and for those representatives to be questioned by both governmental and non-governmental delegates.[63] Though criticized as 'unconstitutional'—Ernest Mahaim warned that these 'innocuous experts' were likely to become a 'tribunal' of 'inspectors'[64]—this further layer of procedure nevertheless provided yet another, generally welcomed opportunity to divert and defuse political conflict through hybrid legal-expert means.

A kind of expert legal authority likewise provided the basis for a growing range of technical advice provided by the Office to governments. ILO officials on 'mission' to member states were asked for advice on drafting labour legislation, and increasingly on the implementation of such legislation through administrative means. Over time, this developed into a practice of technical assistance *avant la lettre*, whereby ILO officials provided solutions for a wide range of problems in various issue-areas, including refugees, factory inspections, and, above all, social insurance schemes, in particular to states on the southern and eastern European peripheries. From the late 1920s onwards, and especially in the aftermath of the Great Depression, the organization's 'centre of gravity' began to shift away from Europe and ILO missions extended as far as Southern Africa (1928), Soviet Union and East Asia (1928–29), India and Middle East (1933), and South and southeast Asia (1937–38). Accordingly, ILO officials provided more and more technical advice to members in Asia, such as Japan and China, and the Americas, including the United States, which became a member in 1934.[65]

The development of international labour jurisprudence within the Office represents a further innovation in the legal-expert authority exercized by the ILO. Part XIII supplied no authority for the Office to provide authoritative interpretations of labour conventions produced under ILO auspices. Nevertheless, the concentration of legal expertise and collation of international legislation and state practice within the Office provided useful

---

62 E A Landy, *The Effectiveness of International Supervision* (Oceana 1966) 16-17 and 21 fn 6 (citing Albert Thomas).

63 ibid 36–37.

64 ibid 20.

65 On the development of technical assistance practices in the ILO, see generally Guy Fiti Sinclair, 'A "Civilizing Task": The International Labour Organization, Social Reform, and the Genealogy of Development' (2017) 20 JHIL 1–53.

guides to interpretation, and the Office regularly published the advice it had rendered as a result of member-state inquiries in the Bulletin for the benefit of others. While such publication was invariably accompanied by an explicit disavowal of interpretive authority, a presumption gradually emerged that the Conference must be presumed to have intended a particular provision to be understood in the manner in which the Office had previously interpreted an identical or equivalent provision in another Convention, if that opinion had been submitted to the Governing Body and published in the Bulletin and had met with no adverse comment.[66]

Finally, if ILO practice indicated a merging or blurring of legal and expert authority, it also soon became apparent that the boundaries between law, social reform, and economy had been breached. In addition to the high moral sentiments it articulated, the Preamble to Part XIII alluded to a powerful economic motivation: 'Whereas also the failure of any nation to adopt humane conditions of labour is an obstacle in the way of other nations which desire to improve the conditions in their own countries ... '[67] At least part of the purpose of international action on labour standards, therefore, was to remove the competitive advantage enjoyed by countries that imposed lower standards of protection. In addition, the report issued by a Commission of Enquiry appointed under Article 411 of Part XIII could indicate 'measures, if any, of an economic character against a defaulting government which it considers to be appropriate, and which it considers other Governments would be justified in adopting':[68] another indication that the ILO was concerned with economic relations. The ILO's early inquiry into production in the Ruhr, its involvement in the Economic and Financial Conference held in Genoa in 1922,[69] and, especially, its massive inquiry into post-war industrial production, which lasted for four years and resulted in a five-volume report,[70] further indicated a view of the ILO as an integral part of the wider international economic framework established after the War.

---

66 'Interpretation of the Decisions of the International Labour Conference' (10 April 1938) 23:1 International Labour Office Official Bulletin 30, 32.

67 Part XIII, Section I (Preamble).

68 Part XIII, Art 414.

69 Patricia Clavin, *Securing the World Economy* (OUP 2013) 23–25; 'The International Labour Organisation and the Genoa Conference' (21 June 1921) 5:25 International Labour Office Official Bulletin 3.

70 See generally ibid 51–52.

6. *Conclusion*

What were the lasting legacies of these modes and technologies of liberal government, embedded in the text of the Treaty of Versailles and elaborated through the early actions of ILO officials? Certainly, it is not possible to draw a straight line from the varied and often conflicting intentions of the negotiators at Paris, through the text of the Treaty, to the present day. The interplay of exogenous events (such as wars, economic and other crises), endogenous feedback effects, institutional interactions, and leadership choices are too diverse and unpredictable over the span of a century to suggest so simple a narrative.[71] Nevertheless, it is possible to pick out a few features that might, with some deference to path dependency, be seen as significant precursors or antecedents of practices, whether in the present-day ILO itself or more broadly in international economic law and governance.

First, it is clear that certain concepts embedded in Part XIII were subsequently taken up in a variety of international instruments and organizations, including some of the most significant in operation today. As noted above, Part XIII articulated a set of 'social' goals and policies, which by 1937 James Shotwell was already characterising as part of a 'vast field of social and economic rights'.[72] Among these goals was 'the prevention of unemployment';[73] in 1944, the Conference recognized the ILO's 'solemn obligation … to further among the nations of the world' programmes that would achieve, among other things, 'full employment and the raising of standards of living'.[74] The same ideal appeared in the Charter of the United Nations, now linked to the twin enterprises of development and human

71 See generally Laurence R Helfer, 'Understanding Change in International Organizations: Globalization and Innovation in the ILO' (2006) 59 Vanderbilt Law Review 649; Deborah D Avant, Martha Finnemore and Susan K Sell, 'Who Governs the Globe?' in Deborah D Avant, Martha Finnemore and Susan K Sell (eds), *Who Governs the Globe?* (CUP 2010) ch 1; Orfeo Fioretos (ed), *International Politics and Institutions in Time* (OUP 2017).

72 Shotwell, *At the Paris Peace Conference* (n 27) 55.

73 Part XIII, Section I (Preamble).

74 'Declaration Concerning the Aims and Purposes of the International Labour Organisation' (Declaration of Philadelphia), 10 May 1944, Annex to the Constitution of the ILO, Art III(a).

rights;[75] in the General Agreement on Tariffs and Trade (GATT);[76] and in the Agreement Establishing the World Trade Organization (WTO).[77] These and other social goals have retained a powerful hold on international imagination, even if they are perhaps more often than not honoured in the breach.[78]

The ILO also pioneered techniques of governance that have been integrated into the practices of other international organizations. Methods of international supervision—such as in the ILO's reporting and complaints, or 'naming and shaming,' procedures described above—have since been adopted by other institutions of global governance, notably in human rights area.[79] So-called 'soft law'-making techniques of the kind undertaken by the ILO—in the recommendations adopted by the Conference and the 'jurisprudence' generated by the Office—have become much more widely reflected in the practice of international institutions, including in

75 Charter of the United Nations (26 June 1945), Article 55: 'With a view to the creation of conditions of stability and well-being which are necessary for peaceful and friendly relations among nations based on respect for the principle of equal rights and self-determination of peoples, the United Nations shall promote:

a. higher standards of living, full employment, and conditions of economic and social progress and development;
b. solutions of international economic, social, health, and related problems; and international cultural and educational co-operation; and
c. universal respect for, and observance of, human rights and fundamental freedoms for all without distinction as to race, sex, language, or religion.'

76 General Agreement on Tariffs and Trade (10 October 1947), Preamble: 'Recognizing that their relations in the field of trade and economic endeavour should be conducted with a view to raising standards of living, ensuring full employment ....'

77 Marrakesh Agreement establishing the World Trade Organization (15 April 1994), Preamble: '*Recognizing* that their relations in the field of trade and economic endeavour should be conducted with a view to raising standards of living, ensuring full employment ....'

78 See generally Steve Charnovitz, 'What the World Trade Organization Learned from the International Labour Organization' in Adelle Blackett and Anne Trebilcock (eds), *Research Handbook on Transnational Trade Law* (Elgar 2015) 411 (ch 29) 413–16.

79 See generally Hellen Keller and Geir Ulfstein (eds), *UN Human Rights Treaty Bodies: Law and Legitimacy* (CUP 2012); James H Lebovic and Erik Voeten, 'The Politics of Shame: The Condemnation of Country Human Rights Practices in the UNCHR' (2006) 50 International Studies Quarterly 861. On the ILO's supervisory mechanisms, see Landy (n 62); Laurence R Helfer, 'Monitoring Compliance with Unratified Treaties: The ILO Experience' (2008) 71 Law and Contemporary Problems 193.

the general comments of human rights supervisory mechanisms, as well as a source of significant controversy among international law scholars.[80] Indeed, in recent decades the ILO itself has increasingly turned to the use of 'soft law', in the form of codes, standards, and declarations.[81]

What then of the view, for which I have suggested some evidence above, that the ILO should be understood as part of the wider international economic framework born from the Versailles settlement? In the aftermath of the Great Depression, the ILO became increasingly concerned with economic issues and became a leading advocate of national and even international economic planning.[82] As I have argued elsewhere, ILO technical assistance to non-Western societies profoundly shaped notions and practices of development as they emerged as the dominant ideology of international law after World War II.[83] Moreover, the notion of 'special and differential treatment' for developing countries that emerged within the GATT/WTO jurisprudence may be traced back to the provisions of Part XIII.[84] Alexandrowicz's treatise on *World Economic Agencies* thus included a substantial chapter on the ILO,[85] and it is still occasionally included in surveys of international economic law.[86] It can hardly be doubted that other institutions such as the WTO, the World Bank, and the International Monetary Fund are now considered much more central to the field. However, if the current moment may be acknowledged as presenting an unusually acute crisis in the international economic order—albeit a lesser one than a centu-

---

80 See generally Dinah Shelton (ed), *Commitment and Compliance: The Role of Non-binding Norms in the International Legal System* (OUP 2000).

81 See generally Philip Alston, '"Core Labour Standards" and the Transformation of the International Labour Rights Regime' (2004) 15 EJIL 457; Claire La Hovary, 'The ILO's Supervisory Bodies' "Soft Law Jurisprudence"' in Blackett and Trebilcock (n 78) ch 22.

82 See generally Anthony M Endres and Grant A Fleming, *International Organizations and the Analysis of Economic Policy 1919-1950* (CUP 2002); Sinclair, 'A "Civilizing Task"' (n 65).

83 Sinclair, 'A "Civilizing Task"' (n 65).

84 Part XIII, Art 427 (recognising that 'differences of climate, habits and customs, of economic opportunity and industrial tradition, [made] strict uniformity in the conditions of labour difficult of immediate attainment', while holding that 'there are methods and principles for regulating labour conditions which all industrial communities should endeavour to apply, so far as their special circumstances will permit'). See generally Charnovitz, 'What the World Trade Organization Learned' (n 78).

85 Charles Henry Alexandrowicz, *World Economic Agencies* (Stevens 1962) ch 3.

86 See, eg, Steve Charnovitz, 'The Field of International Economic Law' (2014) 17 Journal of International Economic Law 607.

ry ago—we might yet expect to see a rearrangement of international institutional relations and, just possibly, a renewed role for the values which the ILO represents.

Chapter 7 The Role of Private International Law: UNIDROIT and the Geneva Conventions on Arbitration

*Herbert Kronke**

1. *Introduction: Terminology and the Historical Context*

As is obvious from the title, the term 'private international law' is not intended to be synonymous with 'conflict of laws' but, in the North American tradition, as the entirety of international law *not* relating to state-to-state relationships. It is clear that World War I and its aftermath mark key moments in the development of organized and institutionalized research in the fields of comparative law, conflict of laws, the law of dispute resolution and transnational commercial law. To a varying extent they were driven by economic expansion and rivalry, the war and, following its catastrophic outcome, the quest for peace. For many post-WWI lawyers, one of the main functions of harmonized law was to build and maintain this peace by fostering an orderly and universally beneficial commercial exchange. As I used to tell visitors, this historic peace-making and peace-building function is still an integral part of UNIDROIT's present-day mission.

Within this historical development, the years 1916 and 1926 are particularly significant. The former sees the founding of the first two academic institutions with staff and funding devoted exclusively to private international law, that is, the institutes affiliated with the universities in Heidelberg and Munich. In 1926, at the national level, the Kaiser Wilhelm Institute in Berlin (now Max Planck Institute for Comparative Law and Private International Law in Hamburg) and, at the international level, the International Institute for the Unification of Private Law (UNIDROIT) in Rome see the light of the day. The—explicit or implicit—objectives of these institutions differed widely. In the deed of trust of the Heidelberg institute, its founder, the elder of the Berlin merchants Carl Leopold Netter, expressed the desire 'to testify that, even in times of war, the work for peace is not forgotten.' Consequently, the aim of that institute was to fund research and

* Professor emeritus, Heidelberg University School of Law. Arbitrator, Iran–United States Claims Tribunal. Former Secretary-General of UNIDROIT.

the study of non-German law, primarily private law, commercial law, civil procedure as well as the relationship between law and the economy. The Kaiser Wilhelm Institute, on the other hand, was intended to build up the necessary expertise for dealing with the fall-out of the war, in particular non-performed commercial contracts and Germany's foreign debt.

2. *UNIDROIT*

2.1. *The Institutional Framework*

The International Institute for the Unification of Private Law/*Institut International pour l'Unification du Droit Privé* (UNIDROIT) was set up in 1926 as an auxiliary organ of the League of Nations pursuant to Article 24 of the Covenant.[1] Remarkably, if looked at with knowledge of how intergovernmental organizations are working today, it took the League's Council not more than twenty minutes to complete its creation. Then, more than now, it was really all about the individuals involved. One of these figures was Antonio Scialoja, distinguished professor of Roman law at the University of Rome, Senator of the Kingdom and Deputy Secretary-General of the League. Scialoja was convinced that after a century of nationalization of private law the time was ripe for returning to a common law of 'civilized' nations—at least in Europe. He had identified ways and means to work towards achieving this, and he had even won over the king. In 1924, the Council of the League had accepted[2] the offer of the Italian Government to establish and maintain an institute for the purpose of 'harmonising and coordinating the rules of Private Law of the different states or groups of states, with a view to promoting gradually the adoption of a uniform system of Private Law by the various states'.[3] At a meeting of the Council on 15 March 1926, Scialoja 'read his report (Annex 849) and submitted the following draft resolution. "The Council adopts the present report and the draft Statutes annexed thereto" (Annex 849a)'. And, following a brief exchange relating to the correct translation of the Italian term '*argomento*' in-

1 For a detailed account, see Lena Peters, 'International Institute for the Unification of Private Law (UNIDROIT)' in *International Encyclopedia of Laws, International Organisations*, Suppl 55 (Kluwer 2014).

2 LoN, Council, 30th session, 19th meeting (3 October 1924) 5 LNOJ 1369, 1375.

3 Letter dated 3 October 1924, League of Nations document C.262.M.101.

to French (*'matière'*), the report of the meeting concludes, 'The resolution proposed by M. Scialoja was adopted.'[4]

On 30 May 1928, in the presence of the King of Italy, the members of the Diplomatic Corps, other dignitaries, and the members of the Governing Council of UNIDROIT, the Prime Minister of Italy, Benito Mussolini —a journalist turned politician—opened the session with brief remarks on the intended role of the country and the now established institute to conduct research on the relationship between law and commercial activity with the intention of promoting the latter by harmonising the former. The representative of the President of the Council of the League of Nations replied:

> To unify the rules of private law means working toward the creation of a universal law ... [I]t means knocking down one of the most formidable barriers separating individuals of different origins; it means, in short, ensuring the peaceful and productive development of peoples... In Savigny's time, the focus lay purely on scientific work. Today's enterprise is essentially a practical one. However, it is also more difficult and more useful to humanity. The League of Nations' working method and its ultimate aim in different fields of action is to overcome existing divergences through superior unity. This is also the working method and the ultimate aim of the new institute.[5]

Initially, the members of the Governing Council, the body in charge of shaping the Organization's policies and, in particular, its work programme, were appointed by the Council of the League of Nations. Among the 14 members appointed for the period 1928-1933, there were three Judges at the Permanent Court of International Justice (one of them, Sir Cecil J.B. Hurst, had been a British negotiator at the Versailles conference), one international-law adviser and, previously as well as again later, Foreign Minister and Prime Minister of Sweden (Östen Undén) and Mussolini's Minister

4 LoN, Council, 38th session, 3rd meeting (15 March 1926) 7 LNOJ 504, 506.

5 French original: '*Unifier les règlements du droit privé, cela signifie travailler à la création d'une loi universelle, ... cela signifie abattre une des barrières les plus formidables qui séparent les individus d'origine diverse; cela signfie, en un mot, assurer le développement tranquille et productif de la vie des peuples ... Il s'agissait, au temps de Savigny, d'accomplir un travail purement scientifique. Il s'agit aujourd'hui d'une œuvre essentiellement pratique, et, pourtant, plus difficile et plus utile à l'humanité. Réunir dans une unité supérieure les divergences qui se présentent: voilà la méthode de travail et le but suprême de la Société des Nations dans les différents champs d'action, voilà la méthode de travail et le but du nouvel institut.*'

of Justice (Alfredo Rocco). These names reflect, on the one hand, the political weight member states accorded to this particular initiative of the League and, on the other hand, the still widely held view that private international law (including comparative law) was somehow a function of public international law. Of greater importance for the work programme was the presence on the Governing Council of two of the most distinguished private-law scholars of the time: Henri Capitant (France) and, even more so, Ernst Rabel (Germany), whose seminal comparative studies of the law of sales[6] was already far advanced and who proved to be the decisive voice when it came to defining the first triennial work programme.

2.2. The Work Programme, and the Individuals

From the beginning, there was no shortage of ideas, projects, and demands as regards the work the Organization should take up: intellectual property, negotiable instruments and arbitration, to name but a few.

Arbitration is particularly associated with the name René David, one of the exceedingly rare examples of a universally known jurist. David had become a tenured professor in 1929 at the age of 23. One year later, he took office as one of UNIDROIT's two Deputy Secretaries-General, together with Hans Gerhard Ficker, a scholarly minded head of department in the German Ministry of Justice. David's interests were not limited to comparative law and approaches to the harmonization of law generally, but also included arbitration[7]. UNIDROIT as such, however, was never involved in the development of any instrument in this field, such as the Geneva Conventions.[8]

Ernst Rabel, who was since 1926 director of the Kaiser Wilhelm Institute[9] and also served as an ad hoc judge at the Permanent Court of International Justice and the German–Italian Mixed Arbitral Tribunal as well as the Permanent German–Italian and German–Norwegian Arbitral Commissions, had a clearer notion than others as to the limits of resources member states would be willing to make available and the need to focus

---

6 Eventually published as Ernst Rabel, *Das Recht des Warenkaufs* (vol 1, de Gruyter 1936/vol 2, de Gruyter 1958).

7 René David, *Les grands systèmes de droit contemporains* (1st edn, Dalloz 1964); id, 'The Unification of Private Law' in *International Encyclopedia of Comparative Law*, vol 2 (JCB Mohr 1971) ch 5.

8 See below, 3.

9 See above, 1.

the Organization's work in a realistic direction. The Governing Council followed his advice, and UNIDROIT provided the institutional framework for the harmonization of the law of the international sale of goods.

Interrupted by Rabel's forced emigration to the United States in 1939 and World War II, the work was taken up again after the war and, in 1964, lead to the adoption of the two Hague Conventions.[10] Both the Conventions and the preparatory work were, in turn, to serve as the basis for the 1980 United Nations Convention on the International Sale of Goods (CISG). Only in the post-World War II period, released from the shackles of political considerations, did the Governing Council effectively live up to its reputation as a 'republic of scholars.' Not only the scholars in the true sense, who, according to certain member states' traditions, were put forward for election by their respective governments, but also high-ranking civil servants in ministries of justice, trade or foreign ministries who served —in some cases—for decades conducted Governing Council business as though they were under no instructions, but only with regard for the substance, such as the economic rationale, the inherent legal merit and the feasibility of a project. Indeed, under the UNIDROIT Statute—ie from 1940 onward—the members of the Council have been elected by the Organization's own General Assembly, which is composed by the member states' governments. But, once elected, they serve in their personal capacity as experts. Without a shadow of a doubt, it is this intellectual freedom which shaped UNIDROIT as a uniquely innovative and productive private-law formulating agency.[11]

2.3. 1937: Not the End, but a Transition into the Unknown

In March 1933, immediately after the Nazis had come to power, Germany gave notice of its withdrawal from the League of Nations, eventually becoming effective in 1935. Italy, the host state and principal funder of the Organization, followed in 1937. This, however, did not entail the demise of the Institute. Diplomatically shrewd, and skilled, the Italian Government

---

10 Convention relating to a Uniform Law on the Formation of Contracts for the International Sale of Goods (done 1 July 1964, entered into force 23 August 1972) 834 UNTS 169 (ULF). Convention relating to a Uniform Law on the International Sale of Goods (done 1 July 1964, entered into force 18 August 1972) 834 UNTS 107 (ULIS).

11 For details, see Herbert Kronke, 'UNIDROIT' in *Encyclopedia of Private International Law*, vol 2 (Edward Elgar 2017).

circulated a draft Statute in 1939 for a—now independent—international Organization, and by 1942 practically all countries previously involved had adhered to the new treaty. As a matter of fact, however, the work was put on hold and did not recommence until well after the war had ended.

3. *The Geneva Arbitration Conventions*

3.1. *Political Background*

It is a highly plausible hypothesis that the rationale for negotiating the two instruments relating to dispute settlement was the desire to facilitate trade by providing legal certainty regarding the specific dispute-resolution mechanism typical for certain areas of trade and types of transactions, such as distance sales and maritime transport of the goods sold. The equation, quite in line with the conference's framework theme, would have been 'peace through trade'. Indeed, there are traces in reports on the meetings suggesting that participants would have preferred to see the work on arbitration move faster. Moreover, and even if not explicitly reflected in the documents, recourse to and reliance on arbitration necessarily implied the assumption of a reduced emphasis on sovereignty as the basis of authority to resolve disputes.

Incidentally, notwithstanding the appetite for work on the law of arbitration shown by many during UNIDROIT's early years, the Organization was, as is obvious from the dates of their adoption, not involved in the preparation of the Geneva instruments. They were principally creatures of the International Chamber of Commerce.

The Geneva Protocol was adopted and signed by 25 states and eventually entered into force for 34 contracting states.

3.2. *The 1923 Protocol on Arbitration Clauses*

The principal purpose of this treaty was to overcome an arbitration-adverse peculiarity of certain legal systems, notably the French legal system. These systems refused to recognise simple arbitration clauses, eg those included in a sales contract or a charter party. Instead, they required a fully fledged 'arbitration agreement' relating to a dispute that had already arisen.[12] That agreement had to identify the subject matter of the dispute and even the arbitrators who were to serve on the tribunal. Given that, at the time when a contract is entered into, merchants were generally unwilling to even contemplate a future dispute and the details regarding its solution, this requirement obviously posed a significant problem for international commercial transactions.

The Protocol on Arbitration Clauses, signed on 24 September 1923 apparently remedied this unsatisfactory situation. Article 1(1) provides that the contracting states recognise the

> validity of an agreement whether relating to existing or future differences between parties subject respectively to the jurisdiction of different Contracting States by which the parties to a contract agree to submit to arbitration all or any differences that may arise in connection with such contract ...

The seemingly straightforward language turned out to be the first stumbling block, as 'subject ... to the jurisdiction of different Contracting States' was construed in a widely diverging manner in various contracting states. Both political factors—eg, in relation to colonies and mandates—and legal considerations in a strictly technical sense—eg, questions about the circumstances in which a person is subject to the jurisdiction of a state—contributed to these disharmonies. In addition, Article 1(2) provided for a reservation each contracting state could make to limit that obligation 'to contracts which are considered as commercial under its national law.' Given the different mechanisms adopted in legal systems for distinguishing 'commercial' and 'civil' contracts (eg 'objective' v 'subjective' characterization) and, moreover, the absence of any meaningful distinction in some major legal systems, this was a significant carve-out that would eventually undermine the potential effect the Protocol was going to have. Indeed, half of the initially 25 contracting states did avail themselves of the right to make that reservation.

---

12 Peter Schlosser, *Das Recht der internationalen Privaten Schiedsgerichtsbarkeit*, vol 1 (1st edn JCB Mohr 1975).

3.3. The 1927 Convention on the Execution of Foreign Arbitral Awards

This treaty built on the 1923 Protocol, Articles 6 and 7. It applied only to awards made after the coming-into-force of the Protocol and was open to signature only of signatories of the Protocol. Its principal purpose was to provide for a solution of a fundamental shortcoming reflected in Article 3 of the Protocol. Pursuant to that provision, contracting states had undertaken to ensure that only arbitral awards made in their respective territories would be executed by their authorities and in accordance with the provisions of their respective national laws. Article 1 of the Convention provides that in the territories of a contracting party to which the Convention applies, an award made in pursuance of an arbitration agreement covered by the 1923 Protocol shall be recognized and enforced in accordance with the rules of procedure of the territory where the award is granted, provided the award has been made in the territory of a state party to the Convention and between persons who are subject to the jurisdiction of one of the contracting states. In other words, while awards were now, in principle, capable of being granted in jurisdictions other than the one where they were made, other obstacles limited the creation of an effective 'space of free movement' for arbitral awards. First, two major restraints, or uncertainties, flowed from the 1923 Protocol, ie, the parties to the arbitration agreement were subject to the jurisdiction of one of the contracting states, and, in many instances, the relevant state characterized the contract as commercial. Second, the rules of procedure of the enforcement state had been complied with.

Conversely, the system of grounds for denying recognition and enforcement, as laid out in Articles 1, 2 and 3 of the Convention may seem relatively modern, at least at first sight. In addition to bringing the award within the (limited) scope, as outlined above, according to Article 1, five requirements must be met to obtain recognition or enforcement: (a) the award was made pursuant to a valid arbitration agreement; (b) the subject-matter was capable of settlement by arbitration under the law of the country in which the award is sought to be relied upon; (c) the award was made by the tribunal provided for in the submission agreement and in conformity with the law governing the procedure; (d) the award has become final in the country in which it has been made; (e) recognition or enforcement is not contrary to the public policy 'or to the principles of the law' of the country in which it is sought to be relied on. Article 2, in turn, states three grounds for refusing recognition and enforcement: (a) annulment of the award in the country in which it was made; (b) due-process violations, such as insufficient notice of the proceedings or lack of proper representation; (c) the tribunal exceeded the scope of the submission.

However, the Geneva system had a major drawback. Article 4(2) provides that the party relying upon an award or claiming its enforcement must supply, inter alia, documentary evidence to prove that the award has become final—in the sense defined in Article 1(d)—in the country where it was made. Practically, this introduced a system of double exequatur, which, in effect, undermined the very purpose of this body of purportedly transnational rules.[13]

The Convention was adopted and signed by 18 states and eventually entered into force for 28 contracting states.

3.4 Overall Assessment

The principal merit of preparing and adopting the two Geneva instruments was that, afterwards, governments made a very significant effort to respond to businesses' needs to legitimise, in a harmonized manner, rules relating to transnational commercial dispute resolution. One might say that, after centuries of continued nationalization of the institutions administering and the rules governing commercial dispute resolution, it moved back to where it had belonged up until the mid-17th century—at least in parts of the world and as regards important branches of trade. However, an important difference was, and continues to be, that it was now the national legal systems of sovereign states that provided a rule-based framework for such privately conducted judicial function.

There are no reliable data or reports on the application and the practical relevance of the two instruments as we have for the current regime of the 1958 New York Convention. Certain details, such as the positive and negative lists in Articles 1, 2 and 3 of the 1927 Convention, were remarkable. Yet much was left for the adoption of the New York Convention—as a truly global regime—and the 60 years that followed.[14]

13 Schlosser (n 8).

14 Herbert Kronke and others (eds), *Recognition and Enforcement of Foreign Arbitral Awards: A Global Commentary on the New York Convention* (1st edn, Kluwer 2010).

4. Conclusion

After such a devastating conflict, the awareness that not only state-to-state relationships were in need of repair but that rebuilding functioning national economies and international commerce also required work on relevant private international law, or transnational commercial law, fortunately bore fruit. It was not governments, or the League of Nations, alone that were to be credited for the achievements briefly outlined in this paper but farsighted and intellectually strong personalities, such as Antonio Scialoja, Ernst Rabel, René David and a few others; they provided the leadership needed for transforming ideas into sound and coherent analysis and, eventually, legal texts that were adopted by states and became binding and relevant in commercial transactions. That has not changed since. And nothing, or very little, would have been achieved had there not been the support, indeed very substantial input, from the organizations of industry and commerce. That has not changed either. Finally, critics who might take issue with the, as they may feel, modest volume of work that actually came to fruition must be reminded of the exceedingly short period of time at the disposal of the individuals and institutions involved. For all practical purposes, work begun in the mid-1920s already came to a halt only ten years later. More specifically, work at UNIDROIT on the harmonization of the law of international sales, which to no small extent depended on its *spiritus rector* Ernst Rabel, remained an orphan six years after its effective commencement. Taking post-World War II experience with work cycles in the private-law formulating agencies into account, what was achieved—and ready to be built upon starting in the 1950s—was by no means disappointingly little. Finally, governments' resources available for participating in negotiations aimed at the modernization and international harmonisation of commercial law were limited then, as they are limited now. Taking into account, therefore, that the 1920s also witnessed major progress in relation to the law of carriage of goods by sea (1924 Brussels Convention 'Hague Rules') and by air (1929 Warsaw Convention), one cannot but admire the conscientiousness and the determination shown by many governments in such historically difficult circumstances.

Chapter 8 Article 231 of the Versailles Treaty and Reparations: The Reparation Commission as a Place for Dispute Settlement?

Jean-Louis Halpérin[*]

It is more inspiring to speak about a success story in international law than about a failure. It is more exciting to study a completely new subject in legal history than to try to elbow one's way into a rich literature about a well-known matter. The issues of Article 231 of the Versailles Treaty and of Reparations present concurrently the two less desired positions.

It is widely known that the process of reparations was abandoned after ten years of successive attempts to adapt it to the economic and political context of the period between 1921 and 1931, leading from the end of World War I to the Great Depression. Concerning Germany, the reparations process gave rise to the payment of less than twenty-two billion gold marks, which amounts to one sixth of the foreseen sum of the 1921 Bill and Schedule of Payments.[1] While the Allied powers, especially the successive governments of France, were dramatically disappointed by this low score, the German people were upset by Article 231 and the debt linked with this reparations process, one of the main elements of Nazi propaganda.

Furthermore, this fiasco has been broadly analyzed by jurists and economists of the interwar period, as well as by historians. Concerning France, it is noteworthy that several doctoral theses in law (at a time when economics was taught inside the Law Faculties) were devoted to reparations issues, even if they are not so interesting from the perspective of international law.[2] The contrast is strong between this relatively poor litera-

---

* Professor of Legal History at the Ecole Normale Supérieure PSL, Chairman of the Centre of Legal Theory and Analysis (UMR 7074).

1 Richard Castillon, *Les Réparations allemandes: Deux expériences, 1919–1932, 1945–1952* (PUF 1953) 65–66.

2 André Garrigou-Lagrange, *Le Problème des réparations. La technique des règlements* (doctoral thesis Paris 1923); Pierre Noël, *L'Allemagne et les réparations* (doctoral thesis Paris 1924); Louis Imbert, *Le Règlement des réparations* (doctoral thesis Aix-Marseille 1935).

ture and the 1938 doctoral thesis in history written by Étienne Weill-Raynal, which contains many developments and analyses of great interest.[3]

What is worth saying today about reparations in a symposium about the history of international law with a focus on dispute settlement? I have chosen the Reparation Commission as a focal point, although I do not claim to make and to present an exhaustive examination of it. On one hand, many things have been written by Étienne Weill-Raynal, who himself worked in the French Delegation of the Reparation Commission. On the other hand, the records of the Reparation Commission, kept in the French National Archives, are collected in more than four thousand boxes, of which I have not been able to consult all.[4] Having made spot checks in these Archives for the period between 1920 and 1924, I would like to analyze the working process of the Reparation Commission until the implementation of the Young Plan, which was a kind of divestiture for the Commission. As a very original kind of international organization, the Reparation Commission was a hybrid institution based on the cooperation of national delegations of the Allied powers that tried to dialog with the German diplomats. With an ambivalent status, it was a political and administrative authority with some competences that could be compared to those of a tribunal. Before studying the attempts to make the Reparation Commission a place for dispute settlement of the reparations issue, it is necessary to begin with Article 231 of the Versailles Treaty as an important milestone to settle the double-pronged dispute about reparations: the dispute between Allied powers and Germany and the dispute among the Allied nations.

1. *Three Steps Towards Drafting Article 231 of the Versailles Treaty and One Step Towards the Reparation Commission*

The process leading to the establishment of the Reparation Commission has to been understood as a sequence of three steps in the writing of Article 231 of the Versailles Treaty and one step to establish a commission to settle the amount of reparations.

---

3 Étienne Weill-Raynal, *Les Réparations allemandes et la France* (Nouvelles Éditions Latines 1938, 3 vol).

4 French National Archives, AJ/6/76 to AJ/6/4342. The study focuses on the minutes of the Reparations Commission meetings from 1920 to 1924. On the issues about the Dawes and Young plans, see d'Argent (ch 9).

1.1 An American Idea

On January 1918, President Wilson issued a statement known as the Fourteen Points, saying in point seven that Belgium had to be 'restored.' For the American President, this meant that compensation would be paid by Germany to Belgium because of the violation of its neutrality. Behind this statement was the idea that the German war against Belgium was a severe breach of international law, whereas the war against the other Allied powers was not a radically unjust or illicit one. At the beginning of November, 1918 the German Government and the Allied Powers accepted to discuss an Armistice on the basis of the Fourteen Points. In a note, written by the United States Secretary of State Robert Lansing and accepted by the Allies, it was specified that the Armistice would imply the reparations of all damages caused to civilians by the German aggression.[5] This note, enlarging the field of reparations (henceforth extended to other countries than Belgium), was transmitted to Germany and accepted on 4 November 1918.

1.2 A British Enlargement

During the Peace Conference, the British proposed first to include the war costs in the reparations (at the beginning the British claims were harsher than the French ones), but then had to take account of the American opposition towards a war indemnity, like the one in the 1871 Frankfurt Peace Treaty.[6] Nevertheless, it was decided to include into reparations the pensions paid to war widows and disabled veterans, which was not exactly in line with the principle of compensating (only) civilians as laid out in the Armistice talks. At the same time, two Commissions—one on the Responsibility of the Authors of the War and on Enforcement of Penalties, the other of Reparation for Damages—were established. Whereas the first (with the Dean of the Paris Law Faculty, Larnaude, among its members) failed to create an international Tribunal on war crimes, the second (with Klotz and Loucheur as French delegates) laid the foundations of the reparations process.

5 Weill-Raynal (n 3) vol 1, 25.
6 Marc Trachtenberg, 'Reparations at the Peace Paris Conference' (1979) 51 The Journal of Modern History 24.

1.3 An Inter-Allied Compromise

The American Delegation proposed to separate the issues of sanctions and of reparations and prepared the draft for articles 231–243, which were to be included into Part VIII of the Versailles Treaty devoted to 'Reparation'.[7] The most famous of these provisions, article 231, went as follows:

> The Allied and Associated Governments affirm and Germany accepts the responsibility of Germany and her allies for causing all the loss and damage to which the Allied and Associated Governments and their nationals have been subjected as a consequence of the war imposed upon them by the aggression of Germany and her allies.

The article implies that it is not the matter of a penal responsibility for a war of aggression, but of a civil liability; ie, Germany must restore the *status quo ante* for civilians of the Allied Powers that have suffered damages (which was not the case for the American people). The German liability, as a source of reparations, was conceived according to the rules of the Napoleonic Code and of the more recent German Civil Code (BGB), both of which were quoted by the French delegation.[8] The Reparations system was considered as an expression of social solidarity towards the civilian victims of the war and, as a German writer called it in a 1928 dissertation, of 'neo-collectivism' or the socialization of risks.[9] It was also in the spirit of French statutory laws voted for before the Versailles Treaty that concerned war pensions and devastated regions (laws of 31 March and 17 April 1919).

Article 231 must neither be read in isolation nor in the erroneous German translation, which transformed Germany into the 'author of the war', entailing the idea of criminal guilt. On the contrary, Allied Governments recognized in Article 232 that the resources of Germany were not adequate, and they limited the reparations to 'compensation for all damage done to the civilian population', while separating the special case of Belgium with the reimbursement by Germany of the sums borrowed by Belgium during the war. Furthermore, Article 235 provided a sum of 20 billion gold marks to be paid before the 31 March 1921.

---

7 The English version of the Versailles Treaty uses the singular, whereas the French version uses the plural Reparations. It is the same for the Reparation Commission, in French the *Commission des Réparations.*

8 Camille Bloch and Pierre Renouvin, 'L'article 231 du Traité de Versailles. Sa genèse et sa signification' (1932) 10 Revue d'histoire de la Guerre mondiale 1.

9 Wolfgang Bonde, *Das Problem der Reparation* (Jena dissertation 1928) 23.

1.4 The Reparation Commission as a New Deal

As accepted by the German Government and Parliament (through the ratification of the Versailles Treaty), Articles 231 and 232 appeared as a preliminary judgment to resolve the dispute settlement about reparations. The question of fixing the amount of reparations was delegated to the Reparation Commission, as the Allied Governments were not able to find an agreement about an achieved process of evaluation or a lump sum. As a second deal based on American proposals in April and May 1919, it was decided in Article 233 to create an 'Inter-Allied Commission' in order to settle this part of the dispute. The Treaty insisted that the German Government recognize the power and authority of the Reparation Commission (Art 240): the Germans had to provide for the salaries and expenses of the Reparation Commission, to supply all necessary information to the Commission and to accord to its members the same rights and immunities as diplomatic agents. As a counterpart, the Reparation Commission had 'to give to the German Government a just opportunity to be heard' and to consider from time to time 'the resources and capacity of Germany.' The Reparation Commission was empowered to determine before 1 May 1921 the amount of the damage for which compensation was to be made by Germany (Art 233), to draw up a schedule of payments, then to modify it according to the evolution of German resources. The power to cancel any part of the reparations debt was reserved to the Allied Governments. The compromise gave birth to an ambiguous institution that could claim to be an international authority, if not a tribunal.

2. The Failure to Affirm the Reparation Commission as an Independent Tribunal

From 1920 to 1923, the Reparation Commission worked hard and tried to affirm its competences as a kind of tribunal. But the gap between this idea of an independent judiciary and reality appeared quickly, with this model of dispute settlement being strongly challenged as early as December 1922.

2.1 The Ambiguous Status of the Reparation Commission

The fact that Part VIII of the Versailles Treaty was prepared inside the Peace Conference by the Commission of Reparation for Damages (with a special

Organization Commission of the Reparation Commission presided by Loucheur and with future members of the Reparation Commission like Bradbury, Bertolini and Theunis) explains why many features of the Reparation Commission were determined by Part VIII and its Annex I and II (which could be amended by the state members of the Commission, unlike the Treaty itself).[10] Whereas Annex I gave the list of damages to be compensated by reparations, Annex II fixed the main characteristics of the Reparation Commission in 23 paragraphs. The Commission was composed of one Delegate and one Assistant Delegate (present in the meetings, but without the right to vote, except when taking place of the Delegate in case of illness or necessary absence) for each of the four great Allied Powers (United States, Great Britain, France and Italy) and in addition one Delegate of a fifth nation, alternatively Belgium, Japan (only for damages at sea) and the Serb–Croat–Slovene State (for reparations paid by Austria, Hungary or Bulgaria).

The principal permanent Bureau of the Reparations Commission was placed in Paris. Under the authority of a Chairman and a Vice-Chairman, elected by the Delegates, the Commission was authorized to appoint officers, agents and employees. All proceedings of the Commission were required to be private, except for special reasons decided by the Reparations Commission. It was also repeated that the Commission had to hear the German Government (if this Government so desired). More original were the clauses of paragraphs 11, 12 and 13 of Annex II. The first one said that the Commission should 'not be bound by any particular code or rules of law or by any particular rule of evidence or of procedure,' but should be 'guided by justice, equity and good faith' through the creation of 'rules relating to methods of proof of claims.' The price of this autonomy and of the power to interpret the provisions of the Treaty about 'the whole reparation problem' (§ 12) was the required unanimity for questions involving the sovereignty of any of the Allied Powers, for any postponement of the payment of instalments falling due between 1921 and 1926 and questions of the interpretation of the provisions of Part VIII of the Treaty (§ 13). In case of default by Germany in the performance of any obligation concerning the reparations, the Reparation Commission could only provide recommendations to the Allied Powers (§ 17). It was determined that the Reparation Commission would be dissolved after payment of all the

10 The German text of Annexes I and II can be read in Calmette (ed), *Recueil de documents sur l'histoire de la question des réparations* (Alfred Coste 1924) 131.

amounts paid to Germany. Unlike a Tribunal, the Reparation Commission was not linked by law and was not able to decide self-executing rulings.

The nature of the Reparation Commission remained largely undetermined when its first meeting took place in Paris, on 24 January 1920 (after a British-French conference in December 1919 decided that the chairman of the Reparation Commission would be the French delegate). Among the Delegates, the British John Bradbury (former Head of the Treasury and acquaintance of Keynes), the Belgian Georges Theunis (who was originally trained as an engineer, but dealt with economic questions after World War I) and the American Albert Rathbone (Assistant Secretary of the Treasury) were specialized in financial issues, whereas the other delegates were administrators or judges (the French Jonnart, ex-governor of Algeria and senator re-elected in January 1920, the Italian Bertolini, ex-minister, and the judge D'Amelio, future president of the Court of cassation under the fascist regime).[11] After electing Jonnart as chairman, the members of the Reparation Commission agreed quickly about their work methods: meetings of the Delegates (generally with the presence of Assistant Delegates) at least two times each week, adoption of standing orders, choice of a British Secretary General (Salter, then after July 1922 McFadyean, who was formerly the secretary general of the British Delegation), and the organization of different services (Financial, Restitutions, Legal).[12] The Reparation Commission, was confronted with the two refusals of the American Senate (in November 1919 and in March 1920) to ratify the Versailles Treaty. It was decided to maintain the two American Delegates as Observers (with a period of suspended participation between February and May 1921 until the decision of the new United States President to keep the Delegation): these American Delegates (Roland Boyden, who was trained as a lawyer, and Colonel Logan), while unofficially attending the meetings of the Reparation Commission without the right to vote, were very active in proposing solutions of compromise in the discussions.

As said in the standing orders of the Reparation Commission, the Commission comprised a national organization, with delegates defending their national interests, and an international organization.[13] There is no doubt that the Delegates, accompanied by civil servants of their country (directed

---

11 Andrew Williams, 'Sir John Bradbury and the Reparation Commission 1920–1925' (2002) 13 Diplomacy and Statecraft 81.

12 AJ/6/76; Commission des Réparations, *Rapport sur les travaux de la Commission des Réparations de 1920 à 1922* (Félix Alcan 1923, 2 vol), notably the introduction by Andrew McFadyean, 1–132.

13 AJ/6/76, 80.

by a Secretary General, Aron for France), represented their respective Governments. If they did not agree with the instructions of their governments, they had logically to resign. The French Delegation was particularly unstable: after one month, Jonnart resigned for health reasons and was replaced by Poincaré, whose mandate as President of the French Republic had come to end in February 1920. The presence of Poincaré should have increased the influence of the Commission, but Poincaré resigned in May 1920 after the San Remo Conference, considering that the Reparation Commission would 'be inevitably deprived of the most important part of its powers'.[14] The new French Delegate and chairman, Louis Dubois (a politician and ex-minister) had less prestige than Poincaré (whom he consulted as French Prime Minister in 1922–1923)[15] and was replaced in September 1922 by Louis Barthou, the most active French President of the Reparation Commission from 1922 to 1926. Finally, the last French President was Fernand Chapsal (senator and ex-minister). Poincaré, Barthou and Chapsal conjoined the Presidency of the Commission with their mandate in the French Senate, which was not in favour of the political independence of the Reparation Commission. Poincaré recognized in April 1920 that 'the Delegates represented their respective government' and could not agree with too great sacrifices for their country'.[16] Despite a feeling of Inter-allied constitutional distrust, the votes inside the Commission were in general unanimous, with the French President used his casting vote only three times.[17] It is noteworthy that his casting vote was not used for the 26 December 1922 ruling about the German default in wood deliveries, the French and Belgian justification for the Ruhr occupation, because of the Belgian and Italian votes.[18]

2.2 *The Obstacles for Transforming the Reparation Commission into an Independent Tribunal*

While the idea of a French preponderance has to be nuanced, the possibility for the Reparation Commission to act as a true international organization was limited. The Legal Service of the Commission, in which the most famous member was Massimo Pilotti (the future first President of the

14 AJ/6/77 (19 May 1920).
15 Weill-Raynal (n 3 vol 2, 234–235.
16 AJ/6/77 (26 April 1920) 14.
17 Weill-Raynal (n 3) vol 1, 153.
18 AJ/6/80 (26 December 1922) 21.

European Court of Justice at Luxemburg), and which was endowed to prepare the leasing contract of the Hotel Astoria in Paris, talked about a 'legal personality in the view of international law' for the Reparation Commission.[19] The Legal Service argued that the Reparation Commission was more powerful than the 1856 Danube European Commission or the pre-existing International Offices. If this argumentation justified the capacity of contracting and of transferring payments to the Commission, as per the diplomatic privileges of its members, it remained an 'uncertainty as regarded its civil personality' according to Poincaré.[20] When the Commission decided to open a secondary office in Berlin, it was very difficult to 'dilute the principle of national' representation of each Delegation and to develop the idea of independent international agents (especially with respect to chief economists) for the members of the services.[21] Keeping the deliberations secret (the minutes of the Reparation Commission were labelled confidential, but there were problems with leakages of information, as is said in a meeting on 20 May 1921) did not contribute to establish the Commission as an autonomous organ, whereas the reading of these minutes bear witness of serious efforts of friendly cooperation between the Delegates.[22]

One can also speak of a gap between discourse and reality regarding the nature of the powers of the Reparation Commission. It was repeated that the Commission had to be 'impartial and just',[23] as a kind of sovereign tribunal (a court of appeal or a court of cassation in the French version)[24] judging the claims of the Allied powers and taking account (in some hearings) of the arguments of the German *Kriegslastenkommission*.[25] But it cannot be seriously said that the Reparation Commission made impartial rulings among equal litigants. The Delegates were both judges and parties (or advocates, as wrote Weill-Raynal)[26], distrusting the fantastic (because very low) figures presented by the German Government about the Reparations and establishing the non-performance of coal deliveries (very soon in June 1920, then in December 1922).[27]

19 AJ/6/76, 149.
20 AJ/6/77 (26 April 1920).
21 AJ/6/77 (5 May 1920).
22 AJ/6/78 (20 May 1921).
23 AJ/7/77, Speech by Jonnart (24 January 1920).
24 AJ/6/77, Speech by Theunis (17 May 1920); McFadyean (n 12) 7.
25 AJ/6/79 (30 August 1922).
26 Weill-Raynal (n 3) vol 1, 157.
27 AJ/6/77 (23 June 1920); AJ/6/80 (26 December 1922).

The Commission had to decide issues of interpretation of the Versailles Treaty and was not obliged to follow the opinions (that could be mixed between a majority and a minority of dissenting opinions) of its legal service.[28] It had to determine its relationship with other bodies, including arbitration tribunals (about the issue of tank steamers claimed by the United States in April 1920), which made clear that the Commission itself was not an arbitration tribunal.[29] The Commission took on the important work of checking the calculations of the claims presented by each country about its own active reparations debt. The 1921 payment statements were established sixteen months after serious reports, for example, from Bradbury about the French claims.[30] But the Reparation Commission did not create explicit rules relating to methods of proving these national claims. All of this substantial amount of work, which was kept in the Archives of the Commission, was in the end useless for establishing the amount of payments.

2.3 *The Turning Point of 1922*

The Commission was quickly by-passed in 1920 and 1921 by a succession of governmental conferences that set out to reconsider the agenda of German payments.[31] The establishment of the 1921 Schedule of Payments was the outcome of a bargain (the official meeting lasted only 45 minutes) between the national Delegates rather than the result of deep deliberation inside the Reparation Commission.[32] The Reparation Commission was then short-circuited by the French–German agreement about reparations in kind, decided in Wiesbaden in October 1921 and needing derogations to part VIII and its Annexes of Versailles Treaty.[33] In March 1922, the Reparation Commission unanimously imposed severe conditions in exchange for the allowance of a delay for Germany.[34] But, a few months later with the 'sensational fall' of the mark and the German request for a new moratori-

28 AJ/6/76, 128–131.
29 AJ/6/77 (26 April 1920).
30 AJ/6/78 (20 April 1921).
31 Bruce Kent, *The Spoils of War: The Politics, Economics and Diplomacy of Reparations 1918–1932* (Clarendon Press 1989) 92.
32 AF/6/78 (27 April 1921); Pierre d'Argent, *Les Réparations de guerre en droit international public* (LGDJ and Bruylant 2002) 87–88.
33 Weill-Raynal (n 3) vol 2, 150–156.
34 AJ/6/79 (21 March 1922).

um, the Reparation Commission was clearly divided: Bradbury proposed (in August, and in a more developed way in October 1922) a complete plan for rescheduling the German debt and initiating foreign loans to Germany, but was rejected by a vote on 31 August 1922 (two votes against from France and Belgium, one abstention from Italy) and replaced by an Italian–Belgian proposal (supported by France) enjoining the German Government to make a deep financial and monetary reform.[35] In December 1922, the Commission was unanimous in taking note of the non-execution of timber (then coal) deliveries, but the British Delegate did not vote for the declaration qualifying this non-execution as a 'default' (the United States Delegate acted as an *amicus curiae* to attenuate the German default).[36] Bradbury accused Barthou of acting 'behind [the] back' of the Commission, with the support of some bureaucrats, but only in favour of the French Government. Bradbury said that 'the Commission had to judge as fairly as it could, having regard to its composition,' the way in which to acknowledge the inconsistence between this composition and a judicial status. When Barthou suggested that the Commission must not live in an 'atmosphere of politics' ('politics must remain outside the scope' was also one of his sentences) but that 'its role was essentially judiciary,' he was contradicted by the different appreciations of the consequences of the German default, the source of the division among Allied Powers about the Ruhr Occupation.[37] The end of the Ruhr crisis, decided in a London Conference with the participation of the Reparation Commission, was a divestiture of the Commission in favour of a pool of bankers and conducted by the Americans Dawes and Young.[38] The Commission was then reorganized, with fewer meetings in Paris and only attended by Associate Delegates, before being disbanded in 1930.[39] The idea of such a body, internationally representative in scope, although not judicial in practice, had definitely sunk following the reparations process, but it can be said that the debates of December 1922 showed the true deadlock of the Reparation Commission. It was impossible for the Commission to decide like a Tribunal with members consisting of representatives of their Government who were deprived of any guarantee or spirit of independence. In the final analysis, Delegates are not Judges.

35 AJ/6/79 (31 August 1922).

36 AJ/6/80 (26 December 1922) 20.

37 AJ/6/80 (26 December 1922), 13.

38 Weill-Raynal (n 3) vol 2, 500–522.

39 ibid vol 3, 206; Leonard Gomes, *German Reparations 1919–1932* (Palgrave Macmillan 2010) 177.

Chapter 9 The Conversion of Reparations into Sovereign Debts (1920–1953)

Pierre d'Argent[*]

1. *Morality, Law, and the Economists*

As an early critique of the Versailles settlement, notably because of the inclusion of war pensions as head of damage,[1] John Maynard Keynes foresaw the economic unsustainability of the overall reparation regime and famously wrote, 'International morality, interpreted as a crude legalism, might be very injurious to the world.'[2]

That sentence says it all: after the first total war of modern times during which all classes of citizens had been called to fight and to die; after a war that was for the first time not left to professional soldiers; after an industrialized war of unprecedented scale; after a war that invented war cemeteries and implanted them in the European landscape for centuries to come—after such a war, the demands of morality were running high.

Those demands were turned into law through a treaty that was imagined to be a founding stone of a lasting peace. However, there is only so much that law can achieve and deliver, and it was later for the economists and the financiers to fix the sort of monster that politicians and diplomats, turned legislators of peace, had invented. Indeed, the history of the interwar period in relation to the reparation issue makes a fascinating story that mixes together the insistence of complying with legal obligations (after all, *pacta sunt servanda*), how hurtful such insistence can be for the creditor itself, and the disillusion stemming from unmet naïve legal expectations. It also provides an important point of departure in world history because it is then that, progressively, a professional class of experts—the economists—

* Professor at the University of Louvain (UCL), Associate Member of the Institute of International Law, Member of the Brussels Bar.

1 Such inclusion doubled the reparation claim. After lengthy debates between the Allied Powers at Versailles, it was finally included in order to satisfy the demands of the United Kingdom and the Commonwealth nations since most of the material destruction occurred in Belgium and Northern France: see Pierre d'Argent, *Les réparations de guerre en droit international public* (Bruylant and LGDJ 2002) 66–68.

2 John Maynard Keynes, *The Collected Writings* (CUP 1978) vol 3, 94.

took over and intellectually dominated the rest of the 20th Century, replacing morality turned into law by pragmatism and finance.

2. The Magnitude of the German Reparation Debt

The history covered by this contribution begins just after the 1921 London Schedule of Payments by which the Reparation Commission decided that the German reparation debt amounted to 132 billion gold marks. According to the Schedule, that sum was to be paid in various instalments until 31st March … 1988.[3] The political confidence in a stable and predictable future stemming from such a schedule of payment seems simply incredible today: it is as if we would make plans today about the repayment of the Greek debt until 2085. Furthermore, 132 billion gold marks is a very abstract figure.

In order to measure the magnitude of the reparation debt, not only over time but also in economic terms, it is useful to put it in today's value: 132 billion gold marks is the equivalent of about 450 billion in today's US dollars,[4] an amount close to today's GDP of countries such as Belgium or Austria.[5] In 1913, Germany's GDP was approximately 441 billion in today's US dollars.[6] In other words, 132 billion gold marks was a claim equivalent to the German pre-war GDP. To put it differently, under Versailles, Germany was supposed to transfer to its creditors an amount equivalent to the market value of all final goods and services produced in Germany in one year just before the war. Of course, that was to be diluted over 67 years—but it is still a huge amount.

To make it even more concrete, consider the following: in 2017, the total education budget of Germany was approximately 20.7 billion dollars.[7] In other words, the 132 billion gold marks to be paid by Germany under the Versailles reparation scheme roughly amounts to 22 years of today's German expenditure for education. Economically speaking, claiming 132

---

3 'The Reparation Commission to the German War Debt Commission, Paris, 28 April 1921' (1922) 16 AJIL Supp 214. The London Schedule of payment divided the German debt into A, B and C bonds and Germany was actually only required to pay the first two categories of bonds, totalling 50 billion gold marks.

4 <www.westegg.com/inflation> accessed 14 June 2018.

5 <https://data.worldbank.org> accessed 14 June 2018.

6 ibid.

7 Or EUR 17.6 bn : <https://www.bmbf.de/en/education-and-research-priority-areas-of-federal-government-policy-1410.html> accessed 14 June 2018.

billion gold marks is the same as requesting today, that during a whole generation, Germany be turned into a pastoral country of uneducated citizens; or, if payments are postponed until 2085, to request that the German education budget be cut by a third for the next 67 years.

It is no surprise that Versailles has been characterized as 'economic vivisection.'[8]

3. *The Ruhr Crisis and the Dawes Plan*

In January 1923, after Germany stopped certain deliveries, the new French government of Poincaré requested productive guarantees for German payments, which was rejected by Britain. French and Belgian troops entered and occupied the Ruhr region. The purpose of the occupation was to seize, as a means of direct payment, part of the German coal and industrial output.

Of course, France and Belgium pretended to act in accordance with the Versailles Treaty provisions, while the United Kingdom and Germany disagreed. However, as Charles De Visscher aptly put it, the legal argument was a 'caustic dead end.'[9] Indeed, the fact of the matter was that the creditors had fatally wounded their debtor. While, in April 1923, one gold mark was worth about 6000 marks used in the real economy, it was worth 1 trillion (ie 1000 billion) marks in December of the same year. Collecting the needed gold marks to comply with the London Schedule of Payment became simply impossible after such an unmatched devaluation of the currency—unmatched devaluation that is still part of the collective political imagination in Germany and explains its obsession about having the containment of inflation through price stability as the core policy objective of the European Central Bank.[10] The past is so much present.

Chancellor Cuno was replaced by Stresemann, who decided to end passive resistance in the Ruhr, and a return to a negotiated settlement was agreed. In November 1923, the Reparation Commission appointed a com-

8 John Wheeler-Bennett, *The Wreck of Reparations: Being the Political Background ofthe Lausanne Agreement* (Allen & Unwin 1932) 255.

9 Charles De Visscher 'Revue des revues' (1924) 5 Revue de droit international et de législation comparée 469, 476. On the debate relating to the legality of the Ruhr occupation, see also Étienne Weill-Raynal, *Les réparations allemandes et la France* (Nouvelles Éditions Latines 1947) vol 2, 368–383.

10 See Treaty on the Functioning of the European Union (signed 13 December 2007, entered into force 1 December 2009) [2008] OJ C115/47, arts 127 and 140.

mittee chaired by the United States General Charles Dawes, who was tasked with the return of monetary stability in Germany.

The Dawes plan is a complex set of five interrelated agreements approved in London on 16 August 1924.[11] The basis of the Dawes plan was the return to German fiscal and economic unity, which meant the end of the Ruhr occupation. The basic novelty of the Dawes plan was to distinguish between the capacity of Germany to pay reparation and the transfer of massive wealth to the creditor nations. Under the Dawes plan, Germany was made to pay yearly instalments partly defined by a prosperity index, which were designed to include all debts owed by Germany under the Versailles Treaty. What was precisely included in those instalments was subject to interpretation by the Reparation Commission established pursuant to Article 232 of the Versailles Treaty.[12] The Reparation Commission issued several awards, the details of which are unimportant here.[13] What is important, however, is to recall that the German payments were made by Germany in German currency and in Germany, to an account open in the books of a profoundly reformed *Reichsbank*, in the name of the 'Agent-General for Reparation Payments.'

The purpose of such internal collection of debt and the avoidance of a massive international transfer of wealth was to prevent an increased competition by German manufacturers on the world market. Indeed, as it was said at the time of Versailles by economists critical of the settlement, deciding on the amount of reparation exacted from Germany was actually, in economic terms, deciding on the extent of the services that the creditor nations were willing to see Germany render to the world. In other words, prior to the Dawes plan, the reparation payments made by Germany were actually detrimental to their legal beneficiaries: indeed, in order to pay the various instalments in the currencies of the creditor nations, Germany had to compete on world markets with the producers from those beneficiary nations, therefore limiting their own exports and creating economic downturn at home while turning Germany into the 'workshop of the world.'

11 See Charles Dawes, *A Journal of Reparations* (MacMillan 1937). For the text of the 1924 London Agreements incorporating the Dawes plan, see Final Protocol of the London Conference (16 August 1924) 41 LNTS 429. For references and details about the Dawes plan, see d'Argent (n 1) 91–95.

12 See Halpérin (ch 8).

13 *Interpretation of London Agreement of August 9, 1924*: Awards Nos 1 (24 March 1926) 2 (29 January 1927) and 3 (29 May 1928) 2 RIAA ch XXI, 873–899. See John Fisher Williams, 'The Tribunal for the Interpretation of the Dawes Plan' (1928) 22 AJIL 797.

Over time the Dawes plan worked: economic stability, together with German capital that had fled during the Ruhr inflation times, was brought back to Germany. At the same time, the political mood had changed for better: the pact of Locarno was concluded in 1925, Germany joined the League of Nations in September 1926, the Kellogg–Briand pact was concluded in Paris in 1928.

Because the Dawes plan remained open-ended while, legally speaking, leaving the London Schedule of payments unaffected, the need was felt to finally settle the reparation debt issue in order to achieve financial predictability and prolonged stability. Furthermore, the European creditors of Germany came to realize that the sums of money collected by Germany and transferred to the victorious belligerents through the Agent-General were immediately used in their national budgets to pay back the loans they had contracted with the United States during the conflict in order to sustain their war effort. In a way, and in light of the financial cycle by which the payments received from Germany were immediately used to repay United States war loans, the reparation payments did not really make good on any damage in the countries that had suffered from the German invasion.[14]

Therefore, the European creditors felt that it was the right time to change the Dawes plan into a final settlement, which would link what was legally distinct but financially linked, ie the German reparations and the repayment of the United States war loans.

4. *The Young Plan and Its Aftermath*

Under the leadership of Owen D Young, who was a former member of the Dawes committee and former Agent-General, a committee of independent experts jointly appointed by the Reparation Commission along with, the United States Government and, for the first time, the German Government issued a report on 7 June 1929. The Young report was approved in The Hague on 20 January 1930 and incorporated in treaty law.[15]

---

14 See d'Argent (n 1) 95–96.

15 Agreement regarding the Complete and Final Settlement of the Question of Reparations (with Annexes) (signed 20 January 1930) 104 LNTS 243; Arrangement as to the Financial Mobilisation of the German Annuities (with Annex) (signed 17 January 1930) 104 LNTS 243. On the Young plan, see eg, A Pépy, 'Après les ratifications du Plan Young: Révision et sanctions' (1930) 5 Rev Dr Int 441–477; GA Finch, 'The Settlement of the Reparation Problem' (1930) 24 AJIL

Under the Young plan, the Reparation Commission was dissolved, together with various guarantee mechanisms under the Dawes plan. The Bank for International Settlements, an institution that still exists,[16] was established as trustee of the creditor nations and tasked with allocating to each of them new yearly instalments.

According to the Young plan, during a first period of 37 years, ending in 1966, each German instalment was composed of two parts: on the one hand, an unconditional part (about one third of the total due) and, on the other hand, a deferrable part that Germany could decide to postpone in case of economic hardship. After 1967, the instalments due until 1988 were only made up of the deferrable part. That part incurred interests and was financed by a consortium of United States banks coordinated by JP Morgan.

That latest, deferrable part of the instalments corresponded to the sums needed for the service of the inter-allied war loans. In such a way, Germany was somehow subrogated in the obligations owed by its war reparation creditors to the United States. A link between war reparations and inter-allied war loans was thus established, but it was not specifically agreed that the postponement by Germany of the variable part of the instalments would authorize the European powers to suspend the service of their debts to the United States. However, it was agreed that if the United States were to cancel or reduce the war loans, Germany would automatically benefit from it.

In addition, 'reparation bonds' were issued on the deferrable part of the instalments in order to cash-in and depoliticize the payment issue. Financial instruments were used and 'the public' (ie individuals, banks and corporations), instead of States, became creditors of Germany by purchasing those bonds that could be exchanged and traded on the world market.

Under its own terms, the Young plan was a complete and final settlement of the financial issues that arose out the Great War; it operated a kind of juridical *novatio* for all the previous conventional arrangements—however, without prejudice to Article 231 of the Versailles Treaty which remained unaffected.

The Young plan entered into force in May 1930, but very soon the disastrous economic consequences of the 1929 financial crisis were felt and Germany requested a new moratorium on its obligations. In August 1931,

339–350; Chandler P Anderson, 'Final Liquidation of German War Reparations' (1931) 25 AJIL 97–101; and also the references in d'Argent (n 1) 97.

16 < www.bis.org> accessed 14 June 2018.

such a moratorium was agreed by United States President Hoover for one year, and it applied on all interstate payments, be them of reparation or for war loans. A new revised plan was designed in Lausanne in July 1932. Most of the Young plan was to be terminated and replaced by the issuance by Germany of tradable bonds for total value of 3 billion gold Reich marks, with 5% interest.[17]

However, the Lausanne agreement never entered into force because Belgium, France, Italy and the United Kingdom agreed to postpone its ratification 'until a satisfactory settlement has been reached between them and their own creditors',[18] ie the United States. Such settlement of the war loans issue never occurred and the Lausanne agreement failed to replace the Young plan. However, Germany considered that a new situation had arisen since the Young plan was not brought back in full force, and it called for a new diplomatic conference.

This conference never met: on 30 January 1933, Hitler became Chancellor and very soon suspended the payments, including the service of the reparation bonds that were constituted as private legal titles, distinct and separate from the interstate debts. As a matter of law, the bonds remained unaffected by the legal uncertainties surrounding the legal status of the Young plan resulting from the failed Lausanne settlement.

After the Second World War, the 1953 London Agreement on German External Debts[19] deferred *sine die* the settlement of the World War I governmental claims while the World War II claims were deferred until German reunification. As far as the latter are concerned, the *Bundesverfassungsgericht* (BVerfG) has interpreted the Two Plus Four Agreement of 1990[20] that paved the way to German reunification as putting an end to the deferral of World War II claims.[21]

As far as the World War I reparation bonds issued on the world market are concerned, Annex I of the London Agreement of 1953 set out a com-

17 See d'Argent (n 1) 100–103, with references.

18 'Procès-verbal relating to the Ratification of the Agreement concerning German Reparations, Lausanne, 2 July 1932' in Manley O Hudson (ed), *International Legislation* (vol 6, Carnegie Endowment 1937) no 311b, 83.

19 London Agreement on German External Debts (signed 27 February 1953, entered into force 16 September 1953) 333 UNTS 3.

20 Treaty on the Final Settlement with Respect to Germany (signed 12 September 1990, entered into force 15 March 1991) 1696 UNTS 115 (Two Plus Four Agreement).

21 BVerfG, 13 May 1996, 94 *BVerfGE* 315. There is no need to enter here into a discussion about the adequacy of such understanding of the Moscow Treaty: on that issue, see d'Argent (n 1) 220–228.

plex scheme of gradual payments with deferred maturities and interests rates. Arbitration was initiated in 1979 against Germany by Belgium, France, Switzerland, the United Kingdom and the United States about the Young plan loans and the interpretation of depreciation provisions in the Agreement after the revaluations of the Deutsche Mark in 1961 and 1969.[22] Overall, the bonds were roughly paid back by 1983. One outstanding debt relating to the service of interest over a loan contracted by the Weimar republic to finance war reparation instalments was finally paid back after German reunification, with a final payment in October 2010, some 92 years after Versailles.[23]

5. The Versailles Reparations in Perspective

From such long and complex history, what can be gathered?

First, as we know from personal experience through our own mortgages and bank debts, finance is an incredible time machine since it helps to get cash now, while deferring the service of the debt to a later point thanks to a promise solidified in a private law instrument, ie a contract. It also confirms what everybody suspects: while it seems to depoliticize governmental debts by diluting them into the anonymity of the public, resorting to financial instruments paradoxically make debts stronger and more lasting over time. It is a lesson of humility for public international lawyers: on the long term, private law instruments are more resilient and beat public law instruments. The reason for this is probably due to the subjects at stake, ie the anonymity that goes with the market and the exchange of privately owned bonds. After all, who is a 'bond bearer' that needs to be serviced? It could be anyone, including German citizens themselves.

Second, public international law builds states as abstract legal entities having debts *vis-à-vis* each other, and it only governs the debt obligation.

22 *Case concerning the question whether the re-evaluation of the German Mark in 1961 and 1969 constitutes a case for application of the clause in article 2 (e) of Annex I A of the 1953 Agreement on German External Debts between Belgium, France, Switzerland, the United Kingdom of Great Britain and Northern Ireland and the United States of America on the one hand and the Federal Republic of Germany on the other* (decision of 16 May 1980) 19 RIAA 67–145.

23 David Crossland, 'Germany Closes Book on World War I With Final Reparations Payment (*Spiegel Online*, 28 September 2010) <www.spiegel.de/international/germany/legacy-of-versailles-germany-closes-book-on-world-war-i-with-final-reparations-payment-a-720156.html> accessed 14 June 2018.

However, it is absolutely blind and wants to ignore the issue of the contribution to the debt. The civil law distinction between the *obligation à la dette* and the *contribution à la dette* does not exist in international law. International law does not pierce the veil of sovereignty, and how states collect the debt domestically is of no interest to international law. Moreover, international law is premised on the paradigm of state continuity. So, as a matter of principle and if we think abstractly as international law invites us to do, over an infinite period of time, even the poorest nation on the planet has, theoretically speaking, an unlimited capacity to pay. In other words, the state remains, it is always the same, and a huge sum of money can always be paid through instalments stretching over a huge number of years. However, Versailles teaches us that such oversimplifications are unsustainable in real life: paying odious debts generation after generation simply does not make sense, politically speaking. Therefore, despite the fine legal abstractions built by international law, time—time that governs our own lives—is of the essence. Therefore, when designing reparation regimes for historical events, time should never be ignored. If the temporal dimension of war settlements is ignored, it can be feared that, to paraphrase Keynes by swapping morality for legality, 'International legality, interpreted as a crude moralism, might be very injurious to the world.'

Part 4:
The Institutionalization of International Adjudication

Chapter 10 Peace Through International Adjudication: The Permanent Court of International Justice and the Post-War Order

Christian J Tams[*]

1. *Introduction*

That 'peace' should be sought 'through law' is one of international law's prominent themes. Over the centuries, the theme has been varied significantly. The post-WWI variation of the theme stands out as a particularly ambitious one. Just as after earlier upheavals, peace was sought through international treaties and territorial re-ordering. But not all was *déjà vu*; much was not in fact. Breaking with precedent, the task of preserving international peace and security was entrusted to a World Organization, the League of Nations.[1] And as part of the move to international institutions, the World Organization was quickly supplemented by a World Court, the Permanent Court of International Justice (PCIJ).

The second of these innovations is at the heart of the present contribution, which seeks to offer a bird's eye view on the role of the World Court in the post-war attempt to ensure peace through law. The argument proceeds in two steps: section 2 revisits the cirumstances of the PCIJ's creation and assesses its relevance in the 1919 variation on the peace through law theme; section 3 outlines the experience of the court, once created. The treatment is selective and impressionistic, and it is aimed throughout at assessing whether the PCIJ's experience has shaped future approaches to peace through law.

---

* Professor of International Law, University of Glasgow.

1 According to the opening lines of the Covenant's Preamble, the League was set up '[i]n order to promote international co-operation and to achieve international peace and security.'

2. A New, but Modest, Beginning: Binding Dispute Resolution in the Post-war Order

The starting point for the discussion is a new beginning. The post-war settlement, with a brief delay, resulted in the establisment of the PCIJ—a permanent world court, not part of the League's institutional structure, but linked to it in manifold ways. Article 14 of the Covenant called upon the League Council to 'formulate and submit to the Members of the League for adoption plans for the establishment of a Permanent Court of International Justice', and clarified the dual basis of that future court's jurisdiction: it would be

> competent to hear and determine any dispute of an international character which the parties thereto submit to it [and] ... also give an advisory opinion upon any dispute or question referred to it by the [League's] Council or by the Assembly.[2]

The 'Council quickly got down to work':[3] it set up an Advisory Committee to produce a Report, which the Council considered (and modified in significant respects) in mid-1920, and which it placed before the League Assembly in late 1920.[4] In mid-December 1920, ten months after the Advisory Committee had been set up, the Protocol of Signature of the PCIJ Statute was adopted. Another nine months later, it entered into force; two

---

2 As Rosenne notes, 'When the Covenant of the League of Nations ... was being negotiated at the Paris Peace Conference of 1919, there were suggestions to include a Court amongst its organs. However, in the short time available, this idea could not be pursued'. The language of Article 14 of the Covenant offered a pragmatic way out. See Shabtai Rosenne, 'Permanent Court of International Justice' in Rüdiger Wolfrum (ed), *Max Planck Encyclopedia of Public International Law* (OUP 2006), para 4.

3 ibid para 5.

4 For a clear summary of the process see Ole Spiermann, 'Historical Introduction', in Andreas Zimmermann, Christian Tomuschat, Karin Oellers-Frahm and Christian J Tams (eds), *The Statute of the International Court of Justice. A Commentary* (2nd edn, OUP 2012) 47, paras 6–22. The primary documents are all available via the 'PCIJ section' of the website of the International Court of Justice (<www.icj-cij.org/pcij/other-documents.php?p1=9&p2=8>); see notably (i) *Advisory Committee of Jurists, Documents presented to the Committee relating to existing plans for the establishment of a Permanent Court of International Justice, 1920*; (ii) *Advisory Committee of Jurists, Procès-verbaux, 1920;* (iii) *Documents concerning the action taken by the Council of the League of Nations under Article 14 of the Covenant and the adoption by the Assembly of the Statute of the Permanent Court, 1921.*

weeks later, the first generation of PCIJ judges was elected; and on 15 February 1922, the new court was inaugurated.[5]

2.1. *A World Court at Last*

All this was no mean feat, and not just because of the record time in which the PCIJ was established. More importantly, the League succeeded where internationalists of earlier eras had failed: many of them had argued for the establishment of an international tribunal and placed great hopes in it.[6] Jeremy Bentham had seen access to an international court as a means of removing the need for conflict: 'Establish a common tribunal, the necessity of war no longer follows from difference of opinion. Just or unjust, the decision of the arbiters will save the credit, the honour, of the contending party'—things were fairly straightforward in his *Plan for an Universal and Perpetual Peace.*[7] At the Hague Peace Conferences of 1899, and more so in 1907, many delegates had fervently argued for a system of compulsory dispute settlement, and had claimed that it was time to move from institutionalized arbitration to a proper, permanent court. (A firm minority, in what Arthur Eyffinger would later describe as a 'titanic debate', succeeded in blocking both.[8]) Fifteen years later, the move from arbitration to adjudication was accomplished, and without anything approaching a titanic debate. The new World Court was set up quickly, and efficiently.

Unsurprisingly, many saw in this the triumph of an idea whose time had come: the culmination of a long process of establishing the rule of law, impartially administered, over states who would no longer meet on the battlefield, but in the 'hushed calm of courtrooms',[9] in a palace dedicated to

---

5 For the record see PCIJ Rep Series D no 1, vol 1.

6 The following section draws on Christian J Tams, 'World Peace through International Adjudication?' in Heinz-Gerhard Justenhoven and Mary Ellen O'Connell (eds), *Peace Through Law: Can Humanity Overcome War?* (Nomos/Hart 2016) 215–54.

7 Jeremy Bentham, 'Plan for an Universal and Perpetual Peace' (Principles of International Law, Essay IV) in *The Works of Jeremy Bentham, Part VIII* (William Tait 1839) 552.

8 See Arthur Eyffinger, 'A Highly Critical Moment: Role and Record of the Second Hague Peace Conference' (2007) 54 Netherlands International Law Review 197, 219; and further Christian J Tams/Christelle Bouguillon, 'La deuxième conférence de La Haye et le règlement pacifique des différends' (2009) 113 RGDIP 75.

9 Stephen C Neff, *Justice Among Nations: A History of International Law* (HUP 2014) 346.

peace, the *Palais de la paix*. James Brown Scott, ever the enthusiast, was one of them; he felt that '[w]e should ... fall upon our knees and thank God that the hope of ages is in process of realization.'[10] Sir Eric Drummond, the League's first Secretary-General, not otherwise known as an enthusiast, was not to be outdone. At the PCIJ's inaugural ceremony, he praised the Court's establishment as 'the greatest and ... most important creative act of the League' and noted that

> there have been various well-distinguished marks in the progress of mankind. The opening of the Court is not the least of these. Indeed, we believe and hope that it will prove the greatest. After all, the ideal to which I presume all men of goodwill look forward is that not only individual nations but the whole world shall be ruled by law.[11]

It is important to bear in mind this perspective, and to appreciate the sense of triumph and accomplishment felt by some observers at the time. It is particularly important because what Brown, Drummond and others said about the PCIJ fits will with broader perspectives on the era, which emphasizes the League's efforts to have 'the whole world ... ruled by law.'[12] Josef Kunz and many others–partly enthusiastically, increasingly critically —described the prominence of international law in a world gradually moulded by 'Geneva men' and the 'Geneva spirit': 'legal arguments were at the core of every debate,' according to Kunz.[13] The establishment of a world court nicely fits this vision of the post-war era—and it adds a further dimension: for while at Geneva, legal arguments were presented by state delegates and League officials in political and technical arenas, at The Hague they were assessed, scrutinized and tested by a court that was *solely* guided by considerations of law, that was required by Statute to apply it *impartially*, and given the power to do so with *binding force*. The World Court, in this perspective, was to give authoritative voice to the international rule of law.

10 James Brown Scott, 'The Permanent Court of International Justice' (1921) 15 AJIL 52, 55.

11 PCIJ Rep ser D no 2, 320.

12 ibid 320.

13 Josef L Kunz, 'Swing of the Pendulum: From Overestimation to Underestimation of International Law' (1950) 44 AJIL 135, 137.

2.2. *A World Court with a Modest Brief*

Not everyone shared this perspective. Where Brown, Drummond and others felt an important step had been taken, others saw a missed opportunity. This other perspective was not as prominent, and is ignored in some retrospective assessments,[14] but it deserves attention too. Its focus was not on what had been created (a court), but on how that court differed from the 'hope of ages'[15] of earlier generations. Two points stand out.

The first concerns the operating conditions of the new court, and it boils down to a relatively straightforward proposition.[16] The system of binding dispute resolution established under the PCIJ Statute was optional, not mandatory. It was optional in two respects. For one, to participate in the new system, states had to agree to be bound by the Statute: this was obvious and inherent in the functioning of a system of law based on treaties. Things did not end there, though; the system was optional also in another, less obvious, respect. Leaving aside marginal, incidental questions, the Statute itself did not provide the Court with competence in contentious proceedings. It was an invitation to provide the Court with jurisdiction: a vessel waiting to be filled with (jurisdictional) life—life that could, as per Article 36 of the Statute, come from special agreements, treaty-based compromissory clauses or optional clause declarations.[17] The Court's jurisdiction, in other words, was not compulsory, not even in the sense that it would be implicit in a state's sovereign decision to join the Statute; it was derivative.

---

14 See eg Rosenne, MPEPIL (n 2).

15 See Scott (n 10).

16 For more on this point see Christian J Tams, 'The Contentious Jurisdiction of the Permanent Court' in Christian J Tams andMalgosia Fitzmaurice (eds), *Legacies of the Permanent Court of International Justice* (Brill 2013) 11, 16–21.

17 In pertinent part, Article 36 of the PCIJ Statute (which, without major change, became Article 36 of the ICJ Statute) provided as follows:
'The jurisdiction of the Court comprises all cases which the parties refer to it and all matters specially provided for in treaties and conventions in force.
The Members of the League of Nations and the states mentioned in the Annex to the Covenant may, either when signing or ratifying the protocol to which the present Statute is adjoined, or at a later moment declare that they recognize as compulsory *ipso facto* and without special agreement, in relation to any other member or state accepting the same obligation, the jurisdiction of the Court in all or any of the classes of legal disputes.'

This derivative character set the newly-established court apart from the 'hope[s] of [earlier] ages'.[18] The plans of Bentham and others, had sought to make jurisdiction compulsory, not dependent on a second 'opt in'. Similarly, at The Hague in 1907, as noted above, it took a 'titanic debate'[19] for a minority to block plans for an obligatory system of dispute settlement. After World War 1, the titans had tired. Compulsory jurisdiction was not off the table; in fact, during the Advisory Committee debates, it was very much on it. But the Committee's proposed draft provision that would have given the PCIJ jurisdiction, without a further opt-in, over *all* disputes that had ben 'impossible to settle ... by diplomatic means'[20] did not survive the Council debates.[21] In fact, unlike in 1907, the great powers all insisted that jurisdiction would have to be based on dual consent. The post-war order, in other words, moved from arbitration to adjudication, but it did not take a 'leap of faith' towards compulsory jurisdiction.[22]

The PCIJ differed from earlier proposals in a second, and more significant, respect: it was set up as part of an overarching re-design of the international order: a particular variation of the peace through law theme. As hinted at in the Introduction, in this variation, the PCIJ was part of a move to international institutions, and its establishment overshadowed by the more momentous creation of the League of Nations. While earlier peace plans had put courts centre stage, in the new post-war order, the PCIJ occupied a relatively modest place. For around half a century, peace through law proposals had been dominated, in David Caron's words, by a 'profound and widespread nineteenth-century faith [still strongly felt during Hague Peace conference, CJT] in the peacekeeping ability of an interna-

18 See Scott (n 10).
19 Eyffinger (n 8).
20 See article 33 of the Advisory Committee Draft, reproduced in Advisory Committee of Jurists, Procès-verbaux (n 3) 727.
21 For details see Spiermann, 'Historical Introduction' (n 4) paras 11–17.
22 During the inter-War era, states would once more seek to introduce compulsory arbitration or adjudication through a universal dispute settlement treaty, the (Geneva) General Act for the Pacific Settlement of International Disputes (concluded 26 September 1928, entered into force 16 August 1929) 93 LNTS 344; yet limited ratification and far-reaching reservations affected its relevance.

tional court.'[23] To a powerful 'legalist movement'[24]—a broad church in which international lawyers would find their place alongside, pacifists, United States Secretaries of State, socialists and the Pope[25]—international courts and tribunals were crucial instruments of world peace, and arbitration and adjudication natural ways of resolving international conflicts in a civilized world society, which would no longer need to espouse war. This was always primarily a civil society movement, which states (who would have had to endorse it) viewed with some caution. But during the roughly half-century before 1919 it had significant strength. No more than a few snapshots must suffice here, which are chosen to illustrate the movement's diversity. The literary-minded will find in Strindberg's *German Lieutenant* a little gem of a scene in which Lieutenant Bleichroden and his wife, during a dinner party in Vevey on Lake Geneva, witness an Englishman celebrate the *Alabama* award: In it he saw not the massive British defeat (that it had also been), but a victory of justice; 'while a waiter placed a tray with filled champagne glasses on the table,' the Englishman expressed pride in his country which 'ha[d] appealed to the verdict of honourable men, instead of to blood and iron. … I wish you all many such defeats as we have had to-day, for that will teach us to be victorious.'[26] More traditionally inclined students of international law might turn to Westlake's 1886 textbook, which concluded on a decidedly optimistic note: '[I]nternational arbitration is in the air … It is the season to raise our hopes, and do our utmost to try what the idea of international arbitration can accomplish.'[27] To scholars

23 David D Caron, 'War and International Adjudication: Reflections on the 1899 Peace Conference' (2000) 94 AJIL 1, 9. For a highly accessible account of earlier peace plans see notably Mark Mazower, *Governing the World: The History of an Idea* (Penguin 2013) ch 3.

24 Terminology is not uniform. Others speak of the 'international arbitration campaign' or 'movement' (see eg Mazower, n 23, at 83), but that risks ignoring the push to move from arbitration to adjudication and 'proper courts.'

25 Mark W Janis underlines the limited influence of trained (international) lawyers (but probably undersells the role of activists from outside the United States): given how much debate about today's international courts has become 'the erudite province of lawyers and judges,' he notes that 'it is easy to suppose that it was a juridical impulse that was principally responsible for their creation. However, to a surprising extent, the international courts of today were the work of nineteenth-century American Utopians by and large untrained in law': Mark W Janis, *The American Tradition in International Law: Great Expectations 1789–1914* (OUP 2004), 95.

26 August Strindberg, *The German Lieutenant and Other Stories* (translated by Field, A C McClurg 1915) 64–65.

27 John Westlake, *International Law*, vol 1 (Cambridge 1896) 368.

of civil society movements, the proceedings of the annual Lake Mohonk conferences (annual gatherings of the faithful until 1916) provide much material: the first 1895 conference considered '[t]he feasibility of arbitration as a substitute for war … [to have been] demonstrated'.[28] And when looking at emerging global debates of the time, one cannot fail to notice that advocates of international legalism—Asser, Fried, Root, Cramer, the *Institut de droit international*, Theodore Roosevelt—dominated the lists of early Nobel Peace laureates;[29] and that at the global summits of The Hague, in 1899 and more so in 1907, binding dispute settlement was perceived to be the key to world peace. Notwithstanding setbacks, by 1914, 'the campaign for international arbitration' was 'probably the single most influential strand of internationalism'.[30] All this matters because, to quote again David Caron, '[internationalist] movements could have chosen other strategies to promote peace'; precisely for that reason, their 'focus on a permanent international court deserves attention'.[31]

By 1919, things had changed markedly. Arbitration, which prior to 1914 had helped resolve low- and mid-level conflicts, had proved powerless to stop a major global conflict from spiralling out of control. This was not lost on statesmen and observers, and it led to an (under-appreciated[32]) reassessment of the role of international courts and tribunals. When the leaders of the Allied and Associated Powers began to design the post-war order, they viewed an international court as useful, but no longer as a central guardian of world peace. And so the PCIJ was set up in a system that 'chos[e] other strategies to promote peace'.[33] The world court was designed to operate on the margins of the new world organization, the League of Nations: not part of the League's machinery for preserving peace and barely integrated in the League collective security system. The League's

28 See 'Resolution Adopted at the First Mohonk Conference on International Arbitration' (1895), 57 The Advocate of Peace 181.

29 For details, short biographies, and acceptance speeches, see <www.nobelprize.org/nobel_prizes/peace/laureates> accessed 29 November 2018.

30 Mazower (n 23) 83.

31 Caron (n 23) 8.

32 For an intriguing account see Stephen Wertheim, 'The League of Nations: A Retreat from International Law?' (2012) 7 Journal of Global History 210. For much more on 'legalist' and 'anti-legalist' trends in the establishment of the post-WWI order see David Kennedy, 'The Move to Institutions' (1987) 8 Cardozo Law Review 841; condensed accounts can be found in Mazower (n 23, 119-123); and Jochen von Bernstorff, *The Public International Law Theory of Hans Kelsen* (CUP 2010) 193–195.

33 Cf Caron (n 23) 8.

founders were idealists, too, but theirs was not the idealism of the legalists. It did not centre on arbitration or adjudication but on collective decision-making within international organizations: It was not the force of law administered by impartial judges, but the strength of political action backed by public opinion that was to ensure the League's success.[34] If the League, in Josef Kunz' terms, 'overestimated international law', then the Covenant hid this fairly well. It 'enshrined the primacy of politics over international law institutionally within the powerful organ of the Council',[35] and it 'focused on the political rather than judicial settlement of disputes'.[36] Courts were not ruled out—they were useful if states had consented to their involvement. But nothing required them to give such consent. What the League set up was a watered-down version of Scott's 'hope of ages': a world court, yes, but one with a modest brief. Elihu Root's assessment of the Covenant reflects this second perspective. Where his long-time protegé James Scott Brown saw progress, Root was disappointed at the 'relegation' of legalist thought in new post-war order:

> Nothing has been done to provide for the reestablishment and strengthening of a system of arbitration or judicial decision ... We are left with a program which rests the hope of the whole world for future peace in a government of men, and not of laws, following the dictates of expediency, and not of right.[37]

---

34 Mazower (n 23) speaks of 'Woodrow Wilson's impatience with the entire legalist paradigm' (at 121).

35 von Bernstorff (n 32) 195.

36 Anthony Giustini, 'Compulsory Adjudication in International Law: The Past, The Present, and Prospects for the Future' (1985) 9 Fordham International Law Journal 213, 224.

37 Note by Root to Henry Cabot Lodge, 19 June 1919, cited in Wertheim (n 32) 228. See further Jonathan Zasloff, 'Law and the Shaping of American Foreign Policy: From the Gilded Age to the New Era' (2003) 78 New York University Law Review 239, 348–49: 'Root's legalism, however, diverged sharply from Wilsonian diplomacy, a point obscured by frequent references to Wilson's "legalism." As Root noted, neither the Versailles Treaty nor the Fourteen Points called for international legal institutions (such as a world court) or compulsory arbitration of legal disputes; indeed, Wilson rejected the legal-political distinction that served as the essential framework of Root's thinking.'

3. *A Pragmatic Pioneer: the PCIJ in Operation*

What did the PCIJ make of all this? And what did states make of the new world court? The quarter-century of the Court's history yields many answers, and the PCIJ's experience in many ways remains instructive. As one of a number of 'great experiments' of the inter-War era, the PCIJ was to be a pioneer, simply because it was 'the framework within which the world first experienced the development of an international judiciary'.[38] So it was within the PCIJ's framework that mundane questions were first addressed—yes, judges would wear robes, but not the proposed caps, which Judge Moore had felt looked 'like a miter, with gold bands around them, making us look like a cross between bishops and clowns'[39]—and crucial decisions taken—jurisdiction was consensualist, preliminary objections could be addressed *a limine*, jurisdictional titles would cover consequential disputes about remedies, etc.[40] Through dealing, as a first of its kind, with the mundane and crucial issues of everyday judicial life, the PCIJ set the tone: future courts could look to it and decide to follow the pioneer or take a different approach.

As regards 'peace through law' schemes, the PCIJ's experience is perhaps best seen as a process of consolidation and adjustment: of 'finding its way'[41] in the new international legal order of the inter-War period and of testing out what a permanent court could bring to it. With the benefit of hindsight, two aspects stand out. First, as an agency of dispute settlement, the PCIJ filled with life the role accorded to it in the peace through law design of the post-WWI order, without stretching it all too much. Second, through its jurisprudence, the Court emerged relatively quickly as an authoritative interpreter of international law. Both aspects are taken up in the following.

---

38 Ole Spiermann, 'The Legacy of the Permanent Court of International Justice—on Judges and Scholars, and also on Bishops and Clowns' in Christian J Tams and Malgosia Fitzmaurice (eds), *Legacies of the Permanent Court of International Justice* (Brill 2013) 399, 412.

39 See references in Spiermann, in Tams/Fitzmaurice (n 38), 401.

40 For much more on these legacies see Tams, in Tams/Fitzmaurice (n 16), 29–37.

41 Rosenne, MPEPIL (n 2) para 38.

3.1. Sticking to the Brief: the Court as a Dispute Settler

The first point is closely related to the opening discussion of the Court's place in the post-war order designed in 1919/1922. If the architects of that era had foreseen a limited role for international adjudication in the settlement of major conflicts, they were to be proved right. (This may be worth mentioning as in many other respects, the post-war order evolved rather differently than its architects had foreseen.) The PCIJ played no major role in major conflicts, simply because it was hardly ever asked to 'address the main political issues of the day'.[42] However, those that it was asked to address, it typically handled competently—and through its work demonstrated the usefulness of binding dispute resolution by a standing international court. With the benefit of hindsight, the experience of the PCIJ can be summarized in three points:

(i) First, the Court had relatively few cases and not too many clients.[43] Over the two decades of its existence, the PCIJ addressed 33 contentious disputes (circa 1 ½ per year) and rendered twenty-seven Advisory Opinions (a little over one per year). Its *clientèle* remained decidedly European. In only four cases did non-European States appear at all, and in only one single case did a non-European state (Brazil) play a decisive role.[44] This was not principally a problem of jurisdiction. Even in the absence of automatic, compulsory jurisdiction, during the 1920s and 1930s, states regularly agreed on compromissory clauses establishing the jurisdiction of the PCIJ over specific types of disputes.[45] Many states went further and accepted the

42 Ole Spiermann, *International Legal Argument in the Permanent Court of International Justice. The Rise of the International Judiciary* (CUP 2005) 132.

43 The following draws on Tams, in Tams/Fitzmaurice (n 16), 21–28.

44 Namely in the *Brazilian Loans*, PCIJ Rep ser A no 21. Other non-European states participating in contentious proceedings were Japan (as joint applicant in *SS 'Wimbledon'* PCIJ Rep ser A no 1, and *Statute of Memel*, PCIJ Rep ser AB no 47) and China (in *Denunciation of the Sino-Belgian Treaty of 2 November 1865*, PCIJ Rep ser A no 18).

45 While the precise figure is difficult to establish, estimates suggest that in the two decades of the PCIJ's existence, as many as 500 compromissory clauses were concluded, ie between twenty and twenty-five per year. To help put this figure in perspective, it is useful to compare it to developments since 1946. These in fact are revealing: the ICJ has seen roughly 300 clauses in seventy years, ie less than five per year, and few true compromissory clauses (ie those permitting for some opt-out by way of declaration) at all since the 1970s.
A list of compromissory clauses referring to the PCIJ agreed before 1932 can be found in PCIJ Series D no 6 (4th edn). After 1932, the PCIJ no longer produced a consolidated list, but included information on new clauses in the respective

Court's jurisdiction over all disputes under the so-called optional clause.[46] The PCIJ's jurisdictional potential was, in fact, enormous. But this enormous potential was never 'translated' into real cases. States decided to use the Court only exceptionally. To illustrate, of the circa 500 compromissory clauses agreed in the inter-war period, only eight were ever invoked.[47] The World Court, as became clear quickly, was to be a court for rare occasions.

(ii) Second, beyond numbers, the disputes that did come before the Court were typically not the stuff of headlines. The bulk of its case-law—occasional exceptions such as the *Customs Union* opinion[48] notwithstanding—concerned disputes of limited reach and relevance. Maritime incidents of the *Lotus* type,[49] a dispute about the property of a foreign university,[50] the competence of an international organization,[51] and State interference with shipping on the River Congo[52] were some of the themes. More than anything else though, were issues raised by the post-war settlement: from questions relating to the territorial re-ordering of Europe (as in the

---

Chapter X of its Annual Reports (published as Series E nos 8, 9, 10 etc). Useful data can be found in Louis B Sohn (ed), *Systematic Survey of Treaties for the Pacific Settlement of International Disputes, 1928–1948* (United Nations 1949); and C Wilfred Jenks, *The Prospects of International Adjudication* (Stevens 1964) 71. A (non-exhaustive) list of compromissory clauses referring to the ICJ is available at <http://www.icj-cij.org/jurisdiction/index.php?p1=5&p2=1&p3=4> accessed 29 November 2018.

46 States parties to the PCIJ Statute made use of the 'option' of Article 36 (2) in large number: after a modestly successful start, the figure of states recognising the PCIJ's jurisdiction rose quickly: In 1939, of the fifty-two states parties to the Statute or otherwise entitled to appear before the PCIJ, forty had submitted an optional clause declaration; this amounted to roughly 75%. In total, the number of states that at some point submitted a declaration amounted to 45: See Shabtai Rosenne, *The Law and Practice of the International Court, 1920–2005* (The Hague 2006), 797–798; and Manley O Hudson, *International Tribunals: Past and Future* (Carnegie Endowment 1944) 76–78.

47 CW Jenks has details: see n 45, at 72–73.

48 PCIJ Rep ser AB no 41.

49 *Lotus*, PCIJ ser A no 10.

50 See the *Peter Pázmány University case*, PCIJ Rep ser A no 61.

51 See eg *Competence of the ILO to Examine Proposal for the Organization and Development of the Methods of Agricultural Production*, PCIJ Rep ser B no 3; *Competence of the ILO to Regulate Incidentally the Personal Work of the Employer* (Advisory Opinion) [1926] PCIJ Rep ser B no 13.

52 See *Oscar Chinn* (Jurisdiction) [1934] PCIJ Rep ser AB no 63.

many Silesian cases),[53] to the internationalization of the Kiel canal,[54] and to rights of minorities under the post-war treaties.[55] Set up to inaugurate a new era, the Court, in practice, was mainly busy addressing the 'follow up' of the previous War.

None of this was, it needs to be said, the PCIJ's fault: as all courts, it could only react to cases brought before it; and in fact, through its involvement in the matters that were brought before it, it often helped defuse tensions. But in the practice of the Court, it soon became clear that the reality of international adjudication could be quite mundane. Whereas in the debates of the late 19th and early 20th century, binding dispute resolution had been presented as an alternative to war, in the 1920s and 1930s, states saw in it a useful means of solving small-scale disputes: to adapt a phrase coined for the League, the PCIJ could perhaps be said to have dealt with the 'small change' of international affairs.[56]

(iii) That said, third, in dealing with smaller and mid-level conflicts and questions, the Court quickly established for itself a reputation as an agency for the settlement of disputes and (through advisory opinions) the provision of legal advice to international organizations. To illustrate by reference to a random sample of issues: once the Court had decided the *Wimbledon* case, ships would be permitted to pass the Kiel canal; Mr Mavrommatis was granted new concessions after the PCIJ's merits judgment of 1925; following the Court's opinion on the Treaty of Lausanne Turkey did accept

53 Among them *Certain German Interests in Polish Upper Silesia* (Merits) PCIJ Rep ser A no 7; *Factory at Chorzów* PCIJ Rep ser A no 9 and PCIJ Rep ser A no 10; *Rights of Minorities in Upper Silesia*, PCIJ Rep ser A no 15; *Access to German Minority Schools in Upper Silesia* (Advisory Opinion) PCIJ Rep ser AB no 40.

54 *SS 'Wimbledon'* PCIJ Rep ser A no 1.

55 See eg *Rights of Minorities in Upper Silesia (Minority Schools)* (Judgment) PCIJ Rep ser A no 15; *Interpretation of the Convention Between Greece and Bulgaria Respecting Reciprocal Emigration, Signed at Neuilly-Sur-Seine on November 27th, 1919 (Greco–Bulgarian Communities)* (Advisory Opinion), PCIJ Rep ser B no 17; *Access to German Minority Schools in Upper Silesia* (Advisory Opinion), PCIJ Rep ser AB no 40; *Treatment of Polish Nationals and Other Persons of Polish Origin or Speech in the Danzig Territory* (Advisory Opinion), PCIJ Rep ser AB no 44; *Minority Schools in Albania* (Advisory Opinion), PCIJ Rep ser AB no 64.

56 Cf Frederick S Northedge, *The League of Nations: Its Life and Times, 1920–1946* (Leicester University Press 1986) 72.
Ole Spiermann goes further when noting (with clinical Nordic precision) that '[i]n the political history of the League of Nations, the Permanent Court [was] but a footnote': Spiermann, *International Legal Argument* (n 42) 132.

the Council's decision in the *Mosul* dispute; etc.[57] While many of the PCIJ's judgments were declaratory in nature, it is worth noting that in 'no case' did states 'refus[e] … to comply with a PCIJ judgment'.[58]

As regards the PCIJ's overall performance, Rosenne rightly observes that during the inter-war period, 'the value of the settlement of international disputes through an international Court of the standing of the PCIJ, whether through its contentious jurisdiction or through its advisory competence, became widely accepted in modern diplomatic practice'.[59] This acceptance was a key factor explaining the almost seamless continuation of the Court after World War II: when another generation of peacemakers began to design another post-war order, they quickly agreed that a World Court should continue to be a part of it. To quote Rosenne again,

> [i]n the process of the reconstruction of organized international society following World War II, there was no serious demand to abandon the idea of a standing international judicial organ or to require any major change in its practices and procedures. The focus of attention was on the Court's place in the renewed international organization for the maintenance of international peace and security.[60]

Put differently, while the organizational detail required attention, the continued existence of the Court was soon agreed. The general impression was that, while not preventing wars,[61] the PCIJ had done its job as a dispute settler quite well.

***

The PCIJ's experience as a dispute settler can perhaps be seen as an exercise in consolidation. The Court and its clients quickly embraced the role foreseen by the peace architects of 1919. This was a more limited role than that of courts in earlier peace designs, but one that fit expectations. States and the League tended to prefer other means of dealing with major political

57 See *SS 'Wimbledon'* [1923] PCIJ Ser A No 1; *Mavrommatis Palestine Concessions* (Merits) PCIJ Rep ser A no 5; *Article 3, Paragraph 2, of the Treaty of Lausanne (Frontier between Turkey and Iraq)*, PCIJ Rep ser B no 12.

58 Constanze Schulte, *Compliance with Decisions of the International Court of Justice* (OUP 2004) 50.

59 Rosenne, MPEPIL (n 2) para 38.

60 Rosenne MPEPIL (n 2) para 38.

61 Yuval Shany, 'No Longer a Weak Department of Power? Reflections on the Emergence of a New International Judiciary' (2009) 20 EJIL 73, 80.

conflicts. But European states did make use of the new option of 'going to court' to solve disputes of a legal nature—not frequently, let alone lightly, but with some regularity. International organizations did so too: they relied on the Court's advisory jurisdiction as a useful 'in-house counsel.' By 1945, when the ICJ was established, international adjudication by an international court had been accepted as a new addition to the 'general arsenal of diplomatic processes'[62] for the peaceful resolution of international disputes.

3.2. *'Gradually Moulding International Law': the Court as an Agent of Legal Development*

Not seriously in demand as a 'war-prevention tool,'[63] the PCIJ soon carved out for itself other functions. 'Debarred from *directly* acting as an important instrument of peace,'[64] it made significant indirect contributions. One of these has particular relevance: through its jurisprudence, the Court became an important 'agent of legal development,'[65] a guide to the proper construction of international law. It did not do so over night, but in retrospect, it grew into this new role surprisingly quickly.

One reason for this swift role adjustment is that in the World Court's case-law, international law gained a new edge: principles of law formulated in books became tangible when applied to concrete disputes with a view to solving real-life problems—and their application by a court, with binding force upon the parties, gave them 'bite.' Of course, the PCIJ was not the first body to apply international law; arbitral tribunals had done so for decades. And yet, the creation of the Court marked a change.[66] From the

---

62 Rosenne MPEPIL (n 2) para 36.

63 Shany (n 61) 77.

64 Hersch Lauterpacht, *The Development of International Law by the International Court* (Praeger 1958) 5.

65 The term is borrowed from Sir Franklin Berman: see his 'The ICJ as an Agent of Legal Development,' in Christian J Tams and James Sloan (eds), *The Development of International Law by the International Court of Justice* (OUP 2013) 9.

66 In a perceptive study, Oliver Lissitzyn noted in 1951: 'Although the various arbitral tribunals have made a substantial contribution to the development and refinement of international law, their authority has been impaired by lack of continuity in functions, personnel and traditions the narrowness of the basis of their powers..., the differences in the personal characteristics and professional standing of the persons composing them.' As this was so, 'The International Court of Justice, like its predecessor, is undoubtedly a more effective instrument for the devel-

beginning, the new Court's decisions were publicly available. Individual opinions laid bare points of disagreement,[67] which were dissected in a new genre of legal writing, annual reviews of the Court's activity.[68] Most importantly, as a permanent institution, the Court could—and would—build a body of jurisprudence, case by case, and regularly referencing its earlier decisions.[69] In later Annual Reports, the Court would go out of its way to note that it 'ha[d] in practice been careful not to reverse precedents established by itself in previous judgments and opinions, and to explain apparent departures from such precedents'.[70]

Wise observers had expected something like this.[71] In fact, the possibility of seeing the emergence of a systematic body of case-law had been one

---

opment of international law than an arbitral tribunal': see Oliver Lissitzyn, *The International Court of Justice: Its Role in the Maintenance of International Peace and Security* (Carnegie Endowment 1951) 10 and 13.

67 According to Article 57 of the PCIJ Statute, 'If the judgment does not represent in whole or in part the unanimous opinion of the judges, dissenting judges [were] entitled to deliver a separate opinion'. In the PCIJ's practice, this was read expansively, to permit reasoned opinions by judges dissenting from and concurring with the majority, incl. in advisory proceedings and with respect to orders. This marked a change compared to earlier arbitral practice, notably under the 1907 Hague Convention which did not mention the possibility of dissent. Article 57 of the ICJ Statute would consolidate the PCIJ's approach. For a clear summary of developments see Rainer Hofmann and Tilmann Laubner, 'Commentary to Article 57' in Zimmermann/Tomuschat/Oellers-Frahm/Tams (n 4) paras 5–11.

68 See notably the reviews by the 'chronicler of the World Court' (Manfred Lachs), Manley O Hudson, entitled the 'xth year of the World Court', in successive volumes of the *American Journal of International Law*. For Lachs' remark see his *The Teacher in International Law: Teachings and Teaching* (Martinus Nijhoff 1982) 100.

69 The practice has continued to this date, and it bridges the divide between the two incarnations of the World Court. In the words of Judge Winiarski, '[t]he present Court [ICJ] has since the beginning been conscious of the need to maintain a continuity of tradition, case law and methods of work [with the PCIJ]. … Above all, without being bound by *stare decisis* as a principle or rule, it often seeks guidance in the body of decisions of the former Court, and the result is a remarkable unity of precedent, an important factor in the development of international law': see *ICJ Pleadings, The Temple of Preah Vihear,* vol 2, 122.

70 Third Annual Report [1926–27], PCIJ, Rep ser E no 3, 218, 226.

71 See eg, Manley O Hudson, 'The Permanent Court of International Justice and World Peace' in *The Annals of the American Academy* (1924) 122: 'It may reasonably be anticipated
that the Permanent Court of International Justice will contribute to
the maintenance of the world's peace … [by] building a cumulating body of international case law'.

of the arguments supporting the move from arbitration to adjudication.[72] But (adapting Hersch Lauterpacht's statement), 'the lawyers and statesmen who in 1920 drafted the Statute of the Court did [indeed] not fully appreciate all the possibilities, in this direction, of the activity of the Court about to be established'.[73] In fact, while the drafters certainly contemplated the possibility of court decisions 'gradually moulding and modifying international law',[74] they saw this with scepticism as much as anticipation: a scepticism that militated against expressly encouraging the Court 'to assure the continuity and progress of international jurisprudence based on judgments' (as proposed by Baron Descamps[75]) and that led to the adoption of a firmly worded Article 59 of the Statute (precluding anything remotely resembling a doctrine of *stare decisis*).[76]

Once the Court took up its work, these concerns soon gave way. This is not to say that doctrines of precedent were embraced—the Court never claimed that it could 'legislate'[77]—but its jurisprudence shaped, clarified and developed important areas international law, and it did so through the means of persuasion. Once the first handful of decisions had been ren-

---

72 As Hersch Lauterpacht would later observe, 'the necessity of providing for a tribunal developing international law by its own decisions had been the starting-point for the attempts to establish a truly permanent international court as distinguished from the Permanent Court of Arbitration': 'The so-called Anglo-American and Continental Schools of Thought in International Law' (1931) 12 BYBIL 59.

73 Lauterpacht, *Development* (n 64) 8. Lauterpacht prefaced this by a cautious 'it may be possible that...'.

74 See *Documents concerning the Action Taken by the Council of the League of Nations* (n 4), 46.

75 *Advisory Committee of Jurists, Procès-verbaux* (n 4), 373.

76 According to Article 59, '[t]he decision of the Court has no binding force except between the Parties and in respect of that particular case'. As Chester Brown observes, the inclusion of this provision 'was primarily intended to underline the opinion that the Court should not be considered to be a law-making or law-creating institution': see his Commentary to Article 59, in Zimmermann/Tomuschat/Oellers-Frahm/Tams (n 4) para 9.
Along the same lines, Léon Bourgeois, Arthur Balfour and others, during the drafting, had considered ways and means of limiting the Court's influence; Balfour felt 'there ought to be some provision by which a state can enter a protest, *not* against any particular decision arrived at by the Court, but against any ulterior conclusions to which that decision may seem to point': *Documents concerning the Action Taken by the Council of the League of Nations* (n 4), 38. No such provision was adopted.

77 Its successor would clarify that it could not: see *Nuclear Weapons*, ICJ Rep 1996, 226, para 18.

dered, commentators began to assess the Court's contribution to the development of international law.[78] Hardly a decade after the first judgment, Hersch Lauterpacht wrote about it in book-length form.[79] In the practice of the Court, the question of principle—can courts make law? —was left to a side, and the PCIJ's pronouncements were recognized as important points of reference.

To illustrate, by the late 1930s, there had emerged building blocks of a law of treaties: the lenient, non-formalist, approach to the notion of a 'treaty' in the jurisprudence of the PCIJ; gradually consolidated principles of interpretation; clear statements on treaties and third parties; pointers towards special categories of treaties, eg those establishing territorial regimes, etc. In all of these respects (and many more) a later generation of international lawyers would draw on the PCIJ's case-law when codifying the modern law of treaties.[80] Curious disputes provided the Court with an opportunity to formulate general principles of state responsibility—its autonomy from domestic law; the principle of full reparation; the conceptual hierarchy between its different modalities.[81] Still obscurer cases would yield timeless pronouncements on diplomatic protection.[82] The rather many PCIJ findings on minority rights, rendered 'without much doctrine or precedent to rely on', 'have kept their relevance' even though the League's minority protection system was wound up unceremoniously.[83] To these one can add holdings on expropriation, on sovereign debts, on jurisdiction

78 See William E Beckett, 'Decisions of the Permanent Court of International Justice on Points of Law and Procedure of General Application', *British Yearbook of International law* 11 (1930), 1.

79 Hersch Lauterpacht, *The Development ofInternational Law by the Permanent Court of International Justice* (London 1934). Admittedly, it was a rather short book, subsequently much expanded to cover the early work of the ICJ: see Lauterpacht, *Development* (n 64).

80 In the words of Stephan Wittich, 'the experience of the Permanent Court … left clear marks on the modern law of treaties': see his 'The PCIJ and the Modern International Law of Treaties' in Tams/Fitzmaurice (n 16) 89, 120.

81 For much more on this see Christian J Tams, 'Law-making in Complex Processes: The World Court and the Modern Law of State Responsibility' in Christine Chinkin and Freya Baetens (eds), *Statehood, Sovereignty and State Responsibility. Essays in Honour of James Crawford* (CUP 2014) 287, 292–296.

82 Notably the Court's state-centred interpretation of diplomatic protection claims, by which a state was 'in reality asserting its own rights': see *Mavrommatis Palestine Concessions*, PCIJ ser A no 2 (1924) 12.

83 Catherine Brölmann, 'The PCIJ and International Rights of Groups and Individuals' in Tams/Fitzmaurice (n 16) 123, 142 and 141.

—the PCIJ's jurisprudence reflected the expanding reach of international law.

The Court's holdings did not, to reiterate, have a binding effect beyond the immediate case at hand. But to state as much is to miss the essential point: the Court's jurisprudence, readily available and generally well-received,[84] became a natural point of reference for anyone seeking guidance on disputed questions of international law. It 'require[d] no doctrine of judicial precedent to explain th[e] *inevitable practice*' of 'looking to previous decisions for guidance in the solution of similar problems'.[85] Rendered in the early stages of the international legal community's 'move to institutions',[86] decades before international courts would proliferate, PCIJ decisions stood out as 'the most authoritative pronouncements on questions of international law … that can be made while the family of nations remains as at present constituted'[87]—viz lacking recognized law-interpreters and structured processes for spelling out the meaning of legal rules.

The aggregate effect of these 'authoritative pronouncements' was significant. They marked a general shift in the understanding of international law, which Ole Spiermann describes as a trend 'From *Buchrecht* to practice'.[88] From today's perspective, the point may seem almost trite, but the crucial relevance of the trend was not lost on contemporary observers. To Lord McNair, writing in the early 1960s, 'the feature of the past half-century has been the gradual transformation of international law from a book-law occasionally supplemented by treaties into a case-law constantly supplemented by treaties'.[89] In Sumner Lobingier's assessment, offered towards the end of World War II, the World Court appeared as 'The Molder of an International Law System', which (like the jurisconsults of Ancient Rome) had begun to transform international law—as yet 'little more than a mass of heterogeneous and often disputed doctrines'—'into a scientific system'.[90] Looking back, Robert Jennings would later speak of 'a change in the sources of international law [a term presumably not used in the formal,

84 As noted above, Balfour's idea of a 'protest option' (see n 76) was not formalized.
85 Sir Arnold Duncan McNair, *The Development of International Justice* (New York University Press 1954), 13–14 (emphasis added).
86 See Kennedy (n 30).
87 Beckett (n 78) 1.
88 Spiermann, *International Legal Argument* (n 42), 23.
89 Arnold D McNair, *The Expansion of International Law* (Magnes Press 1962) 54.
90 Charles Sumner Lobingier, 'What of the World Court Now?' (1945) 43 Michigan Law Review 833, 855–856.

technical sense, CJT], which had already begun to be felt even in the early 1930s: international law has become a case law.'[91]

Of course, international law is not just case-law, and certainly not in areas in which other processes of law-clarification or codification exist. In this sense, international courts do not dominate the interpretative process: international law is much more than 'what the judges say it is.'[92] But international courts make important contributions to the process of legal development. Their pronouncements become 'beacons' and 'orientation points'[93] and to this date continue to be accorded a 'truly astonishing deference.'[94] An excerpt from the fourth edition of Hall's influential textbook illustrates how much our perception has changed: writing in 1895, Hall thought there to be 'no place for the courts in the rough jurisprudence of the nations.'[95] Today, it is difficult to think of areas of international law that have not been shaped, in one way or the other, by international decisions. That process began in earnest with the PCIJ, and its quick acceptance and recognition in international legal discourse reflected an adjustment in the functions to be performed by international courts.

4. *Concluding Thoughts*

With the benefit of hindsight, it is clear that the 1919 variation of the peace through law theme has had a lasting effect. The key innovations then tried out have shaped our understanding of the task. Since 1919, 'peace through law' has primarily been approached as a study of 'The problem and progress of world organization.'[96] While the League failed in its core purpose, its concept of merging, under one institutional roof, the aims of 'achiev[ing] international peace and security' and 'promot[ing] international co-operation' remains the blueprint. The idea of an international

91 Robert Y Jennings, 'An International Lawyer Takes Stock' (1990) 39 ICLQ 513, 519.

92 Cf Charles Evans Hughes, Speech to Chamber of Commerce, in *Addresses and Papers of Charles Evans Hughes, Governor of New York, 1906–1908* (GP Putnam's Sons 1908) 139: 'We are under a Constitution, but the Constitution is what the judges say it is.'

93 Sir Franklin Berman, 'The ICJ as an Agent of Legal Development' in Tams/Sloan (n 4) 21.

94 Daniel P O'Connell, *International Law*, vol 1 (2nd edn, Stevens 1970) 32.

95 William E Hall, *International Law* (4th edn, Clarendon 1895) 356 (his note 2).

96 Cf the sub-title of Inis L Claude's influential study *Swords into Plowshares: The Problem and Progress of World Organization* (4th edn, Random House 1971).

rule of law authoritatively administered by permanent international courts has not gone away either; in a number of fields, it has risen to prominence. Yet in rising to prominence and relevance, international adjudication has largely remained de-coupled from war prevention. It now is relatively uncontroversial to state that 'the hope of the peace movement of the late 19th and early 20th centuries, that international adjudication was the substitute for war, was … ill-founded and unduly idealistic.'[97] After 1919, the maintenance of international peace and security has come to be seen primarily as a project of collective security to be pursued by an institutionalized 'peace machinery',[98] with courts (unlike in the legalist project) limited to some form of associated role.

International courts—and in this respect, too, decisions taken after World War I have remained influential—have adjusted to that role and filled it with life. Just as the PCIJ, so too have its successors succeeced in defusing simmering tensions through the competent handling of disputes below the level of major contriversies. (The PCIJ's successors have occasionally been asked to do more viz engaging with major controversies; but these instances have remained exceptional.) Just as importantly as the PCIJ, so too do its successors today contribute to international peace not just through the settlement of disputes, but also through their clarification and development of international law. In Yuval Shany's apt description, generalist international courts like the PCIJ and ICJ 'have transformed themselves from providers of heroic and life-saving emergency treatment into providers of preventive health care and quality-of-life related treatment.'[99] This transformation began with the PCIJ. In the history of binding dispute resolution, its establishment, almost a century ago, remains a watershed.

---

97 Stephen M Schwebel, 'The Performance and Prospects of the World Court' (1994) 6 Pace International Review 253, 257.

98 The term is Jessup's: see Philip C Jessup, 'A Half-Century of Efforts to Subtitute Law for War' (1960) 99 Recueil des Cours 1, 18.

99 Shany (n 61) 80. International courts set up in specialized fields such as regional economic integration or human rights protection have, if anything, taken the process further—to the point they are said to be 'no longer primarily dispute-settling bodies' but 'have assumed two other primary functions … : norm-advancement and regime maintenance': ibid, 80–81.

Chapter 11 International Adjudication of Private Rights: The Mixed Arbitral Tribunals in the Peace Treaties of 1919–1922

Marta Requejo Isidro[*] / *Burkhard Hess*[**]

1. Origins and Legal Framework

1.1. Private Rights in the Peace Treaties

1.1.1. War Measures Against the Property of 'Ennemis Nationaux'

The First World War was not only the greatest war mankind had experienced to that point in history, it also triggered many adverse consequences for private commerce and investment. In the course of the war, all belligerent nations adopted legislative measures against the so-called property of enemies.[1] According to these measures, trading with enemy nationals was generally prohibited, and any property of these nationals located in the belligerent state was strictly controlled and—often—seized. Measures of sequestration were usually applied to corporations and branches of foreign investors of the belligerent nations.[2] As the nationals of enemy countries had been denied standing in the domestic courts, they faced default judg-

* Professor of Private International Law, Universidade de Santiago de Compostela; Senior Research Fellow, Max Planck Institute Luxembourg for Procedural Law.

** Director, Max Planck Institute Luxembourg for Procedural Law.

1 Christian Dominicé, *La notion du caractère ennemi des biens privés dans la guerre sur terre* (E Droz/Minard 1961) 14–15; Michael Bazyler, 'Trading with the Enemy' in Frauke Lachenmann and Rüdiger Wolfrum (eds), MPEPIL (2011), paras 5 and 9 (only describing the practice of the UK and the US—but not of other belligerent states); Dirk Hainbuch, *Das Reichministerium für Wiederaufbau 1919 bis 1924* (2016) 127–136 (describing the German '*Treuhänder für feindliches Vermögen*').

2 In this respect, IP rights (especially brands and patents) and insurance contracts were mostly affected, see art 310 VPT.

ments and other detrimental decisions.[3] It was clear that these adverse consequences had to be remedied by the peace treaties.[4]

1.1.2. *Private Rights and Interests in the Peace Treaties*

The Versailles Peace Treaty (VPT) addressed private rights and relationships in the so-called Economic Clauses (Part X, arts 264–312 VPT) which firstly addressed inter-state commercial relations in general (arts 264–270 VPT)[5] and imposed the (most favourable) treatment of nationals of the Allied and Associated Powers in Germany—without any reciprocity (arts 276–295 VPT). As a matter of principle, the Allied and Associated Powers obtained full access to the German markets and a most favourable treatment while Germany and its nationals were not accorded any reciprocal treatment.

Sections III to XI of Part X of the VPT addressed private law relationships. Section III of the VPT, under the headline 'Debts' dealt with unsettled monetary claims arising out of pre-war contracts. These claims were resolved through so-called *Ausgleichsämter* (clearing offices) to be established by all contracting parties within three months after the signature of the Peace Treaty (art 296 VPT). All payments of debts between allied, associated creditors and national debtors of the 'opposite states' had to be cleared through these offices.[6] Article 296 VPT reads as follows:

> There shall be settled through the intervention of Clearing Offices … the following classes of pecuniary obligations: (1) Debts payable before the war and due by a national of one of the Contracting Powers, residing within its territory, to a national of all Opposing Power, residing within its territory; (2) Debts which became payable during the war to

3 The German legislation related to enemy property is described by Dominicé (n 1) 132–36; the French legislation at 113–23; the English legislation at 51–63.

4 This paper mainly addresses the Versailles Peace Treaty (with Germany) of 28 June 2019 (VPT), but also contemplates the parallel provisions in the peace treaties of Neuilly of 9 August 1920 with Bulgaria (NPT), Trianon of 26 June 1921 with Hungary (TPT) and of Saint-Germain of 16 July 1920 with Austria (SGPT) as well as of Lausanne with Turkey of 1922 (LPT).

5 Especially shipping (arts 271–73 VPT), unfair competition (arts 274–75 VPT).

6 Karl Strupp, 'The competence of the Mixed Arbitral Courts of the Treaty of Versailles,' (1923) 17(4) The American Journal of International Law 661 ff; Jakob Zollmann, 'Reparations, Claims for Damages, and the Delivery of Justice. Germany and the Mixed Arbitral Tribunals (1919–1933)' in David Deroussin (ed), *La Grande Guerre et son droit* (LGDJ 2018) 379, 383.

> nationals of one Contracting Power residing within its territory and arose out of transactions or contracts with the nationals of an Opposing Power, resident within its territory, of which the total or partial execution was suspended on account of the declaration of war.

According to Sections IV and V of Part X of the VPT (addressing property, rights and interests as well as contracts and prescription periods), all measures taken by Germany against enemy property were discontinued and the property had to be restored to its owners (arts 297(a) and 298 VPT).[7] On the other hand, the property of German nationals within the allied countries was liquidated by the Allied and Associated Powers[8] and used for the full compensation of their own nationals (art 297(b) VPT).[9]

This basic regime also applied to judgments given by German courts during the war against allied nationals to defend their property. In these proceedings, the latter not had been able to put forward their defence, and the respective judgments were reversed (art 302 VPT). The rationale of the regime demonstrated that the settlement of private rights and interests was aligned to the (full) reparation of war damages as foreseen in Articles 231ff VPT.[10] However, the legal regime of private rights was conceptually and formally clearly separated from the reparation regime.[11]

---

7 Art 297 (a) VPT read as follows: 'The exceptional war measures and measures of transfer (defined in paragraph 3 of the Annex hereto) taken by Germany with respect to the property, rights and interests of nationals of Allied or Associated Powers, including companies and associations in which they are interested, when liquidation has not been completed, shall be immediately discontinued or stayed and the property, rights and interests concerned restored to their owners, who shall enjoy full rights therein in accordance with the provisions of Article 298.'

8 The German government only paid partial compensations (of less than 10% of the original value of the affected assets) to its nationals.

9 Art 297 (b) VPT read as follows: 'Subject to any contrary stipulations which may be provided for in the present Treaty, the Allied and Associated Powers reserve the right to retain and liquidate all property, rights and interests belonging at the date of the corning into force of the present Treaty to German nationals, or companies controlled by them, within their territories, colonies, possessions and protectorates, including territories ceded to them by the present Treaty. The liquidation shall be carried out in accordance with the laws of the Allied or Associated State concerned, and the German owner shall not be able to dispose of such property, rights or interests nor to subject them to any charge without the consent of that State.'

1.2. The Establishment of the Mixed Arbitral Tribunals

1.2.1. The Pertinent Provisions in the Peace Treaties

The Allied and Associated Powers did not entrust the German, Austrian and Hungarian courts with the implementation of the substantive provisions[12] of the peace treaties[13] as they mistrusted the willingness of these courts to fully implement the one-sided regimes of the peace treaties.[14] Under the applicable national jurisdictional rules, these courts had the competence to address private law issues regarding assets located on their soil.[15] Instead, the peace treaties established a self-standing court system, the Mixed Arbitral Tribunals (Articles 304 VPT, 256 TPSG, 187 TPN, 239 TPT). The pertinent provision, Article 304 of the VPT, stipulated in a technical way:

> (a) Within three months from the date of the coming into force of the present Treaty, a Mixed Arbitral Tribunal shall be established between

10 At the 1919 Peace Conference the German delegation challenged these provisions which were deemed to be unilateral and unfair, but the Allied and Associated Powers did not make any concession in this regard. They considered the regime as a direct consequence of the war caused and lost by Germany.

11 In practice, the delineation proved to be difficult. Example: PCIJ, 12 September 1924, *Traité de Neuilly, Article 179, paragraphe 4 (interprétation)*, Series A no 3; on the reparation regime cf Pierre d'Argent, *Les réparations de guerre en droit international public: la responsabilité internationale des États à l'épreuve de la guerre* (Bruylant 2002) 46 ff.

12 German authors disqualified them as *Vorrechte* (privileges), not as *Rechte* (rights): Walter Schätzel, 'Die Gemischten Schiedsgerichte der Friedensverträge' [1930]) Jahrbuch Öffentliches Recht 378, 380.

13 Judicial decisions in the Allied States characterized the Treaty provisions as 'mesures de défiance à l'égard des tribunaux allemands': Tribunal de commerce de Bruxelles (29 December 1920) 1 Recueil MAT 132, 134; Cour d'appel de Bruxelles (20 March 1922) 1 Recueil MAT 959, 961. In a similar vein, Romanian–German MAT, *Mr Kirschen senior v Sobotka, ZEG et Empire allemand* (3 January 1925) 4 Recueil MAT 858, 863–64: '*Les tribunaux arbitraux mixtes ont été créés uniquement pour soustraire la partie alliée à la juridiction ordinaire des tribunaux allemands, les alliés craignant que le ressentiment contre d'anciens ennemis pût influer sur la décision de ces Tribunaux. Il s'agit donc avant tout d'un avantage accordé aux ressortissants alliés*.' Same opinion: Reichsgericht (16 April 1924) 108 Entscheidungen des Reichsgerichts in Zivilsachen 5052.

14 Rudolf Blühdorn, 'Le fonctionnement et la jurisprudence des Tribunaux Arbitraux Mixtes créés par les traités de Paris' (1932) 41 Recueil des Cours 141, 170.

15 Cf Sections 24, 29 and 32 German Code of Civil Procedure of 1877.

> each of the Allied and Associated Powers on the one hand and Germany on the other hand. Each such Tribunal shall consist of three members. Each of the Governments concerned shall appoint one of these members. The President shall be chosen by agreement between the two Governments concerned …
> (b) The Mixed Arbitral Tribunals established pursuant to paragraph (a), shall decide all questions within their competence under Sections III, IV, V and VII.

The name of these tribunals was due to their international composition: two arbitrators were nominated by the respective governments, and a presiding judge who was a national of a neutral state was chosen by agreement between the two governments. The most prominent and innovative feature of the peace treaties was the standing of individuals before these courts.[16]

1.2.2. The Competences of the MATs

The Mixed Arbitral Tribunals (MATs) had the competence to decide the various disputes regarding the treatment of private rights according to the peace treaties. In the Versailles Peace Treaty, their main competences were as follows:

> (1) The tribunals were competent to hear disputes relating to outstanding debts which had not been settled by the Clearing Offices (art 296 and Annex no 16 VPT[17]).
> (2) The MATs were competent to reverse judgments of Austrian, German and Hungarian courts which were given against allied nationals during the war and to award compensation (art 302(2) VPT[18]).

---

16 Burkhard Hess, 'The Private-Public Divide in International Dispute Resolution' (2018) 388 Recueil des Cours 49, para 89.

17 See text of art 296 (n 6). Annex 16 para 1 provided that 'Where the two Clearing Offices are unable to agree whether a debt claimed is due, or in case of a difference between an enemy debtor and an enemy creditor or between the Clearing Offices, the dispute shall either be referred to arbitration if the parties so agree under conditions fixed by agreement between them, or referred to the Mixed Arbitral Tribunal provided for in Section VI hereafter.' Substantive and procedural rules followed, Annex 18–24.

18 Art 302 VPT stated as follows: 'If a judgment in respect of any dispute which may have arisen has been given, during the war by a German Court against a national of an Allied or Associated State in a case in which he was not able to make his defence, the Allied and Associated national who has suffered prejudice thereby

(3) They decided on restitution and compensation claims concerning property rights and interests located in the enemy countries (art 297 VPT[19]).
(4) With regard to the Associated Powers Poland and Czechoslovakia, the MATs were competent to review the liquidation of the property of German, Austrian and Hungarian nationals within their territory by those Powers and to fix the compensation to be paid (art 297(h) VPT[20]).
(5) The Mixed Arbitral Tribunals were competent to review judgments of national courts[21] regarding their conformity with the VPT (art 305 VPT). In these constellations, the MAT acted functionally as a kind of second instance court.[22]
(6) Apart from these main competences, the MATs acted in additional settings, especially in the granting of new licenses for IP rights (art 310 VPT). The German Polish MAT and the MAT for Upper Silesia played

---

shall be entitled to recover compensation, to be fixed by the Mixed Arbitral Tribunal provided for in Section VI.'

19 Especially art 297(e) and (f) VPT. Art 297 VPT stated: '(e) The nationals of Allied and Associated Powers shall be entitled to compensation in respect of damage or injury inflicted upon their property, rights or interests, including any company or association in which they are interested, in German territory as it existed on 1 August 1914, by the application either of the exceptional war measures or measures of transfer mentioned in paragraphs 1 and 3 of the Annex hereto. The claims made in this respect by such nationals shall be investigated, and the total of the compensation shall be determined by the Mixed Arbitral Tribunal provided for in Section VI or by an Arbitrator appointed by that Tribunal. This compensation shall be borne by Germany, and may be charged upon the property of German nationals within the territory or under the control of the claimant's State.'

20 Art 297 (h) (2) stated: 'In the case of liquidations effected in new States, which are signatories of the present Treaty as Allied and Associated Powers, or in States which are not entitled to share in the reparation payments to be made by Germany, the proceeds of liquidations effected by such States shall, subject to the rights of the Reparation Commission under the present Treaty, particularly under Articles 235 and 260, be paid direct to the owner. If on the application of that owner, the Mixed Arbitral Tribunal, provided for by Section VI of this Part, or an arbitrator appointed by that Tribunal, is satisfied that the conditions of the sale or measures taken by the Government of the State in question outside its general legislation were unfairly prejudicial to the price obtained, they shall have discretion to award to the owner equitable compensation to be paid by that State.'

21 The same regime applied to enforcement measures taken in German territory to the prejudice of a national of an Allied or Associated Power during the war, art 300 (b) VPT.

22 Blühdorn (n 14) 141 ff.

an important role in the protection of labour and minority rights in the transferred territories.[23]

1.2.3. The German–US Peace Treaty of 1922

A specific situation existed with regard to the United States[24] as the Peace Treaty of the United States and Germany of 10 August 1922 provided for the establishment of a Mixed Commission which dealt with the individual claims of American nationals against Germany and German nationals. It also decided on the reparation of war damages. However, these proceedings were different from the ones before the Mixed Arbitral Tribunals, as individuals had no standing in the Mixed Commission; their losses were taken up and claimed before the Commission by state agents.[25]

2. The Organization of the Mixed Arbitral Tribunals

2.1. Historical and Statistical Background

2.1.1. A New Model for the Settlement of International Disputes

In 1919, the idea of establishing international arbitral tribunals competent for the resolution of disputes between individuals (or individuals against states) at the international level was innovative. There had been, in the 19th century, a couple of international mixed commissions competent to decide on the legal consequences of war affecting private property. However, in these bodies, individuals were not granted any standing,[26] but were represented by their home state under the traditional rules of diplomatic protec-

23 It must be noted that the statute of the MAT for Upper Silesia was different although it borrowed from the structure of the MAT. Cf Erpelding (ch 12).

24 The United States did not ratify the peace treaties, cf Arthur Burchard, 'The Mixed Claims Commission and German Property in the United States of America' (1927) 21 AJIL (1927) 472 ff.

25 The procedure of the Commission was based on diplomatic protection where the rights of the individual are represented by its home state at the international level, Hess (n 16) 49, paras 83 ff.

26 Kate Parlett, *The Individual in the International Legal System: Continuity and Change in International Law* (CUP 2011) 52 ff.

tion.[27] A first attempt of establishing an international tribunal competent to hear claims brought by individuals was founded in the 1907 Hague Convention on the International Prize Court. Shortly before the war, comprehensive rules of procedures had been established.[28]

These procedures were taken up by Germany and Russia when they concluded a separate peace treaty, the German–Russian Agreement on Private Rights of 27 August 1918, which aligned with the Peace Treaty of Brest of 3 March 1918.[29] However, there were considerable differences between these courts and the Mixed Arbitral Tribunals. The main difference related to the limited access of German parties and other nationals of the defeated states to the Mixed Arbitral Tribunals of the 1919/1920 peace treaties. Their jurisdiction depended almost entirely on the initiative of allied and associated states and their nationals that were solely empowered to bring individual actions before the Mixed Arbitral Tribunals.[30] German individuals, however, were not entitled to bring their own claims against allied parties[31]—even counterclaims were largely excluded.[32] This 'unilateralism' might explain why the Mixed Arbitral Tribunals were not associated with the Permanent Court of Arbitration at The Hague which had been established for the settlement (and the administration) of international disputes.[33]

2.1.2. Statistical Data

There is not much reliable information available about the case law addressed by the Mixed Arbitral Tribunals. The most reliable source of empir-

27 Hess (n 16) 49, para 84.

28 Schätzel (n 12) 378, 380 f (with further references). Günther Küchenhoff, 'Erinnerungen an das Schiedsgericht für Oberschlesien' in Manfred Abelein and Otto Kimminich (eds), Festschrift für Raschhofer (Michael Laßleben 1977) 143, 149 ff.

29 Carl Friedrich Ophüls, 'Gemischte Schiedsgerichte' in Karl Strupp and Hans Jürgen Schlochauer (eds), *Wörterbuch des Völkerrechts* (vol 3, De Gruyter 1962) 173; Schätzel (n 12) 378, 379 f.

30 The peace treaties did not provide for specific provisions on the standing of the individual, cf art 304 VPT and Annex.

31 The only exception was art 297 (h) VPT with regard to the liquidation of (mainly) German assets in Poland, text above (n 20).

32 See nevertheless the French–German MAT, art 14 (e), the Italian–German MAT, art 19, or the one corresponding to the Czechoslovakian–German MAT, art 24.

33 The PCA did not even act as an appointing authority with regard to the respective presidents of the MAT. It was completely outside the framework of the MATs.

ical information is an article written by Walter Schätzel.[34] According to this author, there were 36 Mixed Arbitral Tribunals, which decided almost 70,000 cases.[35] Germany established Mixed Arbitral Tribunals with Belgium, France, Greece, Italy, Japan, Yugoslavia, Poland, Romania, Thailand, Czechoslovakia and the United Kingdom. Austria established Mixed Arbitral Tribunals with Belgium, France, Greece, Italy, Japan, Yugoslavia, Romania and the United Kingdom. Hungary had Mixed Arbitral Tribunals with Belgium, France, Italy, Yugoslavia, Romania and the United Kingdom. Bulgaria formed Mixed Arbitral Tribunals with Belgium, France, Greece, Italy and the United Kingdom. The situation of Turkey was different as it established more self-standing Mixed Arbitral Tribunals via the Treaty of Lausanne (1922) with Belgium, France, Greece, Italy, Romania and the United Kingdom.[36] These MATs had their seat in Istanbul.

As already mentioned, the number of cases processed by the arbitral tribunals was remarkable: According to Göppert, the French–German Mixed Arbitral Tribunal heard 23,996 cases, while the Polish–German Mixed Arbitral Tribunal dealt with 28,670 cases[37]. The UK–German Mixed Arbitral Tribunal heard almost 10,000 claims, while the Belgian–German Mixed Arbitral Tribunal decided 2,200 cases.[38] The Italian–German MAT was seized by thousands of small claims brought by Italian workers who had to leave Germany after the outbreak of the war.[39] All other arbitral tribunals decided less than 1,000 cases; the Siamese–German MAT only 3 cases.[40] The Mixed Arbitral Tribunals between Austria and the Allied Powers heard 2,845 cases in total, most of them (2,142) related to Italy.[41] The Mixed Arbitral Tribunals of Hungary decided almost 5,000 claims, and the Bulgarian

34 Schätzel (n 12) 378, 449 ff. Additional information is found in an unpublished memorandum by Otto Göppert, *Zur Geschichte der auf Grund des Versailler Vertrages eingesetzten Schiedsgerichte*, (typoscript March 1931, on file with the authors).
35 Hess (n 16) 49, para 89.
36 Schätzel (n 12) 378, 389.
37 Göppert (n 34) 90, 194.
38 Göppert (n 34) 91.
39 Eventually, these claims (which related to unpaid wages, loss of personal property as clothes) were settled between the state agents, Schätzel (n 12) 378, 392. The MAT received 3,860 claims, almost all were settled, the MAT gave only 49 contradictory judgments, Göppert (n 34), 152–153.
40 Schätzel (n 12) 378, 450; Ophüls (n 29) vol 3, 173, 175. According to Göppert (n 34), 90, the French–German MAT received 23,996 claims; by December 1930, 21,093 cases were closed.
41 Schätzel (n 12) 378, 450 (footnote 2).

Mixed Arbitral Tribunal heard more than 1,000 cases. Most of these claims were processed within less than 10 years.[42]

Overall, the work of the Mixed Arbitral Tribunals appears impressive. These courts were confronted with a multitude of claims, and the tribunals (largely supported by the state agents[43]) were able to develop the first techniques for the processing and settlement of mass claims. The work of the Mixed Arbitral Tribunals is documented in a series of decisions published between 1921 and 1930.[44] These *Recueils* also contain information about the procedures applied, the composition of the courts, and the origin and representation of the parties. Remarkably, this collection of case law, which has been described as comprehensive, was chosen by its French editor in collaboration with all presidents of the MATs and the state agents of all state parties involved.[45] However, it must be noted that this collection is in fact not comprehensive and includes only the most important decisions of the MATs and some important decisions of national courts.[46]

---

42 The Mixed Commission under the American–German Treaty of 10 August 1922 decided altogether 20,434 claims which were submitted to it: Department of State (ed) *The Treaty* of *Versailles and After: Annotations of the Text of the Treaty* (US Government Printing Office 1947) 629 f (providing for statistical information).

43 See infra text at n 51.

44 Office français des biens et intérêts privés (ed), *Recueil des décisions des tribunaux arbitraux mixtes institués par les traités de paix* (Librairie de la Société du Recueil Sirey, 1922–1930), hereafter Recueil MAT.

45 The decisions of the American–German Mixed Commission were documented by the German Commissioner Wilhelm Kiesselbach, *Probleme und Entscheidungen der deutsch-amerikanischen Schiedskommissionen* (Bensheimer 1927).

46 Schätzel (n 12) 378, 424.

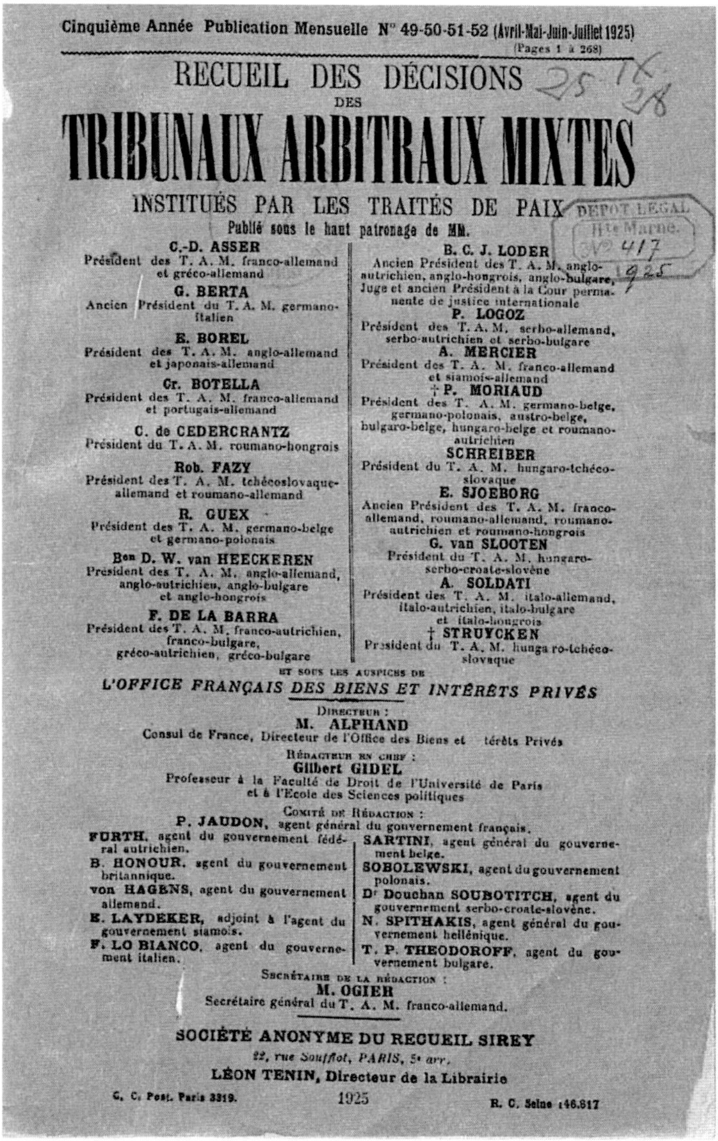

Cinquième Année Publication Mensuelle N° 49-50-51-52 (Avril-Mai-Juin-Juillet 1925)
(Pages 1 à 268)

RECUEIL DES DÉCISIONS
DES
TRIBUNAUX ARBITRAUX MIXTES
INSTITUÉS PAR LES TRAITÉS DE PAIX

Publié sous le haut patronage de MM.

C.-D. ASSER
Président des T. A. M. franco-allemand et gréco-allemand

G. BERTA
Ancien Président du T. A. M. germano-italien

E. BOREL
Président des T. A. M. anglo-allemand et japonais-allemand

Gr. BOTELLA
Président des T. A. M. franco-allemand et portugais-allemand

C. de CEDERCRANTZ
Président du T. A. M. roumano-hongrois

Rob. FAZY
Président des T. A. M. tchécoslovaque-allemand et roumano-allemand

R. GUEX
Président des T. A. M. germano-belge et germano-polonais

Bon D. W. van HEECKEREN
Président des T. A. M. anglo-allemand, anglo-autrichien, anglo-bulgare et anglo-hongrois

F. DE LA BARRA
Président des T. A. M. franco-autrichien, franco-bulgare, gréco-autrichien, gréco-bulgare

B. C. J. LODER
Ancien Président des T. A. M. anglo-autrichien, anglo-hongrois, anglo-bulgare, Juge et ancien Président à la Cour permanente de justice internationale

P. LOGOZ
Président des T. A. M. serbo-allemand, serbo-autrichien et serbo-bulgare

A. MERCIER
Président des T. A. M. franco-allemand et siamois-allemand

† P. MORIAUD
Président des T. A. M. germano-belge, germano-polonais, austro-belge, bulgaro-belge, hungaro-belge et roumano-autrichien

SCHREIBER
Président du T. A. M. hungaro-tchéco-slovaque

E. SJOEBORG
Ancien Président des T. A. M. franco-allemand, roumano-allemand, roumano-autrichien et roumano-hongrois

G. van SLOOTEN
Président du T. A. M. hungaro-serbo-croate-slovène

A. SOLDATI
Président des T. A. M. italo-allemand, italo-autrichien, italo-bulgare et italo-hongrois

† STRUYCKEN
Président du T. A. M. hungaro-tchéco-slovaque

ET SOUS LES AUSPICES DE
L'OFFICE FRANÇAIS DES BIENS ET INTÉRÊTS PRIVÉS

DIRECTEUR :
M. ALPHAND
Consul de France, Directeur de l'Office des Biens et Intérêts Privés

RÉDACTEUR EN CHEF :
Gilbert GIDEL
Professeur à la Faculté de Droit de l'Université de Paris et à l'École des Sciences politiques

COMITÉ DE RÉDACTION :
P. JAUDON, agent général du gouvernement français.

FURTH, agent du gouvernement fédéral autrichien.
B. HONOUR, agent du gouvernement britannique.
von HAGENS, agent du gouvernement allemand.
E. LAYDEKER, adjoint à l'agent du gouvernement siamois.
F. LO BIANCO, agent du gouvernement italien.
SARTINI, agent général du gouvernement belge.
SOBOLEWSKI, agent du gouvernement polonais.
Dr Douchan SOUBOTITCH, agent du gouvernement serbo-croate-slovène.
N. SPITHAKIS, agent général du gouvernement hellénique.
T. P. THEODOROFF, agent du gouvernement bulgare.

SECRÉTAIRE DE LA RÉDACTION :
M. OGIER
Secrétaire général du T. A. M. franco-allemand.

SOCIÉTÉ ANONYME DU RECUEIL SIREY
22, rue Soufflot, PARIS, 5e arr.
LÉON TENIN, Directeur de la Librairie

C. C. Post. Paris 3319. 1925 R. C. Seine 146.817

The 10-volume Recueil des décisions des Tribunaux arbitraux mixtes institués par les Traités de Paix *contains a selection of decisions made by various MATs. The collection was edited by the presidents of the MATs and demonstrated the effort to provide for a coherent set of case-law. Pictured here is volume 4, published in 1925. Source: gallica.bnf.fr / Bibliothèque nationale de France.*

2.2. The Composition of the Tribunals

2.2.1. The Judges and the Secretariats

The rules for the appointment of arbitrators and—especially—the presiding judges were contained in Article 304(a) VPT. The judges were nominated by the respective governments, which also appointed the presiding judge by common agreement. In case of failure to reach agreement, the Council of the League of Nations would appoint the MAT's president (art 304(a) VPT).[47] Once nominated, all judges of the MATs were independent.[48] Often, the presidents and the judges of the MATs were prominent international lawyers and law professors of the 1920s and 1930s: CD Asser acted as president of the French–German MAT; Ernst Rabel acted as a member of the Italian–German MAT, Victor Bruns was a member of the Polish–German MAT, Albert de Geouffre de Lapradelle usually acted as a party representative. In the 1920s and 1930s, the case law of the MATs was regularly documented and commented on in international journals.[49]

The tribunals were supported by secretariats. Their staff came from (and was paid by) the contracting states; the '*secrétaire général*' usually came from a neutral state. The secretaries-general were usually jurists with language skills covering both contracting states. In some MATs, the presidents were supported by personal secretaries.[50]

---

47 Usually, the governments were able to agree on the presiding judge. Therefore, the procedure to nominate a judge (when the government failed to designate its judge) was seldom applied. However, after the occupation of the Ruhr by French and Belgian troops (1922/23), the German judges no longer participated in the Belgian and French MATs. After the crisis, the German arbitrators joined the court again and one president of the French–German MAT, *Mercier*, was replaced by common agreement of the two governments.

48 According to the case law of the German Supreme Court for civil and criminal matters, the *Reichsgericht*, the German Government could not unilaterally terminate the appointment of the judges: Reichsgericht (9 June 1925) 111 Entscheidungen des Reichsgerichts in Zivilsachen 115.

49 See for instance Jean Paulin Niboyet, 'Tribunal arbitral mixte germano-roumain, 16 juin 1925. P. Negreanu v Meyer' [1927] Revue de Droit International Privé 97; Lewald, 'Internationalprivatrechtliche Fragen vor den GSchHöfen' [1926] Juristische Wochenschrift 2815; Max Gutzwiller, 'Das Internationalprivatrecht der durch die Friedensverträge eingesetzten Gemischten Schiedsgerichtshöfe' [1932] Internationales Jahrbuch für Schiedsgerichtbarkeit 123 ff (footnotes 1 and 2 with numerous references).

50 Schätzel (n 12) 378, 398–99.

2.2.2. The State Agents

One of the salient features of the MATs was the involvement of 'state agents' before the tribunals.[51] The agents were formally representatives of the contracting states (especially in cases directly involving the states as parties), but they often acted as intermediaries between the individual parties and the MAT. They were not independent, receiving orders from their respective governments.[52] In practice, the state agents played a paramount role in the processing of the individual claims and in assisting the claimants. At the same time, the state agents were empowered to supervise their respective nationals and their representatives in the proceedings.[53] Their activities eventually amounted to a kind of filtering of claims.[54] This empowerment was based on their right to oversee the conduct of private parties.[55] Furthermore, the state agents were also able to directly settle many claims between the states involved.[56] The most important function related to their right to intervene directly in the proceedings and to preserve the rights of the contracting states. In this respect, they limited the standing of the individual parties in the proceedings.[57] Sometimes, state agents even contradicted the legal or factual allegations of individual plaintiffs of their nationality.[58]

---

51 The German state agents were supported by a specific unit, the 'Commissariat for the MATs' (about 100 public servants and additional staff), organized within the Ministry of Foreign Affairs. It was led by a Commissioner for the MATs (*Otto Göppert,* 1872–1943). In 1924, there were 4 sub-divisions monitoring the proceedings in the different MATs, 79 qualified lawyers and 215 additional officials performed their duties in Berlin, Paris, London and Rome. Schätzel (n 12) 378, 399–400 (n 1), Zollmann (n 6) 379, 385; Göppert (n 34), 25–40.

52 Zollmann (n 6) 379, 385.

53 Piero Calamandrei, 'Il Tribunale Arbitrale Misto Italo–Germanico e il suo Regolamento Processuale' [1922] Rivista del Diritto Commerciale 293, 305–306.

54 Schätzel (n 12) 378, 400, reports that the state agents developed a filtering system for individual contract claims similar to the proceedings before the cleaning offices. Finally, the state agents were able to settle 5 out of 6 cases of the French–German MAT.

55 According to Section 18 of Annex to art 296 VPT, the state agents were competent to supervise the representatives and lawyers of their respective nationals.

56 Schätzel (n 12) 378, 400; Zollmann (n 6) 379, 385.

57 Obviously, the old '*leitmotif*' of diplomatic protection reinforced the role of the state agents.

58 Schätzel (n 12) 378, 400.

2.2.3. *The Position of the Individual Claimants*

The most innovative feature of the dispute resolution mechanism was the standing of private individuals before the Mixed Arbitral Tribunals. Representation by lawyers was not required, although it was the rule in major cases; in small cases, parties were represented by the respective state agents. However, in most of the proceedings, participation was not limited to private parties; state agents also pleaded (and eventually settled the claims). This situation clearly distinguished the Mixed Arbitral Tribunals from private arbitration.

It is worth mentioning that the contemporary literature did not generally regard the standing of individuals before the Mixed Tribunals as a positive experience. Some authors clearly preferred individuals to be represented by state agents as foreseen in the German–American Mixed Claims Commission.[59] According to this opinion, the direct involvement of individuals complicated the proceedings. The unsettled legal position of the individual was highlighted in the compensation proceedings under Article 297 VPT: Some authors considered these claims as part of the reparations, thus qualifying the individual plaintiffs as a kind of representative of their home states. However, several MATs clearly stated that the economic rights of the VPT were the subjective rights of individuals.[60]

The strong position of the states in the proceedings became evident when the activities of most of the MATs[61] with Germany were terminated by international agreements related to the so-called Young plan in 1930: The state parties terminated the activities of the tribunals (including pending cases) by waiving the claims of individuals. Eventually, the special regime of the MATs was terminated by an international settlement based on diplomatic protection and the power of the states to espouse and to set-

59 Schätzel (n 12) 378, 400 ff; Rudolf Blühdorn, 'Die Prozessführung vor den Gemischten Schiedsgerichten in der Praxis' [1930] Rabels Zeitschrift für ausländisches und internationales Privatrecht 488 ff. This perspective was obviously influenced by the personal function of those authors who had acted as state agents.

60 French–German MAT, *Sigwald v Germany* (27 August 1926) 6 Recueil MAT 888, 890; British–German MAT, *Exors of F Lederer v Germany* (13 December 1923) 3 Recueil MAT 762, 768. Same opinion: PCIJ, *Certain German Interests in Upper Silesia* (25 May 1926) Rep ser A no 7, 33.

61 With the exception of the MAT for Upper Silesia, cf Erpelding (ch 12).

tle the claims of their nationals.[62] It seems that the latter were (partially) compensated at the domestic level.[63]

A similar situation occurred in the context of the Hungarian MAT when Hungary agreed with Czechoslovakia, Yugoslavia and Romania on a structural reform of the MAT. A Treaty of 28 April 1930[64] augmented the number of neutral judges of the MAT and introduced an appeal to the PCIJ. This 'appeal' operated under international law according to the Statute of the PCIJ whereby the states took up the cases of their nationals and presented them before the PCIJ.[65] As a result, diplomatic protection was reintroduced as the appropriate mechanism to settle the disputes at the level of public international law.

2.3. The Procedures Applied

According to Article 304(d) VPT, each MAT had to develop its own procedure. They did so in such detail that the outcome was described as 'miniature civil procedure codes'.[66] The MAT regulations addressed the internal organization of the tribunals (for instance where the headquarters would be), the rules of the proceedings (for example the principle according to which each court is the judge of its own competence, or those related to representation and legal aid, as well as costs) and also explained the unfolding of the procedure (its different phases, the regime of evidence, enforcement and appeals).[67]

There were many similarities between the regulations as earlier drafts acted as templates for later drafts. Nevertheless, the procedures were not

---

62 Hess (n 16) 49, para 91. The prerogative of the states to espouse the claims of their nationals was clearly stated by the French–German MAT *Sigwald v Germany* (27 August 1926) 6 Recueil MAT 888, 891. Example: the Polish–German MAT Bilateral Agreement of 31 October 1929, Reichsgesetzblatt 1930 II, art III: mutual waiver of all pending claims in the MAT.

63 Göppert (n 34), 208–209 on the dissolution of the Polish–German MAT.

64 121 LNTS 80.

65 Eventually, the PCIJ, *Pazman University (Hungary) v Czechoslovakia* (15 December 1933) Rep ser AB no 61, 222, openly addressed the relationship with the MAT. The Court stated: 'The fact that a judgment was given in a litigation to which one of the Parties is a private individual does not prevent this judgment from forming the subject of a dispute between two States capable of being submitted to the Court, in virtue of a special or general agreement between them.'

66 Calamandrei (n 53) 293.

67 Schätzel (n 12) 378, 402–18.

identical. The contemporary legal literature even identified three different 'model' regulations: 1. the French–German MAT's rules of procedure, which would later inspire those of the Italian–German MAT; 2. the Anglo–German MAT's rules, which borrowed many of their original features from English civil procedural law, and would later serve as a model for the regulations of the Japanese–German MAT; 3. the Belgian–German MAT's regulations, which differed from those used by the French–German MAT and would serve as a reference for the MAT regulations with Yugoslavia, Czechoslovakia and Poland. Despite these common origins, there were also relevant divergences among the MAT regulations based on the same model.[68] Moreover, identical rules were not always identically implemented.[69] Decisions were also drafted in very different styles (and in different languages), closely following the typical formulations of the local decisions of the country where the MAT involved had its headquarters. In this respect, there was no uniformity at all in the manner the awards/judgments were drafted.[70] As a consequence, cross fertilization among the different courts (or, even more challenging, the development of a '*jurisprudence constante*') was difficult.[71]

---

68 Blühdorn (n 59) 488 490, highlights the peculiarities of the Anglo–German MAT's regulations; Calamandrei (n 53) 293, *passim*, those of the Italian–German MAT's regulations.

69 Such as for instance the more or less lenient attitude towards accepting time-barred claims: Blühdorn (n 59) 488, 493.

70 As a result, the decisions of the French–German and Belgian–German MAT were drafted in French and in the French style of judgments, the British–German MAT as English judgments and the decision of the Italian–German MAT appeared as Italian judgments. However, the decisions were short. They usually did not comprise more than five pages. This was due to the huge amount of cases.

71 It must be noted that the '*Recueil des décisions*' (supra n 44) contained, in addition to the text of the decision in the languages of the countries involved, a short summary in French, Italian, English and German.

Differences of style between the different MATs were also of a vestimentary nature. Whereas the members of the British–German MAT sat in lounge suits, the members of the Belgian–German MAT, pictured here in 1924 (from left to right: the German arbitrator, Richard Hoene, the MAT's neutral president, Paul Moriaud from Switzerland, and the Belgian arbitrator, Louis Fauquel), wore robes in the Franco–Belgian tradition. Press photograph by Meurisse news agency. Source: gallica.bnf.fr / Bibliothèque nationale de France.

The procedures followed a similar pattern: The claims had to be filed within a limited period (generally one year after the establishment of the tribunal), the lawsuit had to clearly designate the facts and the pertinent legal provisions, and the means of evidence had to be presented.[72] Usually, documentary proof prevailed—in large part because the state agents encouraged parties to provide for witness testimonies protocolled by the domestic

72 In practice, parties often pleaded according to their national procedural laws and backgrounds. Accordingly, Austrian parties easily complied with time limits which, as a matter of principle, corresponded to their national civil procedure.

courts.[73] Representation by lawyers was not mandatory. Often, the state agents assisted the claimants in formulating the claims, even preparing their forms.[74] However, there were also specialized lawyers involved who 'collected' similar claims (on the basis of forms) and brought them collectively before the MAT.[75]

The procedures of the MATs favoured one comprehensive hearing—a concept which has been taken up by many modern procedural rules. The rationale behind this concept was easy to understand: As the parties to the individual disputes were often domiciled in different countries, the MATs tended to avoid several hearings, which would have been a time-consuming and costly burden on the parties. In order to speed up the proceedings, the procedural rules empowered the tribunals to set time limits and to sanction non-compliance by preclusion.[76] However, these provisions were seldom applied in practice.[77] Nevertheless, from a contemporary perspective, these procedural provisions appear to be progressive and modern.[78]

Among the elements common to all MATs, it is worth mentioning those which provoked criticism from contemporary scholars, who pointed to elements which are essential to any court and all processes, such as impartiality of the arbitrators and equality of arms between the parties. The allegation that arbitrators favoured the nationals of the Allied or Associated Powers or were imbued with the general idea of retaliation against or punishment of Germany is found in some authors with regard to specific MATs: Calamandrei made this observation about the regulations of the Italian–German MAT,[79] while Zitelmann cited examples from the practice of Franco–German MAT, whose tendentious character was commented on by oth-

73 Blühdorn (n 58) 488, 496–97. In the British–German MAT, German parties were confronted with cross-examinations by English barristers and had considerable difficulties to understand and to cope with the unknown procedural technique, Göppert (n 34), 143.

74 Blühdorn (n 58) 488, 495.

75 This was the case in Alsace and Lorraine where some lawyers and state agents collected thousands of claims of farmers with regard to requisite chattels and cars, cf Schätzel (n 12) 378, 391 and 426. Here, the issue was whether the inhabitants of Alsace and Lorraine could qualify as French citizens. The French–German MAT held that arts 72 and 73 VPT provided standing to these groups: *Heim et Chamant v Germany* (7 August and 25 September 1922) 3 Recueil MAT 50.

76 Calamandrei (n 53) 293, 313, regarding the Italian–German MAT Regulation.

77 Schätzel (n 12) 378, 404.

78 Cf Peter Gottwald, *Zivilprozessrecht* (18th edn, CH Beck 2018), § 1, paras 39 ff.

79 Calamandrei (n 53) 293, 339.

er authors as well.[80] The complaints, nevertheless, seem to be general, although it is usually added, in defence of the MATs, that partiality was not the result of bad faith but rather the natural consequence of the origin and training of the arbitrators, who were more easily convinced by arguments presented from a familiar point of view—the one corresponding to their nationality or to their national law.[81] Besides, it could not reasonably be expected from the arbitrators that in cases involving strong interests of their respective states they would act to the detriment of their own country.[82]

Another fact which was usually pointed to as an explanation for the partiality was the selection of London[83] and, in particular, of Paris[84] as the headquarters of the arbitrations. An anti-German feeling was palpable in those environments.[85] Finally, the question of the language of the process was considered key to the inequality of the parties. According to section 8, the VPT itself foresaw the election by the Allied Power among French, English, Italian or Japanese, except if otherwise agreed.[86] In practice, the regulations chose the language of the Allied Power, or, in the case of Greece and Romania, French; only in some cases was German also admit-

80 Ernst Zitelmann, 'Zwischenstaatliche Gerichtsbarkeit und die Gemischten Schiedsgerichtshöfe des Versailler Vertrags' [1923] Niemeyer's Zeitschrift für internationales Recht 303, 316, 320, 320; Blühdorn (n 14) 141, 171. The conflict within the French–German MAT was largely influenced by the occupation of the Ruhr region by French troops in 1923, cf Schätzel (n 12) 378, 391 f.

81 In addition, the provisions of the peace treaties were one-sided and discriminated against the (nationals of) defeated nations. This basic situation explains the bitterness of some commentaries of German scholars. Generally, German scholars had difficulties in understanding the official language of the Peace Treaties, which did not provide for an official translation into German and were based on legal concepts which did not fully correspond to the domestic concepts of German law, Zollmann (n 6) 379, 389. Eventually, the isolated situation of German private law led to the establishment of the *Kaiser-Wilhelm-Institut für Internationales Privatrecht* in Berlin (1926): cf Jürgen Basedow, 'Der Standort des Max-Planck-Instituts: Zwischen Praxis, Rechtspolitik und Privatrechtswissenschaft' in *Aufbruch nach Europa, 75 Jahre Max-Planck-Institut für Privatrecht* (Mohr Siebeck 2001) 3, 6 ff.

82 Blühdorn (n 14) 141, 165.

83 The seat was at 21 St James' Square, London SW1, 6.

84 The seat was firstly at Hôtel Matignon (the former Austrian Embassy), later at 145 avenue Malakoff.

85 Blühdorn (n 14) 141, 179; Zitelmann (n 80) 303, 321–322; Hermann Isay, *Die privaten Rechte und Interessen im Friedensvertrag* (3rd edn, Vahlen 1923) 424. Geneva was chosen for the Yugoslavian–German MAT as well as for the one with Czechoslovakia.

86 Annex to Article 304 VPT s 8, Göppert (n 34), 9–10 stressing the 'considerable advantage' of the allied parties because of the language.

ted (Czech Republic and Yugoslavia). Apart from the greater difficulties that this generated for the German members of the MATs,[87] the authors acknowledged that this fact translated *de facto* into an advantage for the allied litigant who simply used his mother tongue.[88] This discriminatory character of the proceedings was reinforced by the fact that the decisions were given in the language of the Allied Power and were immediately enforceable (without exequatur) in the defeated states (art 302 (1) VPT).[89]

2.4. The Interfaces with Domestic Procedures

2.4.1. The Basic Regime

The relationship between any given MAT and the domestic courts largely depended on the provisions on the different competences of the MAT. Sometimes, these provisions allocated disputes under the VPT either to the national courts or to the MAT.[90] Consequently, Article 304(b) VPT generally defined the jurisdiction of the MATs by referring to the economic clauses of the provisions of the VPT.[91] As a result, the relationship of the MATs to national courts was differently delineated in the individual constellations.[92] These crucial interfaces were defined by the (limited) competences of the MATs:

(1) The first major competence of the MATs related to debts arising out of ongoing legal relationships at the outbreak of the war. Here, the VPT addressed several categories:
   (a) With regard to outstanding debts all private parties were treated equally.[93] As a matter of principle, all claims had to be filed

---

87 The German Government had considerable difficulties in recruiting sufficient legal experts to be sent to the MATs as 'German' arbitrators or agents. The former allies of Germany faced the same problem, Zollmann (n 6) 379, 388–389.

88 Blühdorn (n 14) 141, 178; Schätzel (n 12) 378, 405; Isay (n 85) 425, Zitelmann (n 80) 303, 321–322.

89 See below (n 114).

90 The most prominent examples were Section 16 of the Annex to Article 296 VPT, Article 300(b) and Article 304(b), 2.

91 Article 304(b), para 1 VPT, see text above (n 15).

92 Attempts by German scholars to restrict the competences of the MATs by referring to their *Ausnahmecharakter* (extraordinary nature) were not taken up by the MATs, cf Strupp (n 6) 661, 664 ff.

93 Art 296 VPT, see text above (n 6).

through the Clearing offices. When a clearing (by mutual agreement between the offices) was impossible, the private parties could pursue their claims either before the MAT or bring them before an arbitral tribunal. Alternatively, with the permission of the clearing office of the creditor, the claim could also be brought before the civil court at the debtor's domicile.[94]

(b) Regarding judgments which the courts of the defeated states had rendered against allied defendants during wartime, the MATs were competent to revise these judgments and to award compensation to the allied parties (Article 302(2) VPT). The same legal regime applied to enforcement measures (Article 300(b) VPT).

The revision of war-time judgments under Article 302(2) to (4) VPT generated much case law. A typical example was the sale of the furniture of a tenant who was a national of an enemy country and had fled Germany after the outbreak of the war, leaving the rent unpaid for months.[95] The defendant's absence and the lack of representation in court constituted a recurrent case of a judgment by default,[96] although situations were also accepted in which the defence could not be carried out effectively.[97] There were different positions on whether 'damage' had been caused: only when the Ger-

---

94 Art 296 (2) VPT stated that 'At the request of the Creditor Clearing Office the dispute may, however, be submitted to the jurisdiction of the Courts of the place of domicile of the debtor.' A lawsuit at the creditors domicile (based on art 14 Code Civil) was not admissible: Cour de Cassation, *Schwartzmann v Société Disconto Gesellschaft* (13 March 1929) 8 Recueil MAT 1013 f.

95 In these cases Article 300(b) VPT applied although no judicial decision preceded the enforcement measure —a consequence of the right of pledge that the German civil law gave to the lessor on the furniture of the lessee in case of non-payment of rent.

96 The defendant was outside of Germany as a result of an expulsion order: French–German MAT, *Wilhem v Germany* (21 July 1922) 2 Recueil MAT 426, 427; or he was out of the country at the beginning of the war and could not go back: French–German MAT, *Burtin v Germany and Magdeburger Bank* (15 September 1922) 2 Recueil MAT 450, 453. The presence of a lawyer made it difficult to consider the requirement had been met: Belgian–German MAT, *Ch Petit et Co v Gewerkschaft Glueckaufsegen* (7 October 1922) 2 Recueil MAT 539.

97 The existence of a defence did not automatically exclude art 302(2) VPT. On the other hand, had it been possible it would not have been enough, for art 302 VPT to apply, to claim that it had been a difficult endeavour: British–German MAT, *F L Cook v Germany* (17 and 29 June 1925) 5 Recueil MAT 299–303. The material impossibility of providing evidence was accepted as a case of Article 302, provided it was a consequence of the war, and not of negligence: Italian–German MAT, *Del Favero v Ditta Bassermann e C* (12 January 1925) 5 Recueil MAT 190–200, 197.

man decision was incurred in error[98] or if the situation involved the impossibility of voluntarily satisfying the judgment, exposing the defendant to the consequences of a forced execution.[99] Another practical problem related to the revision of German wartime judgments by the MATs: It was not clear against whom the claim had to be filed—whether against the original claimant or against Germany.[100]

(c) A similar solution applied to contractual claims (outside of Article 296, Article 299 VPT). Here, the competence of the MATs was modified in favour of the nationals of the Allied and Associated Powers: According to Article 304(b)(2) VPT they could either bring their claims before the competent courts in their home states or in Germany.[101] Alternatively, they could sue directly before the MATs. However, Austrian, German and Hungarian nationals could only bring these claims before the MATs.

(2) The second major competence of the MATs related to individual claims of nationals of the allied or associated powers for restitution and compensation of loss of property resulting from extraordinary war measures by Germany and its allies (Article 297(e) and (f) VPT). In this constellation, claims were brought before the MATs against the defeated state represented by its state agent. Here, the main task of the MATs was the assessment of the (individual) losses and the determination of

---

There was an involuntary default when the defendant had not been able to file an appeal because of the shortness of the deadlines: Belgian-German MAT, *Ville d'Anvers v Germany* (19 October 1925) 5 Recueil MAT 712–719, 718.

98 Isay (n 85) 404–405; Belgian-German MAT, *Charles Petit et Cie v Sauer* (1 August 1923) 3 Recueil MAT 545–549: the damage requirement had not been met because '*même habilement défendus, en effet, ils* [the claimants] *eussent dû être condamnés*'.

99 Yugoslav-German MAT *Alexandra et Spasenije Pritza v dame Kathi Fahry* (3 October 1922) 2 Recueil MAT 668–675.

100 For the former Ernst Wolff, *Privatrechtliche Beziehungen zwischen früheren Feinden nach dem Friedensvertrag* (Vahlen 1921) 37, as well as French-German MAT, *Schmidt v Plath* (9 January 1923) 2 Recueil MAT 906, 910. For the latter Isay (n 85) 406, as well as French-German MAT, *Burtin v Germany and Magdeburger Bank* (15 September 1922) 2 Recueil MAT 450, 453; Belgian-German MAT, *Ch Petit et Co c Gewerkschaft Glueckaufsegen* (7 October 1922) 2 Recueil MAT 539; Yugoslavian-German MAT, *Alexandra et Spasenije Pritza v dame Kathi Fahry* (3 October 1922) 2 Recueil MAT 668, 673.

101 Examples: Reichsgericht (16 April 1924) 108 Entscheidungen des Reichsgerichts in Zivilsachen 50, 53; Reichsgericht (15 June 1923) 107 Entscheidungen des Reichsgerichts in Zivilsachen' 76; Reichsgericht (18 October 1926) 114 Entscheidungen des Reichsgerichts in Zivilsachen 421.

the compensation to be paid. The MATs replaced the competent courts in Germany and its former allies.[102]

(3) The third major competence of the MATs related to claims of Austrian, German or Hungarian nationals whose property within the new (associated) states (ie Poland, Czechoslovakia) had been liquidated after the war. The former owners could challenge the compensation provided by those states directly before the MAT under Article 297(h)(2) VPT.[103] Here, the MATs replaced the competent courts of the newly created states.[104]

2.4.2. *Concurrent Pending Jurisdiction in National Courts*

Although the VPT determined the competences of the MAT and delineated them from the jurisdiction of national courts, it did not address the constellation of pending claims at domestic courts when the peace treaty entered into force. In practice, this constellation was resolved with the termination of the national processes. According to Belgian courts, Article 296 VPT '*fait obstacle, pour les dettes visées par lui, à la poursuite de toute procédure entamée comme à l'introduction de toute nouvelle procédure*'.[105] Under Article 304(b) VPT, the wording 'all questions, whatsoever their nature' was interpreted in the sense that it covered ongoing processes, regardless of the procedural state of the pending case.[106] Later, the MATs endorsed the same opinion.[107]

A similar situation of concurring claims arose when the VPT itself opened up more than one forum for the same claim (as provided for by Article 304(b)(2) VPT).[108] Here, the examples we are aware of do not relate

102 Direct conflicts with national courts did not arise as those claims were exclusively filed before the MAT.
103 Ophüls (n 29) vol 3, 173, 175.
104 For additional competences of the MATs, see above (n 20–23).
105 Tribunal de commerce d'Anvers (24 January 1921) 1 Recueil MAT 139, 143.
106 Tribunal supérieur de Colmar (18 January 1922) 2 Recueil MAT 176–77; Cour d'appel de Paris (23 October 1920) 1 Recueil MAT 77; Tribunal supérieur de Colmar (1 March 1922) 2 Recueil MAT 503, 504. Jean Paulin Niboyet, 'Les tribunaux arbitraux mixtes organisés en exécution des traités de paix' [1922] Bulletin de l'Institut Intermédiaire International 215, 234, confirmed that the French courts '*se sont dessaisis d'office*'.
107 French–German MAT, *Héritiers Appel and Germany v Chemin de fer PLM and Office Français* (30 December 1923) 3 Recueil MAT 918–23, 921–22.
108 See above (n 16).

to simultaneous proceedings, but to consecutive ones: Creditors tried to reproduce the dispute before an MAT only after the national court had already delivered an unfavourable decision to them. The (correct) reaction of the MAT was to bar the subsequent proceedings.[109] The question about the admissibility of a *lis pendens* or *res judicata* exception was raised in some cases, albeit only theoretically.[110] The *Reichsgericht* did not permit an action before the German courts (for the repayment of a pre-war debt) once the period for bringing the claim before the MAT had expired.[111]

2.4.3. Finality and Enforceability

According to Article 304(g) VPT, the decisions of the MATs were final and the contracting parties agreed to render them binding upon their nationals. As a rule, there was no appeal opened against them.[112] The judgments of the MATs were directly enforceable in Germany, without any exequatur procedure, Article 302(1) VPT. This was implemented in Germany through the Law of 10 August 1920 conferring on the Landgericht Berlin competence for all enforcement.[113] The same favourable treatment applied to all judgments given by courts of Allied or Associated Powers related to the Peace Treaty.[114]

---

109 French–German MAT, *Banque Meyer v Well Gebrueder* (19 July 1923) 3 Recueil MAT 639, 642; Belgian–German MAT, *Nicaise v Germany and Hoopmann* (21 December 1925) 6 Recueil MAT 93, 94; Belgian–German MAT, *Kairis v Erckens and Germany* (27 June 1928) 8 Recueil MAT 183, 185.

110 Bulgarian-Belgian MAT, *Héritiers de Backer v Municipalité de Philippoli* (27 January 1927) 6 Recueil MAT 144, 146: *Lis pendens* between national courts and an MAT was rejected because it was only possible between courts of the same system and acting on the same degree.

111 Reichsgericht (18 October 1926) 114 Entscheidungen des Reichsgerichts in Zivilsachen 421, 423 f.

112 The parallel provision of the Treaty of Trianon was modified in 1930 by a multilateral convention concluded between Hungary and Czechoslovakia. According to this convention, the PCIJ was the competent appellate instance against the decisions of the MAT, see PCIJ, *Pazman University (Hungary) v Czechoslovakia* (15 December 1933) Rep ser AB no 61, 222.

113 Nevertheless, the enforcement itself was entrusted to the state agents of the MATs, and carried out in accordance with the pertinent national provisions, under the condition that they did not frustrate the objective of the VPT rule. *Landgericht* (regional tribunal) Stettin (15 March 1924) 4 Recueil MAT 140–42.

114 The full suppression of exequatur proceedings and of grounds for non-recognition went further than the present situation in European procedural law (cf art

An additional empowerment of the MATs related to the cassation of the judgments of Austrian, German and Hungarian courts. Whereas Article 305, first sentence VPT gave the MATs the general power to review national judgments with regard to their conformity with the peace treaty, they were empowered to directly set aside German judgments in favour of allied or associated creditors, Article 305, second sentence VPT.

Yet, German creditors (and creditors of the (former) allies of Germany) were not entitled to any preferential treatment if they won their case before the MAT. Recognition and enforcement of these judgments were based on the general rules regarding the recognition and enforcement of foreign civil judgments.[115]

3. *The Legal Nature of the Mixed Arbitral Tribunals*

3.1. *The Contemporary Debate*

One of the most debated issues in the literature between the 1920s and the 1930s was the nature of the MATs. Were they national adjudicatory bodies, international ones, or rather a *tertium genus*? Should they be considered as an exceptional jurisdiction or as a general one? Both questions, especially the latter, had a significant impact in practice.

3.1.1. *National or International Tribunals*

Scholars addressing the issue of the national or international nature of the MATs reached different conclusions depending on what decisive criterion they followed: the origin of the institution or its function. Based on origin, MATs were indisputably international bodies.[116] However, a functional approach led to further distinctions following the taxonomy of the controver-

---

45 of the Regulation (EU) 1215/2012). Contemporary observers, however, considered the MATs as *Sondergerichte* (special national courts). Consequently, exequatur proceedings were not required, Reichsgericht, 15 June 1923, 'Entscheidungen des Reichsgerichts in Zivilsachen' vol 107, 76, 77.

115 Schätzel (n 12) 378, 418.

116 Burchard (n 24) 472, 476 (addressing the specific constellations of the German-US claims tribunal); Hans Joachim Hallier, *Völkerrechtliche Schiedsinstanzen für Einzelpersonen und ihr Verhältnis zur innerstaatlichen Gerichtsbarkeit: Eine Untersuchung der Praxis seit 1945* (Heymann 1962) 14, 15.

sies allocated to the MATs. Taking as starting point the idea that international tribunals deal with disputes between states, Blühdorn excluded the MATs from the category when they addressed individual conflicts within the framework of Article 304(b)(2) VPT. The same was done in cases falling within their competence under the scope of Article 296 VPT. Conversely, MATs were considered international when they fixed the compensations referred to in Article 297 VPT. In this constellation, the individual was not considered bringing a right of his own, but one of the allied or associated Power. [117]

Other authors shared this opinion only to some extent. As a starting point, the view on Article 304(b) was uncontroversial: The competence of the MATs for contractual disputes between individuals was said to be tantamount to the one of the national courts to the point that some scholars considered MATs as internal civil courts, with the particularity that their decisions deployed effectiveness simultaneously in two legal spheres: those of the states of the nationals involved.[118] Some major difficulty was experienced in relation to Article 296 VPT due to the presence in these cases of a state on the side of both the debtor and the creditor. However, the fact that the state's intervention was not carried out as an exercise of sovereignty—the obligation of the state being ancillary to the private obligation relationship—allowed the conclusion that MATs were internal bodies as well.[119] Finally, the greatest controversy that arose regarding Article 297 VPT was the nature of the right to claim of the individual; the question about whether he acted in his own name, on behalf of the state or even as an organ of the state remained unclear.[120] In opposition to Blühdorn, Geier argued that the right conferred by Article 297 VPT found its root in the German legal system. According to him, it was a consequence of the state trespassing into a private right in the name of the common good; thus, it corresponded to the field of administrative law. In this context, the MATs were also considered as internal jurisdictional bodies of the states. [121]

117 Blühdorn (n 14) 144–146.

118 Georg Geier, *Das internationale Privatrecht der Gemischten Schiedsgerichte des Versailles Vertrages* (1930) 7; Calamendrei (n 53) 293, 333, called them '*tribunali anfibi*'.

119 Geier (n 118) 10–11, with further references.

120 See supra n 60 on the position of the MAT.

121 Geier (n 118) 13. From a modern point of view, this debate demonstrates that the access of the individual as a party to an international adjudicative body was an unknown concept in the 1920s.

3.1.2. General/Special Jurisdiction

The question whether the MATs were bestowed with general or special jurisdiction received different answers both in literature and in the case law, although it seems that among the MATs, as well as before the national courts, the idea of an exceptional jurisdiction prevailed. As a consequence, the prevailing view was that the competences of the MATs had to be interpreted narrowly. However, for other authors, the MATs' jurisdiction was general (or comprehensive) for all the subjects included in sections III, IV, V and VII of the VPT. A third group of scholars qualified the jurisdiction as special or common according to the type of controversy at stake: special jurisdiction for claims between individuals and common for the claims opposing an individual and the enemy state.[122]

The lack of agreement extended to practice. An early decision of the French–German MAT, *Société vinicole de Champagne v Mumm*,[123] defended the broadest interpretation: the MATs' jurisdiction 'is general for all matters corresponding to sections III, IV, V and VII', without it being possible to interpret the list of subject matters enumerated in the VPT as limitative, because it would be absurd not to allow MATs to decide about issues equal to those for which jurisdiction had been expressly conferred to them.[124] However, the decision was soon contested: the Polish–German MAT's decision in *Leo von Tiedemann v Poland*, of 21 May 1923, was frequently quoted as the leading case in this regard;[125] others followed where the jurisdiction of the MATs was literally confined to the cases where it clearly[126] resorted from the peace provisions that the contracting states '*ont entendu distraire le*

---

122 Calamandrei (n 53) 293, 299, represents the former opinion. Gilbert Gidel and Henry Émile Barrault, *Le Traité de Paix avec l'Allemagne du 28 Juin 1919 et les Intérêts Privés: commentaires des Dispositions de la Partie X du Traité de Versailles*, (Librairie Générale de Droit et de Jurisprudence 1921) 19, are representatives of the second view. For the third opinion Hermann Isay, 'Die Zuständigkeit der Gemischten Schiedsgerichte' [1924] Juristische Wochenschrift 596, 597. All opinions were strongly influenced by the respective nationality of the authors.

123 French–German MAT, *Société vinicole de Champagne v Mumm* (5 March 1921) 1 Recueil MAT 22–27, for a critique Strupp (n 6) 661, 663. The economic and political background of the case was explained by Göppert (n 34), 60–62.

124 Here one should consider that the decision was about the infringement (or distribution) of IP rights between the parties in third states.

125 Polish–German MAT, *Leo von Tiedemann v Poland* (21 May 1923) 3 Recueil MAT 596, 601–606; Belgian–German MAT *Joseph Zurstrassen et Cie v Germany* (22 May 1924) 4 Recueil MAT 326, 338.

126 Although without a requirement of an *expressis verbis* endowment.

défendeur de son juge naturel pour le soumettre à la juridiction exceptionnelle des TAM.'[127]

The idea of a restricted jurisdiction was echoed by national courts. Although the were willing to give up their own jurisdiction—even by closing on-going procedures upon the VPT entering into force—they understood the material scope of the MATs' assignment as limited and conducted a strict reading of the VPT terms. In this regard, an English judge explicitly stated that an MAT decision 'can only be conclusive within the limits assigned to it by the Treaty. It cannot ... assume jurisdiction in matters outside its province'.[128] Other national decisions concurred in that MATs only disposed of an exceptional or special jurisdiction. Consequently, the VPT provisions, to the point, had to be narrowly interpreted.[129]

The specific nature of the MATs was also highlighted by several decisions of the PCIJ. Repeatedly, the PCIJ was asked to interpret the peace treaties, especially to delineate the part on reparations (Article 231ff VPT) from the economic provisions.[130] Another dispute related to the issue of whether liquidated assets in Upper Silesia had been in the ownership/possession of the German State or of German nationals, who would be entitled to compensation under Article 297(h) VPT.[131] In *Certain German Interests in Upper Silesia*, the PCIJ clearly stated that there was no pendency between the MATs and the PCIJ because the MATs were only competent to decide about the restitution of a company whereas the PCIJ was asked to interpret the peace treaty (as a whole).[132] Eventually, the PCIJ considered

127 Serb–Austrian MAT, *Wapa v Austria and others* (23 March 1923) 3 Recueil MAT 720, 728; Serb–Bulgarian MAT, *Raffinerie et Sucrerie serbo-tchèque Tchoupria v Bulgaria* (3 April 1923) 3 Recueil MAT 185, 191; Czechoslovakian–German MAT, *Paalen v Germany* (27 April 1923) 3 Recueil MAT 993, 997.

128 Decision of the English Controller and Registrar of Patents (5 and 8 May 1922) 2 Recueil MAT 164, 172.

129 Cour d'appel de Bruxelles (20 March 1922) 1 Recueil MAT 959, 961; Cour d'appel de Liège (28 March 1924) 4 Recueil MAT 160 ff.

130 PCIJ, *Treaty of Neuilly, Article 179, Annex, Paragraph 4 (Interpretation)* (12 September 1924) Rep ser A no 3.

131 PCIJ, *Certain German Interests in Upper Silesia* (25 May 1926) Rep ser A no 7, 33.

132 PCIJ, *Certain German Interests in Upper Silesia* (Admissibility) (25 August 1925) Rep ser A no 6, 19–20. From a dogmatic point of view, this argument was not convincing as the PCIJ did not take up the facts and the (direct) applicable law of the case at hand in order to assess whether the same claims were involved. Instead, it adopted a formalistic view.

itself as a court of general jurisdiction (competent for the interpretation of international law) and the peace treaties being a part of it.[133]

3.2. *Modern Parallels*

The debate about the legal nature of the MATs recalls the debate about the legal nature of other modern international courts and tribunals deciding on claims of individuals against states and international organizations such as the Iran–US Claims Tribunal,[134] the United Nations Compensation Commission[135] or the Eritrea–Ethiopia Claims Commission.[136] The most interesting parallelism relates to investment arbitration.[137] Although both areas of law are different and the current structure of investment arbitration does not correspond to the institutionalized dispute resolution by arbitral tribunals, there are some similarities to be mentioned here.

First of all, there is a basic resemblance. In a non-technical way, the MATs protected private investments (especially in the case of Article 297(e) VPT) in the belligerent states which had been affected by economic warfare.[138] The procedural standing of the individuals before the bodies corresponds to the position of individual investors before modern arbitral tribunals. The similarities might even increase if permanent investment courts were to be established.[139] Today, the relationship between domestic courts and investment arbitral tribunals is sometimes described as that of jurisdictions belonging to two different spheres, ie domestic and international law. In this context, some authors refer to the case law of the PCIJ

133 Surprisingly, this judgment is still quoted as an authority for the distinction between international and domestic courts, especially in the context of investment arbitration, cf Hess (n 16) 49, para 242 (with further references).

134 Hans Van Houtte, 'International Tribunals and Conflict of Laws: Recent Examples' in Rafaël Jafferali, Vanessa Marquette and Arnaud Nuyts (eds), Liber amicorum Nadine Watté (Bruylant 2017) 517, 522 ff.

135 Hess (n 16) 49, para 95 ff.

136 Van Houtte (n 134) 517, 526 ff.

137 Hess (n 16) 49, para 104 f.

138 Eg, factories owned by enemy nationals had been put under trusteeship, see above (n 3).

139 Cf the proposals of the EU Commission concerning a multilateral investment court. See the negotiating directives for a Convention establishing a multilateral court for the settlement of investment disputes (20 March 2018) <http://data.consilium.europa.eu/doc/document/ST-12981-2017-ADD-1-DCL-1/en/pdf> accessed 29 November 2018.

regarding the MATs as belonging to a different order. However, in the case law of the PCIJ, the MATs were (somewhat) more assimilated to domestic courts than to international tribunals. Therefore, the parallel is not entirely convincing.

4. Private International Law in the Case Law of the Mixed Arbitral Tribunals

4.1. Nationality and Standing

As the jurisdiction of each MAT (and the admissibility of the claim) depended on the nationality of the claimant, disputes about nationality played a pivotal role in the case law of the MATs. As a starting point, each plaintiff had to bring a claim to the MAT established by his 'home state'.[140] This rule also applied to claims brought by a variety of plaintiffs.[141] The crucial moment for this requirement was the filing of the claim.[142] From the defendants' perspective, contesting the nationality of the claimants was often the most promising (or even the only) defence available (especially in the context of Article 297 VPT).[143] Against this background, it is no surprise that considerable case law of the MATs related to the nationality of the parties—especially to the control of moral persons by shareholders.[144] However, the principles applied in this context were specific to the extraordinary war measures. As a result, the case law regarding corporations was contradictory.[145]

140 Belgian–German MAT, *Charles Petit et Cie v Thun* (29 October 1922) 2 Recueil MAT 401–402: A claim of a Belgian creditor against a Dutch debtor resident in Germany was declared inadmissible because the defendant was not a German national.

141 British–German MAT, *Koch v Landauer Nachfolger* (7 and 17 December 1923) 3 Recueil MAT 772, 774. The nationality was determined according to the domestic laws of the state concerned, Kurt Lipstein, 'Conflict of Laws before International Tribunals. A Study in the Relation between International Law and Conflict of Laws: Part II' (1943) 29 Transactions of the Grotius Society 51, 68.

142 Again, a uniform approach was missing, Schätzel (n 12) 378, 426–430; Lipstein (n 141) 51, 67–69.

143 Schätzel (n 12) 378, 424; Kurt Lipstein, 'Conflict of Laws Before International Tribunals: A Study in the Relation Between International Law and Conflict of Laws: Part 1' (1941) 27 Transactions of the Grotius Society 142 ff.

144 Lipstein (n 143) 142, 160 ff.

145 Schätzel (n 12) 378, 429; Lipstein (n 141) 51, 69. Some MATs applied the incorporation theory, others the control theory.

A much contested issue in the context of Article 296 VPT was the nationality of the inhabitants of Alsace-Lorraine. Here, the German government argued that this group had to be considered as Germans until November 1918. The French government argued that this group had always had a 'virtual French citizenship.' Eventually the French–German MAT endorsed this concept.[146] As a result, more than 20,000 additional claims from Alsace-Lorraine were filed with the MAT; German observers criticized this, arguing that these claims had been systematically collected by 'French agents.'[147]

4.2. The Application of Conflict of Law Rules by the MATs

One of the most interesting questions about the disputes allocated to the MATs relates to the determination of the applicable law, an issue that came up frequently before the MATs. On the one hand, there was almost no explicit provision in this regard; thus, for many questions the MATs did not find a direct response in the Peace Treaties.[148] On the other hand, MATs did not belong to the judicial systems of the contracting states and therefore had no *lex fori*: The determination of the applicable law could not be made by reference to the conflict of law rules of these legal systems.[149]

4.2.1. The Debate Among Scholars

Many contemporary authors of diverse nationalities addressed the issue of which law was to be applied by the MATs, either in general terms, or in

146 French–German MAT, *Veuve Heim v Germany* (30 June 1921 until 19 August 1921) 1 Recueil MAT, 381; French–German MAT, *Chamant v Germany* (23 June–25 August 1921) 1 Recueil MAT 361.

147 Schätzel (n 12) 378, 425 ff. This phenomenon can be seen as a precursor of the current practice of 'ambulance chasing.'

148 The VPT referred to the applicable law only exceptionally: It is worth mentioning Article 296, Annex no 4, where the laws on prescription in force in the country of domicile of the debtor were mentioned in relation to the bar of a debt. The situation was entirely different for the Reparations Commission. Here, art 244 Annex II no 11 VPT stated: 'The Commission shall not be bound by any particular code or rules of law or by any particular rule of evidence or of procedure, but shall be guided by justice, equity and good faith. Its decisions must follow the same principles and rules in all cases where they are applicable …'

149 The *lex fori* solution was nevertheless supported by some scholars, see below.

their comments on specific decisions. A reading of the scholarly texts of the time reveals two perspectives: a merely narrative one, limited to describing the treatment that the conflict of laws problem received on the part of the MATs; and a normative one, which focuses critically on what the MATs should do or should have done on this point. Seen from a distance, the latter is more interesting. The very question about private international law and the MATs, the lack of response thereto or, when there was one, the lack of uniformity spurred the doctrine to develop different theories—in the framework of which essential issues of the discipline were addressed.

Interestingly, many contemporary scholars proposed that the conflict of law rules should be common to all countries; great hopes had been placed on the MATs in this regard,[150] leading, as we will see, to equally great disappointments.[151] Another group of authors favoured instead the application of national conflict of rules, albeit without consensus on which ones these should be. The point of departure for each opinion was the corresponding view on the nature, national or international, of the MATs.[152] The proponents of the former, in spite of sharing a common starting point, disagreed as to which national law should be applied. A first, not very successful proposal, advocated for the application of a national system to the exclusion of its PIL rules, arguing that the VPT always favours the national of the Allied or associated powers. The representatives of this view concluded that German law would never be applied, but always that of the other party.[153]

150 Niboyet (n 49) 97,104: '*les tribunaux arbitraux mixtes … ont la mission de dire le droit et se trouvent dans la situation enviable où l'on peut choisir la solution qui paraît la meilleure sans être lié par aucun texte. Comme tels ils peuvent être des véritables fondateurs du droit international privé. Ils bâtissent à neuf et leur jurisprudence pourrait devenir une source importante pour l'avenir s'ils le voulaient*'. Similarly, Calamandrei (n 53) 293, 337, MATs are called to '*risolvere la questione secondo i criteri che esso Tribunale adotterebbe ove fosse chiamato come legislatore internazionale a formulare un sistema di principi relativi alla competenza legislativa e giudiziaria dei vari Stati*'.

151 Jean Paulin Niboyet, 'Le rôle de la justice internationale en droit international privé: conflit des lois' (1932) 40 Recueil des Cours 153, 230 f; Lipstein (n 141) 51, 67 f.

152 The 'bilateral' nature of the MAT supported this approach.

153 Sipsom, 'Mémoire', quoted by Romanian–German MAT, *P Negreanu v Meyer* (16 June 1925) 5 Recueil MAT 200, 207, 211, which explicitly rejects it. See as well British–German MAT, *S Hardt & Co v M B Stern* (27 March 1922) 3 Recueil MAT 14, 17, on the equal treatment of allies and German nationals.

The idea of a *lex fori*, firmly rejected by some scholars, was still supported by others who in turn differed as to the prevailing criterion to identify it: the nationality of the arbitrators of the two countries involved, provided the designated legal systems coincided contents-wise;[154] or the law that the competent judge would have applied had he been seized of the dispute.[155] The cumulative application of the legal systems of the states represented in a given MAT was defended by those who believed the MATs were state bodies through which the states exercised their jurisdiction, having thus the expectation (even the right) to have their own private international law rules applied by the Mixed Arbitral Tribunals.[156]

Scholars who claimed that the jurisdiction of the MATs did not have national but international roots derived different solutions in terms of applicable law. For some, the MATs were not subject to specific, predetermined conflict of law rules. Rather, they should try to identify common substantive answers in the legal systems present, which, when added to general principles, would sustain an '*internationales Weltprivatrecht*' for international trade.[157] Other scholars who believed, in addition, that MATs were free from a specific PIL system argued that for any divergence between the conflict of law rules between the different legal systems MATs should look for '*einem überstaatlichen internationalen Privatrecht irgendwelcher Art*',[158] to be derived from public international law and the principles of personal and territorial sovereignty.[159]

In a similar vein, in the light of the Treaty's silence, these scholars preferred a '*völkerrechtsgemäße*' solution (ie a solution in accordance with inter-

154 It was proposed, but finally rejected, by Albrecht Mendelssohn-Bartholdy, 'Die Vorkriegsvertraege (Art. 299 des FV) und das internationale Privatrecht' [1921] Juristische Wochenschrift 133, 134. Geier (n 118) 20, with further references. Niboyet (n 49) 97, 104, who criticizes the solution for its pragmatic—as opposed to dogmatic—character, nevertheless accepts it as 'comfortable and legitimate'.

155 Schauer, 'Zur Frage der Anwendung des internationalen Privatrechts durch die Ausgleichsämter und die gemischten Schiedsgerichtshöfe' [1920] Deutsche Juristen-Zeitung 425, 427. For Blühdorn (n 14) 141, 194, in cases where the MATs acted as equivalent to national courts, the applicable law had to be the one a German court would have applied, for the MATs were set up to take over their role.

156 Geier (n 118) 47–59.

157 Walter Grau, 'Versailler Frieden (Privatrechliche Bestimmungen)' in Karl Strupp (ed), *Wörterbuch des Völkerrechts und der Diplomatie* (3rd vol, 1st edn, Walter De Gruyter & Co 1929) 48, 65.

158 Ernst Zitelmann, *Internationales Privatrecht* (1st edn, vol 1, Duncker & Humboldt 1897) 77.

159 The contemporary debate was thoroughly analysed by Lipstein (n 143) 34, 37–38.

national law). Accordingly, MAT decisions should be based on the minimum requirements imposed by public international law relating to private law, referred to as *'überstaatliche Internationalprivatrechtssätze'*,[160] such as: the recognition of vested rights; connecting points which are generally accepted and can be qualified as customary, such as the *lex rei sitae* for real estate rights; with more reservations, the closest connection, meaning the national legal system to which the circumstances of the case pointed preponderantly. These rules were deemed not only relevant per se, but because they should also inspire the MATs when addressing remaining issues.[161]

4.2.2. The Case Law of the MATs

Questions about the applicable law arose frequently before the MATs as it could not be assumed that all controversies submitted to them necessarily presented a cross-border element. The attitudes were very diverse, evolving over time and changing from MAT to MAT. It is possible to detect an evolution that goes from seeking support in good faith, or in equity,[162] to the application of the positive rules in force in the national legal systems. However, a common approach in that sense did not exist, either from the perspective of the method or in terms of concrete solutions. As a rule, disputes were solved on a case by case basis, and most often pragmatically. Without pretending to systematize an incomprehensible casuistry, one can ascertain the following trends: avoiding the issue (eg when the systems of the two states involved present, or are assumed to do so, an identical material solution);[163] absence of any pronouncement on the method accounting for the solution adopted (the MAT proceeds to the immediate application of a substantive solution, replacing those provided in all potentially applicable

160 Franz Kahn, 'Abhandlungen zum internationalen Privatrecht I' (1928) 284–87.

161 Especially Gutzwiller (n 49) 123, 126 ff.

162 In some regulations, the principles of justice and equity were referred to as grounding both the procedural and the material solutions: see for instance Rules of Procedure of the French–German MAT (2 April 1920) 1 Recueil MAT 57, art 99.

163 French–German MAT, *Rumeau v Schmidt* (26 July 1922) 2 Recueil MAT 325, 327; French–German MAT, *Munzing et Cie v Still* (24 November 1922) 2 Recueil MAT 747, 749. Jean Paulin Niboyet, 'Quelques considérations sur la justice internationale et le droit international privé' [1929] Mélanges Antoine Pillet 163. See criticism by Romanian–German MAT, *P Negreanu v Meyer* (16 June 1925) 5 Recueil MAT 200, 210, '... *car dans bien des cas, l'étude approfondie des deux droits révèle des divergences, qui n'apparaissent pas à première vue*'.

legal systems); [164] resort without further justification to connecting points (especially to more than one, when either of them would lead to the same final outcome;[165] or to an alleged choice of the parties to the controversy).[166] Finally, some decisions were based on (assumed) general principles of law: respect for vested rights,[167] the application of the personal law of the deceased in succession matters,[168] the law of the place where the contract is concluded for contractual obligations,[169] and others whose 'universal' character today would certainly be disputed (such as applying the law of the nationality of each of the parties to determine the content of their respective obligations).[170]

From a modern perspective, one must assume that the MATs did not develop a comprehensive jurisprudence on conflict of laws. They addressed outstanding issues on a case-by-case approach. Generally, their perspective was influenced by the specific bilateral situation of the case at hand. Often, conflict of law issues remained undecided because the MAT came to the conclusion that potentially applicable substantive laws of the two states involved were identical.[171] This solution was criticized by the legal doctrine[172] but appears understandable against the background of the huge case load on which the MAT had to decide. As a result, the case law of the MATs appeared to be scattered and fragmented. Finally, there are only a

164 Niboyet (n 163) 105; Geier (n 118) 30, would nevertheless support a less critical reading, according to which the MATs were simply not disclosing the connecting point.

165 Romanian–German MAT, *S Landes v W Schuster* (25 July 1927) 7 Recueil MAT 747, 750; Romanian–German MAT, *Société Phoenix v Germany* (24 July 1926) 7 Recueil MAT 103, 110.

166 Czechoslovakian–German MAT, *Gellert v Kolker* (24 October 1923) 4 Recueil MAT 515, 520; Czechoslovakian–German MAT, *Goldschmiedt v Heesch Hinrichsen et Cie* (30 November 1923) 4 Recueil MAT 530, 534; Czechoslovakian–German MAT, *Loy and Markus v Germany and Deutsch Ostafrikanische Bank AG* (22 April 1925) 5 Recueil MAT 551, 563.

167 Romanian–Hungarian MAT, *Emeric Kulin père v Romania* (10 January 1927) 7 Recueil MAT 138–150.

168 French–German MAT, *Zeppenfeld v Germany* (30 March 1926) 6 Recueil MAT 243, 247.

169 Belgian–German MAT, *Medts v Graff* (9 January 1924) 3 Recueil MAT 798, 800.

170 Romanian–German MAT, *P Negreanu v Meyer* (16 June 1925) 5 Recueil MAT 200, 211.

171 In this respect, the composition of the tribunal was helpful as familiarity with the two applicable legal systems was represented at the bench.

172 Niboyet (n 151) 153, 221 ff; Gutzwiller (n 49) 123, 137.

few decisions where the MATs developed general principles of conflicts of law which could serve as a general reference.[173]

5. Assessment

5.1. A Preferred Way of Dispute Settlement in the 1920s

After the First World War, the settlement of private disputes arising out of the war by international arbitral tribunals was considered a positive step. This attitude even applied to the defeated countries, although the one-sided approach of the peace treaties triggered considerable resistance and frustration. However, within the small group of arbitrators, state agents and the ministries involved, a more cooperative spirit grew over the years, except for when political crises like the occupation of the Ruhr Region between 1923 and 1925 created considerable tension within the MATs. Nevertheless, the regime of the MATs did not always work to the detriment of German parties (and Germany's former allies). For instance, the competence of the Polish–German MAT operated in favour of the expropriated German owners of factories and (large scale) farms. In this context, it was reported that the Polish–German MAT was not less unpopular in Poland than the MATs with the Allied powers in Germany.[174] The abrupt termination of most of the MATs by the Young Agreements in 1930 was the main reason why the experiment of the MATs was quickly forgotten—despite their case law being widely discussed in the 1930s.

5.2. A Practical Drawback: The Fragmentation of the Case Law

One feature of the MAT decisions was the lack of uniformity of the case law. MATs addressed disputes on a case-by-case basis and not through decisions of principle.[175] They were not bound by their previous decisions or by those of others (although cross-references may be identified); thus, it is not surprising that they did not create a true body of jurisprudence. Like the Clearing Offices, which developed a spontaneous practice to hold regu-

173 As highlighted by Lipstein (n 141) 51, 68 ff.

174 Schätzel (n 12) 378, 391.

175 Lipstein (n 143) 142, 150; Gutzwiller (n 49) 123, 128 f; Niboyet (n 151) 153, 222.

lar conferences which allowed for solving problems uniformly,[176] some attempts were made to unify the case law—for instance, the four sections of the French–German MAT created a collegiate body composed of the four presidents plus one arbitrator of each state—but this attempt did not come to fruition.[177] Finally, and decisively, the state parties were not interested in establishing a self-standing judiciary competent to interpret the peace treaties. In this respect, the 'bilateralization' of the individual MATs is telling. On the other hand, the PCIJ was asked to decide on precise aspects of the peace treaties, but there was no intention of the state parties to entrust the PCIJ with the task of being the last arbiter with regard to the peace treaties.[178] In the political tensions of 1930s, the idea of a peaceful settlement of political disputes was quickly lost.[179]

5.3. Are There Lessons to be Learned?

After 1945, the Mixed Arbitral Tribunals were more or less forgotten in international practice. The peace treaties after World War II did not foresee MATs but did provide for some mixed commissions.[180] Obviously, the lack of interest was due to the negative perception of the work of the MATs in contemporary practice. They were disregarded because of the fragmentation of the case law, the politicization of the disputes and also because their dissolution occurred so quickly in the 1930s.[181]

On the other hand, regional international courts were established in the Western (democratic) post-war societies. The ECtHR and the CJEU are powerful examples of international judiciaries with far-reaching competences to set a level playing field where human rights and fundamental val-

---

176 Gidel & Barrault (n 122) xxiv.

177 Walter Schätzel, *Das deutsch-französische Gemischte Schiedsgericht, seine Geschichte, Rechtsprechung und Ergebnisse* (Stilke 1930) 16.

178 See above (n 133). One should not forget that the PCIJ had been set up by art 14 VPT.

179 In this respect, it is telling that most doctrinal articles on the MATs were published in the early 1930s.

180 Dolzer Rudolf, 'Mixed Claims Commissions' in Wolfrum Rüdiger (ed) *Max Planck Encyclopedia of Public International Law* (OUP 2011).

181 Ernst Rabel, 'International Tribunals for Private Matters' (1948) 3 Arbitration Journal 209: 'International tribunals ought to be established totally different from the Mixed Arbitral Tribunals of the Versailles Treaty'. No further explanation was given regarding this bold statement.

ues are respected and implemented. Here, the role of the individual as a party on the international plane has been recognized.[182]

From a modern point of view, the work of the MATs should be reassessed. The MATs worked in a very difficult political and one-sided environment, but the tribunals were able to handle a multitude of claims—in modern terms, mass claims—in an efficient and fair way. In this regard, the modernity of the procedures applied is impressive. They were able to process claims via standard forms and, under the control of state agents, to accelerate the proceedings by time limits, by standardizing claim forms and by concentrating the proceedings in one hearing. Finally, the design of the proceedings permitted the settlement of important parts of the cases. On the other hand, the fragmentation of the case law of the individual adjudicative bodies is a phenomenon which is equally found in modern dispute resolution, especially in investment dispute settlement. The main reason was (and still is) the lack of a superior instance which might be able to establish a 'jurisprudence constante'. This problem is still found in modern dispute resolution, and it remains to be seen whether the efforts of the European Union to establish a permanent investment court might change the situation. All in all, it seems to be high time to appreciate the work and the achievements of the Mixed Arbitral Tribunals in a more comprehensive and more positive perspective.

182 It should be noted that many jurists who had been involved in the work of the MATs were later involved in the establishment of the European Court of Justice as well. Cf Erpelding (ch 12).

Chapter 12 Local International Adjudication: The Groundbreaking 'Experiment' of the Arbitral Tribunal for Upper Silesia

Michel Erpelding[*]

1. *Introduction: Mitigating the Side-Effects of Self-Determination*

On 20 March 1921, French tanks and infantrymen could be seen patrolling the streets of Kattowitz—or Katowice, as it was known to its Polish-speaking inhabitants—in Upper Silesia.[1] The troops were part of a multinational force comprising up to 20,000 British, French, and Italian soldiers under the command of French general Jules Gratier (1863–1956). They had been dispatched to Upper Silesia in February 1920 to keep the peace and guarantee the safety of the Inter-Allied Government and Plebiscite Commission of Upper Silesia based in Oppeln/Opole.[2] Presided by another French general, Henri Le Rond (1864–1949), the Commission had been tasked with organizing a referendum of self-determination in parts of the region pursuant to article 88 Treaty of Versailles and the new principle of self-determination. In the meantime, it also replaced the German *Reich* and the Prussian State in administering the plebiscite area.[3] This made Upper Silesia

---

* Senior Research Fellow, Max Planck Institute Luxembourg for Procedural Law. I would like to thank Professors Hélène Ruiz Fabri and Burkhard Hess for their encouragement and guidance. My gratitude also extends to Martyna Fałkowska-Clarys, Aravind Ganesh, Luca Pasquet, Lidia Sokolowska, and Derek Stemple for their help.

1 Agence Rol, 'Kattowitz [Katowice en Pologne], tanks et soldats français assurant l'ordre, place du Théâtre [lors du plébiscite de la Haute-Silésie du 20 mars 1921]' (press photograph) <http://gallica.bnf.fr> accessed 25 May 2018.

2 Karsten Eichner, *Briten, Franzosen und Italiener in Oberschlesien, 1920–1922* (Scripta Mercaturae 2002) 50–52.

3 Art 88 Versailles Treaty included the following provisions: 'In the portion of Upper Silesia included within the boundaries described below, the inhabitants will be called upon to indicate by a vote whether they wish to be attached to Germany or to Poland … Germany hereby renounces in favour of Poland all rights and title over the portion of Upper Silesia lying beyond the frontier line fixed by the Principal Allied and Associated Powers as the result of the plebiscite.' The Annex to art 88 Versailles Treaty described the Inter-Allied Commission's wide-ranging powers:

one of several theatres of international territorial administration in the interwar period.[4]

The presence of heavily armed foreign troops in Upper Silesia was linked to the area's long history as a disputed border region. Although Upper Silesia had not been under the Polish Crown since the 14th century, and had been conquered by Prussia in 1742,[5] the majority of its population spoke either Polish, or the related Upper Silesian dialect, as their mother

'§ 2. The plebiscite area shall be immediately placed under the authority of an International Commission of four members to be designated by the following Powers: the United States of America, France, the British Empire, and Italy. It shall be occupied by troops belonging to the Allied and Associated Powers, and the German Government undertakes to give facilities for the transference of these troops to Upper Silesia.
§ 3. The Commission shall enjoy all the powers exercised by the German or the Prussian Government, except those of legislation or taxation. It shall also be substituted for the Government of the province and the Regierungsbezirk. It shall be within the competence of the Commission to interpret the powers hereby conferred upon it and to determine to what extent it shall exercise them, and to what extent they shall be left in the hands of the existing authorities.
Changes in the existing laws and the existing taxation shall only be brought into force with the consent of the Commission.
The Commission will maintain order with the help of the troops which will be at its disposal, and, to the extent which it may deem necessary, by means of gendarmerie recruited among the inhabitants of the country.
The Commission shall provide immediately for the replacement of the evacuated German officials and, if occasion arises, shall itself order the evacuation of such authorities and proceed to the replacement of such local authorities as may be required.
It shall take all steps which it thinks proper to ensure the freedom, fairness, and secrecy of the vote. In particular, it shall have the right to order the expulsion of any person who may in any way have attempted to distort the result of the plebiscite by methods of corruption or intimidation.
The Commission shall have full power to settle all questions arising from the execution of the present clauses. It shall be assisted by technical advisers chosen by it from among the local population.
The decisions of the Commission shall be taken by a majority vote.' Treaty of Peace between the Allied and Associated Powers and Germany (signed 28 June 1919, entered into force 10 January 1920) [1919] 225 CTS 188.

4 Four other Inter-Allied plebiscite commissions organized plebiscites after the First World War. The votes took place in Schleswig, Allenstein and Marienwerder, Klagenfurt, and Sopron. Alan James, 'The Peacekeeping Role of the League of Nations' (1999) 6 International Peacekeeping 154, 159.

5 Eichner (n 2) 11–12.

tongue.[6] During the 19th century, it had become Germany's second-largest industrial area after the Ruhr.[7] Its demography had also evolved over that period, due to an influx of German specialized workers and administrators, the emigration of Polish-speaking Upper Silesians to the Western parts of the Reich, urbanization, a general increase in education levels, and German assimilation policies. The period between 1871 and 1914 had seen an increasing antagonism between German and Polish nationalists. This binary confrontation did not necessarily reflect the complex cultural situation in the region—a situation comparable to that of other European border regions, such as Alsace, Carinthia, Schleswig, South Tyrol, or Luxembourg.[8] But nationalism was clearly on the rise. After Germany's defeat in 1918 and the announced rebirth of the Polish State, the tensions within Upper Silesia intensified. To complicate the situation even further, the region became a major point of contention between the Allies. During the Versailles treaty negotiations, Germany managed to drive a wedge between France and Britain regarding the fate of Upper Silesia. While the French were determined to uphold the Allies' original plan attributing the region to Poland, the British soon endorsed the German argument that losing Upper Silesia would render the country unable to meet its reparation payments. Recourse to self-determination under international supervision eventually emerged as the only viable compromise.[9]

---

6 Ryszard Kaczmarek, 'Menschen—Bevölkerungsverhältnisse, soziale Struktur, religiöse und ethnische Gliederung' in Joachim Bahlcke, Dan Gawrecki and Ryszard Kaczmarek (eds), *Geschichte Oberschlesiens: Politik, Wirtschaft und Kultur von den Anfängen bis zur Gegenwart* (De Gruyter Oldenbourg 2015) 47, 63–65.

7 Eichner (n 2) 12. See also Piotr Greiner, 'Die Entwicklung der Wirtschaft vom 16. bis zum 20. Jahrhundert' in Bahlcke/Gawrecki/Kaczmarek (n 6) 427, 447–48.

8 Roland Gehrke, 'Vom Völkerfrühling bis zum Ersten Weltkrieg (1848-1918)' in Bahlcke/Gawrecki/Kaczmarek (n 6) 264–69.

9 Eichner (n 2) 18–30. See also Margaret MacMillan, *Paris 1919: Six Months that Changed the World* (Random House 2003) 219–21.

French patrol in Katowice/Kattowitz during the plebiscite of 20 March 1921. Press photograph by Rol news agency. Source: gallica.bnf.fr / Bibliothèque nationale de France.

However, calling on Upper Silesians to decide on remaining with Germany or joining Poland did not defuse local tensions. As a matter of fact, both before and after the plebiscite of 20 March 1921, Polish insurgents clashed with German paramilitary forces in order to influence the outcome. Putting the region under international administration for at least a year before holding the plebiscite was supposed to prevent this eventuality, and provide local populations with a 'cooling off period.'[10] In practice, the Inter-Allied Commission did little to calm nationalist mobilization. Quite to the contrary: while the French, whose contingent was by far the biggest, more or less openly backed the Polish insurgents, the British and Italian detachments tolerated the armed activities of right-wing German *Freikorps*.[11] The results of the plebiscite showed another limitation of the plan

10 Eichner (n 2) 31.

11 Guido Hitze, 'Das Komplott von Oberschlesien' *Frankfurter Allgemeine Zeitung* (Frankfurt, 20 May 2011) <http://www.faz.net/frankfurter-allgemeine-zeitung/bilder-und-zeiten/das-komplott-von-oberschlesien-1638106.html> accessed 25 May 2018. See also Marek Masnyk, 'Provinz Oberschlesien (1918/19-1938/39)' in Bahlcke/Gawrecki/Kaczmarek (n 6) 290, 296–97.

devised at the Peace Conference. Pursant to Annex 5 of article 88 Versailles Treaty, the Allies had intended to divide Upper Silesia according 'to the wishes of the inhabitants as shown by the vote, and to the geographical and economic conditions of [each] locality.' This turned out to be all but impossible. While the overall vote showed a 59.6 % majority in favour of Germany and a neat divide between Polish and German rural areas, results in the region's cities and industrial area did not allow for a continuous border line based on ethnic or linguistic criteria. Moreover, the prospect of having an international border carve up Upper Silesia's deeply interconnected industrial area threatened the whole region's economic viability. Unsurprisingly, the Inter-Allied Commission failed to resolve the issue. The Supreme Council of the Principal Allied Powers then referred the matter to an ad hoc Committee of Experts. The experts issued a report but were also unable to draw a new frontier. Eventually, the Allies submitted the matter to Council of the League of Nations. The Council entrusted a Committee of small powers (Belgium, Brazil, Chile, and Spain) to come up with a detailed plan.[12]

The actual work of drafting this plan was done by the League's Secretariat, under the supervision of its young Deputy Secretary-General, Jean Monnet (1888–1979). Monnet and his team came up with a new partition plan. Rather than handing over the industrial area to either Germany or Poland, they suggested dividing it between the two states. In order for the partition to go down smoothly, both for the people of Upper Silesia and its industries, Germany and Poland would conclude a bilateral convention. This instrument would organize the provisional cross-border functioning of essential infrastructure while also guaranteeing special rights to the inhabitants and companies of Upper Silesia. In keeping with the will of the Supreme Council of the Principal Allied Powers, this regime would be limited to a transitional period of 15 years. Two international organs, a 'Mixed Commission', and an 'Arbitral Tribunal', were to supervise the application of these measures.[13] The Conference of Ambassadors, successor to

12 Georges Kaeckenbeeck, *The International Experiment of Upper Silesia* (OUP 1942) 6–9.

13 Jean Monnet, *Mémoires* (Fayard 1976) 102–106. For the Council's recommendation to the Conference of Ambassadors, see: Recommendation of the Council of the League Forwarded to the Supreme Council of the Principal Allied Powers (21 October 1921) 2 LNOJ 1223–226. The decision to subject Upper Silesia to a transitional period of 15 years was consistent with Art 90 Treaty of Versailles pursuant to which Poland had the obligation 'to permit for a period of fifteen years the ex-

the Allies' Supreme Council, eventually accepted this solution on 20 October 1921.[14]

Negotiations for the German–Polish Convention regarding Upper Silesia started shortly thereafter. Compared to previous (and even subsequent) international negotiations, they were certainly atypical. First and foremost, although the resulting instrument was officially a bilateral treaty, the League was given extraordinary powers to make sure that both parties would reach a consensus, whether they wanted it or not. The Conference of Ambassadors had decided that the German and Polish plenipotentiaries would negotiate the Convention under the supervision of a third-national appointed by the Council of the League. The choice fell on Felix Calonder (1863–1952)[15], who had been President of the Swiss Federal Council in 1918. As President of the Conference, Calonder was given a casting vote in case of disagreement between the parties. Although ultimately he did not have to use this prerogative, he had considerable influence on the negotiations' outcome. A second important feature of the conference was that it was partly held *in situ*. After an opening session in Geneva in November 1921, the conference moved to Upper Silesia from December 1921 to January 1922. This allowed all participants, including Calonder, to establish direct contacts with the local actors on whose fate they were to decide. After this stage, the negotiators returned to Geneva, where final talks took place from February to May 1922. A third distinctive feature of the negotiation process had to do with language. Since Upper Silesia was still nominally a part of Germany and all participants were fluent in German, the first draft of the Convention was negotiated in that language.[16] However, rather than having to authentic texts of the Convention—the German version and its Polish translation—the Polish negotiators insisted on a single

portation to Germany of the products of the mines in any part of Upper Silesia transferred to Poland in accordance with the present Treaty.' This provision seems to have been suggested during the Versailles treaty negotiations by General Le Rond, then head of the commission on Germany's Eastern borders. Le Rond made this proposal on 11 June 1919, referring to the duration of the Saar regime. Vincent Kroll, *Die Genfer Konvention betreffend Oberschlesien vom 15. Mai 1922* (dissertation, Cologne 1956) 24.

14 Decision of the Conference of Ambassadors (20 October 1921) 2 LNOJ 1226–32.

15 Letter of the President of the Council of the League of Nations to the Presidence of the Conference of Ambassadors (16 Novembe 1921) United Nations Archives at Geneva, R633-11A-17237-17237.

16 Kaeckenbeeck (n 12) 11–19.

version, written in French.[17] On 15 May 1922, the parties were finally able to sign the *Convention germano-polonaise relative à la Haute-Silésie*, known to its contemporaries as the Geneva Convention (hereafter GC). With its 606 articles, it was then the longest international treaty that had ever been adopted, making even the Versailles Treaty and its 440 articles look comparatively short.[18] The Geneva Convention entered into force on 15 June 1922, thus putting an end to the period of Inter-Allied administration.[19] It would remain binding on both parties until 15 July 1937.

Nathaniel Berman has characterized the Geneva Convention as establishing the most elaborate of all international regimes of the interwar period,[20] a veritable *Gesamtkunstwerk* of post-Versailles internationalism.[21] Indeed, the Upper Silesian conventional regime comprised several deeply innovative international legal obligations destined to mitigate the effects of nationalism on the local population and economic actors. These obligations comprised, amongst others: the freedom of movement of certain goods (arts 216–258 GC); the freedom of movement of a substantial part of the region's inhabitants (arts 259–305 GC); the maintenance of protective labour and social legislation (art 1 GC); the guarantee of private rights acquired before partition, also known as vested rights (art 4 GC); the right of residence and of non-discrimination of Upper Silesians who chose to retain their domicile on one side of the territory while opting in favour of the nationality of the other state (arts 40–45 GC). Moreover, the Geneva Convention was the only international instrument of the interwar period that organized the protection of minority rights through bilateral and reciprocal obligations under international supervision rather than through a unilateral commitment of one state toward the League Council (arts 64–158 GC).

---

17 German–Polish Conference Regarding Upper Silesia, 1st session, 2nd and 3rd meetings (23 and 24 November 1921) United Nations Archives at Geneva, R633-11A-17237-18172.

18 Convention Between Germany and Poland Relating to Upper Silesia (signed 15 May 1922, entered into force 15 June 1922) 9 LNTS 465; 118 BSP 365. For the full text of the Convention, see: Kaeckenbeeck (n 12) 567–822.

19 The Inter-Allied Commission left Oppeln/Opole with the last remaining troops on 9 July 1922. Eichner (n 2) 246–248.

20 Nathaniel Berman, 'But the Alternative is Despair: European Nationalism and the Modernist Renewal of International Law' (1993) 106 Harvard Law Review 1792, 1893–98.

21 See Berman (ch 1).

During its third meeting, held on 24 November 1921 at the League of Nations Secretariat in Geneva, the German–Polish Conference on Upper Silesia adopted French as the future Convention's authoritative language. Conference president Felix Calonder is pictured in the centre front row (with moustache). The Polish delegation was led by Kazimierz Olszowski (on the right, leaning forward), Germany's by Eugen Schiffer (on the left, looking at the camera). Schiffer, a former minister of Justice, would later act as counsel for his country in the SS 'Wimbledon' *case before the PCIJ. Source: United Nations Archives at Geneva.*

However, most importantly, by establishing two international organs that were based in Upper Silesia itself, namely a Mixed Commission and an Arbitral Tribunal[22], the Geneva Convention also included procedural mechanisms that would guarantee the effective enforcement of these rights. For Calonder, the existence of these mechanisms was decisive in guaranteeing the Geneva Convention's broader aims. As he remarked in his speech on 15 May 1922, the Geneva Convention would not only defuse tensions in

22 With regard to nomenclature, it should be noted that the authoritative French text of the Geneva Convention defines these organs as the 'Upper Silesian' Mixed Commission/Arbitral Tribunal (*'de Haute-Silésie'*), whereas both organs' official publications in German and in Polish designate them as the Mixed Commission/ Arbitral Tribunal 'for Upper Silesia' (*'für Oberschlesien'*/*'dla Górnego Śląska'*). As most English-language publications tend to use the latter translation, this study will predominantly do so as well.

Upper Silesia. It would also demonstrate how international law, backed up by international adjudication, could bring peace to Europe:

> International arbitration and the Permanent Court of Justice are the most important foundations for establishing and consolidating peace between peoples. Providing governments with easy access to these means would, in my view, critically increase the stability of international treaties. I would like this convention to set an example in this regard …
> This Treaty can and should become, so to say, the charter of economic and social life in Upper Silesia for the fifteen years to come. However, this conventional regime must not only constitute a period of economic adjustment to a new political situation; it should have another effect as well. In drawing up this Convention, my aim has been the establishment and consolidation of peace …
> Of all the questions whose resolution had been postponed by the Treaty of Versailles, none was as disturbing, as painful, and even as dangerous as the Upper Silesian question. And yet, this question has now been solved once and for all … Who would dare say after this that European cooperation is impossible?[23]

Although Calonder was wrong to assume that the Geneva Convention had 'solved once and for all' the Upper Silesian question, his remarks regarding international adjudication were partly confirmed by his own subsequent experience. As President of the Mixed Commission for Upper Silesia, Calonder would make a substantial contribution to the protection of mi-

23 *'L'arbitrage international et la Cour permanente de Justice sont les bases essentielles de la pacification entre les peuples et la facilité offerte aux gouvernements d'y recourir me paraît devoir apporter un élément de solidité des plus importants dans les traités internationaux. Je voudrais que cette convention en fût l'exemple. … Ce Traité peut et doit devenir en quelque sorte la charte de la vie économique et sociale de la Haute-Silésie pendant les quinze années à venir. Mais le régime conventionnel ne doit pas constituer seulement la période d'adaptation économique à une situation politique nouvelle; elle doit avoir encore un autre effet. En préparant cette Convention, j'ai eu la volonté de faire une œuvre de pacification. … De toutes les questions dont le Traité de Versailles a différé la solution, il n'en était pas de plus troublante, de plus douloureuse, de plus redoutable même que celle de la Haute-Silésie. Or, elle est définitivement résolue aujourd'hui … Qui osera soutenir après cela que la coopération européenne est impossible?'* 'Discours du Président' (Geneva 15 May 1922) Archives MAE, SDN 280, Haute-Silésie mars–mai 1922, 185–187.

nority rights,[24] including by forcing Nazi Germany to suspend its anti-Jewish legislation in German Upper Silesia until 1937.[25] I have written elsewhere about this pioneering quasi-judicial body.[26] In this contribution, I would like to focus on what was arguably the Geneva Convention's most substantial contribution to international procedural law, namely its Arbitral Tribunal. After presenting the innovative procedural tools that had been bestowed on the Tribunal, I will give an account of its work, including its attitude towards claimants and the states parties. In my concluding remarks, I will address the possible relevance of the Upper Silesian Arbitral Tribunal's precedent for the history of post-WWII European integration.

2. *Procedural Innovations: The Tribunal's Toolbox*

Among the distinctive features of the Upper Silesian international organs, Nathaniel Berman has especially highlighted their hybrid nature as 'local, *yet* international' organs.[27] With regard to the Arbitral Tribunal, this hybrid nature was manifest in several provisions of the Geneva Convention. For instance, art 563 § 3 (2) GC specified that the Arbitral Tribunal would render its decisions in accordance with both the Geneva Convention and applicable local (ie mostly German) legislation, unless this legislation was contrary to the Convention. Art 593 GC noted that the implementation of the Tribunal's awards and enforcement actions would be subject 'to the same conditions and formalities than those applied to an analogous deci-

24 On Calonder, see Paul Stauffer, '"Staatsmann des kommenden Europa"? Felix Calonder und seine Tätigkeit im deutsch-polnisch-jüdischen Spannungsfeld Oberschlesien 1921–1937' in Paul Stauffer, *Polen—Juden—Schweizer: Felix Calonder (1921–1937), "Exilpolens" Berner Emissäre (1939-1945), Die Schweiz und Katyn (1943)* (Neue Zürcher Zeitung 2004) 14–117.

25 On this subject, see Brendan Karch, 'A Jewish "Nature Preserve": League of Nations Minority Protections in Nazi Upper Silesia, 1933-1937' (2013) 46 Central European History 124–60.

26 See Michel Erpelding, 'Mixed Commission for Upper Silesia' in Hélène Ruiz Fabri (ed), *Max Planck Encyclopedia of International Procedural Law* (OUP forthcoming 2019). Also available as Michel Erpelding, 'Upper Silesian Mixed Commission' [2017] MPI Luxembourg Working Paper 5 <http://www.mpi.lu> accessed 29 May 2018.

27 Berman (n 20) 1896.

sion of a national authority'.[28] Moreover, the Tribunal had wide-ranging evidentiary and disciplinary powers that were impossible to distinguish from those of a local court. It could issue witness and expert summonses which would also serve as safe-conducts before the authorities of both states (art 606 § 1 (1) GC). It could collect evidence either through one of its members or, if the evidence was located outside the plebiscite area, through the competent state representative (art 601 § 2 (1) GC). The authorities of both states had the obligation to assist the Tribunal in these endeavours free of charge (art 601 § 2 (2) GC). Acts of perjury or false testimonies before the Tribunal would be prosecuted by both states as if they had taken place before a domestic tribunal (art 606 § 1 (2) GC). Similarly, the Tribunal could request from the domestic courts of both states to inflict disciplinary sanctions on individuals failing to appear before it, disobeying its commands, or refusing to testify or to take an oath before it without without due justification (art 602 GC). The Tribunal's President could even take the initiative to file a demand for prosecution before the competent national authorities if an offense had been committed against the Tribunal, its members, or its staff (art 570 (2) GC).

However, the Tribunal's special position with regard to German and Polish authorities was even more conspicuous in several other procedural provisions of the Convention. These provisions had been specially devised to maximize the Tribunal's effectiveness in dealing with the matters falling under its jurisdiction and, more generally, in ensuring a uniform interpretation and implementation of the Geneva Convention.

2.1. Direct Individual Claims for Compensation

Pursuant to art 4 § 1 GC, and without prejudice to art 256 Versailles Treaty which defined the private property of German 'royal personages' as German state property,[29] Germany and Poland committed themselves to

---

28 Original French text: '*L'exécution ou l'application [de la sentence ou des mesures d'application] se font dans les mêmes conditions et avec les mêmes formalités que l'exécution ou l'application d'une décision analogue d'une autorité nationale*'.

29 The first two paragraphs of this provision were formulated as follows: 'Powers to which German territory is ceded shall acquire all property and possessions situated therein belonging to the German Empire or to the German States, and the value of such acquisitions shall be fixed by the Reparation Commission, and paid by the state acquiring the territory to the Reparation Commission for the credit of the German Government on account of the sums due for reparation.

> recognize and respect the rights of every kind, and in particular concessions and privileges acquired before the transfer of sovereignty by private individuals, companies or bodies corporate, in their respective parts of the plebiscite area, in conformity with the laws relating to the said rights and with the following provisions [of the Convention].[30]

The drafters of the Convention had fleshed out this general obligation to recognize and respect vested rights with a series of 'principles' established by subparagraphs under art 4 § 2 GC. Pursuant to subparagraph (1), measures taken otherwise than through general legislation were inadmissible, if they were not applicable to the nationals of the state that took them. As per subparagraph (2), recourse to courts or authorities could not be suppressed through modification of the existing law. Following subparagraph (3), the state had to pay full compensation for the suppression or diminution, as a result of general legislation or other measures (*'d'autres dispositions'*), of concessions or privileges authorizing or concerning installations, enterprises, establishments or undertakings located or to be located within the plebiscite area, or relating to an object situated within that territory, or of subjective rights not arising out of a concession, such as claims (*'créances'*), for which even one of the places of performance mentioned by Section 269 German Civil Code was situated in the plebiscite area. As this enumeration of principles was preceded by the words 'in particular' (*'en particulier'*), it was not meant to exhaust the general obligation under art 4 § 1 GC.[31] However, the Tribunal's role in upholding this general obligation was limited to the principle of compensation established by subparagraph (3) of art 4 § 2 GC. Art 5 GC defined the Tribunal's jurisdiction in matters relating to vested rights as follows:

> The question as to whether or to what extent an indemnity for the abolition or diminution of vested rights must be paid by the state, will

For the purposes of this Article the property and possessions of the German Empire and States shall be deemed to include all the property of the Crown, the Empire or the States, and the private property of the former German Emperor and other Royal personages.'

30 Original French text: *'l'Allemagne et la Pologne reconnaîtront et respecteront les droits de toute nature, et notamment les concessions et privilèges acquis avant le transfert de la souveraineté par les particuliers, des sociétés ou des personnes morales, dans leurs parties respectives du territoire plébiscité, et cela en conformité des lois relatives aux dits droits et des dispositions [de la Convention] qui vont suivre.'*

31 Kaeckenbeeck (n 12) 44–45.

> be settled directly by the Arbitral Tribunal on the complaint of the person enjoying the right.[32]

In granting individuals the right to bring claims against a sovereign state before an international judge without exhausting internal remedies, the Arbitral Tribunal for Upper Silesia followed in the footsteps of the Mixed Arbitral Tribunals (MATs) established under the Paris Peace Treaties.[33] As a matter of fact, the Upper Silesian Arbitral Tribunal even modelled its own procedural rules regarding individual compensation claims on those used by the MATs.[34] However, as we shall see, the formulation of art 5 GC would allow it to extend its jurisdiction beyond the limits set for these Tribunals.

2.2. *Indirect Individual Claims*

While persons seeking compensation for an alleged infringement upon their vested rights could file direct claims before the Arbitral Tribunal for Upper Silesia, individuals involved in disputes regarding nationality, domicile and option, or disputes regarding circulation permits, had to take the issue before a binational administrative body first.

Under Part II of the Geneva Convention, individuals living in either part of Upper Silesia were given wide-ranging rights in matters of nationality. In principle, Germans domiciliated in Polish Upper Silesia before 1 January 1908[35] would automatically lose their German nationality at the

32 Original French text: '*La question de savoir si et dans quelle mesure une indemnité pour la suppression ou la diminution de droits acquis doit être payée par l'État, sera directement tranchée par le Tribunal arbitral sur plainte de l'ayant droit.*'

33 On the MATs, see Requejo Isidro and Hess (ch 11). Although there are substantial differences between the Arbitral Tribunal for Upper Silesia and the MATs of the Paris peace treaties, notably with regard to jurisdiction, the former was clearly inspired from the latter. An early draft of the League Council's reply to the Conference of Ambassadors expressly noted that, with regard to the future Upper Silesian Arbitral Tribunal's composition and rules of procedure, 'one could draw on' [original French: '*on pourrait s'inspirer de*'] art 304 Versailles Treaty (which established the MATs with Germany). Anonymous draft recommendation (4 October 1921) United Nations Archives at Geneva, R632-11A-14724-16712, 3.

34 Kaeckenbeeck (n 12) 485.

35 In March 1908, Germany had passed a colonization law (*Ansiedlungsgesetz*) which allowed it to expropriate Polish estates for redistribution to German settlers. However, since there were no Polish large landowners in Upper Silesia, the law was never implemented in that region. Gehrke (n 7) 279.

moment of the transfer of sovereignty and become Poles (art 25 § 1 GC). They could, however, opt in favour of the German nationality for a period of two years after the sovereignty transfer (art 25 § 4 GC). Poles were subject to similar rules, with the exception of the time limit of 1 January 1908 (art 27 GC). Germans born in Polish Upper Silesia but not domiciliated there at the time of the transfer would acquire the Polish nationality in addition to their German nationality if they had family ties to the region, and vice-versa. During a period of two years, they would have to renounce one of the nationalities; otherwise, their nationality would be determined by their domicile (art 26 GC).[36] Optants had the right to transfer their domicile and their belongings to the territory of the state in favour of which they had opted (art 33–39 GC). However, they could also choose to remain domiciliated on the territory of the other state. In this case, their right of residence included the right to exercise the profession or economic activity they practised before the transfer of sovereignty, and to be treated on an equal footing with nationals. This did not prevent state parties from ordering the departure of optants on a limited number of grounds, such as national security (arts 40–45 GC). Declarations of option, or applications for annulment of an option, were subject to a number of procedural rules (arts 46–54 GC). Claims regarding a person's alleged nationality, their right of option or of domicile, or infringements of these rights (art 56 GC), had to be referred to a Conciliation commission in matters of nationality created within the framework of the Tribunal and composed of one representative of each government (art 55 GC). The Conciliation commission was supposed to establish the facts and find a solution, while national authorities remained competent to make a decision on the merits of the case (art 57 GC). The Arbitral Tribunal could only take up the matter at the request of one of the state agents or, if the Conciliation commission had declared itself unable to resolve the issue, at the request of one of the individuals concerned. In this case, national authorities (excluding courts or administrative authorities not subject to superior orders) had the obligation to refrain from any decision on the matter (arts 58–59 GC). The Tribunal had direct jurisdiction over cases where both governments disagreed on a person's right of option (art 60 GC) and cases where individuals objected to the annulment of an act of option (art 61 GC). However, the Convention specifi-

36 It should be noted that although the Geneva Convention did not mention the possibility of dual citizenship, it did not categorically exclude it either. In practice, however, both states were reluctant to grant full rights to double nationals (see below, 3.3).

cally mentioned that the Arbitral Tribunal did not have the right to award compensation for the infringement of individual rights in these matters (art 62 GC). This would significantly reduce the Tribunal's ability to provide applicants with effective redress.[37]

The second Title of Part V of the Convention created a system of annually renewable circulation permits allowing a substantial part of the Upper Silesian population to move freely between both parts of the territory for professional or for private reasons.[38] National authorities could refuse to deliver circulation permits to social outcasts such as prostitutes, beggars and vagabonds, and to individuals convicted of various offenses or of having made a fraudulent use of their circulation permit (arts 259–270 GC). On similar grounds, they could strip an individual of their permit, or limit the rights derived from the permit (art 286–289 GC). Moreover, the validity of these permits was limited in several ways. For instance, they did not give access to the other state's territory outside of the plebiscite area (art 271 (2) GC); the border could only be crossed on designated border posts (art 272 GC); carriers of circulation permits remained subject to customs formalities at the border (art 276 GC). Circulation permits, which were standardized and bilingual, were issued by a 'Permit Office' (*'Office des permis'*) created within each state's lower domestic administration (arts 279–285 GC). Individuals who had been refused a permit, stripped of their permit, or deprived of some rights deriving from their permit, would have to challenge this decision before the Permit Office, which had the obligation to refer the matter to its superior authority (arts 292–293 GC). If the superior authority upheld the decision of the Permit Office, it had the obligation to refer the matter in turn to the Arbitral Commission for Circulation Permits, composed of a German and a Polish government delegate (art 294 GC). Only if this Commission was unable to reach a decision would the matter become subject to the Arbitral Tribunal's binding jurisdiction (art 296 GC).

While direct claims regarding vested rights were reminiscent of actions governed by civil procedure, both types of indirect individual claims were more administrative in nature, and did usually not lead to oral hearings.[39] The binational administrative commissions (ie the Conciliation commission and the Arbitral Commission for Circulation Permits) proved to be

37 Kaeckenbeeck (n 12) 203 and 206–207.

38 During the 15 years of the conventional regime, the authorities issued or renewed between 400,000 and 500,000 circulation permits every year. The region's total population amounted to roughly 2 million. ibid 428.

39 ibid 485–486.

useful supplements to the Arbitral Tribunal, acting as filtering instances and providing solutions mutually acceptable to both governments. The absence of a neutral third party acting as a conciliator between the representatives of both states sometimes led to periodic breakdowns of these commissions. However, owing to their institutional ties with the Arbitral Tribunal, the Tribunal's President was often able to exert a certain influence on their activities.[40]

2.3. *Evocation Procedure*

One of the Upper Silesian Arbitral Tribunal's most distinctive features was the fact that it had been entrusted not only with the resolution of individual disputes, but also with the Geneva Convention's uniform interpretation. The fact that the Conference of Ambassadors had chosen to attribute this task to the Arbitral Tribunal was very likely a concession to Germany's and Poland's need to retain a higher degree of influence on the judicial interpretation of their mutual obligations than they would have had before a multilateral organ such as the Permanent Court of International Justice.[41] The procedural solution that the drafters of the Geneva Convention eventually came up with under article 588 GC was highly original. This was true with regard to both its nomenclature and its substance.

Interestingly, art 588 GC used the term 'evocation' to describe a procedure by which national authorities would ask the Arbitral Tribunal to provide them with an authoritative interpretation of a given provision of the Convention.[42] In continental legal systems, evocation refers to the ability of a higher authority or court to withdraw a given case from a competent lower court or authority. In German lands, the term traditionally evoked the sometimes strained relations between local and royal or imperial courts.[43] In France, it had long been associated with the powerful *cours de parlement*, but also with the king's prerogative to intervene in judicial mat-

40 Georges Kaeckenbeeck, 'The Character and Work of the Arbitral Tribunal of Upper Silesia' (1935) 21 Transactions of the Grotius Society 27, 31.

41 Kaeckenbeeck (n 12) 487.

42 It should be noted that the Arbitral Tribunal had also been endowed with the capacity to render non-binding motivated opinions ('*consultations motivées*') at the request of the Mixed Commission (art 580 GC).

43 Peter Oestmann, *Wege zur Rechtsgeschichte: Gerichtsbarkeit und Verfahren* (Böhlau 2015) 86–90, 354.

ters.[44] Suggesting the idea of hierarchy within a same legal system, the term 'evocation' was perfectly in line with the characterization of the Upper Silesian Tribunal as an organ that was both 'local' and 'international' (or, indeed, 'supranational' *avant la lettre*).[45]

However, from a substantial point of view, the use of the term 'evocation' might have been somewhat misleading. As a matter of fact, art 588 GC did not go as far as giving the Arbitral Tribunal the right to withdraw a case from a domestic court. More modestly, it enabled parties to an 'Upper Silesian case' whose resolution depended on the interpretation of an article of the Convention to request, up to the conclusion of the proceeding in the second instance, that the case be submitted to the Arbitral Tribunal (art 588 § 1 (1) GC). The notion of 'Upper Silesian case' was defined as including cases before tribunals or administrative authorities not subject to orders from a superior authority in the plebiscite, provided that said tribunals or authorities were situated in the plebiscite area, or that the relevant case emanated from that area and had been subject, in the first instance, to its tribunals and authorities (art 588 § 1 (2) GC). Evocation was not a right, as the competent tribunal or authority could refuse it on four grounds: 1) if it considered that the judgment or decision did not depend upon the interpretation of the Convention; 2) if evocation did not seem admissible under the terms of the Convention; 3) if the Tribunal had already answered the question in an award published in its official collection of decisions; 4) if the purpose of the demand was manifestly dilatory (art 588 § 2 GC). However, the power of national authorities and judges to refuse evocation was not unlimited, as refusals based on erroneous grounds had to be regarded by the tribunals and authorities of both countries as 'an essential fault of procedure' ('*un vice essentiel de procédure*', art 588 § 3 GC). Similarly, once evocation had taken place, local tribunals and authorities were bound by the Arbitral Tribunal's interpretation (art 588 § 4 GC).

---

44 In a generally well-informed article, France's most authoritative newspaper at the time noted that the term and concept of evocation were 'based on pre-revolutionary French law' ('*inspirés de l'ancien droit*'). 'La Convention germano-polonaise sur la Haute-Silésie', *Le Temps* (Paris, 23 May 1922). For an overview of evocation in 18th century France, see Claude-Joseph de Ferrière, *Dictionnaire de droit et de pratique contenant l'explication des termes de droit, d'ordonnances, de coutumes et de pratique avec les jurisdictions de France* (Théodore Le Gras 1749) 860–865. In 19th century France, evocation had become a much rarer phenomenon: Albin Le Rat de Magnitot and Huard-Delamarre, *Dictionnaire de droit public administratif* (Joubert 1836) vol 1, 566–67.

45 Berman (n 20) 1896.

All in all, the Arbitral Tribunal for Upper Silesia only treated a limited number of evocation cases. However, as we shall see, the very existence of this procedure was undoubtedly a major innovation of the Geneva Convention, raising questions about this instrument's legacy on contemporary international instruments.

2.4. *Power to Create General Binding Precedent*

In principle, as per art 591 GC, awards rendered by the Tribunal were binding *inter partes*.[46] Only awards rendered in nationality cases had an *erga omnes* effect.[47] However, the drafters of the Geneva Convention had supplemented this classical feature of international adjudication[48] by another much more innovative rule. Under this provision, the Arbitral Tribunal was granted the right to publish some of its decisions as precedent generally binding upon the authorities of both states.[49] Art 592 GC went as follows:

---

46 Art 591 (1) GC: 'The award of the Arbitral Tribunal shall produce its effects, in both states, only with regard to the parties and in respect of that particular case.' French original: '*La sentence du Tribunal arbitral ne produit ses effets, dans les deux États, qu'à l'égard des parties en cause et pour l'affaire seule au sujet de laquelle elle est prononcée.*'

47 Art 591 (2) GC: 'In cases regarding the determination of the nationality of a party pursuant to the provisions of the second part of this Convention or to article 588, the awards of the Tribunal regarding nationality shall produce its effects erga omnes on the territories of both Contracting Parties.' French original: '*Si, conformément aux dispositions de la deuxième partie de la présente Convention ou à l'article 588, il s'agit de déterminer la nationalité d'une des parties en cause, la sentence du Tribunal arbitral relative à la nationalité produire ses effets erga omnes dans les territoires des deux Parties contractantes.*'

48 See, for instance, art 59 PCIJ Statute: 'The decision of the Court has no binding force except between the parties and in respect of that particular case.' Protocol of Signature of the Statute of the Permanent Court of International Justice (opened for signature 16 December 1920, entered into force 1 September 1921) 6 LNTS 379.

49 Considering that both Germany and Poland are civil law countries, the use of the term 'precedent' might be somewhat puzzling here. However, it seems an adequate characterization of the Tribunal's power to issue what Kaeckenbeeck himself described as '*jurisprudence obligatoire*' and '*précédents*'. Georges Kaeckenbeeck, *Le règlement conventionnel des conséquences de remaniements territoriaux: Considérations suggérées par l'expérience de Haute-Silésie* (Éditions Polygraphiques 1940) 17.

> 1. The Arbitral Tribunal publishes its awards of actual relevance from the point of view of case law in an official collection in German and in Polish.
> 2. If, in an Upper Silesian case, a tribunal or an administrative authority wants to depart from an award thus published, the said tribunal or administrative authority shall refer the matter to the decision of the Arbitral Tribunal with a statement of its reasons. The award of the Arbitral Tribunal is binding upon the tribunal or authority concerned.[50]

In the eyes of the Arbitral Tribunal's President, art 592 GC was arguably the most powerful tool at its disposal, since it blurred the lines between judicial and legislative powers:

> Nothing was more important than this provision in shaping the character, or in enhancing the utility, of the Arbitral Tribunal's activity. Nothing contributed more to economy of litigation and to certainty and unity in the application of the Geneva Convention by the courts and authorities of both countries. This provision made the Arbitral Tribunal more than a deciding agency; it turned it into a law-creating and law-defining agency by giving its interpretations and the principles of its decisions equal legal force in both countries.[51]

As we shall see hereafter, the Tribunal's heavy reliance on its precedent-creating capacity would have a major impact not only on the substance of the law applied in Upper Silesia, but also on the effectiveness of the procedures before the Arbitral Tribunal.

3. *Implementing Local International Adjudication: The Tribunal at Work*

During the 15 years of its existence, the Arbitral Tribunal for Upper Silesia successfully solved almost 4,000 cases.[52] In 127 cases, ie less than 3% of the

---

50 Original French text: '*1. Le Tribunal arbitral publie ses sentences dans un recueil officiel en allemand et en polonais, lorsqu'elles sont d'un réel intérêt jurisprudentiel. 2. Si, dans une affaire relative à la Haute Silésie, un tribunal ou une autorité administrative veut déroger à une sentence ainsi publiée, ce tribunal ou cette autorité administrative devra soumettre la question à la décision du Tribunal arbitral avec l'exposé de ses raisons. La sentence du Tribunal arbitral lie le tribunal ou l'autorité intéressée.*'

51 Kaeckenbeeck (n 12) 28.

52 At the expiration of the Upper Silesian Convention on 15 July 1937, the Arbitral Tribunal had solved 3,726 cases while 227 cases were still pending before it. 'Allocutions du Président Kaeckenbeeck à la séance solennelle du Tribunal Arbitral le

total, the Tribunal chose to publish its decision in its 8-volume official collection.[53] Most of these cases related to vested rights, nationality and circulation permits; only four gave rise to an evocation procedure.[54] The Tribunal's ability to successfully deal with a caseload of this magnitude until the very end of the transitional regime was not only due to the wide-ranging powers it derived from the 1922 Geneva Convention. Arguably, the Tribunal's composition and its attitude toward all parties involved also contributed to its success.

3.1. Setting Up the Tribunal

As opposed to the Upper Silesian Mixed Commission, which sat in Katowice/Kattowitz, in Polish Upper Silesia, the Arbitral Tribunal's seat was in Beuthen/Bytom, on the German side of the border.[55] While the Mixed Commission's President was a former head of the Swiss executive and its

---

15 juillet 1937' in Kaeckenbeeck (n 12) 854, 857. During the three winding-down sessions organized from September 1937 to February 1938 and additional negotiations between the President and the states parties, the Tribunal was able to solve most of them. However, due to a lack of cooperation between Poland and Germany, 'three suits [ie procedures regarding vested rights], thirty-four dismissal cases and half a dozen other matters'remained unsettled. Kaeckenbeeck (n 12) 512. Based on statistics provided by Kaeckenbeeck and its official collection of decisions, the Tribunal's caseload can be broken up as follows: about 1670 cases relating to the diminution or suppression of vested rights, 1,328 circulation permit cases, about 1,000 cases regarding nationality and the right to residence, 4 evocation cases, and one single motivated opinion. ibid 212, 428, 495.

53 Schiedsgericht für Oberschlesien/Trybunał Rozjemczy dla Górnego Śląska (ed), *Amtliche Sammlung von Entscheidungen des Schiedsgerichts für Oberschlesien, veröffentlicht gemäß der Bestimmung des Art. 592 des Genfer Abkommens vom 15. Mai 1922/Zbiór urzędowy orzeczeń Trybunału Rozjemczego dla Górnego Śląska ogłoszony wedle postanowienia art. 592 Konwencji Genewskiej z dnia 15 maja 1922 r* (8 vol, Walter de Gruyter 1930–1938), hereafter Arb Trib Dec.

54 Nos 17, 18, 32, 115.

55 Between 1922 and 1923, the Tribunal's offices were situated within the Beuthen Civil and Administrative Court House (now the Bytom City Government Office situated on ulica Parkowa 2). The Tribunal's first own premises were situated within a former Prussian officers' mess on Guttenbergstraße 12 (today ulica Powstańców Śląskich 6). Pictures of this building and its courtroom were published in the weekly supplement of the region's main German-language newspaper: 'Das Schiedsgericht bei der Gemischten Kommission [sic]', *Oberschlesien im Bild: Wöchentliche Unterhaltungsbeilage des Oberschlesischen Wanderers* (Gleiwitz, 14 March 1924) 2. The Tribunal subsequently moved to a stately townhouse located

Polish and German members were high-ranking civil servants, diplomats and politicians who, pursuant to art 562 GC, had either been born in Upper Silesia or had intimate knowledge of the local circumstances, the Arbitral Tribunal's composition was meant to reflect its 'truly judicial character':[56] as per art 563 GC, the two arbitrators had to possess the qualifications necessary to be appointed as ordinary or administrative judges in the legal system of the state that appointed them.

Pursuant to the same provision, the arbitrators were appointed for renewable terms of three years. It also emphasized that arbitrators were independent, that they were not bound by any government instructions, and that they were subject to the same guarantees of irremovability as judges of courts of second instance in their country. If either government wanted to intervene before the Tribunal, it would have to do so exclusively through its Representative, whom it could appoint and revoke *ad nutum* (art 569 GC). Nevertheless, the fact that 'their' arbitrator's term was limited to three years gave Poland and Germany some control over the organ's evolution, and could have jeopardized its independence from the outset. In fact, the Tribunal's composition proved to be rather stable. Poland appointed only two arbitrators: Juliusz Kałużniacki (1869–1928), who kept signing the Tribunal's decisions even on his deathbed,[57] and Bronisław Stelmachowski (1883–1940?). Germany made two replacements. In 1933, shortly before the Nazi takeover, Rudolf Schneider (1875–1956) was replaced by August Herwegen (1879–1945?), who in 1936, after only one term, had to make way for Walter von Steinaecker (1883–1956).[58] However, none of these replacements was the result of political persecution, since all three German arbitrators were, or turned out to be, loyal national-socialists.[59]

---

on Gartenstraße 20 (today ulica Powstańców Warszawskich 12). The Tribunal's three addresses are mentioned in internal documents of the Upper Silesian Mixed Commission and advice of receipt forms conserved with the Tribunal's individual case files in the United Nations Archives at Geneva. The precise locations corresponding to these addresses can be determined by comparing pre-WWII maps of Beuthen with house numbers to present-day maps of Bytom. The three buildings are still extant as of 2018, although the second has undergone substantial modifications, having been integrated into a modernist building. Neither seems to bear a commemorative plaque.

56 Kaeckenbeeck (n 12) 28.

57 'Allocutions du Président Kaeckenbeeck …' (n 51) 855.

58 Each volume of the Arbitral Tribunal's collected decisions mentions the Tribunal's composition on its second page: Arb Trib Dec.

59 Rudolf Schneider had been a member of the catholic *Zentrum* party during the Weimar Republic. However, he had no qualms converting to the new ideology in

The Tribunal in 1924: Schneider (Germany), Kaeckenbeeck (Belgium), Kałużniacki (Poland), Oberschlesien im Bild, *14 March 1924. Source: Śląska Biblioteka Cyfrowa/Silesian Digital Library.*

Most importantly, the Tribunal had only one President, namely the Belgian Georges Kaeckenbeeck. Born in 1892, Kaeckenbeeck, who had never worked before as a judge or practiced as a barrister, was barely 30 years old

1933 and ultimately joined the NSDAP in 1940. By contrast, Steinaecker and Herwegen, who had become members in 1931 and 1932 respectively, were among the few judges affiliated to the party before 1933. Herwegen's non-renewal was very likely the result of an administrative tax fraud conviction instrumentalized by a rival faction of Nazi jurists. As for Schneider and Steinaecker, both played central roles in the conviction of 10,000 alleged sympathizers of the communist party by the Hamm *Oberlandesgericht* between 1933 and 1936. With regard to Herwegen, see Philipp Spiller, *Personalpolitik beim Kammergericht von 1933 bis 1945* (Berliner Wissenschafts-Verlag 2016) 192–196. With regard to Schneider and Steinaecker, see 'Justiz' (*Gedenkbuch für die NS-Opfer aus Wuppertal*), < http://www.gedenkbuch-wuppertal.de/de/justiz> accessed 9 March 2018.

when he became head of the most sophisticated international tribunal of his day. However, Kaeckenbeeck made up for his relative lack of experience in the domestic legal system by an impressive academic curriculum and solid practical expertise in the field of international law. A brilliant law student at the Free University of Brussels, Kaeckenbeeck had been evacuated to England due to severe illness at the outbreak of the First World War. Admitted at Magdalen College (Oxford) after his recovery, he had specialized in international law and provided legal advice to both the British and Belgian governments. After joining the League of Nations Secretariat's Legal Section as early as July 1919, and accumulating experience as a legal adviser to several international conferences, he was appointed head of the Geneva Convention's drafting committee in 1922.[60] Impressed by Kaeckenbeeck's abilities,[61] both parties recommended making him President of the Arbitral Tribunal—a choice which the League Council was 'glad to approve.'[62] It would not come to regret it: while ensuring that the Arbitral Tribunal provided effective relief to the local population, Kaeckenbeeck also adopted strategies to placate both states' susceptibilities.

3.2. *Engaging with the Local Population*

Conceiving itself as an institution that was international and local at the same time, the Arbitral Tribunal for Upper Silesia made efforts to ensure that the local population would be able to access it, both legally and in practice.

From a legal point of view, the Tribunal made it clear from the outset that it would take full measure of the Geneva Convention's innovative provisions regarding direct complaints by private individuals. In its first published decision, rendered on 30 March 1928 in the case of *Steiner & Groß v Poland*, the Tribunal held that individuals of all nationalities—including of the defendant state—could file compensation claims under art 5 GC, and

60 Fernand Vanlangenhove, 'Georges Kaeckenbeeck (1892–1973)', in Académie Royale des Sciences, des Lettres et des Beaux-Arts de Belgique (ed), *Biographie nationale* (vol 40, Bruylant 1977) 544, 544.

61 According to the head of the Polish delegation, Zygmunt Kazimierz Olszowski (1865–1933), the members of the drafting committee unanimously recognized that nobody was better qualified than Kaeckenbeeck to preside over their work. 'Discours de Monsieur Olszowski' (Geneva 15 May 1922) Archives MAE, SDN 280, Haute-Silésie mars–mai 1922, 198.

62 LoN, Council, 18th session, 9th meeting (16 May 1922) 3 LNOJ 541, 542.

that they could do so without prior exhaustion of domestic remedies. In this case, Steiner, a Czechoslovak national, and Groß, a Polish citizen, had been obliged to close their tobacco factory in Katowice/Kattowitz following the introduction into Upper Silesia of the Polish tobacco monopoly. Poland responded to the industrialists' claim by challenging the Arbitral Tribunal's jurisdiction. According to Poland, there was clear support for a 'principle of the inadmissibility of claims of individuals against their own state' in both international legal doctrine and the practice of the Mixed Arbitral Tribunals instituted pursuant to the post-WWI peace treaties.[63] As a matter of fact, even those non-European states that had consented to Mixed Courts for foreigners had consistently refused to extend the jurisdiction of these courts to cases between their own nationals and themselves.[64] As for giving the national of a third state the right to file a claim before an international Tribunal where his state was not represented, this would be a 'severe violation' of the rights of that state; it would also be 'grotesque', as in principle individuals were not subjects of international law.[65] Finally, Poland argued that although art 5 GC provided that the Arbitral Tribunal would judge complaints filed by individuals 'directly', this was merely an acknowledgment of the exceptional nature of a procedure allowing individuals to file claims before an international tribunal, not a waiver of the obligation to exhaust domestic remedies before doing so.[66] Using an argument not unlike the one put forward by the German government,[67] the Arbitral Tribunal rebutted all these claims by invoking the *lex specialis*-character of the Geneva Convention, whose provisions it deemed sufficiently clear to prevent any challenges based on principles of general international law. Since art 5 GC did not distinguish between claimants of different nationalities, neither should the Tribunal;[68] as it provided that claims by individuals for the violation of vested rights would be decided 'directly' by the Tribunal, arguing that this somehow referred to an obligation to exhaust local remedies did not make any sense.[69]

From a practical point of view, the Tribunal took several measures to ensure that Upper Silesians from all backgrounds could make their voices heard before it. The Geneva Convention had addressed the question of the

63 No 1, C 7/27, *Steiner & Groß v Poland* (30 March 1928) 1 Arb Trib Dec 8–10.
64 ibid 12.
65 ibid 10.
66 ibid 16.
67 ibid 16–18.
68 ibid 18–30.
69 ibid 32.

international organs' accessibility almost exclusively from a linguistic point of view. Thus, it had ensured that all decisions of the Arbitral Tribunal and the Mixed Commission would be translated into German or Polish, that oral translation would be provided during debates (art 576 § 1 GC) and that requests written in German or in Polish would be answered in the same language (art 576 § 3 GC). In its hearings, the Tribunal adopted an even more inclusive practice. When questioning parties or witnesses, the President would always ask them which language they wished to use. The Tribunal would then directly address them in that language.[70] Kaeckenbeeck himself adapted to his adoptive Beuthen and the region's inhabitants by becoming fluent in German, which he spoke with a slight Upper Silesian accent.[71] In addition, the Tribunal could rely upon a bilingual Secretariat, presided by an Austrian government lawyer, Otto Grafl, who was 'perfect in both languages.'[72] The Tribunal also made sure that no Upper Silesian would be compelled by economic reasons to renounce filing a claim before it. For instance, while the Geneva Convention provided that parties could be represented by lawyers and law professors registered either in Germany or in Poland or, in intellectual property cases, by a patent agent (art 587 GC), art 6 of the Tribunal's Rules of Procedure extended this possibility to 'any other suitable persons.'[73] In practice, individuals were allowed to resort to self-representation.[74] Inevitably, this led to many cases being badly prepared. As a reaction, the Tribunal adopted flexible procedural standards, sometimes ordering parties to revert to written proceedings when a hearing had shown that they had not grasped which arguments were actually relevant in their case.[75] Similarly, although the Geneva Con-

---

70 Kaeckenbeeck (n 12) 501.

71 Günther Küchenhoff, 'Erinnerungen and das Schiedsgericht für Oberschlesien,' in Manfred Abelein and Otto Kimminich (eds), *Studien zum Staats- und Völkerrecht: Festschrift für Hermann Raschhofer zum 70. Geburtstag am 26. Juli 1975* (Michael Laßleben 1977) 143, 151–52. Although Kaeckenbeeck occasionally mentions Polish studies on the the Geneva Conventions, this author has found no bibliographic or archival evidence that he was fluent in Polish.

72 Kaeckenbeeck (n 40) 30.

73 Pursuant to art 596 GC, the Arbitral Tribunal adopted its own Rules of Procedure in 1923: Schiedsgericht für Oberschlesien/Trybunał Rozjemczy dla Górnego Śląska (ed), 'Verfahrensordnung des Schiedsgerichts für Oberschlesien/Regulamin procesowy Górnośląskiego Trybunału Rozjemczego (9 March 1923) [1923] 2 Reichsgesetzblatt 203/Dz Ust No 72 Pos 562. The German version is reprinted in Kaeckenbeeck (n 12) 823–35.

74 Kaeckenbeeck (n 12) 46, 85. See also: Kaeckenbeeck (n 39) 32.

75 Kaeckenbeeck (n 12) 51.

vention had left it free in that matter, the Tribunal made sure not to exact tariffs or costs that would have impeded the most vulnerable social categories from obtaining justice before it.[76] Even the limited sample provided by the Tribunal's 127 published decisions strikes one as broadly representative of Upper Silesia's population of that time. As a matter of fact, only two cases were brought forward by members of the landed nobility[77] and a few others by industrialists,[78] companies[79], doctors,[80] and one by a lawyer.[81] The vast majority of claims were filed by factory,[82] mine[83], railway[84] and agricultural workers,[85] civil servants[86], employees,[87] small business owners[88] and self-employed workers.[89] Remarkably, the Tribunal also received several cases filed by abandoned spouses,[90] unemployed workers,[91] paupers,[92] and even one by a communist inmate of the Esterwegen concentration camp.[93] The preponderance of working class applicants before the Tribunal was not merely due to the particular sociology of Upper Silesia. As Kaeckenbeeck himself recognized in 1935 before the Grotius Society, the biggest economic players could have done without the Tribunal:

> In fact, the very rich seem to have less need of such a Court than the less well situated who cannot so easily obtain access to the authorities and compromise or arrange matters with them. Our experience shows that the biggest industrial and banking concerns do not as a rule find it necessary to appeal to the Tribunal.[94]

---

76 ibid 500.
77 Nos 11, 62.
78 Nos 1, 34, 35, 43.
79 Nos 57, 58, 75, 76.
80 Nos 6, 93.
81 No 99.
82 Nos 24, 27, 29, 40, 44, 50, 60, 118, 127.
83 Nos 12, 16, 18, 22, 28, 39, 45, 59, 65, 90, 102, 106, 113.
84 Nos 21, 31, 87, 101, 103.
85 Nos 55, 124.
86 Nos 3, 8, 9, 62, 73, 77117, 126.
87 Nos 5, 17, 46, 66, 81, 100, 105, 116, 119.
88 Nos 30, 33, 42, 78, 84, 104, 110, 115.
89 Nos 7, 71, 92.
90 Nos 14, 15, 69, 107, 109, 111.
91 Nos 25, 37, 54.
92 Nos 26, 36, 41.
93 No 64.
94 Kaeckenbeeck (n 40) 32.

Apart from guaranteeing its accessibility, the Arbitral Tribunal also made sure that claims filed before it would receive a timely response. One of the key factors that allowed the speeding up of proceedings was the arbitrators' decision to depart from the letter of the Geneva Convention and adopt German as their working language for all internal discussions and drafts.[95] In order to avoid backlog, the Tribunal used its case-law-making capacity under art 592 GC to issue what can only be described as an early version of pilot judgments: rather than examining several similar cases simultaneously, the President of the Arbitral Tribunal would ask national authorities to refer only one of these cases to the Tribunal and apply the resulting decision to the remaining cases.[96] According to Kaeckenbeeck, '[n]othing contributed more to economy of litigation and to certainty and unity in the application of the Geneva Convention by the courts and authorities of both countries.'[97] With regard to cases filed by private individuals but covered by negative precedent or otherwise clearly irreceivable, the Arbitral Tribunal adopted a summary procedure which it used in more than 1,300 cases. No fees were exacted in these cases.[98] As for art 599 GC regarding interim measures,[99] it proved of great practical value in at least one case. Informed by the German State Representative that the Polish police were about to expell a German family in violation of their right of residence, Kaeckenbeeck convened the Tribunal, decided with his colleagues that

95 ibid.

96 This procedure was first used in the 1933 *Wagner* case. The Tribunal described it as follows: 'Since 105 similar cases are also pending before the Conciliation Commission and the German State Representative has requested to refer all of these cases to the Arbitral Tribunal for binding decision prior to the end of the conciliation procedure, both Governement Representatives, at the suggestion of the President of the Arbitral Tribunal, have agreed to submit only one of these cases to the Arbitral Tribunal for a statement of principle. As a result, the Conciliation Commission chose to refer the case of August Wagner to the Arbitral Tribunal.' No 49, St 42/32, *August Wagner regarding right of residence* (11 January 1933) 4 Arb Trib Dec 2, 4.

97 Kaeckenbeeck (n 12) 28.

98 ibid 85.

99 Art 599 GC read as follows: '1. At the request of one of the State Agents or one of the parties and in cases that they deem appropriate, the Mixed Commission or the Arbitral Tribunal may render provisional resolutions and decisions. This is notably the case where it has been reasonably established that an immediate measure is necessary to protect a right under threat or to avoid considerable damage. 2. Provisional decisions of the Arbitral Tribunal must not include injunctions, but should be limited to a provisional solution to, or confirmation of, an existing situation.'

considerable damage could only be avoided by suspending the police operation pending a decision on the merits, and read the decision by phone to the commanding police officer in the field and to the Polish State Representative. The Polish authorities complied.[100]

While the Arbitral Tribunal made efforts to ensure that the inhabitants of Upper Silesia would not be prevented from obtaining effective and quick relief before it, it also adopted strategies to avoid alienating the states parties.

3.3. Dealing with the States Parties

As an international judicial body endowed with unprecedented powers resulting from a treaty that had been largely forced upon the states parties, the Arbitral Tribunal for Upper Silesia undoubtedly had a legitimacy issue, which could have prevented it from properly working as an institution at all. As a matter of fact, during the first years of the Tribunal's existence, industrialists generally refrained from bringing any cases regarding vested rights before it, because they thought that doing so might lead to backlash.[101] Having participated in the drafting of the Geneva Convention, President Kaeckenbeeck had always been closely aware of the context in which his Tribunal operated, and also knew that his colleagues were far from being totally indifferent to their political environment.[102] Under his leadership, the Tribunal adopted a two-fold approach which allowed it to avoid open conflict with Poland and Germany: while constantly affirming and upholding its legal authority, it also demonstrated deference towards both states.

To avoid that disagreements between its members would undermine the Tribunal's authority in the future, Kaeckenbeeck decided from the outset that there would be no dissenting or separate opinions.[103] Moreover, contrasting with the decisions of the Permanent Court of International Justice, but not unlike those of the Polish–German Mixed Arbitral Tribunal created pursuant to the Treaty of Versailles,[104] the awards rendered by the Arbitral Tribunal for Upper Silesia were generally only a few pages long, thus

100 Kaeckenbeeck (n 12) 208–209.
101 ibid 46.
102 'Allocutions du Président Kaeckenbeeck …' (n 50) 854–55.
103 Kaeckenbeeck (n 12) 58.
104 Eg: Polish–German MAT, *Poznanski v Lentz & Hirschfeld* (22 March 1924) 4 Recueil MAT 353–362.

displaying a distinctly continental *imperatoria brevitas*.[105] As already mentioned with regard to its decision in the case of *Steiner & Groß v Poland*, the Tribunal also avoided lengthy discussions of general international law. Instead, it motivated its decisions by giving authoritative interpretations of the *lex specialis* enshrined within the Geneva Convention.[106] Moreover, regarding the interpretation of this *lex specialis*, the Tribunal made clear from the outset that it would rely mostly on the text on the Convention itself, supplemented by the Decision of the Conference of Ambassadors. By contrast, noting that the negotiation protocols did not cover the final stages of the Geneva Conference, it decided from the outset that it would only give very limited credence to the Convention's *travaux préparatoires*, thus ensuring itself maximum interpretative autonomy.[107]

The Tribunal's will to provide authoritative interpretations of the Geneva Convention to guarantee the rights of individuals had a noticeable impact in the field of nationality. Both states had radically divergent interests in this regard: whereas Poland wanted to have as few Germans with Polish nationality as possible, Germany was bent on securing the maintenance of a large German minority in its neighbouring country.[108] Their conflicting attitudes were especially detrimental to double nationals, notably Germans born in Polish Upper Silesia: even when the Conciliation Commission, established pursuant to the Geneva Convention, had formally recognized their double citizenship, national authorities tended to define them as nationals of the other country. As a result, the individuals in question ended up being virtually stateless.[109] The Arbitral Tribunal eventually put an end to this practice in 1937 by holding that national authorities had a positive obligation to regard individuals whose double nationality had been established by the Conciliation Commission or the Arbitral Tribunal as their own citizens.[110]

The Tribunal had already shown similar concern for the aspirations and needs of individuals in its interpretation of the notion of domicile. Provid-

---

105 Even the seminal decision in the case of *Steiner & Groß* did not exceed 18 rather short pages, only half of which were devoted to motivating the Tribunal's decision.

106 Apart from *Steiner & Groß v Poland*, the only other published case of the Arbitral Tribunal that discussed issues of general international law was decision no 29, C 42/28, *Niederstrasser v Poland* (6 June 1931) 2 Arb Trib Dec 156, 168–170.

107 *Steiner & Groß v Poland* (n 63) 18–20.

108 Kaeckenbeeck (n 12) 123.

109 ibid 134.

110 No 107, St 11/34, *Marta Kirsch regarding nationality* (15 January 1937) 7 Arb Trib Dec 50, 62–64.

ing the parties with such an interpretation was especially important, since under the Geneva Convention a person's nationality often depended on the location of that person's domicile on 15 June 1922. However, art 29 GC had only fixed broad guidelines in this regard, defining domicile as 'the chief place of concentration of an individual's activities and interests, both personal and economic' (*'le principal endroit de concentration de ses activités et intérêts, tant personnels qu'économiques'*). States tended to interpret this provision narrowly. Thus, the German authorities had denied citizenship to a member of the Polish minority who had been born in German Upper Silesia but had found work and accommodation in Polish Upper Silesia at the date of the transfer of sovereignty. The Arbitral Tribunal rebutted Germany's interpretation, noting that neither German nor Polish law, nor indeed 'the notion of merely residing or staying in a given place' (*'ein Begriff des bloßen Wohnens oder Sich-Aufhaltens'*), could determine an Upper Silesian's domicile. Only the *lex specialis* provided by the Geneva Convention, which had been created precisely with regard to 'the special circumstances of Upper Silesia' (*'die besonderen Verhältnisse Oberschlesiens'*), could be of relevance. Simply favouring an individual's economic over their personal centre of interests, or vice-versa, would run counter this *lex specialis*. Conversely, it would also be wrong to expect that an Upper Silesian's domicile concentrate the majority of all his personal activities, economic activities, personal interests, and economic interests. As a consequence, the Tribunal decided that these factors would have to be considered globally given the circumstances of each case. In the case which had come before it, the Tribunal noted that while the individual under consideration had been working and sleeping in Poland, he had spent his weekends in Germany, helping his brother and sisters to run the family farm, resupplying with food and getting his laundry done. In short, his 'home' (*'Heimat'*), and therefore his domicile, lay in Germany—regardless whether he had registered or not with the authorities of that country.[111]

In the case of *Lorenz Puchalla*, decided in 1933, the Tribunal had gone even further. The case concerned a German national who had been domiciled in Polish Upper Silesia before 1908 but had left the territory several times between that date and 1922. The question before the Tribunal revolved around the issue whether Puchalla's absences could be interpreted as 'temporary' abandonments of his Upper Silesian domicile pursuant to the introductory paragraph of art 25 § 2 GC, or whether the fact that they

111 No 7, St 11/27, *Anton Halamoda regarding nationality* (23 March 1928) 1 Arb Trib Dec 122, 124–128.

were unsuccessful attempts at permanent emigration should preclude him from automatically acquiring Polish citizenship. In its award, the Arbitral Tribunal decided that the temporary character of a person's abandonment of its domicile in Upper Silesia had to be analyzed retrospectively. However, rather than simply applying this principle to the facts at hand, the Tribunal devoted several pages to providing the administrative authorities of both countries with a detailed commentary of art 25 § 2 GC, complete with possible other scenarios that might arise before them.[112]

A few years later, after the Tribunal's activity had ended, Kaeckenbeeck would explain its role in interpreting the Geneva Convention by resorting to legal fiction. In his view, the Arbitral Tribunal for Upper Silesia was 'to a very large extent an emanation of both States' (*'dans une assez large mesure une émanation des États'*)—after all, he and his colleagues had been chosen by Poland and Germany. Therefore, the Tribunal's authoritative interpretations—notably in the field of evocation—were not unlike authentic interpretations. In fact, in his view, the Tribunal's activity could even be described as forming an integral part of the domestic judicial system of both states.[113] Although this form of legal fiction might seem a little clumsy at first sight, it was given some credit by the fact that the vast majority of the Tribunal's decisions were taken unanimously.[114]

Operating on a basis of unanimity, the Tribunal had the authority required to force upon the parties the kind of administrative compromises that would have been impossible to reach through negotiations alone. However, this did not mean that the Tribunal asserted its authority con-

112 No 56, St 46/33, *Lorenz Puchalla regarding nationality* (13 December 1933) 4 Arb Trib Dec 126, 146–156.

113 Kaeckenbeeck (n 48) 60–61. '*Ce Tribunal arbitral, spécialisé et se trouvant sur les lieux, était composé d'un juge allemand, d'un juge polonais et d'un président neutre nommé par le Conseil de la Société des Nations, mais dont le choix avait été en fait celui des deux États. Il était donc dans une assez large mesure une émanation des États. Et lorsqu'une question d'interprétation de la Convention lui était transmise par un tribunal ou une autorité, il était compétent pour donner une interprétation qui liait le juge national ou l'autorité, et qui même, si elle était publiée dans la collection officielle de décisions d'intérêt jurisprudentiel du Tribunal arbitral, liait, conformément à l'art. 592, les tribunaux et autorités des deux pays un peu comme le ferait une interprétation authentique. Mais le Tribunal arbitral se bornait à interpréter les dispositions de la Convention. L'élucidation des faits et la décision de l'affaire—sur la base de l'interprétation donnée—restaient dans les mains de l'autorité ou du tribunal national. Le Tribunal arbitral n'agissait donc pas comme une instance internationale superposée aux instances nationales, mais il s'insérait pour ainsi dire dans l'administration nationale du droit.*' See also Kaeckenbeeck (n 12) 487.

114 Kaeckenbeeck (n 39) 43.

stantly. As a matter of fact, it showed considerable deference towards both states. From a procedural view, it often preferred resorting to conciliation, rather than imposing unilateral solutions that would have been binding upon the parties, but might have been felt as so many acts of public humiliation.[115] In this regard, the fact that the Arbitral Tribunal had direct institutional connections with the two conciliation commissions on nationality questions and circulation permits was described by Kaeckenbeeck as especially helpful, since it allowed him to intervene as a neutral in the procedure at a very early stage.[116]

With regard to substantial law, the Tribunal's composition and its consensual approach hardly enabled it to question decisions that resulted from either state's fundamental political or economic choices. In fact, the Tribunal always made a point of acting with judicial restraint when confronted with politically sensitive provisions of the Geneva Convention, using a textual rather than a teleological interpretation. This was especially true with regard to the protection of vested rights. In particular, the Tribunal held that the obligation of states to compensate holders of vested rights that had been infringed upon by general administrative or statutory measures only applied, with regard to vested rights of a public or semi-public nature, to those rights expressly mentioned under art 4 § 2 (3) and (4). These two provisions were respectively limited to concessions or privileges authorising or concerning installations, enterprises, establishments and official certificates of doctors, dentists, veterinary surgeons, as well as authorizations to exercise the professions of midwife, land mine surveyor or farrier. Consequently, other professionals, such as machine operators, could not file compensation claims before the Tribunal after having been stripped of an official authorization or qualification.[117] The Tribunal's interpretation of vested rights also followed a rather narrow and textual ap-

---

115 This policy corresponded to Kaeckenbeeck's conception of his role as an international lawyer, based on the belief that 'the international mindset' correponded, first and foremost, to a 'capacity to seek combination and compromise'. In Kaeckenbeeck's own words: '*L'esprit international est un esprit de synthèse. C'est aussi et avant tout un esprit de bonne volonté active. Il est constructif et organisateur. Il n'est ni antinational, ni révolutionnaire. Il part de l'existence des États pour aboutir à une organisation des rapports entre ces États. Il fait appel au droit et se soumet à lui, pour que cette organisation, étant juste, puisse prospérer en paix.*' Georges Kaeckenbeeck, 'L'expérience du Tribunal arbitral de Haute-Silésie', in Professeurs de l'Institut Universitaire des Hautes Études internationales (eds), *La Crise Mondiale* (Éditions Polygraphiques 1938) 249, 256.

116 Kaeckenbeeck (n 39) 31.

117 *Niederstrasser v Poland* (n 104) 166–170.

proach. This allowed it not to question Poland's will to introduce new economic policies in its part of Upper Silesia, even if these policies had substantial effects on the continued existence of individual businesses. By way of illustration, the Tribunal held that vested rights were of a strictly personal nature. Consequently, it decided that a widow could not claim to have inherited her late husband's right to run a tobacco business, since the business had been established exclusively in her husband's name and had only been inherited by her after the transfer of sovereignty.[118] Similarly, the Tribunal decided that a mere tax increase could not violate the vested right of running an established business, even when it significantly reduced the rentability of that business, since taxing a business implied recognition of its owner's right to run it.[119]

The Tribunal's restrictive and deferential approach led to some rather questionable results after the Nazi takeover in Germany. For instance, the Tribunal refused to award compensation to a notary and solicitor who had been forced to close his legal practice after having been ruined as a result of several anti-Jewish measures adopted by the new German authorities. The Tribunal based its refusal on the ground that the claimant did not have a vested right to run his law practice, since vested rights were concrete in nature, and thus different from mere freedoms, such as the freedom of trade and industry.[120] Similarly, the Tribunal held that informal pressure applied by the Nazi Propaganda Minister Josef Goebbels on the UFA to dismiss Jewish employees could not give rise to reparation under art 4 GC. Relying once again on a textual interpretation, it argued that such an action could not be qualified as 'the application of general statutes or other provisions' ('*l'application générale de lois générales ou … d'autres dispositions*') mentioned by that provision.[121] The Tribunal showed analogous restraint in the field of residence rights, holding for instance that it could not question the facts provided by the German authorities in order to justify their decision to expell a 'privileged alien' pursuant to art 44 GC on grounds of state security.[122] However, while these decisions certainly deserve a critical assessment, they should also not be read out of context. In that context, marked by the general disintegration of the League system, it might already seem remarkable that the Upper Silesian Arbitral Tribunal

118 No 33, C 32/27 *Böhm v Poland* (18 December 1931) 3 Arb Trib Dec 2, 8–12.
119 No 35, C 44/27, *Kügele v Poland* (5 February 1932) 3 Arb Trib Dec 20, 26–28.
120 No 99, C 22/34, *Jablonsky v Germany* (24 June 1936) 6 Arb Trib Dec 218, 234.
121 No 105, C 48/34, *Weißman v Germany* (12 March 1937) 7 Arb Trib Dec 28, 36–38.
122 No 71, St 62/33, *Hochbaum regarding right of residence* (20 December 1934) 5 Arb Trib Dec 140, 160–162.

did not consider the invocation of state security to be self-judging, but stressed that Nazi Germany had a duty to provide the Tribunal with a factual basis for this decision.[123] Similarly, the Tribunal's inability to provide effective relief to minorities was significantly compensated by the existence of minority rights procedures before the Council of the League and, more importantly even, before the President of the Upper Silesian Commission, whose judicial activism eventually led to the suspension of anti-Jewish legislation in German Upper Silesian between 1934 and 1937. While Kaeckenbeeck's background and his later writings clearly indicate that he shared the same hostility towards discrimination as his older colleague and friend, his Tribunal would arguably have been much less well-equipped to win that fight than Calonder, who was an experienced elder statesman, had a clear mandate to protect minority rights and was not bound by any consideration of collegiality.[124]

4. *Defending the Tribunal's Legacy*

On the afternoon of 15 July 1937, after attending the closing ceremony of the Upper Silesian Commission in Katowice, Georges Kaeckenbeeck presided over the last formal sitting of his Arbitral Tribunal in Beuthen. The event was attended by the members of the two international organs, local dignitaries, German and Polish government officials, the British, French and Italian consuls in Katowice, as well as by members of the press.[125] In his speech, which he delivered in French, Kaeckenbeeck took stock of the Tribunal's achievements. Presenting the public with statistics on resolved (3,726) and still pending (227) cases, he made clear that one of the characteristics of the Tribunal had been its ability to deal with an ex-

123 ibid 160–164.

124 Calonder and Kaeckenbeeck both referred to each other as close friends in their respective farewell speeches. 'Procès-verbal de la séance solennelle de clôture de la Commission mixte, tenue le 15 juillet 1937, à 10.30 heures, dans la salle des séances de la Commission mixte à Katowice' in Kaeckenbeeck (n 12) 844, 853; 'Allocutions du Président Kaeckenbeeck ...' (n 52) 857.

125 'Schlußsitzung des Schiedsgerichts für OS', *Oberschlesischer Wanderer* (Gleiwitz, 16 July 1937) 5. It should be noted that while German regional newspapers often gave rather favourable assessments of the Upper Silesian organs' work, the Polish regional press seems to have failed to address this aspect of the question, to the great dismay of the British consul in Katowice—who, while identifying himself as a polonophile, was also an admirer of what he perceived to be Calonder's and Kaeckenbeeck's professional idealism and devotion. Stauffer (n 24) 85–86.

tremely diverse caseload, addressing questions pertaining to legal fields as varied as 'public and private international law, civil law, commercial law, administrative and constitutional law, procedure, industrial law, mining law, labour law, social insurance, pensions, tax law, canon law, [and] railway rates.'[126] As for the Tribunal's case law, and more particularly the rules set out in those decisions that had been published in its official collection, Kaeckenbeeck assumed that they would have a lasting value in at least three ways. First, from a scientific point of view, the Tribunal's decisions regarding vested rights would serve as an illustration of 'the most complete and most far-reaching international experiment which had been attempted in that field.'[127] Secondly, from a procedural point of view, Kaeckenbeeck noted with characteristic restraint that the evocation procedure, 'owing to the possibilities it offers in the international domain … deserve[d] the attention of statesmen and diplomats.'[128] Thirdly, from a practical point of view, Kaeckenbeeck stressed that the Arbitral Tribunal's decisions on nationality would have far-reaching implications for 'thousands and thousands of individuals', since German and Polish authorities would have to resort to them in the future to ascertain a given individual's nationality. Otherwise, 'they would risk jeopardizing hundreds, maybe even thousands, of stabilized situations, depriving many individuals of one nationality without providing them with another.'[129] Both state representatives also acknowledged the Tribunal's legacy, albeit in very general (and strikingly similar) terms: after the Polish state representative had noted that the Tribunal's work included 'valuable material for international legal doctrine' ('*wertvolles Material für die Lehre des internationalen Rechts*'), the German state representative recognized that it had provided 'valuable building blocks for the development of international law' ('*wertvolle Bausteine für den Aufbau des internationalen Rechts*').[130] Their insistence on the Tribunal's theoretical legacy rather than its practical role was hardly surprising. Addressing the Tribunal's role as a guarantor of the Geneva Convention

126 Kaeckenbeeck (n 12) 857.

127 ibid. Original text: '*l'expérience internationale la plus complète et la plus poussée qui ait été tentée dans ce domaine*.'

128 ibid. French original: '*la procédure [d'évocation], qui par les possibilités qu'elle offre dans le domaine international, mérite d'attirer l'attention des hommes d'État et des diplomates*.'

129 ibid 858. French original: '*ils risqueraient de mettre en question des centaines, des milliers peut-être de situations stabilisées et de priver sans raison de nombreuses personnes d'une nationalité sans leur en faire acquérir une autre.*'

130 'Schlußsitzung …' (n 124).

would have entailed acknowledging that many of the individual rights granted under this Convention would disappear once it expired. Upper Silesians could hardly ignore this fact, even those that got their information from publications such as the *Oberschlesischer Wanderer*. Right next to its report on the closing ceremony of the Arbitral Tribunal, the main daily newspaper in German Upper Silesia and official organ of the local Nazi party published an article announcing that pursuant to the termination of the conventional regime several cross-border train services were being discontinued.[131]

Despite paying lip-service to the Tribunal's achievements on 15 July 1937, neither Germany nor Poland actually wanted it to have an enduring legacy on their mutual relations. This became already clear during the Tribunal's winding-up period, organized in three sessions and supplementary conversations between September 1937 and March 1938 at Kaeckenbeeck's residence near Montreux. During this period, which Kaeckenbeeck presented as the 'unhappiest' in the life of the Tribunal,[132] Poland and Germany failed to settle 43 out of 227 cases which had been left over at the expiration of the conventional regime.[133] Although the derailment of the winding-up procedure seems to have been attributable in great part to Poland (which insisted on relying on bilateral negotiations rather than on arbitration by Kaeckenbeeck),[134] it was Germany that physically liquidated the Tribunal's work. The preparations for this process were already in full swing on 15 July 1937. As a matter of fact, during the Tribunal's closing ceremony, the German state representative had gone as far as implying that the Tribunal's contribution to peace in Europe had now been taken up by a new guarantor, namely Nazi Germany and its *Wehrmacht*.[135] Replacing international cooperation and adjudication with great power politics and

131 'Fahrplanänderungen nach Ablauf der Genfer Konvention,' *Oberschlesischer Wanderer* (Gleiwitz, 16 July 1937) 5.

132 Kaeckenbeeck (n 12) 507.

133 ibid 512, 857.

134 ibid.

135 The *Oberschlesischer Wanderer* reported the German state representative's as follows: 'Germany was proud of its recovered equality and military capabilities which, according to the Führer's will, would serve no other purpose than to act as a strong guarantor of European peace. The work of the Arbitral Tribunal had served that very same purpose.' German original text: '*Das deutsche Volk sei stolz auf seine wiedergewonnene Gleichberechtigung und Wehrhaftigkeit, die nach dem Willen des Führers nichts anderes sein sollten, als ein starker Garant des europäischen Friedens. Diesem Ziel habe auch die Tätigkeit des Schiedsgerichtes gedient.*' 'Schlußsitzung …' (n 122).

militarization would ultimately transform Upper Silesia from the world's most advanced 'legal experiment' into a place more commonly associated with the outbreak of the Second World War (the 'Gleiwitz incident' on 31 August 1939 took place less than 20 km from Beuthen) and mass extermination (Auschwitz, which the Nazis had integrated into an enlarged Upper Silesia, was situated a little more than 50 km from the Tribunal's former seat).

Kaeckenbeeck speaking during the Tribunal's closing ceremony, Beuthen/Bytom, 15 July 1937. Also pictured are the Polish arbitrator Stelmachowski (left) and his German counterpart von Steinaecker (right). Source: United Nations Archives at Geneva.

In the years between his departure from Upper Silesia and the end of the Second World War, and despite the increasingly cataclysmic events unfolding in Europe, Kaeckenbeeck repeatedly defended his Tribunal's legacy as a meaningful precedent in the history of international adjudication. He specifically mentioned the system created by the Geneva Convention his course on the international protection of vested rights at the Hague Academy of International law in 1937.[136] In October 1937, speaking in Geneva before an audience of students and interested members of the public, he underlined the 'extreme importance' of the Arbitral Tribunal's decision in *Steiner & Groß v Poland*.[137] In 1940, after the war had already broken out, he defended the Geneva Convention's continued relevance in future post-war situations in a series of conferences at the Geneva Graduate Institute[138] and in a monograph published in Zurich.[139] Kaeckenbeeck's efforts culminated in an authoritative and detailed account of the 'International Experiment of Upper Silesia.' In this book, he insisted heavily on the necessity of providing complex international regimes with judicial guarantees, including for individuals.[140] For him, it could be said that the Geneva Convention had reached its 'climax' with its provisions on the Mixed Commission and Arbitral Tribunal for Upper Silesia.[141] Once again, he highlighted the evocation procedure 'as a new departure in international legal practice susceptible of wide and useful application.'[142]

Although finished shortly before the Second World War broke out, Kaeckenbeeck's book on Upper Silesia was only published in 1942, with the support of the Royal Institute of International Affairs.[143] By that time, he had already left the safety of his Swiss retreat for Britain, where he acted as chief legal adviser for the Belgian government in exile.[144] Kaeckenbeeck's willingness to defend the legacy of the international system developed during the interwar period did not cease after the avent of the United Nations in 1945. In his second course at the Hague Academy of International Law in 1947, Kaeckenbeeck, while insisting on the many elements of continuity between the League of Nations and the United Nations, also criticized the impact of political realism on the new organization.[145] In his view, the UN was 'an instrument for the maintenance of order rather than an association for the maintenance of the law' ('*un instrument pour le maintien de l'ordre, plutôt qu'une association pour le maintien du*

136 Georges Kaeckenbeeck, 'La protection internationale des droits acquis' (1937) 59 Recueil des Cours 317, 396–410.
137 Kaeckenbeeck (n 115) 262–3.
138 *De la guerre à la paix* (Naville & Cie/Librairie du Recueil Sirey 1940) 85–86.
139 Kaeckenbeeck (n 113) 57–67.
140 Kaeckenbeeck (n 12) 529.
141 ibid 479.
142 ibid 486.
143 ibid.
144 Vanlangenhove (n 59) 547–548.
145 Georges Kaeckenbeeck, 'La Charte de San-Francisco dans ses rapports avec le droit international' (1947) 70 Recueil des Cours 113, 304–306.

droit').[146] In an express reference to Upper Silesia, Kaeckenbeeck also deplored that the San Francisco Charter mentioned human rights but failed to build on the League's experience by not providing for any international mechanisms to ensure their implementation.[147]

Kaeckenbeeck's painstaking efforts to save the legacy of the 'Upper Silesian Experiment' as an important precedent in the history of international law yielded little results. True, during the Paris Peace Conference in 1946, Australia, under the impetus of its Minister for External Affairs, the internationalist lawyer and judge HV Evatt (1894–1965), tried to advocate the creation of a European Court of Human Rights based on the Arbitral Tribunal for Upper Sileisa. However, this proposal, which was directly influenced by Kaeckenbeeck's 1942 book, elicited little interest from the other participants.[148] As a matter of fact, Australia's failed proposal seems to have been the last occasion on which a government formally acknowledged the Upper Silesian conventional regime as an important potential source of inspiration in the field of international adjudication. With governments failing to mention it as a model, it is no wonder the Geneva Convention and its enforcement mechanisms all but disappeared from post-WWII international law textbooks. However, their legacy might have survived on a regional level.

5. *Conclusion: From Upper Silesia to Luxembourg?*

Building on his solid experience in international administration, Kaeckenbeeck took an active participation in the post-war reconstruction of Europe. Within Belgium's Ministry of Foreign Affairs, he was appointed head of the Department for Peace Conferences and International Organization —whose work became so closely associated with Kaeckenbeeck that it was internally referred to as '"K" Service.'[149] Between 1949 and 1953, he occupied another international position in a major German industrial centre,

146 ibid 306.

147 ibid 260–264.

148 Annemarie Devereux, 'Australia and the International Scrutiny of Civil and Political Rights' (2002) 47 Aust YBIL 47, 54–55. Kaeckenbeeck himself briefly mentioned the Australian proposal in his 1947 Hague course: Kaeckenbeeck (n 142) 263.

149 Vincent Delcorps, 'The Belgian Ministry of Foreign Affairs and the Challenge of Multilateralism (1944–60)' 44 Revue belge d'histoire contemporaine/Belgisch tijdschrift voor nieuwste geschiedenis 8, 18.

as secretary-general of the International Authority for the Ruhr (IAR)[150] which had been established pursuant to an agreement between the United States, the United Kingdom, France, and the Benelux countries.[151]

On 27 October 1951, Kaeckenbeeck presented a paper about the IAR and the recently adopted Schuman plan establishing the European Coal and Steel Community (ECSC)[152] before the Grotius Society in London. In his presentation, Kaeckenbeeck did not make a single mention of the Geneva Convention and the Upper Silesian international organs. He rather insisted on the changes that had taken place since the Second World War. During that conflict, 'international organization' had emerged as 'the great world saving task,' as illustrated by the replacement of a 'League of Nations' by an 'United Nations Organization.' This new conception implied that international law could not be portrayed anymore as 'a fragmentary limited rule tolerated only within such gaps as are left between political sovereignties.' It had to be seen as 'a law intended to control the actions of men grouped in political entities.'[153] However, when it came to describing the method by which international lawyers could help realizing 'international organization,' Kaeckenbeeck used terms that were clearly reminiscent of his experience in the interwar period:

> No doubt all of us feel that much is amiss in the world. In diagnosing the evil and making plans to combat it, we must, in law, as in all sciences and all arts, use our imagination first. Then, we have a working hypothesis, we must experiment. Experiment implies that a final judgment is reserved.[154]

Kaeckenbeeck thus described the IAR and the ECSC as international 'experiments,' using the very same term he had used to characterize the Upper Silesian conventional regime. Both experiments were part of a continuous process: in his view, the IAR, which '[belonged], with slight deviations, to the classical type of international organization, inspired by a law of co-ordination of sovereignties,' 'almost necessarily' led up to the ECSC, which he described as 'a revolutionary scheme with an enormous political poten-

150 Vanlangenhove (n 60) 550–552.

151 Agreement for the Establishment of an International Authority for the Ruhr (concluded and entered into force 28 April 1949) 83 UNTS 105.

152 Treaty Establishing the European Coal and Steel Community (signed 18 April 1951, entered into force 23 July 1952) 261 UNTS 140.

153 Georges Kaeckenbeeck, 'The International Authority for the Ruhr and the Schuman Plan' (1951) 37 Transactions of the Grotius Society 4, 4–5.

154 ibid 5.

tial.'[155] Kaeckenbeeck did not mention whether he thought that the IAR and ECSC experiments had to be assessed in continuity with the Upper Silesian experiment. However, just like in his book on Upper Silesia, he insisted on the centrality of international judicial guarantees. Indeed, for Kaeckenbeeck, the most striking feature within the ECSC scheme was not the High Authority, with its 'supranational character', but the ECSC Court, and 'the extraordinary advance in the establishment of the rule of law in international life, which [it] [foreshadowed].'[156] In the long run, the Court established by the Schuman plan would possibly give rise to a form of federal organization scheme that might be replicated elsewhere:

> When you consider that [the Court's] judgments will be executory in the territories of the member States with no other formality than the certification of their authenticity, you will realise to what extent this Court will bear a federal character. Like the Assembly, it may well be resorted for similar tasks, in domains other than those of the European and Steel Community. Indeed, men with vision may discern possibility of a number of functional organizations revolving [a]round an Assembly, such as the Council of Europe, and a Court, such as the Schuman plan contemplates. This is no longer pure Utopia. Six European Parliaments are beginning to deliberate on the matter.[157]

Although Kaeckenbeeck himself would be prevented from taking part in this new venture,[158] he would turn out to be right with regard to the Court's political potential. After the failure of the openly federal scheme of the European Defence Community (EDC) in 1954, efforts at European integration shifted to a more limited approach, based on the establishment of a common market. They ultimately resulted in the 1957 EEC Treaty.[159] Within that framework, legal advisers and judges soon found ways to pursue the federalist drive that elected officials had been unable or unwilling to maintain. In 1963–1964, following the lead of the EEC Commission's

155 ibid 5–6.

156 ibid 12.

157 ibid 12–13.

158 During a cabinet meeting on 17 July 1952, the Belgian Minister of Foreign Affairs named Charles De Visscher, Louis Delvaux and Georges Kaeckenbeeck as possible Belgian candidates for the Court of Justice—in that order of preference. Belgium eventually appointed Delvaux, a former Minister of Agriculture with no prior international experience. Vera Fritz, *Juges et avocats généraux de la Cour de Justice de l'Union européenne (1952–1972)* (Vittorio Klostermann 2018) 82–83.

159 Treaty Establishing the European Economic Community (signed 25 March 1957, entered into force 1 January 1958) 294 UNTS 17.

Legal Service and its Director-General Michel Gaudet (1915–2003),[160] the European Court of Justice (ECJ) adopted two seminal judgments[161] which established a 'constitutional practice' of European law.[162] In *Van Gend en Loos*, by holding that individuals could directly invoke EEC law, the Court laid the foundations of the the direct effect principle;[163] in *Costa v ENEL*, it established the principle of supremacy of EEC law over the domestic law of member states.[164] Both cases had come before the Court following a preliminary ruling procedure, under which domestic courts could refer Community law questions to the Court before making a decision on the merits. Under art 41 ECSC, preliminary rulings had been limited to questions relating to the validity of acts adopted by the High Authority or the Council. Under art 177 EEC Treaty, the Court's jurisdiction under the preliminary ruling procedure was expanded to include, amongst others, all questions of interpretation of that Treaty. Despite the difference in nomenclature, the EEC Treaty's preliminary procedure before the ECJ bore a striking resemblence to the evocation procedure before the Upper Silesian Arbitral Tribunal under art 588 GC.[165]

From a purely normative perspective, it might be tempting to analyze this evolution as a timely vindication of Kaeckenbeeck's painstaking efforts to salvage the legacy of the Upper Silesian experiment. As a matter of fact, the ECJ handed down its judgment in *Van Gend en Loos* during Kaeckenbeeck's final year as a practitioner of international law (he retired in 1963 from his functions as a member of the French–German Arbitral Tribunal for the Saar and died in 1973).[166] However, although they might have known about the existence of the Geneva Convention either from literature or from conversations with Jean Monnet, there is no proof that the le-

---

160 Anne Boerger and Morten Rasmussen, 'The Making of European Law: Exploring the Life and Work of Michel Gaudet' [2017] American Journal of Legal History 57, 70–78.

161 For a contextualized analysis of these decisions: Antoine Vauchez, *Brokering Europe: Euro-Lawyers and the Making of a Transnational Polity* (CUP 2015) 116–150.

162 Anne Boerger-De Smedt, 'Negotiating the Foundations of European Law, 1950-57: The Legal History of the Treaties of Paris and Rome' (2012) 21 Contemporary European History 339, 340.

163 Case 26/62 *Van Gend en Loos* [1963], ECLI:EU:C:1963:1.

164 Case 6/64 *Costa v ENEL* [1964], ECLI:EU:C:1964:66.

165 For a comparison between both procedures: Fernando Irurzun Montoro, '¿La cuestión de interpretación ante el tribunal arbitral de la alta silesia (1922–1937) como antecedente de la cuestión prejudicial europea?' (2017) 63 Revista Española de Derecho Europeo 13–45.

166 Vanlangenhove (n 58) 552.

gal experts who created the preliminary ruling procedure used Upper Silesian evocation as their model. While it seems that Maurice Lagrange (1900–1986), who drafted art 41 ECSC Treaty, might have read it as giving the Court a general jurisdiction to interpret that treaty, archives provide almost no information as to his and the other participants' motivations or inspiration.[167] Similarly, while the German delegate Carl Friedrich Ophüls (1895–1970) made an express reference to individual complaints before the Mixed Arbitral Tribunals established by the Treaty of Versailles, he did not mention the procedure before the Upper Silesian Arbitral Tribunal under art 4 GC.[168] With regard to art 177 EEC, sources are just as inconclusive. First, the group of legal experts who elaborated the EEC's adjudication provisions did not record any minutes of their meetings.[169] Moreover, in his often-quoted 1981 recollection of these meetings, the representative of Luxembourg and 'cosmopolitan Euro-lawyer par excellence'[170] Pierre Pescatore (1919–2010) mentioned several models that the group had used as a general inspiration for the EEC Treaties, namely the ECSC, the EDC, the Belgium–Luxembourg Economic Union, and even the German *Zollverein* (1834–1919)—but not the Geneva Convention.[171] More specifically, with regard to art 177 EEC, Pescatore remembered that the provision was the result of a suggestion by the Italian lawyer and member of the ECSC High Authority's legal department Nicola Catalano (1910–1984). According to Pescatore, Catalano had based his suggestion on the existence of a similar procedure before the Italian Constitutional Court. His idea apparently met with immediate approval by the German members of the group, whom their own constitutional law had also rendered familiar with this

167 Anne Boerger-De Smedt, 'La Cour de Justice dans les négociations du traité de Paris instituant la CECA' (2008) 14 Journal of European Integration History 7, 29–30.

168 'Dokument 28: Kurzprotokoll des juristischen Sachverständigenausschusses, Sitzung vom 7.8.1950' in Reiner Schulze and Thomas Hoeren (eds), *Dokumente zum Europäischen Recht. Band 2: Justiz (bis 1957)* (Springer 2000) 45, 46. It should be noted that Ophüls had been commissary for the Mixed Arbitral Tribunals at the German Ministry of Foreign Affairs in 1923–1930. Biographical note: Bundesarchiv, GND:11873637X {{Ophüls, Carl Friedrich}}.

169 Pierre Pescatore, 'Les travaux du "groupe juridique" dans la négociation des Traités de Rome' (1981) 24 Studia diplomatica 159, 167.

170 Vauchez (n 161) 106.

171 Pescatore (n 168) 165–166.

kind of procedure.[172] At no point does Pescatore mention the Upper Silesian evocation procedure as a source of inspiration for the drafters of art 177 EEC. However, this does not constitue proof that nobody in the room was aware of this precedent. Federalists such as Catalano and Pescatore might simply have thought that it was strategically wiser to associate the ECJ with powerful constitutional courts of democratic states than with an Arbitral Tribunal once situated in a region now closely associated with the outbreak of the Second World War. In that case, interwar Upper Silesia and its Arbitral Tribunal could be described as forming part of the repressed memories of post-WWII Euro-lawyers.

Future research might perhaps be able to establish a direct link between the evocation procedure before Kaeckenbeeck's Tribunal in Beuthen and the 'extraordinary judicial gadget'[173] of the preliminary ruling procedure before the ECJ in Luxembourg. This being said, there is one major difference between EEC law and the provisions of the Geneva Convention. The protection afforded to Upper Silesians had been part of a 15 year-scheme destined to ensure the smooth partition of an ethnically diverse and economically interconnected region. True, there are indications that during the negotiations at Geneva, some participants formulated the idea of a permanent economic integration regime for both parts of Upper Silesia.[174] However, it was clear that France would not accept such an ambitious plan,[175] and that both Poland and Germany were impatient to regain full

172 ibid 173. Catalano himself compared the preliminary ruling procedure to the Italian *questione di leggitimità costituzionale* (art 23 Law no 87 of 11 March 1953) in one of his subsequent publications. Nicola Catalano, *Manuel de droit des communautés européennes* (Dalloz/Sirey 1962) 85.

173 Pescatore (n 169) 173.

174 During a discussion with an anonymous French source, the head of the Polish delegation at the League of Nations, Jan Perłowski (1872–1942), described this as a 'British tendency.' 'Compte-rendu d'un entretien avec M. Perlowski' (26 November 1921) Archives MAE, SDN 278, Haute-Silésie 16 octobre–31 décembre 1921, 174.

175 According to Perłowski, the 'French tendency' wanted the economic union of Upper Silesia to cease after 15 years: the region's economic life would have to reflect its political division. A form of 'minimal solidarity' ('*un minimum de solidarité*') might possibly subsist, but it would allow each part of the region to pursue its own interests. Strangely, Perłowski quoted the Belgium–Luxembourg Economic Union established in 1921, which included a customs and monetary union, as this tendency's model. ibid.

sovereignty over their respective parts of the territory.[176] In comparison to the Geneva Convention's limited regime, the provisions of the EEC Treaty went much further. As stated by the ECJ in *Costa v ENEL*:

> By contrast with ordinary international treaties, the EEC Treaty has created its own legal system which, on the entry into force of the Treaty, became an integral part of the legal systems of the member States and which their courts are bound to apply.
> By creating a Community of unlimited duration, having its own institutions, its own personality and its own capacity in law, apart from having international standing and more particularly, real powers resulting from a limitation of competence or a transfer of powers from the States to the Community, the Member States have limited their sovereign rights, albeit within limited fields, and have thus created a body of law which binds both their nationals and themselves.[177]

Just like the EEC's institutions, the Upper Silesian international organs did have 'real powers' and rendered decisions that were both international and integrated within the domestic legal systems of the states parties. However, in Upper Silesia there had been no Community of 'unlimited duration' endowed with its own international legal personality. The ECJ used the existence of such a Community to go further than the Arbitral Tribunal for Upper Silesia. While the latter had generally interpreted limitations on Poland's and Germany's sovereignty in a very restrictive way, the ECJ in *Costa v ENEL* relied on a teleological, rather than literal, interpretation of the EEC Treaty. Thus, from the open-ended nature of the EEC, the ECJ deduced 'a permanent limitation of [its member States'] sovereign rights'.[178] Over the following years, the landmark decisions adopted in *Van Gend en Loos* and *Costa v ENEL* would allow Euro-lawyers to unify different legal-

176 In a confidential letter to Léon Bourgeois, then President of the French Senate, Jean Monnet noted that the Polish delegation wanted the transition period to be as short as possible. Monnet to Bourgeois (Geneva 23 November 1921) Archives MAE, SDN 278, Haute-Silésie 16 octobre–31 décembre 1921, 163. In a subsequent letter, he observed that both parties generally favoured interpretations that would ensure the independence, rather than the mutual interdependence, of their respective parts of the region. He concluded that both states were 'similarly anxious to abandon as little of their sovereignty as possible' ('*paraissent avoir également le souci de perdre le moins possible de leur souveraineté*'). Monnet to Bourgeois (Geneva 9 March 1922) Archives MAE, SDN 280, Haute-Silésie mars–mai 1922, 174.

177 *Costa v ENEL* (n 162).

178 ibid.

political doctrines of integration into a single European integration programme, based on the redefinition of Europe as a 'Community of law.'[179] This characterization undoubtedly echoes Kaeckenbeeck's prediction of an 'extraordinary advance in the establishment of the rule of law in international life.' However, in this author's view, Kaeckenbeeck's writings also remind us that avant-garde schemes for regional integration developed by benevolent lawyers have inherent limitations. Unless they are able to establish a direct connection with the ultimate holders of sovereignty, they will have to live with the danger of joining Upper Silesia on the list of inconclusive international experiments.

179 Vauchez (n 160) 140–146.

Part 5:
Beyond 'Peace Through Law': The Use of Law and Its Records as Vehicles of Resistance and Change

Chapter 13 Resistance Through Law: Belgian Judges and the Relations Between Occupied State and Occupying Power

Didier Boden[*]

The legal aspects of war are not limited to questions of respect or violation by the belligerent states of their obligations under international law. War also has many consequences in domestic law, and more specifically in the criminal law, private law, and private international law of the belligerent states (whether in a situation of occupation or not). Depending on the interpretation given to these consequences, war may turn law from an instrument of peace and reconciliation into an instrument of resistance. During the First World War, German-occupied Belgium and its courts had been a legal laboratory of the greatest interest in this respect. Understandably, neither the drafters of the Versailles Peace Treaty nor the League of Nations made much of this experience, since their priorities were to terminate and prevent war rather than to regulate it. However, despite its limited impact on positive law, occupied Belgium definitely set standards that remained relevant afterwards—both with regard to judicial independence in times of occupation and to the power of judges to resist major violations of international law. That is why this contribution is focalized on that state, even if some judgments from other countries will also be mentioned.

1. *Overall Approach*

The main (but not the only) legal basis of the relations between the occupied state and the occupying power is Article 43 of the Appendix to the 1907 Hague convention. Among Belgian courts, discrepancies with regard to the interpretation of that article arose at the beginning of the First

---

* Associate Professor (*maître de conférences*), SERPI-IRJS (*Sorbonne département d'Étude des Relations Privées Internationales*, department of the *Institut de Recherche Juridique de la Sorbonne*), Sorbonne Law School, Université Paris 1 Panthéon-Sorbonne.

World War. The most audacious of these interpretations (which also happened to be the most interesting one) ended up prevailing.

1.1. Article 43 of the Annex to the 1907 Hague Convention

On 18 October 1907, at the end of the second international peace conference held at The Hague, numerous conventions were signed. One of the most important of these conventions was the Convention Respecting the Laws and Customs of War on Land. It was ratified by Austria–Hungary, Belgium, France, Germany, Luxembourg, Netherlands, Russia, United Kingdom, United States, and 21 other powers at that time. It entered into force before the First World War. The very text of the convention is complemented by a most important Annex entitled Regulations Concerning the Laws and Customs of War on Land.[1]

> Article 43 of the Annexed Regulation provides that:
> The authority of the legitimate power having in fact passed into the hands of the occupant, the latter shall take all the measures in his power to restore, and ensure, as far as possible, public order and safety, while respecting, unless absolutely prevented, the laws in force in the country.[2]

The proceedings of the Hague conference indicate that this provision 'implies no recognition by the legal government, of any right of the occupant on the occupied territory.'[3] As to the meaning of the phrase 'public order and safety [*l'ordre et la vie publics*]', the proceedings indicate that it refers to 'the material order, security or general safety [*l'ordre matériel, la sécurité ou la sûreté générale*]', on the one hand, and 'the social functions and ordinary transactions which constitute the everyday life [*les fonctions sociales, les*

---

1 Convention (IV) Respecting the Laws and Customs of War on Land and its Annex: Regulations Respecting the Laws and Customs of War on Land (adopted 18 October 1907, entered into force 26 January 1910) (1907) 205 CTS 277.

2 ibid. The French version of this provision is written as follows: '*L'autorité du pouvoir légal ayant passé de fait entre les mains de l'occupant, celui-ci prendra toutes les mesures qui dépendent de lui en vue de rétablir et d'assurer, autant qu'il est possible, l'ordre et la vie publics en respectant, sauf empêchement absolu, les lois en vigueur dans le pays*.'

3 Albert Mechelynck, *La Convention de La Haye concernant les lois et coutumes de la guerre sur terre, d'après les Actes et Documents des Conférences de Bruxelles de 1874 et de La Haye de 1899 et 1907* (Hoste 1915) 334–348 (especially 334 and 344).

transactions ordinaires qui constituent la vie de tous les jours];[4] on the other hand.

1.2. The Belgian Interpretation

The Belgian courts had to interpret Article 43 from the very beginning of the First World War. Initially, two opposed interpretations emerged: that of two very courageous judges (Raymond de Ryckère and Maurice Benoidt) on one side, and that of the majority on the other.

1.2.1. The Majority's Interpretation

According to the interpretation, which was initially that of the majority, Article 43 of the Regulation annexed to the Convention of 1907 transferred the legitimate legislative power to the occupier. The opportunity to adopt this interpretation was given by a decree of 20 November 1914 of the German Governor-general of occupied Belgium, which conferred upon Belgian justices of the peace (the lowest courts in Belgium) jurisdiction for all disputes between landlords and tenants resulting from the circumstances of the war (destruction of the rented property, etc). It seems that a majority of the Belgian justices of the peace accepted to exercice that jurisdiction, despite the fact that it had been conferred upon them by the German Governor-general, in violation of the Belgian Constitution and Belgian laws. Their argument was that 'Considering Article 43 of the Annex of the 1907 Hague Convention, the decrees of the German Governor-general have the force of law in Belgium.'[5]

1.2.2. The Interpretation of de Ryckère and Benoidt.

At the same moment, another interpretation was adopted by at least two extremely courageous judges, Raymond de Ryckère (Judge at the Brussels

4 Id, eod loc.

5 J P Châtelet, 19 Febr 1915, *Genard v Stainier*, Pasicrisie belge 1915 (III) 3; J P Antwerp, 5 and 11 Febr 1915, *De Buysscher v Jules van Beylen*, and *F Braed v Alphonse Sillis De Mayer*, Pasicrisie belge 1915 (III) 5–7; J P Namur, 16 March 1915, *Gisquière v Rossel*, Pasicrisie belge 1915 (III) 3–5; and numerous other judgments published in the same journal.

Court of First Instance) and Maurice Benoidt (vice-chairman of the same court). The judgments granted by de Ryckère were the most elaborated:

> a) Currently, there are two legal orders in Belgium: that of the occupying power and that of the occupied state. The Belgian courts must only obey the rules of the Belgian legal order. If the occupant wants to be obeyed by courts in Belgium, it has to create its own courts.
> b) During the occupation, the Belgian courts have the duty to continue to judge as a long as the source of their legitimacy remains.
> c) The source of the legitimacy of the Belgian political powers is the election. The source of the legitimacy of the Belgian judicial power is independence.
> d) As a long as the independence of the Belgian judges is respected, they have to continue to judge; would their independance be infringed, they would have to cease carrying out their functions.[6]

1.2.3. 'Whereas the Independence of the Belgian Courts Has Been Infringed...'

Until 1918, Judges de Ryckère and Benoidt remained isolated in their interpretation of wartime judicial independence—which the Belgian *Cour de Cassation* formally rejected in a 1916 landmark decision.[7] It was the German occupiers' divisive policies that eventually made the other Belgian judges side with their colleagues de Ryckère and Benoidt—in particular, their decision to incite a group of Flemish nationalists to constitute itself as a 'Council of Flanders [*Raad van Vlaanderen*]'.[8] Between 11 November 1917 and 21 January 1918, this German-backed *Raad van Vlaanderen* pronounced the deposition of the Belgian government, proclaimed the 'Inde-

---

6 Trib civ Brux, 8th ch [de Ryckère], 20 Febr 1915, *De S... c J...*, J T 1918, col 991–994; Trib civ Brux, 8th ch [de Ryckère], 4 March 1915, *Debay. Louage*, J T 1918, col 994–995; Trib civ Brux, 1st ch [Benoidt], 22nd Apr 1915, *Veuve Piron c Deridder*, J T 1919, col 7–10; Trib civ Brux, 8th ch [de Ryckère], 6 May 1915, *Wanda Kulpe c Veuve Malherbe-Rubens*, J T 1918, col 995–998; Trib civ Brux, 8th ch [de Ryckère], 31st July 1915, *B... c L...*, J T 1918, col 998–999; Trib arb Verviers [Désiré Godard], 1st March 1917, *D'Aaoust c Torbach*, J T 1919, col 69–72; Trib civ Brux, 8th ch [de Ryckère], 10 Nov 1917, *Bessels c Meulemans*, J T 1919, col 6–7; Trib civ Brux, 8th ch [de Ryckère], 24 Nov 1917, *Piedferme c Spitaels*, J T 1919, col 7–8; Trib corr, ch temp [de Ryckère], 30 Jan 1917, *Proc Roi c Saeremans*, J T 1918, col 999–1000.

7 C cass, 1st civ ch, 20 May 1916, Pasicrisie belge 1915–1916 (I) 375, 416–418.

8 A detailed account of the events, relying on many reproduced documents, can be found in [Anonymous], 'Une page de gloire de la Magistrature belge', J T 1918, col 946–952, 963–967.

pendence of the Flemish State' and appointed its 'ministers'. The judges of the Court of Appeal of Brussels reacted by using an old procedural provision which allowed them, by a unanimous vote, to order to the Public Prosecutor General to initiate proceedings against 'the members of the de facto group having taken the name of Raad van Vlaanderen'. The resolution was voted unanimously by the judges of the Court of Appeal, the prosecutions were initiated, certain members of *Raad van Vlaanderen* were arrested and presented by the Belgian police before the Belgian investigating criminal judge. The German army came to the Brussels Courthouse to free them by force and to arrest the chairmen of all the Chambers of the Court of Appeal. Three days later, on 11 February 1918, and in the following days, all the courts of the Kingdom decided that 'Whereas the independence of the Belgian courts has been infringed', they had to 'cease carrying out their functions'.[9]

This led to a period of anarchy throughout the country. Crime increased considerably. The occupier had to create its own courts and administration by transferring judges and civil servants from Germany. While the war had entered its most difficult phase for the German Reich, the occupier suddenly needed to devote valuable resources to try to regain control of the situation in Belgium. The 'Belgian judges' strike' (even if it was not perfectly followed, for instance in the courts for the protection of the children) certainly contributed—albeit to an extent difficult to determine precisely—to the final defeat of Germany. This had consequences on the interpretation given to Article 43 of the 1907 Regulation during the Second World War.[10] On the Belgian as much as on the German side, the interpretation given by the judges de Ryckère and Benoidt was considered in 1940 as the basis for the new *modus vivendi*.

2. *Variety of Concrete Aspects*

The 'Belgian judges' strike' is the ultimate consequence of a conception of the relations between the legal order of the occupant and that of the occupied state characterized by the principle of non-permeability. When adopted, this principle prevents the application of the legal norms of the occupant by the courts of the occupied state. However, a more precise analysis results in noting that the effects that the occupied state gives to the legal

---

9 C cass, gen assembly, 11 Febr 1918, J T 1918, col 949–950.

10 See below, 3.

norms of the occupant, whether simply conceivable or actually observed, are not limited to the assertion of their non-applicability. This is made understandable by a distinction between categories of effects, supplemented by some illustrations.

2.1. Categories of Possible Effects

Those who study the relations between legal orders (especially in private international law and in domestic legal rules concerning the effects given to religious norms) are accustomed to distinguish between two types of operations, known in German as *Anwendung* (application) and *Berücksichtigung* (taking into consideration).[11]

A norm (A) is taken into consideration on the occasion of the application of a rule (B) when (A) plays a role at the stage of the verification of the conditions of (B).

Ex: Rule (B) provides that b1 + b2 + b3 → X

It is conceivable that a norm (A) plays a role when the conditions b1 + b2 + b3 are checked. This role may consist of an addition of condition, a substitution of condition, or a confirmation of condition.

Addition of condition. A French penal provision applies to the infringements of intermediate category committed by a French citizen in a

11 On that mecanism, see, *inter alia* Patrick Kinsch, *Le fait du prince étranger*, (th Univ Strasbourg Robert Schuman 1992/LGDJ 1994) 323–470; Didier Boden, *L'ordre public, limite et condition de la tolérance. Recherches sur le pluralisme juridique* (th Univ Paris 1 Panthéon-Sorbonne 2002, 2 vol) 174–193, 488–490, 651–653 (note 1346), 702–703 (note 1421), 704–709 (note 1428); Estelle Fohrer-Dedeurwaerder, *La prise en considération des normes étrangères* (th Univ Panthéon-Assas Paris 2 2004/ LGDJ 2008); Hélène Chanteloup, 'La prise en considération du droit national par le juge communautaire. Contribution à la comparaison des méthodes et solutions du droit communautaire et du droit international privé' [2007] Rev crit DIP 539–572; Didier Boden, 'Les effets en droit international privé français de l'appartenance d'une personne à un prétendu groupe ethnique ou d'une appartenance comparable' in Sylvain Bollée and Étienne Pataut (eds), *L'identité à l'épreuve de la mondialisation* (IRJS 2016) 247–260. *Adde*, CJEU, 18 October 2016, *Republik Griechenland v Grigorios Nikiforidis*, case C-135/15, ECLI:EU:C:2016:774, spec pts 40–55.

foreign country if the facts committed abroad carry criminal liability according to the foreign law.[12]
French applicable rule:

French conditions b1 + b2 + b3 → French penalty

Foreign norm about to be taken into consideration:

Foreign conditions a1 + a2 + a3 → Foreign penalty

Application of the French rule taking into consideration the foreign norm by addition of conditions:

b1 + b2 + b3 + a1 + a2 + a3 → French penalty

Substitution of condition. The fulfilment of the requirements of the norm taken into consideration will act as the fulfilment of the requirements of the applicable rule. The simplest way to illustrate it today consists in taking the example of the ERASMUS exchange programme.

French applicable rule:

French conditions b1 + b2 + b3 → French diploma

Foreign norm about to be taken into consideration:

Foreign conditions a1 + a2 + a3 → Foreign diploma

Application of the French rule taking into consideration the foreign norm by substitution of conditions:

b1 + b2 + a3 → French diploma

Confirmation of condition (or re-characterization). The fulfilment of the requirements of the norm taken into consideration and the fulfilment

12 French Penal Code (*Code pénal*), Art 113-6, subpara 2: 'French criminal law ... is applicable to misdemeanours committed by French nationals outside the territory of the French Republic if the conduct is punishable under the legislation of the country in which it was committed'.

of the requirements of the applicable rule are checked separately (hence it is not a substitution), but the requirements of the norm taken into consideration are not presented as necessary (hence it is not an addition). It is odd, but quite frequent.

French applicable rule:

French conditions b1 + b2 + b3 → French consequences

Foreign norm about to be taken into consideration:

Foreign conditions a1 + a2 + a3 → Foreign consequences

Application of the French rule taking into consideration the foreign norm by substitution of conditions:

b1 + b2 + b3 (and, by the way, a1 + a2 + a3) → French consequences

Another classification can be made, according to whether the taking into consideration: (1) expresses respect, friendship and esteem towards the norm taken into consideration and the legal order from which it comes; (2) expresses disrespect, enmity and hostility towards the norm taken into consideration and the legal order from which it comes; (3) expresses neither respect nor hostility.

The two classifications may also be combined as follows: [13]

	Friendly	Hostile	Neither friendly nor hostile
Addition	The present decision will apply after obtaining the agreement of the occupying authority	Law against the wearing of the uniform of the enemy	Law on the compensation by the ex-occupied state for the damage caused by the ex-occupant
Substitution	The decrees of the German Governor-general (GGG) have force of law in this country		
Confirmation	Contracts concluded to evade the decrees of the GGG are *contra bono mores*	Contracts between individuals concluded to pursue projects of the occupant are *contra bonos mores*	The '*fait du prince occupant*'[14] is a cause of exoneration

2.2. *Three Illustrations*

Numerous illustrations could be given of the acceptance or refusal of a given domestic legal order to give effect to the norms of another state's legal order when each one is at war with the other, whether in a situation of occupation or not.

---

13 Some of the following examples are established facts, others are theoretical possibilities.

14 '*Fait du prince occupant*' : specific case of *force majeure*, where the event that prevents one or both parties from fulfilling their obligations under the contract is an act of the occupying power.

2.2.1. Criminal Law

Article 491 of the Belgian Penal Code (*Code pénal*) punishes the *abus de confiance* (*breach of trust*). In 1917, the recruitment office of the German army in Belgium gave 50 Francs to a petty criminal to let him buy the necessary equipment for travel to Germany, where he was to join the German army. A few days later, the German recruit-to-be presented himself at a Belgian police station to turn himself in for various robberies and swindles. He was presented to the Criminal court of Brussels on 8 May 1917. One of the questions the court had to answer was whether the recruitment office of the German army had been victim of a breach of trust. According to the court,

> Article 491 Code pénal does not protect the undertakings that, established under the auspices of the occupant, have the only goal of supporting its military, economic and political interests, eg, by providing recruits, which constitutes a crime against the external security of the Belgian State, punishable by Article 115 Code pénal. Article 491 is not applicable when the diverted money was given to the defendant with the only aim of making an illicit use of it, contrary to the Belgian law, ... an immoral use, or for criminal ends.[15]

This decision can be analysed as a refusal of a friendly taking into consideration by confirmation of condition.

2.2.2. Contract Law

According to Article 1722 Code civil, if, during the term of a lease, the leased property is entirely destroyed by *force majeure*, the lease contract is automatically terminated without any indemnity. If it is destroyed only partly, the tenant can request a reduction of the rent or the termination of the contract. If the property is located in the 'military rear area' (*Etappengebiet*, near the combat zone) and if the occupant prohibits the tenant to use it as it was meant by the contract, is this a case of *force majeure*? The Civil court of Ghent answered affirmatively.[16] This decision can be analysed as a

15 Trib corr Brux, ch temp [de Ryckère], 8 May 1917, *Proc Roi c Terclavers, J T* 1919, col 133–137.

16 Trib civ Ghent, 28 Jul 1915, *Van den Bulcke c épouse Frohberg, Pasicrisie belge* 1915 (III) 116.

taking into consideration by confirmation of condition neither friendly nor hostile.

2.2.3. *International Private Law (Outside Occupied Belgium)*

Let us finish with a last example of relations between state legal orders in wartime which shows once more the variety of the possible effects and how they are sometimes surprising. The British *Trading with the Enemy Act 1914* had legal repercussions in many countries ... including in Germany. The most famous judgment on this subject was given in 1918 by the *Reichsgericht* (the civil and criminal supreme court of the German *Reich*). In this case, a German tradesman and an English company had concluded on 1 January 1914 a framework contract concerning future sales of extract of Quebracho (a tree used for its tannin). When the war started, the English company still needed to deliver 6,360 tons of extract to the German party. The company refused to carry out its obligations with the reason that, in the event of performance of the contract, it would have been liable for heavy penalties under the British *Trading with the Enemy Act 1914*. The German party prosecuted the English party before the German courts, and claimed damages for failure to perform the contract. It was dismissed. According to the *Reichsgericht*, admittedly the German courts had to refuse the application of this British law because it was contrary to public policy of German private international law. But in this case the law of the contract was German law, not English law. Under German civil law, *force majeure* exonerates the debtor from his liability. As the British Act fulfilled the criteria of the definition of *force majeure* in German civil law, the judges concluded that it was not applicable, but had to be taken into consideration.[17] This decision can be analysed as a taking into consideration by confirmation of condition neither friendly nor hostile.

17 RG, 2 ZivS, 28 Jun 1918, *RGZ* 93 [1918] 182–185, Nr 59, *S... F... g Forestal Land Timber and Railways Company*.

3. *Epilogue*

Before the beginning of the Second World War, the *Regierungspräsident*[18] of Cologne, Eggert Reeder, was put in charge of preparing the legal and administrative aspects of the future occupation of Belgium by Germany. He studied what had happened in 1914–1918 and was very impressed by the 'Belgian judges' strike' of 1918. He concluded that, if the *Reich* wanted to occupy Belgium in the least expensive possible way, it would have to respect the independence of the Belgian judges as much as possible and as long as possible. In 1940, the strange relations between occupying power and occupied state resumed, with acceptances and refusals of application, with acceptances and refusals of taking into consideration, and even with a very short judges' strike in 1942.[19]

18 *Regierungspräsident*: German homologue of a French *préfet*, ie a local civil servant appointed by the central government at the head of an administrative district.

19 Didier Boden, 'Le droit belge sous l'Occupation' in Dominique Gros (ed), *Le droit antisémite de Vichy* (30–31 Le Genre humain, Seuil 1996) 543–558; Boden, *L'ordre public…* (n 12) 470–490.

Chapter 14 The Work of Peace: World War One, Justice and Translation Through Art

Jennifer Balint* / Neal Haslem** / Kirsten Haydon***

1. Introduction

What work do we want law to be doing, and what work do we want to do with law and the records of war? In considering the 'peace through law' offered by the Treaty of Versailles, the peace treaty that formally ended the First World War, alongside the records of the war such as letters and artefacts and judgements, this chapter considers what it means to translate these records of war and law in order for them to be integrated and heard. Through considering a range of art practices focused on legal and other records—including *Minutes of Evidence*, which reactivates historical archives of a quasi-judicial body to raise awareness about issues of justice in Australia, and *Flowers of War*, a contemporary artwork that draws from records of the First World War to elicit public engagement—it asks us to consider ways in which legal and other records may be 'translated' and engaged with.

James Boyd White wrote that 'Law should take as its most central question what kind of a community we should be, with what values, motives and aims; it is a process by which we make ourselves by making our language.'[1] We make our community through making law. Yet how to move from statement of intent to sustainable change? From individual or

---

* Associate Professor in Socio-Legal Studies, Criminology, School of Social and Political Sciences, The University of Melbourne; Chief Investigator, Minutes of Evidence Project <www.minutesofevidence.com.au>; jbalint@unimelb.edu.au.

** Senior Lecturer and Associate Dean, Communication Design, School of Design, RMIT University; Collaborator/Artist, Flowers of War <http://flowersofwar.org>; neal.haslem@rmit.edu.au.

*** Lecturer and Studio Leader, Gold & Silversmithing, School of Art, RMIT University; Collaborator/Artist, Flowers of War <http://flowersofwar.org; kirsten.haydon@rmit.edu.au>.

1 James Boyd White, *Heracles' Bow: Essays on the Rhetoric and Poetics of the Law* (University of Wisconsin Press 1989) 42.

state accountability, to structural and societal change? How do we as individuals and communities take carriage of this? How do we contest the absences and exclusions of law? This chapter argues that the critical work of law that must be done is in 'translation' from its record to the individuals and society to which it is directed, and back again. That the 'work' of law —of peace through law—resides in the public as necessary partners.

The process of art as a way of production of meaning is increasingly being recognized as a congruent means to achieve this work of 'translation'. As a process based on individual experience, art has been shown to create that personal space to facilitate recognition and change. Art creates personal spaces within public frameworks. Art does not replace the accountability process of law—yet it can give it personal resonance. Agata Fijalkowski and Sigrun Valderhaug have written of this as both an affective and reflexive experience or encounter.[2] Art can create its own processes of recognition and accountability when law fails. This is not art of, but art as collaboration, that uses existing legal and other records to make visible and engage the participant—verbatim and documentary theatre, public art and installations. Without societal recognition of and engagement with judgments, treaties and legislation—which comes both from personal integration and from structural change—accountability will not go beyond the courtroom or the legislature. Art can enable both a process of integration of law as well as a means of calling law to account, of naming absences in law, and of creating and enabling individual and societal processes of recognition. As a process that is both communal and individual, art works in a different register to law and the state, meaning that it can work at a level of possible transformation and change.

2. *Translating Foundational Moments*

The Versailles Treaty between the Allies and Germany was signed in June 1919. This formal legal treaty with Germany had as its preamble a desire by the Allied and Associated Powers that 'the war in which they were successively involved directly or indirectly … should be replaced by a firm, just and durable Peace'.[3] Peace, however, requires work. The frameworks that

2 Agata Fijalkowski and Sigrun L Valderhaug, 'Legal Decisions, Affective Justice, and Moving On?' (2017) 7 (2) Oñati Socio-legal Series 337, 340.

3 Treaty of Peace with Germany (Treaty of Versailles) (signed 28 June 1919, entered into force 10 January 1920), Preamble.

law establishes require activation. The spaces and stories that law does not recognize need hearing. This can be particularly important when legal records get buried and rewritten through politics, or claims to law get subverted.

That the translation of law must be personally activated, and personally heard, can be seen across much law and society work. In early legal sociological writing, Leon Petrażycki identified that for law to be effective, there must be a personal connection. With a goal of a society based on 'rational and neighbourly active love', he argued that, 'The true practice of civil law or any law is not to be found in the courts, but altogether elsewhere. Its practitioners are not judges and advocates, but each individual citizen…'[4]

He saw law as a form of 'ethical experience', and distinguished between state official law and what he termed 'intuitive unofficial law', 'those legal experiences that contain no references to outside authorities'.[5] The relationship between the two was critical for law to be effective. As Reza Banakar explains: 'For positive [state official] law to become an effective social tool it had to be understood as an integral part of the larger mechanisms of social organization, upon which it is dependent for its existence'.[6] There is a push-pull between this social or 'unofficial law' and 'official law'. Much socio-legal scholarship has built on this—law is less effective when it runs counter to dominant normative orders in a society; yet social change can be motivated by key legal judgments and legislation. As Banakar notes, 'intuitive legal experiences can challenge official law forcing the legislature to revise its rules of application. At the same time, the official law can create the basis for intuitive legal experiences'.[7] Most recently in relation to Petrażycki's legacy, Roger Cotterrell has suggested:

> At a time when law is often seen as a mere technical calculus, divorced from the moral experience of citizens, Petrażycki's voice from a centu-

---

4 Petrażycki, *Wstęp do nauki polityki prawa* [Introduction to the Science of Legal Policy] ([1897] Warsaw, 1968), 138–39. As quoted by Krzysztof Motyka, *Law and Sociology: The Petrażyckian Perspective* in Michael Freeman (ed), *Law and Sociology: Current Legal Issues 2005* (OUP 2006) 119, 134.

5 See further, Adam Podgórecki, 'Unrecognized Father of Sociology of Law: Leon Petrażycki' (1980–81) 15 Law and Society Review 183; Andrzej Kojder, 'Leon Petrażycki's Socio-legal Ideas and their Contemporary Continuation' (2006) 6(3) Journal of Classical Sociology 333.

6 Reza Banakar, 'Sociological Jurisprudence', in Reza Banakar and Max Travers (eds), *An Introduction to Law and Social Theory* (Hart Publishing 2002) 42.

7 ibid 40.

> ry ago insists that studies of law in action can and should be guided by a vision of what an ethical life and a well-organized society might be.[8]

Petrażycki demonstrated the necessity of a personal connection to the law. Law must have meaning. But how to activate this? How to translate this? How to move law from words on a page to translation and integration?

The Treaty of Versailles included the Covenant of the League of Nations, underpinned as outlined in the preamble to Part I,

> by the acceptance of obligations not to resort to war,
> by the prescription of open, just and honourable relations between nations,
> by the firm establishment of the understandings of international law as the actual rule of conduct among Governments, and
> by the maintenance of justice and a scrupulous respect for all treaty obligations in the dealings of organised peoples with one another.[9]

As a 'foundational moment'[10] expected to establish lasting peace, the Treaty of Versailles also had large ambitions for international justice in a broader sense. It was expected to mark a moment between the past and the present, to outline a just and fairer future. As a 'foundational moment', it was expected to create new normative frameworks for the states and nations of the world: that they not resort to war, that they abide by international law, that they maintain justice not only in their dealings with one another, but also with regard to the populations under their jurisdiction. But how was this translated on the ground? What was required and what impact did these ideals have?

Article 23 of the Treaty held many of these ambitions. Going beyond the League's core mandate of settling international disputes and guaranteeing international peace and security, it endowed the new organization with a much broader mission of institutionalized technical, social and economic cooperation at a universal level. According to Article 23, the League 'will endeavor to secure and maintain fair and humane conditions of labour for men, women, and children, both in their own countries and in all countries to which their commercial and industrial relations extend', 'undertake to secure just treatment of the native inhabitants of territories

8 Roger Cotterrell, 'Leon Petrażycki and Contemporary Socio-Legal Studies' (2015) 11(1) International Journal of Law in Context 1, 9.
9 Treaty of Versailles, Preamble (n 3).
10 See further Jennifer Balint, *Genocide, State Crime and the Law: In the Name of the State* (Glasshouse/Routledge 2012) 6, 88.

under their control,' 'will entrust the League with the general supervision over the execution of agreements with regard to the traffic in women and children, and the traffic in opium and other dangerous drugs,' 'will entrust the League with the general supervision of the trade in arms and ammunition with the countries in which the control of this traffic is necessary in the common interest,' 'make provision to secure and maintain freedom of communications and of transit and equitable treatment for the commerce of all Members of the League,' and 'will endeavour to take steps in matters of international concern for the prevention and control of disease.'

We can imagine how critical these statements were at the time, encapsulated in a binding legal document coming at the end of 'the war to end all wars,' with its devastation of an estimated 16–18 million civilian and military deaths. The hope of the League of Nations, was that it be a means of lasting peace and justice. The knowledge of this destruction was acknowledged in this document of law: as criminologist Stanley Cohen has noted, 'Acknowledgment is what happens to knowledge when it becomes officially sanctioned and enters the public realm.'[11]

Despite its forward-looking character, Article 23 of the Treaty of Versailles—which essentially established the League of Nations as an organization that would not only guarantee the peaceful settlement of disputes among its members, but also ensure the interests of humanity as a whole—still encapsulated some knowledge of the war. In particular, Article 23(e) in its provision of equity of commerce, noted that 'the special necessities of the regions devastated during the war of 1914–1918 shall be borne in mind.' This was meant to safeguard certain war-torn industrialized countries, notably France, against unfair competition from abroad. By contrast, the drafters of the League Covenant chose to ignore the aspirations that the war had raised in other regions around the world. Most prominently, despite hundreds of thousands of non-European troops and labourers having served on and behind their frontlines, and countries like Japan and China having joined the fight against the Central Powers, they refused to define racial equality as a key principle of the new organization.[12]

We must ask what conceptions of governance and race informed the new international body which was expected to facilitate peace? What lived realities and injustices inhabited it? Article 22 of the Treaty of Versailles, critically, established the 'mandate' system, whereby former colonies 'in-

11 Stanley Cohen, 'State Crimes of Previous Regimes: Knowledge, Accountability, and the Policing of the Past' (1995) 20(1) Law & Social Inquiry 18.
12 See Castellanos-Jankiewicz (ch 5).

habited by peoples not yet able to stand by themselves under the strenuous conditions of the modem world', could be 'entrusted to advanced nations who by reason of their resources, their experience or their geographical position can best undertake this responsibility'.[13] Colonialism underlay the very concept of international justice, a state-based system where a sovereignty that overrode Indigenous sovereignties was the basis of membership.[14] This framework underlay what stories of harm were heard, and what were not.

3. *Ottoman Courts-Martial*

Another core absence during the Paris peace negotiations was the concept of genocide. While the Treaty of Versailles was being formulated, in another part of the continent the Ottoman State was reckoning with its past in a Courts-Martial that was not only largely ignored by the world, but obstructed. This Courts-Martial, before its demise, was to establish a critical legal record that established accountability for the genocide of the Armenian people by the Ottoman State.[15] An estimated 1.5 million Armenian citizens of the Ottoman State were killed. There had been recognition of this during the war by the Allies, backed up by many eyewitness reports of consular staff and religious clergy.[16] In fact, on 24 May 1915 the Allies had declared:

---

13 See Hébié and Baldini Miranda da Cruz (ch 4).

14 For further discussion, see Jennifer Balint, Julie Evans and Nesam McMillan, 'Rethinking Transitional Justice, Redressing Indigenous Harm: A New Conceptual Approach' (2014) 8 The International Journal of Transitional Justice 194, 203-204; see also James Anaya, *Indigenous Peoples in International Law* (OUP 2004); Anthony Anghie, *Imperialism, Sovereignty and the Making of International Law* (CUP 2005).

15 For a longer discussion of the Ottoman Courts-Martial, see Jennifer Balint, 'The Ottoman State Special Military Tribunal for the Genocide of the Armenians: Doing Government Business' in K J Heller and G Simpson (eds), *The Hidden Histories of War Crimes Trials* (OUP 2013) 77–100. See also, Vahakn N Dadrian and Taner Akçam, *Judgment at Istanbul: The Armenian Genocide Trials* (Berghahn Books 2011).

16 See, eg, Arnold Toynbee, *The Treatment of the Armenians in the Ottoman Empire* (Hodder and Staughton 1916); Henry Morgenthau, *Ambassador Morgenthau's Story* (Gomidas Institute 1918); Suzanne Elizabeth Moranian, 'Bearing Witness: The Missionary Archives as Evidence of the Armenian Genocide' in Richard G Hovannisian (ed), *The Armenian Genocide. History, Politics, Ethics* (St Martin's Press 1992) 103-128; Marjorie Housepian Dobkin, 'What Genocide? What Holocaust? News

> In view of these new crimes of Turkey against humanity and civilisation, the Allied governments announce publicly ... that they will hold personally responsible ... all members of the Ottoman government and those of their agents who are implicated in such massacres.[17]

The Peace Treaty of Sèvres between the Allies and Turkey, signed in August 1920, entailed recognition of this in its Articles 142, 144, and 230 which refer to the establishment of a Tribunal and undertook to 'repair so far as possible the wrongs inflicted on individuals in the course of the massacres perpetrated in Turkey during the war' (Article 142).[18] While genocide was not mentioned, the framer of the concept Raphael Lemkin has said that accounts of the massacres had influenced his development of the term.[19] Yet the court provided for in Article 230 of the Treaty of Sèvres—imitating the solution they had adopted with regard to German war criminals in Article 228 of the Treaty of Versailles, the Allies reserved 'the right to designate the tribunal which shall try the persons so accused'—never eventuated, and in fact the Peace Treaty of Sèvres was abandoned, signed but never ratified. The last paragraph of Article 230 of the Treaty of Sèvres even provided for a court established by the League of Nations to be the designated tribunal. The successor to the Treaty of Sèvres, the Treaty of Lausanne, was to omit all mention of war crimes.[20]

Despite the earlier pronouncements of the Allies, it fell to the Ottoman State to initiate legal proceedings. The process began in the Ottoman Parliament. The Armenian massacres had become the primary topic of conversation in the Parliament, with one parliamentarian decrying '[w]e inherit-

---

from Turkey, 1915–1923: A Case Study' in Richard G Hovannisian (ed), *The Armenian Genocide in Perspective* (Transaction Publishers 1998) 97.

17 Cited in Vahakhn Dadrian, Th*e History of the Armenian Genocide. Ethnic Conflict from the Balkans to Anatolia to the Caucasus* (3rd edn, Berghahn Books 1997), 216.

18 Treaty of Peace between the Allied and Associated Powers and Turkey (signed 10 August 1920) 28 LNTS 225.

19 The first draft, proposed by Russia, contained the phrase 'crimes against Christianity and civilisation', but it was changed to 'crime against humanity and civilisation' by France in light of the Muslim populations in the French colonies: see Ulrich Trumpener, *Germany and the Ottoman Empire* (Princeton University Press 1968), 210, footnote 26. The term 'crimes against humanity' was the original charge, yet due to opposition by the United States, who preferred 'crimes against the law of war', and Japan, it was changed to massacres.

20 Treaty of Peace with Turkey, with Related Documents Signed at Lausanne (signed 24 July 1923, entered into force 6 August 1924) 28 LNTS 11.

ed a country turned into a huge slaughterhouse'.[21] The media also heavily reported the massacres, with one newspaper arguing for Parliament's dissolution, stating that 'It is impossible to appear before humanity and civilization hand in hand with those who had worked with the organizers of the Armenian massacres'.[22]

It was on 2 November 1918 that a motion for a trial of the ministers of the two wartime cabinets was introduced by a Deputy in the Chamber of Deputies of the Ottoman Parliament, invoking 'the rules of law and humanity'. Two inquiries were subsequently established in late November 1918 and the Courts-Martial were established by Imperial authorization on 14 December 1918. The Courts-Martial prosecutors relied on the Ottoman Penal Code for the charges. Prior to the establishment of the trials, over 200 files had been prepared on individual government, military and Party officials as alleged perpetrators. Along with the trial records, these resulted in an extensive documentary record of the genocide.

At least sixty-three trials were held within the framework of the Courts-Martial, organized as follows: Ittihadist leaders and Central Committee members; Ministers of the two wartime cabinets (these first two were merged after the sixty-three prisoners were taken by the British to Malta and Mudros in May 1919); Responsible Secretaries and Delegates (who organized and supervised deportations) and those of the 'Special Organization' (who did the killings); and officials in provinces where the massacres took place. The trials provided a clear record of the crimes perpetrated. For example, in the trials in the province of Yozgat, which held to account local officials responsible for the deportation of Armenians from that community, an affidavit from the Military Commandant of Yozgat noted that 'underlying the entire scheme of deportations lay "a policy of extermination" (*imha siyaseti*)'.[23]

The ascendancy of Kemalism and the establishment of the modern nation state of Turkey resulted in the demise of the Courts-Martial. On 29 April 1920, a bill was introduced in the new Kemalist National Assembly in Ankara that nullified the official decisions and decrees of the Sultan's Istanbul government. In July that year the guilty verdicts of the former Governor of Baiburt, Mehmed Nusret, and Mehmed Kemal, who had been

21 John S Kirakossian, *The Armenian Genocide: The Young Turks Before the Judgment of History* (Sphinx Press 1992) 162.

22 ibid 158.

23 Vahakn N Dadrian, 'The Turkish Military Tribunal's Prosecution of the Authors of the Armenian Genocide: Four Major Courts-Martial Series' (1997) 11 Holocaust and Genocide Studies 37.

sub-district governor of Bogazliyan and subsequently interim district governor of Yozgat, and who had both been executed, were overturned. They were declared 'national martyrs.' On 31 March 1923, a general amnesty was announced for all those convicted by the Courts-Martial as well as by civilian courts, with pensions provided to families and a region, a school and street named in honour of Nusret, and a statue of Kemal erected.[24]

Yet we have these records. The Ottoman Courts-Martial established at the end of World War I provides a clear statement on the genocide of Armenians. With the subsequent and continuing denial of the genocide by the Turkish state, these records are critical. Aside from victim and witness testimony, the only authoritative statement of the fact of the massacres are these records from the trials at the end of World War I. These records—those that still exist, much was destroyed—and the fact the Courts-Martial was held—remain as evidence. In a situation of continued denial by Turkey, this is important.

Legal and other records can create new meeting points, new means of recognition, both inside and outside law.[25] In bringing these outside of law, they can be 'translated' and heard. This process of translation and of engagement is a critical means of social and structural change. Despite the official condemnation and recognition of the genocide through statements in the Ottoman Parliament and the media, the wider population appeared reluctant to accept the legal process and its verdicts. Due to this public unwillingness to accept Armenian testimony during the Yozgat trial, in his closing arguments the Prosecutor-General told the court that he was intentionally excluding all evidence supplied by Armenian witnesses, and was concentrating on documentary evidence and evidence supplied by former government officials.[26] In this failure of translation, the Armenian genocide—although documented and condemned in courts of law—was not effectively heard by the wider community. It remains unheard today.

---

24 Annette Höss, 'The Trial of Perpetrators by the Turkish Military Tribunals: The Case of Yozgat' in R G Hovannisian (ed) *The Armenian Genocide: History, Politics, Ethics* (St Martin's Press 1992) 219. Dadrian (n 26) 52.

25 On the concept of meeting points, see Jennifer Balint et al, *Keeping Hold of Justice: Encounters Between Law and Colonialism* (forthcoming, University of Michigan Press).

26 Höss (n 27) 221.

4. Art as a Means of Making Visible

How do we create this sense of shared humanity? Of hearing the victims and witnesses and their stories? How do we make visible these stories? When these are in courtrooms far away, with limited public access? Or when populations fail to hear them? Organized outreach activities have been a new addition to contemporary international criminal justice. Yet while these are an important means of communicating legal outcomes and processes, 'making visible' is something different to the usual outreach activities, which appear focused on relating what courts are doing, and informing communities of this (sometimes using innovative means, such as drama and visual art), yet not creating an interactive process as such.

Here, we can use the record of law and of other documents to create this. We have many thousands of pages of records of judgments, of transcripts. These reside not only in international courts, but in tribunals and commissions of inquiry. We have many more records from war, including letters that can be brought into the public domain, and used as a basis for interaction and recognition.

Increasingly, we see this process of interaction and engagement through non-legal means. For example, the exhibition *My Body: A War Zone* draws on local and international judgements of sexual violence in the Yugoslav War, as documented at the International Criminal Tribunal for the former Yugoslavia and in local courts. Featuring particular women's stories and their photos, alongside judgments, it opened in Sarajevo in in 2015, and was also shown in Mostar, Banja Luka, Brčko and Zenica. The showings are in public squares, on huge billboards, that are visible and invite engagement. Olivera Simić, who interviewed those involved, notes that 'Many of the young people who joined the discussions around the exhibition stated that visual art in the form of women's portraits revealed stories that would otherwise stay buried in legal documents.'[27] Designed as a key visual awareness raising tool, it was established to demonstrate the need for an *International Protocol on Investigation and Documentation of Sexual Violence in Conflict*. It itself was part of a broader project, *The Legacy of Rape*, which documented the testimonies of women victim survivors of sexual violence from

---

27 Olivera Simić, 'My Body: A War Zone: Documenting Stories of Wartime Sexual Violence in Bosnia, Herzegovina and Nepal' (2016) 8(1,2) Journal of Arts & Communities 11, 20. See also Zuzana Pavelková, 'My Body, a War Zone: Breaking the Silence Surrounding Sexual Violence in Conflict' (Balkan Diskurs, 13 August 2015) <http://balkandiskurs.com/en/2015/08/13/my-body-a-war-zone-breaking-the-silence-surrounding-sexual-violence-in-conflict/> accessed 24 July 2018.

Democratic Republic of the Congo, Nepal, Bosnia and Herzegovina, and Colombia.

When the state refuses to establish a justice process, or to even recognize the harm perpetrated, we see that civil society can establish these records independently. Responding to the failure of any state recognition of the Kurdish 'Anfal,' the campaign of extermination of Kurds in Northern Iraq in 1988 led by Saddam Hussein, which involved mass deportation and chemical weapons, artist Osman Ahmed has worked with survivors to create a visual documentation of the genocide. The drawings that he has done are a result of extensive interviews with survivors, and his own witnessing, and are a clear documentary record of the harms perpetrated.[28] As Ahmed wrote in his exhibition catalogue, 'Since witnessing the genocide in 1988, every drawing has been a renewal of my intent to bear witness; every tableau is a meeting place where memories and flashbacks spring to life out of chaos.'[29] His drawings document the harm perpetrated, as a visual image, in the absence of any state record of harm. Done collaboratively with survivors of the genocide, they have also been a powerful means of recognition for those involved.

Archival records of historical judicial or quasi-judicial proceedings may be used in a similar way. The *Minutes of Evidence* project used theatre, research and education to create new and collaborative ways of understanding Australia's past and the possibilities for its future. Centred on the 'minutes of evidence' of the 1881 Parliamentary Inquiry into the Coranderrk Aboriginal reserve in the colony of Victoria, Australia, this transcript of the Inquiry, alongside letters and petitions from the time, was turned into a verbatim theatre production, *Coranderrk: We Will Show the Country*, performed in theatres, at universities and 'On Country' to descendants of Coranderrk. Unusually for the time, the Parliamentary Inquiry heard evidence from the Aboriginal residents of Coranderrk. This testimony, alongside that of settler supporters, and of settler officials, enables these voices to be heard, that chart out alternative possibilities for living together—the just possibilities that were sought at the time—and also the structural injustices of colonialism that endure.[30]

---

28 For images, see 'Memories of Anfal' (Culture Inside) <http://www.cultureinside.com/homeen/artists-espace/gallery.aspx/viewgallery/2291/24788/> accessed 24 July 2018.

29 Osman Ahmed, *Displaced*, Imperial War Museum London, 31 May–7 September 2008.

30 See 'Minutes of Evidence' <www.minutesofevidence.com.au> accessed 24 July 2018; Jennifer Balint et al, 'The "Minutes of Evidence" Project: Creating Collabo-

Uncle Jack Charles, playing William Barak, testifying at the Coranderrk Inquiry, with Board of Protection Secretary Captain Page, played by Tom Long: Coranderrk: We Will Show the Country, *La Mama Courthouse Theatre, 2011. Photograph: Steven Rhall.*

Thirteen partner organizations, including government and community organizations, universities, education experts, performance artists and theatre practitioners, came together to create 'meeting points' through theatre, education and research. This record of law, the 1881 Parliamentary Inquiry, was used to create spaces for awareness of structural injustice, and consideration of what a just response may require. Alongside the space of theatre, the Inquiry has been used to develop new curriculum resources for government and non-government schools in Victoria in Years 9 & 10 *History* and *Civics & Citizenship* to respond to the paucity of material available to teach Indigenous history and Indigenous-settler relations in Victoria. The *Minutes of Evidence Coranderrk Curriculum and Teacher Resource Package* includes

rative Fields of Engagement with the Past, Present and Future' in Leigh Boucher and Lynette Russell (eds), *Settler Colonial Governance in Nineteenth-Century Victoria* (ANU Press and Aboriginal History Inc 2015) 203; Jennifer Balint et al, 'The Minutes of Evidence Project: Doing Structural Justice' (2018) 7 State Crime Journal.

the development of protocols for engagement with Indigenous communities around educational resources.

These 'meeting points' established in public spaces, schools, theatres, universities, and through research in *Minutes of Evidence* are designed to act as a catalyst for establishing awareness and possibilities in relation to the nation's past, present and future. This record of law was little known in the wider community in Victoria. Re-activating it through theatre and education, and placing it alongside other claims to justice across time and space, has enabled a broader engagement around what justice could look like. The reactivation of these legal records, through creating interactive spaces in which the record can be heard and considered, has enabled the stimulation of public engagement in issues of justice in Australia. It has meant that the claims of justice and injustice on record at the Coranderrk are heard in the present. Critically, it creates a space for consideration of what a structural justice may require.

5. *Flowers of War*

The international commemorative project *Flowers of War* provides an example of the way in which art can do the work to translate historical records from the past and make them vibrant catalysts of discourse in contemporary society.[31] The artists, Kirsten Haydon, Elizabeth Turrell and Neal Haslem, have researched historical records and artefacts from World War I, and looked at the ways these historical objects intertwine with the symbolism and cultural connotations of flora.

The work has, as its foundation, a metal, meccano-like circular structure over two metres in diameter. This framework is given a rigidity through crossed steel members that resonate with the technology of industrialization, bridge-building and the assertion of the power of humankind to dominate and exploit their natural environment. Mounted onto this structure are individual enamelled artworks—wearable brooches—that interweave to create an enamelled steel wreath. With forms based on flowers and leaves that embody connections to the history and social commemoration of war, over 400 individual pieces are attached onto the circular framework. Each individual piece embodies, and translates, different stories and connections. Some trace individual soldier's experiences, often tragic, sometimes heroic, but personal and particular to that individual in time

31 See 'Flowers of War' <http://flowersofwar.org> accessed 24 July 2018.

and space. One example is the piece that recollects the record of Private Arthur Elderton's cotton 'effects' bag in which the traces of his life; gold locket, wallet, badge, coins, compass, scissors and a button were sent home to his mother in New Zealand on 18 July 1916 following his death from shrapnel wounding. Another takes the form and colour of the cornflower; a flower which came to symbolize the war and the human sacrifice of the war for the French in the same way the poppy did for the Anglophone world. Another takes the form of a eucalypt leaf, yet in colouring and surface treatment connotes the rusted and burnt metal wreckage dragged up from old battlefields by farmers wishing to replant crops following the end of the war. With hundreds of these individual pieces intertwined we see the personal bound up in the geo-political—together forming a steel wreath of commemoration.

The wildflowers and leaves forming the steel wreath bring to presence individual moments of World War I. As Australian art historian Ann Elias writes, '[as] living forms, as art, and as symbols, the wildflowers that soldiers encountered in World War I Europe help us negotiate the unimaginable enormity of war and deepen the solemnity of remembrance'.[32] Elias goes on to discuss Elaine Scarry's writing on the strength of flowers as communicative objects.[33] Scarry expands on the 'vivacity' of the arts, and with this the capacity of the floral to hold the imagination in the way that other objects brought to memory, like human faces do not. She speaks to the 'ease of imagining' a flower, and through this the capacity of flowers to provide gateways to imagining, and therefore empathising with, other concepts, ideas and histories less comfortably brought to mind.

In this way *Flowers of War* interweaves innumerable stories, moments and memories from World War I in a complex material artefact able to be walked around, inspected, reflected upon and experienced. As an art object, *Flowers of War* comes alive through individual interpretation. It is in this moment of interpretation, as translation, that the remembrance of war becomes the presence of war, its legacy to us today and its lesson for the future. As a work of art, the work that *Flowers of War* does is non-instrumental representation; it brings to mind but does not close the mind.

---

32 Ann Elias, 'Flowers, Remembrance and the Art of War' (*The Conversation*, 10 November 2017) <https://theconversation.com/flowers-remembrance-and-the-art-of-war-86768> accessed 1 April 2018.

33 Elaine Scarry, 'Imagining Flowers: Perceptual Mimesis (Particularly Delphinium)' (1997) 57 Representations 90.

Another key aspect—and development device—of *Flowers of War* is public participation. When *Flowers of War* has been exhibited publicly, first in New Zealand, and later in the United Kingdom, it has used public participation to grow.[34] In its initial exhibition, the wreath was only half complete—it invited participation and contribution. The exhibition incorporated the opportunity for viewers to create their own flowers or leaves on paper using coloured pencils and watercolour wash. These audience-created paper flowers were, similarly to the steel artwork, combined to form another wreath—a public paper wreath. Through the daily process of paper wreath creation and recreation, the capacity for the artwork to bring historical records into current imagination is activated. This public work contributes to help the artists generate further enamelled pieces for the steel wreath. Participants are encouraged to discuss their paper flowers and provide their own stories or comments relating to the artwork. These conversations, stories and images have been used by the artists to create new enamelled brooches for the artwork. The participatory aspect of the project, along with the steel and enamel wreath itself, supports the artwork to manifest its presence in the contemporary world, as living history, lived through contemporary society and understandings.

34 It will be at the Shrine of Remembrance in Melbourne, Australia from October 2018 to November 2019.

Flowers of War, *(Wreath detail), 2018.*

Enamel, Steel, Silver, Pigments

Photographer Vlad Bunyevich

Image courtesy of the Shrine of Remembrance

Flowers of War, (*Wreath in progress*), 2017.

© Kirsten Haydon, Neal Haslem and Elizabeth Turrell

Installation Canterbury Museum, Christchurch, New Zealand

Photographer Neal Haslem

6. Peace Through Law: Conclusion

When we are talking of 'peace through law', the critical questions remain; how do we translate law into peace, into settlement of conflicts, into prevention? What is in fact required for peace? This chapter has argued that 'peace through law' is dependent on law's findings being translated and heard. While we may establish legal aspirations of peace inside international courts created as a consequence of the Treaty of Versailles, such as the Permanent Court of International Justice,[35] the Mixed Arbitral Tribunals[36] and the Arbitral Tribunal for Upper Silesia,[37] we need to consider what we do with these records, these judgments? These are not foolish questions. How the work of law continues, how it becomes translated, is critical. We must hear these judgments and claims. We must use the records that we have to translate the harm and to generate our own contemporary responses, our own records. In translating our records from the past, we are able to create spaces that enable societies and individuals to take responsibility for their integration while still making visible their limitations, and to practice accountability in the present.

35 See Tams (ch 10).
36 See Hess and Requejo Isidro (ch 11).
37 See Erpelding (ch 12).